CAMBRIDGE LATIN AMERICAN STUDIES

EDITORS
MALCOLM DEAS   CLIFFORD T. SMITH
JOHN STREET

8

ECONOMIC DEVELOPMENT OF
LATIN AMERICA

SECOND EDITION

THE SERIES

Economic Development of Latin America

SECOND EDITION

Historical background and contemporary problems

CELSO FURTADO
Translated by Suzette Macedo

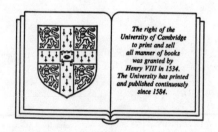

The right of the
University of Cambridge
to print and sell
all manner of books
was granted by
Henry VIII in 1534.
The University has printed
and published continuously
since 1584.

CAMBRIDGE UNIVERSITY PRESS

CAMBRIDGE
NEW YORK   PORT CHESTER
MELBOURNE   SYDNEY

Published by the Press Syndicate of the University of Cambridge
The Pitt Building, Trumpington Street, Cambridge CB2 1RP
40 West 20th Street, New York, NY 10011, USA
10 Stamford Road, Oakleigh, Melbourne 3166, Australia

First published 1970
Reprinted 1972
Second edition 1976
Reprinted 1978, 1981, 1982, 1984, 1985, 1986, 1988, 1990

Printed in the United States of America

Library of Congress Cataloguing in Publication Data

Furtado, Celso.
Economic Development of Latin America.
(Cambridge Latin American studies; 8)
Translation of Formação econômica da América
Latina.
Bibliography: p.
Includes index.
1. Latin America – Economic conditions.
2. Latin America – Social conditions. I. Title.
II. Series.
HC125.F7813 1976 330.9'8 76-14914

ISBN 0-521-29070-8 paperback
(ISBN 0-521-07828-8 hardback – first edition
ISBN 0-521-09628-6 paperback – first edition)

To my students at the University of Paris
A meus alunos da Universidade de Paris

CONTENTS

TABLES

PREFACE TO THE SECOND EDITION

The success of the first edition of this book[1] confirmed my impression that there was a growing interest, both in University circles and among the general public, in Latin American economic issues and in interpretations of these issues originating from within the region itself.

This new edition has been kept more or less to the same length as the first, but many chapters have been extensively rewritten to give greater depth to the study of the institutional framework which is the basis of the structural matrix prevailing in the region, as well as to include up to date information on recent economic developments.

In the six years since the first edition was written, Latin America has emerged from a phase of slackening economic growth to enter an expansionary cycle comparable to that of the first half of the 1950s. Moreover, there has been an intensification of the effort to bring about structural change, particularly in the agrarian sector; at the same time, new economic policy *models* have been introduced, and the ideological bases of these policies have been widened.

The richness of Latin America's historical experience, stemming from a wide variety of situations, which cover the full range of contemporary underdevelopment and the entire spectrum of ideological approaches, accounts for the interest which the region arouses in the so-called developed countries as well as in the countries of the Third World. One of my intentions is to stimulate this interest in Latin American realities and in the view of these realities that has been emerging in the region.

It would be impractical to list all the names of the many individuals whose ideas have helped to form the view of Latin America which this book seeks to communicate. In any case, it is a view developed by writers contemporary with the realities they write of, and I claim no more than to be one of the interpreters of this contemporary generation.

Sao Paulo   C.F.

---

[1] Spanish, French and English translations came out one year after the publication of the original in 1969; Italian, Swedish and Japanese translations followed in the next two years.

PREFACE TO THE FIRST EDITION

The study of the economic development of the Latin American countries has been attracting increasing interest, both in Europe and in the United States and in the countries of the Third World generally. An independent political life, which began practically at the same time as the Industrial Revolution, and an even longer experience of the international division of labour system as exporters of raw materials, single out this group of countries from among the now numerous family of nations with so-called underdeveloped economies. To these reasons must be added the growing awareness that, to a greater extent in Latin America than in any other important areas, obstacles to development are mainly of an institutional nature, a circumstance that makes it doubly difficult to try to identify evolutional trends in the region. Moreover, the problems posed by economic development at its present stage are leading Latin American peoples to see their situation in more truthful terms and to value those aspects that constitute the features of a common cultural personality.

This book was written with the dual purpose of helping students outside the area to form some idea of the socio-economic profile of the region and of contributing to the provision of a wider perspective for studies of the development of individual Latin American countries. In seeking to avoid dealing with each country in isolation – which would be to ignore the existence of a cultural reality in process of becoming homogeneous – I have also tried to avoid giving the false impression that there is a Latin American *economic system*, which would be the result of manipulating aggregate data for the region as a whole. So far as possible, each country is dealt with as an autonomous economic reality, whose experience, at a given historical moment, can be regarded as typical of regional evolutional trends.

C.F.

Paris, April 1969

ABBREVIATIONS

BNDE	Banco Nacional de Desenvolvimento Economico
CIDA	Interamerican Committee for Agricultural Development
ECLA	United Nations, Economic Commission for Latin America
FAO	United Nations, Food and Agriculture Organisation
IDB	Interamerican Development Bank
IMF	International Monetary Fund
INTAL	Instituto para la Integración de América Latina
LAFTA	Latin American Free Trade Area

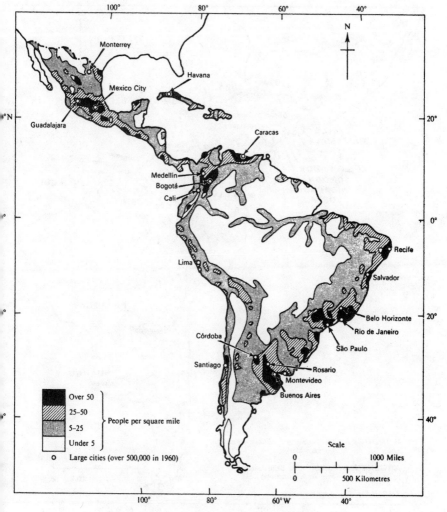

■	Over 50
▨	25–50
▦	5–25
☐	Under 5

People per square mile

o Large cities (over 500,000 in 1960)

Scale

0 ——————— 1000 Miles

0 ——————— 500 Kilometres

Map A   *Latin America: population distribution*

Map B   *Latin America: political divisions*

I. FROM THE CONQUEST TO THE FORMATION OF NATION-STATES

Introduction: the land and the people

Latin America: from geographical expression to historical reality

For a long time the term 'Latin America', popularised in the United States, was used only in a geographical sense to designate the countries situated south of the Rio Grande. Far from showing any interest in what they had in common, the nations that emerged from the Iberian colonisation of the Americas sought to emphasise their distinctive characteristics in an effort to define their own national personalities. With the exception of Brazil, colonised by Portugal, and Haiti, colonised by France, the remaining Latin American republics share much of their colonial history and, in Spanish, a common language. Nevertheless, the fact that the pre-Columbian cultural heritage contributed in such widely diverse ways to the formation of the present national personalities makes the differences between countries such as Argentina and Mexico as great as the similarities. The same can be said of the African ethnico–cultural contribution, which is no less unevenly distributed. Even leaving aside the case of Haiti, whose African–French origins place it in a category of its own, the differences between the countries of the Caribbean region, where there is a marked African ethnico–cultural influence, and the Andean countries, where indigenous ethnico–cultural elements predominate, are as marked as is possible for countries sharing part of their history. None the less, the emphasis on diversity was less a reflexion of the real extent of the differences between the Latin American countries than of their awareness of a common origin. It was as though the new nations felt themselves threatened, in their formative process, by superior forces that would lead them, sooner or later, to be reintegrated in the web of a common history interrupted by the circumstances in which the Spanish colonial empire finally collapsed.

The growth of a Latin American consciousness is a recent phenomenon, deriving from the new problems posed by the region's economic

I

and social development since the Second World War. Generally speaking, traditional development, based on the expansion of exports, had transformed the countries of the region into competing economies. Exporting the same primary products and importing manufactured products from outside the region, they failed to forge any economic links with each other. Thus, in the context of the international division of labour created in the Colonial Pact period and extended during the first stage of the Industrial Revolution, the traditional form of development helped to foster regional fragmentation. The disruption of international trade following the 1929 crisis had profound repercussions in the region. It is the attempt to find the solution for the problems that have arisen since then that has paved the way for the emergence of the present Latin American consciousness. The shortage of traditional imports which became more acute during the Second World War, gave rise to a more diversified regional trade which altered the traditional patterns of trade among countries exporting temperate-zone products, such as Argentina, and those exporting tropical products, such as Brazil. With the end of the war and the reopening of normal channels of trade, there were strong pressures for the re-establishment of the old trading patterns, but the experience had served to create contacts and crystallise possibilities.

In the second half of the 1950s, when industrialisation based on import-substitution began to reveal its limitations, for the first time in Latin America the obstacles to regional development created by the small size of the national markets began to be widely discussed; this discussion shed light on the similarities and contributed to the creation of a regional consciousness.

No less important for the shaping of this regional consciousness is the role played by Latin America's changing relations with the United States. Control by the United States companies of a large part of the region's sources of raw materials, public services and trading activities, created close dependent links with the United States for most Latin American countries, particularly those in the Caribbean area. After the First World War the penetration of United States capital was intensified, not only in the traditional forms of portfolio investment, but also in the form of control over companies. The latter form of penetration gained considerable momentum, during the 1930s, in manufacturing, which was the region's fastest-growing sector. Thus Latin America as a whole was clearly in a position of economic domination by the United States which extended and deepened the traditional political domination in the proliferation of institutionalised 'Pan-American' organisations. This institutionalisation obviously helped to consolidate the system of control but it also served to hasten the realisation that only by seeking closer ties could the Latin American countries hope to bring about any significant change in the conditions of their dialogue with the United States.

A similar process took place within the United Nations framework: the United States consistently used the Latin American countries as a submissive tactical reserve during the cold war years, a period when these countries represented one-third of the votes in the General Assembly. It was not long, however, before the hitherto disciplined Latin American *bloc* began to put forward its own claims, as in the case of the creation of the Economic Commission for Latin America (ECLA) established in 1948 against strong opposition from the United States. ECLA established its headquarters in Santiago, Chile, in marked contrast with the Washington-based Pan-American organisations, and came to play a leading role in the formation of the new Latin American consciousness.

In summary, 'Latin America' ceased to be a geographical term and became an historical reality as a result of the break in the traditional pattern of the international division of labour, the problems created by the belated process of industrialisation, and the evolution of its relations with the United States which, in becoming a hegemonic world power, drew up a special code for the region involving more direct and open control, while at the same time requiring increased co-operation among countries in the area.

Physical background

The Latin American republics form a geographical entity of more than 20 million square km, an area equivalent in size to that of the Soviet Union or of the United States and Canada combined. Crossed by the Equator, much the larger part of Latin America lies in the Southern Hemisphere: its southern tip is in latitude 56° S, whereas its northernmost extremity extends only as far as latitude 32° N. From the geographical viewpoint the region is made up of three sub-regions:

(*a*) northern Mexico, in which the basic relief features of the United States are prolonged,

(*b*) the American isthmus, which extends for more than 2,000 km, narrowing southward to a width of only 70 km in Panama; and

(*c*) the South American continent, whose relief is dominated by the Andean Cordillera, the great alluvial plains, the Guiana and Brazilian massifs, and the Patagonian plateau. The Andean barrier extends from the extreme north to the extreme south of the South American continent, sheltering extensive plateaus such as the Bolivian Altiplano – over 800 km wide – and reaching altitudes of more than 6,000 m. The great South American plains are formed by the basins of the Orinoco, Amazon and Parana rivers.

The west coast of Latin America, extending for more than 12,000 km is bordered by the Andean and Middle American Cordilleras. In Colombia, the Andean Cordillera is divided into three orographic branches, separated by the great southern valleys of the Magdalena and Cauca rivers. In contrast with the Colombian highlands, the highland areas of Peru and Bolivia occupy a large part of the Cordillera, which is between 250 and 400 km in width and over 4,000 in height in this section. Both in the Equatorial–Colombian and Peruvian–Bolivian regions the Cordillera's highest peaks reach altitudes of 6,000 m or higher; but the highest peak of all, Mt Aconcagua (7,000 m) is found in the Argentine–Chilean region, where the Cordillera takes on the form of a monoclinal relief.

The eastern region of the South American continent is made up of the Brazilian and Guiana massifs, fragments of Gondwanaland, which was separated from similar structures in the African block by the widening of the Atlantic Ocean.[1] The Brazilian massif, which extends 3,500 km south of latitude 6° S and some 4,000 km from northeast to southeast, is by far the greater in size. Between these two massifs and the Andean Cordillera there are vast sedimentary basins which support the alluvial plains formed by the Orinoco, Amazon and Paraná–Paraguay rivers.

The existence of extremely diverse general conditions and of certain highly significant peculiarities determines the extraordinarily wide variety of climates found in the Latin American countries, taken as a whole. The two major conditioning elements in the regional pattern of climate are the position of the Equator, which crosses the region close to its widest part, and the importance of the Andean Cordilleras and the Sierra Madre in Mexico – an importance reflected in the fact that several of Latin America's largest cities are situated more than 2,000 m above sea level (Mexico City: 2,240 m; Bogota: 2,591 m). The pattern of climate can be roughly characterised as follows: a humid tropical climate prevails in extensive areas, which are also the least densely populated. A tropical climate with a dry season and a hot semi-arid climate prevails in areas no less extensive but with a greater density of population. Finally, mountain climates, sub-tropical climates, and temperate climates characterise the most densely populated areas.

[1] Cf. Cl. Collin Delavaud, and others, *L'Amerique latine; Approche Geographique Générale et Régionale*, Paris, 1973, vol. I, p. 11.

Population pattern

The Latin American population, which at present exceeds 300 million, represents about 7.7 per cent of the world total and around 15 per cent of the total population of the underdeveloped world, excluding China. The Latin American population is distinguished from any other population grouping of comparable importance by the fact that it combines a low crude death rate – similar to the average rate for the developed countries – with a high crude birth rate – equal to the average rate for the underdeveloped countries.[2] Latin America's peculiar position is shown by the average annual growth rates for the world's major population groupings at the beginning of the 1970s:

	%		%
Latin America	2.8	China	1.7
Africa	2.6	Japan	1.2
Asia (except China and	2.4	United States	0.6
Japan)		Soviet Union	1.0
		Europe	0.5

As a result of these characteristics, the age structure of the Latin American population is characterised by a large proportion of children and young adults. Persons under 15 years of age now make up around 42 per cent of the Latin American total, a percentage which had been showing an upward trend over the last twenty years and is only now beginning to stabilise.

The rapid growth of Latin America's population is a relatively recent phenomenon. Although conclusions in this respect must be regarded as

[2] The average for Latin America as a whole obviously conceals wide differences between the various sub-regions. Thus, in Argentina and Uruguay, both the birth and death rates have already declined significantly and the natural rate of increase of the population is less than 1.5 per cent. Chile and Cuba are in an intermediate position: with a substantial decline in the mortality rate and the birth rate also beginning to show a downward trend, the rate of population increase is nearly 2 per cent but has started to decline. In some special cases (Haiti and Bolivia) the crude death rate has not yet been significantly reduced and this, combined with a high but stable birth rate, produces a rate of population increase of the intermediate type (2.5 per cent), but with a tendency to rise, in contrast to the second group for which rates of increase show a downward trend. Finally, in the remaining fourteen countries, representing 79 per cent of the region's population, the combination of a high birth rate, which has only recently begun to decline, with a mortality rate which has already been significantly reduced, results in a rate of population increase which is close to 3 per cent and in some cases even higher than 3.5 per cent. For details see: Carmen A. Miro, 'The Population of Latin America', in Claudio Veliz (ed.), *Latin America and the Caribbean: A Handbook*, London, 1968.

provisional pending further study, it is now generally accepted that the population of Spanish America at the time of Independence was much smaller than when America was discovered.[3] It is widely held that the total Indian population in the areas occupied by the Spaniards must have been not less than 50 million at the time of the Conquest. The particular circumstances of the Conquest and of the subsequent occupation of the more densely populated areas produced what amounted to a virtual holocaust of the indigenous population. To understand this extraordinary phenomenon, almost without parallel in the history of mankind, one must bear in mind that at the time of the Conquest, the native populations were concentrated in mountainous regions, supported by artisan agricultural economies, using elaborate techniques for the utilisation of soil and water and characterised by complex systems of social organisation. The mining economy introduced by the Spaniards, which required a wide-scale dislocation of the population, disrupted the pattern of food production and led to the break-up of the family units among a sizeable proportion of the population. The actual process of conquest resulted in the forcible transfer of great numbers of people, particularly adult males, who were practically wiped out by the long marches and forced labour imposed upon them by the *Conquistadores*. On the other hand, the need to exact a surplus from the population remaining on the land, in order to provide a steady food supply for the mining communities and cities, made heavy demands on the remaining rural population. Finally, the ravages of epidemics caused by contact with peoples carrying new contagious diseases played a no less significant part in bringing about a holocaust of the Indian population. It has been estimated, for example, that the Mexican population, which probably was not less than some 16 million at the time of the Conquest, was reduced to one-tenth of this total in the course of a century.[4]

[3] For a general survey of data relative to the growth of the population of Spanish America in the Colonial period, see: Rolando Mellafe, 'Problemas Demograficos e Historia Colonial Hispanoamericana', in *Temas de História Económica Hispano-americana*, Paris, 1965. For data relative to Brazil, see: Celso Furtado. *Formação Económica do Brasil*, Rio, 1959; English edition: The *Economic Growth of Brazil: A Survey from Colonial to Modern Times*, tr. Richard W.de Aguiar and Eric Charles Drysdale, Berkeley, Univ. of California Press. 1963. See also the essays by Bailey W. Diffie, Woodrow Borah and S. F. Cook; Peter Boyd-Bowman, Wilbur Zelinsky and Dauril Alden on estimates of the population before the Conquest and during the colonial period, in Lewis Hanke (ed.) *History of Latin American Civilization*, New York, 1967, vol. 1.

[4] The wholesale destruction of Brazil's aboriginal population was equally drastic. The Jesuit, José de Anchieta, observed that 'the number of people used up in this place (Bahia) from twenty years ago until now (1583) seems a thing not to be believed', and

Towards the middle of the seventeenth century the decline of the mining economy, and the development of subsistence agricultural and pastoral activities, together with the consolidation of new social structures and the increased natural resistance to the new diseases, opened a new chapter in the demographic history of Latin America. Attached to large agricultural estates with abundant land resources, in communities which received some protection from the Crown, the population began to increase. The establishment of an export trade in agricultural products in the eighteenth century made possible the continuation and even acceleration of population growth, as the result of the incorporation of a considerable African contingent.

Brazil's demographic history contrasts sharply with that of Spanish America. The aboriginal population was relatively sparse when the Portuguese began to colonise Brazil, which led them to bring in large numbers of Africans who were to provide the basis of the labour force for the tropical agricultural economy established in the Brazilian Northeast in the first half of the sixteenth century. The exploitation of alluvial gold and precious stones from the early years of the eighteenth century prompted a strong current of immigration from Portugal to Brazil. This influx of immigrants altered the demographic and ethnic patterns in Brazil. Up to that time the population had been concentrated in the region of tropical agriculture between Bahia and Maranhão, with the African contingent in the majority. The mining economy, which in Spanish America had brought about the depopulation of certain regions, produced the opposite effect in Brazil. Since what was involved was not the full-scale operation required in the case of silver, but simply the working over of placer deposits, Brazilian gold provided opportunities for the small entrepreneur. Even the slaves, who generally worked under strict supervision, enjoyed far better living conditions than the slave workers on the plantations. By the end of the century dominated by the mining economy, Brazil's population structure had undergone striking changes: the population of European origin now outstripped the African contingent, and the largest and most rapidly expanding population cluster had shifted from the northeast to the centre-south. At the close of the eighteenth century Brazil's population numbered 3 million, whereas that of Spanish America was slightly over 16 million.

During the nineteenth century Latin America's population increased at twice the overall rate estimated for the growth in world population.

proceeds to give figures that reveal a destruction of population on a scale similar to that carried out in Mexico. See J. Capistrano de Abreu, *Capitulos de História Colonial*, 5th ed. Rio, 1934, p. 79.

In fact, the ten-year average for Latin America was as high as 12.8 per cent, as against a growth rate of 6.4 per cent for the world as a whole. Nevertheless, compared with the rate of population increase in North America, for which the ten-year average was as high as 30 per cent, the Latin American growth rate was relatively low. In 1800 the population of the United States and Canada combined was 6 million, whereas that of Latin America was over 19 million. By 1900, Anglo-Saxon America had a population of 81 million and Latin America only 63 million. It is only in the present century that Latin America has taken over the lead in world population growth. Between 1900 and 1930 the decennial average of Latin America's population increase was 20 per cent, whereas that of Anglo-Saxon America was 18.6 per cent, and the world rate was 7.8 per cent. Between 1930 and 1960 the Latin American rate rose to 24.8 per cent, easily overtaking that of Anglo-Saxon America (14 per cent) which for the first time fell below the world average of 14.3 per cent. As a result of these changes in the rate of increase, Latin America's population, which at the turn of the century was approximately one-fifth below that of Anglo-Saxon America, now exceeds it by about 20 per cent.[5]

The significant changes in trend which characterise the present demographic pattern in Latin America began to emerge in the 1940s. Between 1920 and 1940, the growth rate of the region's population remained more or less stable at around 19 per thousand per decade. During the 1920s the fastest growing population was that of Argentina (at an average rate of 3 per cent a year) mainly as the result of a large influx of immigrants. The Mexican population, affected by the aftermath of Civil War, showed the lowest rate of increase: an average of only 1.35 per cent a year. In the following decade, the flow of immigrants to Argentina was reduced considerably, while in Mexico the opposite process occurred: part of the population which had emigrated to the United States returned home during the years of the depression; at the same time, the effects of the Civil War disappeared. The rate of population increase in these two countries was around 1.8 per cent. After the 1940s, the Latin American demographic process was no longer significantly affected by migratory flows; the decisive variable became the mortality rate, which began to decline throughout the region. The average annual growth rate of the population rose from 1.91 per cent in 1935–40 to 2.54 per cent in 1945–50; 2.85 per cent in 1955–60; and 2.91 per cent in 1965–70.[6] In

---

[5] For data on the growth of world population since the nineteenth century see Simon Kuznets, *Modern Economic Growth*, Yale University Press, 1966.

[6] Cf. Centro Latinoamericano de Demografía (CELADE), *Boletín Demográfico*, no. 10, July, 1972.

the two decades between 1950–5 and 1970–5 the crude birth rate (per thousand per annum) declined from 41.31 to 37.21 while the crude death rate fell from 14.51 to 9.28. As a result, the natural rate of increase of the population rose from 26.80 to 27.93. However, these averages obscure the more complex process now under way. Thus, the *overall fertility rate* (the average number of children which a woman has had at the end of her reproductive years) declined, in the period under consideration, from 5.69 to 5.29, after having been as high as 5.72 in 1955–60. The evolution of the fertility rate is one of the most important indicators of the long-term behaviour of a population. There is every likelihood that the downward trend registered over the last fifteen years will persist in the future. The effect of this lower fertility pattern has not yet made itself felt because of the continuing rejuvenation of the Latin American population: the proportion of persons under 15 years of age reached its maximum in 1965–70.

A closer examination of the demographic behaviour of the three most populous countries, which together account for two-thirds of the Latin American population, may provide a clearer picture of the contradictory trends underlying the regional averages. In Argentina, the pattern is similar to that found in highly urbanised countries with a high level of income. Between 1950–5 and 1970–5, the crude birth rate fell from 25.38 to 21.80 per thousand per year and the overall fertility rate from 3.15 to 2.98. The crude death rate declined from 9.16 to 8.76 while the average expectation of life at birth rose from 62.72 to 68.19 years. The natural rate of increase of the population declined from 16.22 to 13.04 per thousand per year and the proportion of persons under 15 years of age from 30.64 to 28.82 per cent, while the group of persons of 64 years and over increased from 4.52 to 7.56 per cent.

In Brazil, the picture is different. During the two decades under consideration, the crude annual birth rate declined from 41.42 to 37.12 per thousand and the overall reproductive rate from 5.70 to 5.15. The crude death rate was reduced from 12.16 to 8.77 and the expectation of life at birth increased from 54.15 to 61.39 years. The natural rate of increase declined from 29.26 to 28.35, the proportion of persons under 15 years of age increased from 42.74 to 43.32 per cent of the population, and that of persons of 64 years and over from 2.44 to 3.14 per cent.

For Mexico we have the following data: the crude birth rate declined from 46.62 to 42.00 and the overall fertility rate from 6.88 to 6.46; the natural rate of increase rose from 30.18 to 32.47; the proportion of the under-15 group increased from 43.54 to 46.18 per cent and that of the older group (64 years and over) rose from 3.30 to 3.53 per cent.

A comparison of these figures shows that mortality rates are low and have been sustained at practically the same level. The similarity is only partial, however, as can be seen by comparing the expectation of life at birth in the three countries. This is far greater in Argentina than in the other two. The proportion of persons in the older group is twice as high in Argentina, a relationship which clearly affects mortality levels. What characterises Brazil and Mexico in relation to Argentina is the extremely rapid pace of the decline in mortality. This feature is the basic cause of the so-called population explosion in Latin America. During the period under review, the death rate in Brazil declined twice as fast as in Argentina, and in Mexico five times as fast. Factors of a social and economic nature are responsible for this acceleration in the decline of mortality. It is known, for example, that the cost of controlling epidemic and endemic diseases has been reduced considerably in the last three decades. Moreover, the rapid growth of the middle classes, the principal beneficiaries of economic development in Mexico and Brazil, was accompanied by the modernisation of public services, including public health, a process which affected the sanitary conditions of the population as a whole. The demographic pattern in Mexico, where the overall fertility rate is extremely high and relatively stable, is of particular interest. It would seem that in that country the urbanisation process has had little effect on the social conditions which influence reproductive behaviour. Notwithstanding the rapid decline in mortality, the average age of the Mexican population is now less than it was two decades ago. The index of dependency – the relation between the population not of working age (less than 15 years of age and 64 years and over) and the economically active population (from 15 to 64 years of age) – is around 1 in Mexico while in Brazil it is 0.83 and in Argentina 0.57.

Rapid urbanisation is another striking feature of Latin America's recent demographic evolution. Unlike the urbanisation of the industrially more advanced countries, which took place in conditions of relative stability or decline in the rural population, the rapid growth of cities in Latin America did not prevent the rural populations from continuing to expand at a relatively rapid pace. If we define 'urban population' as the population living in centres of 20,000 inhabitants or more, this demographic group increased at an average annual rate of 5.4 per cent between 1950 and 1960 while the rural population continued to expand at an annual rate of 1.8 per cent. In the following decade (1960–70) the rates were 5.2 and 1.5 per cent respectively. The urban population increased from 25.6 per cent of the total in 1950 to 41.1 per cent in 1970. In absolute terms, it grew from 40,187,000 to 112,961,000. Of this total,

Brazil accounted for 36.7 million, Mexico for 20.6 million and Argentina for 15.8 million. The total number of cities (centres of 20,000 inhabitants or more) increased from 320 in 1950 to 828 in 1970 and the number of cities of 1 million inhabitants or more increased from 7 to 16. In 1970, the number of persons living in cities belonging to the latter group was 52 million.

The present characteristics of the Latin American population leave no room to doubt the continued demographic expansion of the region over the next few decades. However uncertain forecasts may be in this respect, particularly when the time-scale is extended, it must be recognised that the basic trends will be slow to change. If we accept the projections of specialists, we must assume that by the mid-1980s only two countries in the region (Argentina and Uruguay) will have growth rates of around 1 per cent a year. A third country (Chile) will have a rate of growth closer to 1.5 than to 2.0 per cent a year while a fourth country (Cuba) will have a growth rate nearer 2.0 than 2.5 per cent a year. In 1975, the populations of these four countries totalled 48.6 million, representing less than one-sixth of the Latin American total. Mexico, whose population in that year was around 59.2 million, will probably have a growth rate closer to 3.5 than to 3.0 per cent a year by the middle of the next decade and Brazil, accounting for one-third of the region's total population, will have an annual growth rate closer to 3.0 than to 2.5 per cent. If the fertility rates observed in the various Latin American countries in 1965–70 were to remain stable during the next twenty-five years, the total population of the region would be around 711 million in the year 2000. There is evidence, however, that these rates are already declining. The basic problem is to forecast the pace of this decline. In a study presented to the World Population Congress held in 1974, the Latin American Center on Demography made three assumptions in this respect, estimating the total population of the region at 662 million at the end of the present century on the high growth assumption, 612 million on the medium growth assumption and 560 million on the low growth assumption. Table 1.1 shows the data for the medium growth assumption, by countries and subregions. On this assumption, the average fertility rate will decline from 5.54 (the 1965–70 level) to 3.91 in 1995–2000. Since it is likely that this downward trend will be sustained, it is also likely that the growth of the Latin American population will stabilize at some time in the future, although it is difficult to predict exactly when. It must be borne in mind that a population may continue to expand for a period of 65 to 70 years after reaching the unit reproductive rate of 2. It is very unlikely that this rate will be attained in Latin American in two or three decades. Even if it

TABLE I.I *Latin America: area and population by countries and sub-regions*

Country and sub-region	Area (km²)	Population (000)			
		1920	1950	1975	2000 (forecast)
Bolivia	1,098,581	1,918	3,013	5,410	10,267
Colombia	1,138,338	6,057	11,629	25,890	51,464
Chile	741,767	3,783	6,058	10,621	15,842
Ecuador	270,670	1,898	3,225	7,090	14,773
Peru	1,280,219	4,862	7,968	15,326	30,561
Venezuela	898,805	2,408	5,330	12,213	23,552
Total Andean Group	5,428,380	20,926	37,223	76,550	146,459
Argentina	2,766,656	8,861	17,085	25,384	32,860
Brazil	8,511,965	27,404	52,326	109,730	212,508
Paraguay	406,752	699	1,337	2,628	5,592
Uruguay	186,926	1,391	2,198	3.060	3,993
Total Altantic Group	11,685,373	38,355	72,946	140,802	254,953
Costa Rica	50,900	421	849	1,994	3,695
El Salvador	20,935	1,168	1,922	4,108	7,945
Guatemala	108,889	1,450	3.024	6,130	11,191
Honduras	112,088	783	1,389	3,037	6,271
Nicaragua	130,000	639	1,133	2,318	4,680
Total Central America	422,812	4,461	8,317	17,587	36,907
Cuba	114,524	2,950	5,520	9,528	15,662
Haiti	27,750	2,124	3,380	5,888	10,742
Mexico	1,969,300	14,500	26,640	59,204	132,243
Panama	75,650	429	765	1,676	3,218
Dominican Republic	48,442	1,140	2,303	5,118	11,767
Total Caribbean and others	2,235,666	21,143	38,608	81,414	173,632
Total Latin America	20,019,000	84,885	157,104	316,353	611,951

SOURCES: Areas: Instituto Interamericano de Estadìstica, *Boletin Estadìstico*; population: 1920 and 1950: Centro Latinoamericano de Demografia, *Boletín Demográfico*, no. 10, July 1972; 1975 and 2000 (estimate): Centro Latino-americano de Demografia, *America Latina: Situación Demográfica alredor de 1973 y perspectivas para al Año 2000* (paper prepared for the World Population Conference held in 1974).

were attained by the end of the first quarter of the next century, however, the Latin American population would not be stabilized before it had grown to one billion.

2 Economic and social background of the territorial occupation

Individual action and the 'encomienda' system

The essential features of what was to become the social structure of the Latin American countries originated in the Spanish conquest itself and in the institutions established by the Spaniards and Portuguese to create an economic base which would consolidate their conquest of the new lands.

The circumstances attending the lengthy process of Spain's reconquest of her territory from the Moors permitted the creation of a highly centralised state, although the different regions of the Peninsula retained markedly feudal characteristics. Compared with other regions of Europe, commercial capitalism had made a belated appearance in the Iberian Peninsula. In Portugal the development of commercial capitalism was intimately bound up with the monarchy from the very beginning.[1] By basing its strength on commercial activities and becoming the promoter of a grand commercial design, the Portuguese monarchy achieved autonomous development within the Peninsula. However, placing commercial activities under the aegis of the State led to a centralism not very different from that of Spain.

Adventurous spirits from all over Europe had been attracted to Spain by the war against the Moors and, at the time of the discovery of America, which coincided with the end of the Reconquest, Spain had large numbers of men able and ready to embark on military adventures likely to bring them handsome rewards.[2] The conquest of the American lands was organised along the same lines and guided by the same principles as the long struggle to reconquer the homeland from the Moors. The essential

[1] In this regard see the perceptive study by Antonio Seŕgio, *Breve Interpretaçao da História de Portugal*, Lisbon, 1972.

[2] The Conquest of Granada, the richest of the Moorish kingdoms, was the culmination of a war lasting eleven years; it capitulated in 1492, the year Columbus discovered America.

difference lay in the fact that at home, the enemy possessed considerable technical resources for the time which rendered individual action completely ineffectual. Thus, the religious-military Order became the key factor in organising the struggle. Bringing together knights from very different cultural areas, united by their religious ardour and spirit of adventure, Orders such as that of Calatrava, Santiago and Alcantara appropriated extensive territories reconquered from the Moors and laid the patrimonial and centralist foundations of the future Spanish monarchy. With the union of Castile and Aragon in the persons of Isabella and Ferdinand, and with Ferdinand's successful bid to impose himself as Grand Master of the religious–military Orders, the conditions were created for the establishment of a highly centralised state, in a society where commercial capitalism was only just beginning to emerge. Thus, in different ways, Spain and Portugal had created conditions that enabled the state to assume control of economic activities at the very outset of the commercial revolution.

It is worth noting that during the first stage of the Reconquest, lasting until the eleventh century, the basic objective was to *occupy* the lands held by the Moors and prepare them for self-defence by creating a militia of farmer–soldiers. Since these farmer–soldiers emerged mostly from the lower estates of the Visigothic feudal structures, this initial stage of the Reconquest reinforced the power of the Kings of Castile by contributing towards the creation of a class of free men, that is, men not bound by feudal ties. With the conquest of Toledo (1085), the Moslem power began to wane. The urban populations in the reconquered areas continued to move south, but the rural masses tended to remain on the land and to accept the overlordship of Christian landlords. Once this pattern had been established, the Reconquest tended to reinforce feudal institutions. In this sense, it would seem less accurate to speak of a 'belated feudalism' in Spain than of a revival of feudalism in the thirteenth and fourteenth centuries.[3]

In America, the weakness of the peoples to be conquered and the distance of the Central Power – allowing the conquest to degenerate on many occasions into crude acts of pillage – made it possible to organise the campaigns on a far less elaborate basis than that of the religious–military Order. In fact, individual initiative was responsible for most of the action, promoted by men of relatively modest means who organised groups of hardy adventurers eager to share in the spoils of conquest. Thus, the real driving force behind the shaping of the structure of the new

[3] Cf. Ignacio Sotelo, *Sociologia de América Latina*, Madrid, 1972, pp. 47–8.

empire was the private interest of the Conquistador.[4] 'L'expression *Ost des Indes*', writes a contemporary historian, 'est devenue la meilleure définition du caractère privé des expéditions de conquête. L'État espagnol vérifia en pratique que la meilleure façon de protéger ses intérêts était de céder aux particuliers la possibilité de découvrir et de soumettre les nouveaux territoires à incorporer à la couronne. Les expéditions d'État furent l'exception et quant elles ont eu lieu, elles ont été justifiées par des causes très particulières.'[5]

Individual action, the basis of the occupation of American territories, was carried out within a contractual framework strictly defined by the Spanish or Portuguese State.[6] In the case of Spain, since territorial expansion was almost always the result of the conquest and subjugation of native populations, later exploited as a source of labour, the nexus between individual action and State patronage assumed greater significance. Through the system of *capitulaciones* or concessions, the State ceded certain prerogatives to the individual Conquistador against the fulfilment of certain obligations. The rewards granted by the Spanish State assumed their definitive form in the institution of the *encomienda*.[7] This

[4] Cf. Silvio Zavala, *Los intereses particulares en la Conquista de Nueva Espana*, Madrid, 1933.

[5] Alvaro Jara, *Problemas y Métodos de la História Económica Hispanoamericana*, Universidad Central de Venezuela, Caracas, 1969, pp. 1 and 2. 'Se ha establecido,' writes Jara, 'que los intereses privados de los conquistadores – los componentes de la hueste indiana – fueron el verdadero motor expansivo del amplio movimiento de ocupación del continente americano.' For a more complete version see his *Guerre et Societé au Chili*, translated by Jacques Lafayette, Paris, 1961.

[6] The absence of treasures which could be easily plundered lessened Portugal's interest in Brazil in the early years, particularly as her trade with the East Indies was then at its height. To attract private capital for her American colony, the Portuguese Crown divided it into twelve hereditary captaincies, placed under the direction of proprietary landlords (*donatários*), who took over many of the royal privileges. The want of any economic base, except in the region where the cultivation of sugar cane had been introduced, led to the collapse of this experiment. The Crown had to assume direct responsibility for the cost of defending vast territories which long remained of little economic value. Although formally modelled on Portuguese feudal institutions, the system of hereditary captaincies should be seen as an endeavour to attract private capital for the task of commercial expansion directed by the Crown, comparable to the trading corporations set up in England and Holland during the latter half of the sixteenth century.

[7] On 20 December 1503, Isabella the Catholic passed an act authorising the allotment of Indians (*repartimiento de Indios*) which gave rise to the *encomienda* system. On the *capitulaciones* and *encomiendas*, see the classic work by Silvio Zavala, *Las Instituciones Jurídicas en la Conquista de América* (Madrid, 1935). For a short bibliography on the *encomienda* see Jacques Lambert, *Amérique Latine: Structures Sociales et Institutions Politiques*, Paris, 1963.

term had been used in Spain to designate the lands and rents ceded as a reward to the commanders of religious-military Orders. In America a nucleus of the native population was 'commended' or entrusted to a Conquistador who was to be responsible for ensuring that his 'wards' were instructed in the Roman Catholic faith and, in return, was given the right to use them as a labour force.

The grantee, or *encomendero*, as guardian and protector of the native population entrusted to him, came privately to exercise public law functions, which placed him socially in a position comparable only to that of the feudal lord in medieval Europe. And, like the feudal lord, he had military responsibilities and had to organise local security at his own expense. In regions where the Indians were quickly 'pacified', the *encomendero*'s military obligations became merely formal. But in regions where the war against the Indians dragged on for a very long time, as in the case of Chile, these responsibilities proved a heavy burden.

For security reasons, the Spanish Crown decided to concentrate the native population in certain areas, giving rise to what came to be known as the 'indigenous community', in which elements of the existing Indian communities – the *ayllu* in Peru, and the *calpulli* in Mexico[8] – continued to exist together with elements transplanted from Spain. Since the landlords were obliged to pay taxes in relation to the number of native inhabitants entrusted to their care, the community system helped to defend the interests of the Crown. The regular extraction of a labour surplus was possible only where the native population was relatively dense. The community, by favouring the preservation of the traditional power structure, facilitated the extraction of a labour surplus, as in the case of the *mita* system, whereby the authorities requisitioned one-seventh of the native male population for work in the mines. Nevertheless, the institution of the community did help to preserve many cultural patterns, and to prevent the reproductive rate of the population from declining even further.

Social organisation based on the *encomienda* was most effective in regions where there was a relatively dense native population which had achieved a certain level of material development and had a measure of social stratification. The existence of a local ruling class, traditionally entitled to the surplus produce, and in a position to finance wars or

---

[8] The *ayllu*, a village community of variable size which held its lands in common, was the largest political unit in Peru before the Inca conquest. The *calpulli* was the Aztec clan. The lands held by the clan included certain tracts which were owned and operated by the whole clan in common and other tracts which were partitioned among the heads of families and regarded as essentially private property (Translator).

public works, facilitated the establishment of the *encomienda* system. In fact, *encomenderos* who were allotted native communities managed to persuade the chieftains to increase the traditional surplus and hand over most of it to the new masters. In regions where the Indians had a very low level of material development, the possibility of expropriating their surplus produce through traditional leaders was ruled out. In such cases the *encomienda* proved ineffective as a form of social organisation and the *encomendero* resorted to more direct forms of slavery, forcing the men to perform intensive labour in conditions very different from those to which they had been accustomed. This system resulted in a rapid depletion of the population. In the West Indies, particularly in Hispaniola (Santo Domingo), the *encomienda* took the form of a straightforward apportionment of the native inhabitants among the gold prospectors, and no measures were taken to preserve a communal way of life. The result was the rapid disappearance of the native populations of these islands.

Unlike the feudal lord, who extracted a surplus from the population under his control which was used in one way or another in the same region, the Spaniard who undertook the Conquest or received an *encomienda* was mainly concerned to appropriate a surplus which could be transferred to Europe. Either because he was accustomed to forms of consumption which could be satisfied only by imports from Europe, or because his ultimate aim in embarking on the American adventure was to achieve a coveted economic and social position in Spain, the *encomendero* was not interested in a surplus which could only be used locally. In fact, his aim was to mobilise the surplus so that he could discover, produce and transport precious metals. Apart from gold and silver, little that could be produced in the Americas during the first century of colonisation was marketable in Europe. Unlike the East Indies, which produced articles of great value per unit of weight, such as spices, silks and muslins, the Americas produced nothing that could become the basis of a lucrative trade. The Portuguese who, in the first two centuries of colonisation, had failed to find precious metals in the lands they occupied sought to overcome this handicap by starting commercial production of a tropical crop, using the experience gained in the Atlantic islands since the middle of the fifteenth century. Finding only a sparse and scattered population, ill-suited to the hard work of the sugar plantations, they decided to import African labour, a step calling for considerable investment and hence limiting private action to groups able to mobilise fairly substantial financial resources. It was this that gave the Portuguese action its character of 'colonisation' rather than 'conquest', and it was this that created the distinctive features of the social structures of the Portugese territories in the initial stage.

In the case of Spanish America, the search for precious metals – and their production following discovery – was the determining factor in the action of the private individuals who played the leading role in shaping the structure of the new Empire. On the other hand, the *encomienda* system provided the framework for the concentration of the population whose labour was to be exploited. The various forms taken by the surplus extracted from that population (a labour force used directly for work in the mines or for agricultural production destined for the urban population of the mine-workers) determined the position of the *encomendero* in the social structure. In any event, the commercial character of the enterprise (entry into the exchange circuit) predominated since the principal objective was to effect transfers to the metropolis. The vicissitudes encountered in the achievement of this objective are at the root of the social formations, geared towards the local use of the surplus, which emerged subsequently.

In the Portuguese settlements, the establishment of tropical agriculture created distinctive conditions at the outset, requiring substantial investment which frequently remained under the control of commercial and financial interests in the metropolis.

The production of precious metals

The evolution of the production of precious metals in Spanish America was subject to marked fluctuation. In the early years the treasures accumulated in Mexico and Peru were systematically plundered, an activity serving chiefly to excite the imagination of Spain. The second phase, which lasted until the middle of the sixteenth century, is characterised by the Spaniards' efforts to discover the sources of the precious metals. Production was limited to the alluvial gold which was discovered in several regions, and tended to be rapidly exhausted. In most cases Indians were coerced or cajoled into leading expeditions organised on the initiative of an *encomendero* to rivers or streams with placer deposits from which the Indians had traditionally extracted gold. Indian gold-workings were nearly always found near by. Production was started and rapidly intensified, to be followed by an even more rapid decline once the gold-bearing gravels had been completely worked over. The belated discovery of gold in Brazil was not due to its greater scarcity. In fact, the output of Brazilian gold in the eighteenth century was to outstrip the total gold production of the Spanish territories in the two preceding centuries. The slowness of the Portuguese was due mainly to the absence of a gold-working tradition among the Indians of Brazil. Since gold was unknown to the natives, the Portuguese had to roam the vast Brazilian territory in search of rivers and streams with gold-bearing gravels.

Silver production became paramount towards the middle of the sixteenth century. Unlike alluvial gold production, which declined very rapidly, silver production, involving the opening of mines, attained a much higher level of development and great stability over a long period. The 1570s witnessed a revolution in American silver mining with the introduction of the amalgamation technique, a process for extracting silver from the ore with the aid of mercury, discovered in 1554 in Pachuca, Mexico, by Bartolomeo de Medina. This technological advance made it economically possible to use poorer-grade ores and to reach levels of production undreamed of in earlier periods.

Silver production in Potosí, which had started in 1545 on the basis of traditional Indian mining techniques, began to decline two decades later with the exhaustion of the richest veins. The use of the mercury amalgamation process became possible only after extensive research had been carried out locally by Pedro Fernandez de Velasco with the backing of Viceroy Francisco de Toledo. In addition, considerable investments were needed for the development of the water-power systems which provided mechanical energy for the reduction of the ore.[9] The discovery of a quicksilver deposit at Huancavélica in Peru contributed greatly to the dramatic expansion of production in Potosí.

Throughout the colonial period the supply of mercury, a key factor in silver production, came from the Huancavélica mine and from Almadén in Spain.[10] Mexico, which in the seventeenth century occasionally imported quicksilver from Peru, had to rely almost entirely on supplies from Spain, whose output surpassed that of Peru at the turn of the seventeenth century and was three-times as great in the second half of the eighteenth century.

The organisation of silver-mining in the densely populated Peruvian–Bolivian Cordillera, the backbone of the Viceroyalty of New Castile which had its capital in Lima, provides an insight into the significance of the various institutions on which the colonial economy was based. The Huancavélica mine, situated at a relatively short distance from Lima, was exploited by a small group of *concessionaires* (organised in a *gremio*, or guild) under the direct control of the Spanish Crown which was the only legal buyer. The Crown established production goals, financed produc-

---

[9] Cf. D. A. Brading and Harry E. Cross 'Colonial Silver Mining: Mexico and Peru', *The Hispanic American Historical Review*, vol. 52, no. 4, November, 1972.

[10] When silver production was at its height in Peru and Mexico during the first half of the seventeenth century, significant quantities of quicksilver were imported from Idria in Slovenia.

tion, assured the supply of labour and determined the price paid to producers.[11] Production seldom reached the original goal of 6,820 *quintales*, needed to meet the requirements of Potosí and leave a 15 per cent margin for export to Mexico. There were various reasons for this failure, ranging from administrative mismanagement to the increasing difficulties of recruiting labour, since the *mitayos* (Indians forced into labour under the *mita* system) fled from the region to escape being drafted having been told of the dreadful conditions in a mine so noxious to health that few left it alive. Transportation of the quicksilver was under licence to private groups who assumed responsibility for delivering it over 2,500 km away.

The production of both mercury and silver was based on Indian labour, recruited largely by coercion through the *mita* system. Under this system, which was established in 1570 and lasted until 1810, Indian communities in stipulated areas were required to provide tribute in the form of a supply of labourers. As a rule, it implied the dislocation of the *mitayos* to centres hundreds of miles away, often at considerable cost in human suffering. This was the case notably in the Huancavélica quicksilver mine, in whose galleries many *mitayos* died of poisoning.

Notwithstanding the enormous importance of silver to the Spanish American colonial economy, the direct utilisation of labour in its production remained at relatively low levels. Its chief significance was the creation of a market which provided a focus for many other economic activities. The number of *mitayos* in Potosí probably did not exceed 13,500, and in seventeenth-century Mexico, the mine-workers probably numbered no more than 15,000.[12] Since silver mining was a highly profitable enterprise, the supply of labour never became an effective obstacle to production. In Mexico, where the population had dwindled considerably, and where many of the mines were situated at great distances from the more populated areas, wage labour was resorted to very early. By the end of the sixteenth century, the wage-labour system already prevailed over the forms of enforced labour exacted through the *encomiendas*. Faced with higher labour costs, the Mexican mine-owners persuaded the Crown to halve the royal-fifth, a concession granted to their Potosí counterparts only in the mid-eighteenth century when the difficulties besetting quicksilver production had increased considerably and the richest ores had already been exhausted. The Mexican mine-

---

[11] Cf. Arthur P. Whitaker, 'The Failure of the Huancavelica Mercury Mine', in *History of Latin American Civilisation, Sources and Interpretations*, edited by Lewis Hanke vol. I.

[12] Cf. D. A. Brading and Harry E. Cross, op. cit.

owners also benefited from the steep fall in quicksilver prices which followed the notable expansion of output in Almadén.

According to data compiled by E. J. Hamilton, between 1503 and 1650 Spain received from its American colonies 181 tons of gold and 16,887 tons of silver.[13] Both the data on Spain's imports of silver and those on the consumption of mercury in Peru and Mexico indicate that after a remarkable period of expansion in the half-century following the spread of the mercury amalgamation technique, that is between the 1570s and the 1620s, output remained at a high but declining level in the quarter-century that followed, and suffered three-quarters of a century of decline or stagnation after 1650. It is likely that the initial cause of this decline was the inadequate supply of quicksilver, whose output dwindled first in Spain and then in Peru. Since Potosí's production was more profitable from the viewpoint of the Spanish crown, large shipments of Spanish mercury were diverted to that region and deliveries to Mexico were halved in the second quarter of the sixteenth century. Thus, Mexican silver-mining, with higher costs and scattered over a wider region, tended to be sacrificed at a time when supplies of mercury were insufficient to meet demand. During the 1580s the Zacatecas mines, by far the most productive in Mexico, were unable to refine half the metal extracted.

Towards the middle of the eighteenth century, silver production again began to expand: dramatically in Mexico and more modestly in South America, where mines situated in Chile, New Granada, and even in Peru, managed to compensate for the prolonged and definitive decline of Potosí.

Colonial trade

The external trade of the Spanish colonies was subject to strict control by the metropolitan authorities. This system reflected not only the spirit of the emerging Colonial Pact, but also the particular circumstances of Spain's external relations at a time when that country was involved in constant international conflicts and had to protect a treasure which excited the envy of other nations. Ships bound for the Indies sailed from Seville where they were subject to strict control. The system of convoyed

---

[13] Cf. E. J. Hamilton, *American Treasure and the Price Revolution in Spain, 1501–1650*, Harvard University Press, 1934. For estimates based on the same sources but relating to the whole of the colonial period, see Pierre Chaunu, *L'Amerique et les Amériques*, Paris, 1964. An estimate of production during the period 1571–1700, based on the consumption of mercury, is given in the article by D. A. Brading and Harry Cross cited above.

fleets was introduced in the 1540s, half a century after the voyages of Columbus, in response to the growing loss of ships to pirates and corsairs. In 1543, during the war with France, it was decreed that only ships of more than 100 tons, sailing in fleets of ten sail, could leave for the Indies. Each fleet was escorted by a warship financed from taxes collected from the merchants whose goods were being carried. Finally, in 1561, a system of annual convoys was established.[14] Two fleets sailed each year, one in January, bound for Tierra Firme, and one in August, bound for New Spain. The sale of the merchandise transported in the fleets was also subject to control; once released by the local authorities, the goods were offered for sale at a pre-established centre, giving rise to the famous *fleet fairs*. The organisation of trade in this manner permitted the emergence of a local merchant class, which drew its supplies directly from the annual fairs and enjoyed a position of monopoly (or oligopoly) in the resale of goods.

If we analyse the data on this trade, taking into account bullion exported by private individuals and the goods imported from Spain, it becomes apparent that the value of the imports covered only a fraction of the exports. The averages over long periods indicate that the value of the precious metals shipped by the private sector was about four times that of the total imports.[15] It seems, then, that there can be no doubt that the foremost objective of the work carried out in the Americas was to create a flow of resources for accumulation in Spain. Since production costs could be covered locally by mobilising the labour force of the *encomienda* – which produced the food supply for the men working in the mines and in transport – the imports from Spain essentially reflected the way in which the *encomenderos* used their own income, which included 80 or 90 per cent of the bullion output. Had this income been spent locally, whether in consumption or in productive or unproductive investment, the level of imports would have had to be much higher. The highly favourable balance of trade clearly indicates that the *encomendero* class was able to save a substantial proportion of its income, which was transferred to Spain.

The general pattern of trade changed considerably in the eighteenth century as a result both of the weakening of Spanish naval power and of the changes which had taken place in the colonies during the long period of decline in the production of precious metals. We know that from the

---

[14] Cf. Eduardo Arcila Farías, *Reformas Económicos del Siglo XVIII en Nueva España*, Mexico, 1974, vol. I, p. 76.

[15] For the statistical data see Alvaro Jara, *Tres Ensaios sobre Economía Minera Hispanoamericana*, Santiago, 1966.

first century of colonisation, Spain tended to operate essentially as an entrepôt, supplying the Indies with goods imported from various regions of Europe. The decline in the output of precious metals made this entrepôt trade seem even more burdensome to the colonies. At its height, the total capacity of the Isthmus (Tierra Firme) and Mexico (New Spain) fleets was around 10,000 tons. By the second half of the eighteenth century, trade had dwindled so dramatically that the total tonnage of the fleets was less than a half or a third of what it had been.

The formal breakdown of the Spanish monopoly began in the eighteenth century. With the outbreak of the War of the Spanish Succession in 1701, a French company was granted the privilege of selling slaves in the Spanish Indies for ten years. By the Treaty of Utrecht (1713) this privilege was transferred to the English and a joint-stock company was floated expressly for the purpose of exploiting it, with the Kings of Spain and England each holding 25 per cent of the share capital. The company, which had the right to supply African slaves for the Spanish possessions at the rate of 4,800 a year, for a period of 30 years, established slaving stations at the principal ports between Vera Cruz and Buenos Aires and, shortly afterwards, in the interior, its operations reaching as far inland as the remote mines of northern Mexico. In addition, it had the right to import the goods needed for the maintenance of the slaves while they remained in its hands. Under cover of these slave-trading operations, an extensive illicit commerce developed. In addition to supplying slaves, the company secured the privilege of sending one shipload of English merchandise to the ports of Vera Cruz, Cartagena and Puerto Bello every year. The size of these annual ships was officially restricted to 500 tons. However, this concession was used as a cover for sending not one, but several, shiploads a year, which soon became a regular source of supply.

Realising that trade between the American colonies and Europe was becoming increasingly important and diversified, and that Spanish participation in this trade had suffered a permanent decline, the Spanish Crown promulgated a series of reform measures, which had far-reaching repercussions. Several commercial companies were formed to bring together the financial and technical resources needed to develop exportable production in certain regions. The first to consolidate itself was the Caracas or Guipúzcoa Company, created in 1728 with a capital of three million *pesos*. At that time Venezuelan cocoa had become one of Spanish America's principal exports. Another important company was the Havana company, incorporated in 1740, mainly to foster the tobacco trade.

The breakdown of the old colonial trade system was accelerated in the second half of the eighteenth century. After 1765, a system of so-called *free trade* was introduced. This system signified firstly the end of the prohibition on direct inter-colonial trade. Before this reform, trade between the American provinces had been dependent on licences issued for specific transactions. The concession of this greater freedom was, however, progressive both in respect of the goods traded and of the ports concerned. Secondly, the new system opened trade with the Indies to the shipping of all major Spanish ports, thus putting an end to the monopoly of Seville and Cadiz. Finally, *creoles* (Spaniards born in America) were permitted to sail from American to Spanish ports.

The interests centred around the old commercial structures were, however, by no means negligible. The relations of Buenos Aires with the silver-mining region of Upper Peru are illustrative in this respect. The important trading entrepôt of Lima fought for over two centuries to defend its privileged position as the monopoly supplier in the trade with the silver-producing region, although access to that region was much easier through Buenos Aires.[16] In consequence, an important centre of commercial interests linked to the contraband trade, developed in that city. The proximity of Brazil and, after 1713, the presence of the English engaged in the slave trade, helped to consolidate and widen these parallel commercial relations. On the other hand, the Río de la Plata region was soon to become an important producer of hides, a commodity for which there was little outlet in Spain. Direct trade with the metropolis was prohibited until 1721, when 'register ships'[17] were authorised to engage in regular trade. In 1622, a custom-house had been established in Córdoba to prevent bullion from finding its way to Buenos Aires, where it could be used to foster the contraband trade. There was thus a considerable under-utilised economic potential in the region, a fact which explains why the trade liberalisation measures made a greater impact

---

[16] 'It took 50 days to travel the 350 leagues of flat land separating Buenos Aires from Jujuy and twelve more days to cover the remaining 100 leagues to Potosí; thus, a journey of 72 days separated the Río de la Plata from the silver mines of Potosí. By contrast, the journey from Lima to Potosí over 500 leagues of high mountain passes and difficult trails, lasted four months, adding 150 per cent to the costs of the merchandise, in comparison with that imported through Buenos Aires, not taking into account the fact that carriage from the Spanish ports to El Callao-Lima was several times more costly than to Buenos Aires.' Rodolfo Puiggros, *Historia Económica del Río de la Plata*, 3rd ed. Buenos Aires, n.d., p. 47.

[17] Register ships were ships which sailed singly, outside the annual convoy system, but which might legally be freighted only by members of the Cadiz *Consulado* or merchant guild. (Translator.)

there than anywhere else. Exports of hides alone increased within a few years from 150,000 to 800,000 units.[18]

The mercantile class of New Spain put up considerable resistance to the liberal legislation. Its power was so great that in 1720 the Spanish Crown deemed it necessary to transfer the site of the annual fleet fair from Mexico City to Jalapa in order to prevent the New Spain merchants from having too strong a bargaining position when buying goods arriving from Spain. On the other hand, the merchant houses used every means at their disposal to prevent shipments from exceeding certain volumes, in order to keep prices under strict control. The liberalising trade reforms were introduced into New Spain only in 1789, eleven years after their adoption in Buenos Aires and twenty-four years after they were first put into effect in the West Indies. As a consequence of these reforms, there emerged a new class of merchants, centred in Vera Cruz and having greater financial links with external interests.[19]

Growth poles and the origins of Latin American 'feudalism'

The production of precious metals, which provided the basis for the foundation and organisation of the Spanish Empire in the Americas, took two main forms: the extraction of alluvial gold and the production of silver from ores of varying richness in silver content. The search for gold accounts for the extraordinary scattered pattern of settlement in the early years of colonisation: within a few decades the Spaniards, few though they were, had occupied lands extending from northern Mexico to Chile. Nevertheless, gold production had little importance in the effective organisation of the economic space. As soon as the more accessible alluvial deposits became worked out, the region usually became depopulated. In the West Indies, an important gold-producing area in the first half of the sixteenth century, depopulation followed the exhaustion of deposits because the native populations which survived the hard labour imposed on them were transferred to other regions, where they could be put to work more profitably. In Cuba, Santo Domingo and Puerto Rico, the Spanish presence in the subsequent phase was linked to activities related to the refitting and victualling of the fleets in transit from Seville to the continental ports of Vera Cruz and Puerto Bello. In Chile and Antioquia (New Granada), agricultural activities provided the basis for settlement by populations originally attracted by the presence of alluvial gold.

[18] Rudolfo Puiggros, op. cit., p. 52.
[19] Cf. D. A. Brading, *Mines and Merchants in Bourbon Mexico, 1763–1810*, Cambridge University Press, 1971, pp. 114–19.

The production of silver (extraction from the ores and refining of the metal) played an entirely different role, since it gave rise to genuine growth poles. Silver-mining, unlike surface prospecting for gold, required heavy capital outlays in galleries and shafts, hydraulic works and mechanical plant. A characteristic of the silver mines was that in the initial stages of exploitation, the extraction of the mineral was relatively easy but the ores were of poor quality: as the shafts sank deeper, ore grades improved. Thus, although the industry demanded increased capital investments, its profitability was sustained or even heightened with the passage of time. Since many mines were worked for decades and even centuries, their exploitation gave rise to an important urbanisation process and to the formation of satellite economies. According to the census taken by Viceroy Francisco de Toledo twenty-five years after the discovery of the famous mine at Potosí, there was a population of 120,000 living in the vicinity of the 'prodigious silver mountain'. By 1650 that population had increased to 160,000, the biggest urban concentration in the Americas of the colonial period.[20] The demand created by an urban agglomeration of this size for food, clothing and articles of domestic use, as well as for building materials and draught animals, necessitated the organisation of important satellite economies.

Thus, settlement in Chile, which was at first supported by the production of gold, found a permanent basis in export agriculture for which the market was the Peruvian growth pole. Similarly, the regions of northern Argentina, with their relatively dense Indian population, tended to become a centre for supplying Upper Peru with textiles and draught animals.

A chain of economic interrelations was formed between the silver-producing region, situated in what is now Bolivia, the quicksilver-producing region, in present-day Peru, the Arica region, from which silver was shipped to Lima, Lima itself, which was the chief administrative centre, and the Cordoba–Tucuman region in Argentina, which supplied craft manufactures and draught animals. The dynamic pole of this system was, of course, the production of silver, based on Indian labour drafted by means of the *mita* system, which was used for this purpose throughout Spanish America.

Unlike Potosí, linked to the satellite economies situated between Chile and northern Argentina, without the intermediation of Lima, able to draw on the labour reserves of the Altiplano, and with direct access to the sea through Arica and Buenos Airea, the silver-producing regions of New Spain remained totally tributary to Mexico City, situated

[20] Cf. Lewis Hanke 'The Imperial City of Potosí, Boom Town Supreme', in *History of Latin American Civilization*, vol. I, cit.

between the mining areas and the port of Vera Cruz. The concentration of production in the widely separated mining centres of Pachuca, Zacatecas and Sonora, hindered the formation of an important urban centre capable of providing support for other economic activities. As a result, Mexico City – which besides being a commercial entrepôt between the metropolis and the Philippines, was situated in the region's most densely populated area, from which it derived an important surplus in the form of agricultural products or labour – enjoyed a dominant position unrivalled by any other city in the South American continent. The fleet fair system operated by the Spanish Crown gave the merchant class of Mexico City effective control over trade between the metropolis and the mining region. Consequently, the share of the surplus which remained in the country was used mainly in Mexico City, which played the key role in organising the economic space.

The events of the last century of the colonial period were of equal importance in the organisation of the future Latin American economies. We have already referred to the recovery in population growth, due probably to the greater resistance of the new generations to diseases introduced by the Europeans and to the reconstitution of social structures. With the decline of mining consequent upon the impoverishment of lodes or shortages of mercury, this increased population was no longer requisitioned for long marches in search of gold or drafted into the mines, and could devote itself to agriculture. On the other hand, the acceleration of European development brought about a considerable increase in the demand for products previously consumed only in minute quantities: sugar, cocoa, cotton, hides and indigo, among others. New agricultural activities, geared to the export market, opened up a stage of resettlement for the Spanish West Indies, based mainly on African slaves.

The notable changes which took place in the eighteenth century, including the relative liberalisation of trade, had a decisive effect on the Caribbean region, that is, the area between Caracas and Havana, and on the Río de la Plata. In the case of the first region, the most important factor was the creation of the joint-stock trading companies, with their considerable financial power; in the case of the second, the catalysing effect was provided by the register ships, which made it possible to activate a hitherto under-utilised economic potential. For the region as a whole, however, the developments of the first two centuries of colonisation were undoubtedly of greater importance: the period of prosperity permitted the organisation of the economic space around the mining poles which provided the basis for the Viceroyalties of Mexico

(New Spain) and Peru (New Castile); the decline in the mining economy led to the weakening of links between the satellite regions and to the strengthening of localism.

The prolonged decline of mining activities was to have far-reaching consequences in the region's subsequent social development. With the weakening of demand for agricultural surpluses which could be readily converted into money, the institution of the *encomienda* lost some of its original character. The basis of the system was the principle that part of the surplus extracted from the Indians belonged to the Crown, the *encomendero* acting simply as a collecting agent. With the reduced possibilities for monetising the surplus, transfer to the State of its share of wealth became difficult or even impracticable. As a result, the institution gradually died out and was formally abolished at the beginning of the eighteenth century. Nevertheless, the *mita* system was maintained, as a tribute exacted from the Indian communities, making it possible to subsidise the decadent mining industry.

The organisation of the Indians to create an agricultural surplus is closely related to the introduction of another institution which was to play a fundamental role in shaping the structure of Latin American society: the large agricultural estate. Grants of land were made in the same spirit as grants of Indians: as an incentive to private action so as to pave the way for the Conquest and produce a surplus for the benefit of the Crown. Land, in itself, was not an attraction. However, given the demand for agricultural products, it could become the source of a surplus to be exacted from the population ceded to the *encomendero*.

The decadence of the economic system that had grown up around the poles producing precious metals took the form of a progressive decentralisation of economic and social activities, which tended to transform the ownership of land into the basic institution of social organisation. In effect, once the *encomienda* system had been abolished, it was the control of land that made it possible to continue extracting a surplus from the native population. Since this surplus, by its very nature, had to be used almost entirely locally, the social structure tended to assume the form of isolated or semi-isolated communities. These vast rural domains, essentially based on a subsistence economy and almost entirely cut off from the authority of the State, were to become one of the most characteristic features of Latin American society. The ownership of land became the basis of a system of social domination of the mass of the people by a small ethnically and culturally differentiated minority.

The social evolution of Brazil had its own distinctive features, but its results differed little from those described above. The decadence of the large plantation dependent upon slave labour and export markets began in the second half of the seventeenth century when the Brazilian sugar monopoly was broken and prices started to tumble.[21] Sugar production in the French and English Antilles expanded rapidly after this period, while mercantilist policies closed a great many European markets to sugar from the Portuguese colonies. The loss of foreign markets led to the partial break-up of Brazil's export agriculture and its transformation into a subsistence, or mainly subsistence, economy. The hinterland sector producing meat, draught animals and firewood for the coastal communities declined even more rapidly. The working population on these estates, unlike that of the large coastal plantations which employed African slaves, was largely of Indian origin.

With the breakdown of tribal structures, the residual native populations had been widely scattered and had lost, with their religion and their language, all cultural identity. In the absence of the mediating structure of the 'indigenous community', these populations came under the direct control of the landowners. But both in the regions where the Spaniards had established 'indigenous communities' – these were the most densely settled areas, where more complex forms of social organisation prevailed – and in regions where, under the Portuguese or Spanish yoke, the populations had moved from the tribal structure to the direct control of the landowner, the end result was inevitably the same: extraction of a labour surplus in the form of agricultural production or personal services.

In the one case the relations of the ruling class were established with the community's traditional leaders, in the other, with isolated individuals, giving rise to the *latifundio* – indigenous community and *latifundio* – *minifundio* patterns respectively. These two bi-polar patterns were to leave a permanent mark on the Latin American agrarian structure. Since the Indian communities tended to break up into *minifundios* as their communal lands were gradually appropriated by the ruling class, the similarities between the two patterns became more pronounced. Thus, in

[21] The marketing of Brazilian sugar in Europe was carred out from the very beginning under the control of Dutch interests responsible for refining the product and organising its distribution. The occupation of Portugal in 1580 and Spain's war with Holland made it difficult to carry out satisfactory marketing operations, and the Dutch West Indies Company finally occupied the Brazilian sugar region in 1630. In 1640 Portugal regained her independence, and twelve years later the Dutch were expelled from the Brazilian Northeast. Many of them went to the Antilles where they organised a new sugar-producing area. Thereafter sugar prices showed a persistent downward trend. For a detailed account and bibliography, see C. Furtado, *Formação Económica do Brasil*.

different ways, a large proportion of the rural population came to be scattered in small structural units, self-sufficient from the viewpoint of the organisation of production, but subject to the direct control of a landowning class.

As a result of this pattern of organisation, commercial capitalism, the basis of the land-exploiting enterprise in Latin America, gave rise to social formations almost totally cut off from the markets. Nevertheless, the process seldom culminated in the creation of closed self-contained units, like the feudal social forms of Europe. In almost all cases, the commercial activity, while of secondary importance to the population as a whole, was the main concern of the ruling class. Whenever circum-stances permitted, activities producing a marketable surplus were relatively broadened. Since the principal preoccupation of the ruling class was to integrate part of the surplus into a commercial circuit, there is little point in referring to this class as 'feudal'. The absence of wage-earners indicates the presence of a pre-capitalist social formation, which is not necessarily feudal in character. Wherever the marketable surplus was below a certain level, the landowning class tended to disappear and the working population became scattered in a purely subsistence economy.

The discovery of gold in Brazil at the beginning of the eighteenth century changed the overall trends of the country's evolution.[22] It opened up an important market for draught animals and provided new oppor-tunities for the underemployed labour force of the sugar economy. The São Francisco River, linking the cattle-raising region of the Northeast to the mining area, became an important line of communication. The growth pole formed by the gold- and diamond-producing areas was to have considerable significance in the development of the Brazilian economy. In contrast to sugar production, only feasible for those in a position to mobilise substantial financial resources, alluvial gold could be exploited by lone prospectors and large-scale operators alike. The mining region thus attracted immigration on a far greater scale than that of the preceding two centuries. The rapid development of urban life created an expanding market for food, which was added to the even more important market for draught and pack animals used in the exten-sive transport network linking the vast gold region to the port of Rio de Janeiro. The market for cattle and mules was supplied mainly by the southern regions whose pastoral potential was soon recognised. Thus

---

[22] For an analysis and bibliography of the gold period in Brazil see C. R. Boxer, *The Golden Age of Brazil 1695–1750: Growing Pains of a Colonial Society*, Berkeley, Univ. of California Press, 1962.

the growth pole created by the mining industry made it possible to establish economic links between Northeast, Central and Southern Brazil already in the eighteenth century, i.e. in the period immediately preceding independence. As we have seen, in this same period the links centering on the growth pole constituted by the silver-producing region of Upper Peru, established in the first one and a half centuries of colonisation, were beginning to slacken.

Taking an extremely schematic view, it can be said that the first 150 years of the Spanish presence in the Americas were marked by the spectacular economic successes of the Crown and the Spanish minority that had participated directly in the Conquest; by the destruction of a large part of the existing population; by the worsening of the living conditions of the population that survived the Conquest; and finally, by the impact on vast regions of the development of growth poles whose main function was to produce a surplus in the form of precious metals, which was transferred to Spain on an almost entirely unilateral basis. The 150 years that followed were characterised by the decline of mining; by the slackening of pressures on the population, which slowly began to increase and improve its living conditions; and by the weakening of links between the regions, which gradually became less interdependent. In the first phase the ruling class was composed of men directly connected with Spain, integrated in the apparatus of the State or in key positions of control over the production system that yielded the surplus transferred to the mother country. In the second phase the landowning class, having little connexion with the mother country and a strictly local horizon of interests, became increasingly important. In Portuguese America these two phases were to some extent reversed. In the first 150 years an export agriculture economy was set up, made up of isolated units directly linked to the exterior and cut off from all the other areas of the country, with the exception of the pastoral interior which developed as a dependency of the sugar economy. The first third of the second 150-year phase was marked by an economic depression more rapid than that experienced in the Spanish Empire during the same period. The last century of the colonial era was characterised by the emergence of a growth pole centred on the production of gold and diamonds, which performed the dual role of accelerating settlement of European origin and creating a market that linked up the country's various regions. The ruling class in the first phase consisted of the owners of large sugar plantations who had direct connexions with the metropolis. In the second phase, the ruling class included a sizeable group of individuals whose connexions were with domestic commercial activities and the flourishing mule trade, a sector of economic activity linking together the various regions involved. There is thus some evidence that whereas the evolution of socio-economic structures fostered the tendency to fragmentation in the southern part of the Spanish Empire, in Brazil it created conditions favouring the preservation of territorial unity. It is interesting to note that New Spain (Mexico), whose wealth and population at the time of independence surpassed those of all Spain's South American provinces combined, maintained its territorial unity. In that region, mining activities had enjoyed a period of exceptional prosperity in the last half-century of the colonial period.

3 First half of the nineteenth century

End of the colonial era

The break-up of the Spanish and Portuguesè Empires at the time of the Napoleonic Wars was the last act in the complex historical process that unfolded throughout the eighteenth century, and was intimately related to the economic and social changes that had taken place in Europe. Spain's attempts to diversify the economies of her American colonies encountered two major obstacles: the protectionist barriers erected in the principal European markets as a result of prevailing mercantilist policies and her own inability to supply the colonies with manufactured goods. The colonies sought a way out of this situation by trying to find direct markets (through the contraband trade) or by producing domestically the articles they needed. Both attempts involved direct conflict with the metropolis. In regions with a developed export agriculture, such as Venezuela, or with a flourishing trade, such as Buenos Aires, awareness of these problems had crystallised very early under the influx of liberal ideas from England and France. With the outbreak of the Napoleonic Wars, Spain's isolation and the rapid penetration of British commercial interests precipitated changes difficult to reverse after the establishment of autonomous local authorities in various regions. In most cases, these governments arose in circumstances which did not involve hostility to the metropolis, then occupied by the French. But the very dynamic of the process led to breakaway movements, which in some cases took the form of prolonged and cruel struggle against the obstinate attempts of the Spaniards to restore a situation which had long ceased to exist. The true nature of the problem is clearly revealed by the fact that in this same period Brazil broke away from Portugal, although the seat of government of this country, an ally of England's, had been transferred to the colony itself and remained there from 1808 to 1821. The new conditions created by the rapid advance of the Industrial Revolution in England,

and by the progressive control England was able to exercise over world shipping, were bound to lead to a policy of opening the American ports to international trade, a policy incompatible with the type of relations prevailing between Spain and her colonies. The vast extent of the colonies, and the mother country's inability to supply them with manufactures, called for radical changes in the structure of an empire organised three centuries earlier around the exploitation of precious metals.

In the case of Portugal, the transition had begun much earlier. The Methuen Treaty, signed in 1703, had given England a privileged position in the Brazil trade. By this treaty, Portugal took the irreversible step of opening her own market and that of her colonies to English manufactures in return for the advantages her wines received on the English market. Brazilian gold production, which began in the second decade of the eighteenth century, had a dynamic impact on the Luso–Brazilian demand for manufactures, thus creating exceptional opportunities for English manufacturers. The result was that virtually all Brazil's gold found its way to England, enabling that country to build up the substantial international reserves without which she would have had difficulty in conducting the war against Napoleon.[1] English penetration in Brazil enabled Portugal to survive as a colonial power in the eighteenth century, but it also hastened the break in the link between the colony and the metropolis, whose position as a superfluous entrepot had become increasingly apparent. With the transfer of the Portuguese Crown to Rio de Janeiro in 1808, English interests became directly involved in the Colony, which had become the seat of the Portuguese Court. In this case, too, the process proved irreversible, and set in motion a train of events affecting the Portuguese Crown itself, when one of its members assumed the leadership of the separatist movement.

The first half of the nineteenth century is marked in Latin America by the struggles for independence and by the process of formation of the nation-states. In the Spanish colonies the independence movement spread out from three centres: Caracas, Buenos Aires and Mexico. The first two were centres of regions that had developed most rapidly during the eighteenth century, a development that was largely a reflexion of Spain's weakening naval power and the penetration of English interests. In these regions, independence permitted the rise of a mercantile bourgeoisie, liberal in outlook, progressive in the sense that it was 'European-

---

[1] Cf. W. Cunningham, *The Growth of Modern Industry and Commerce: Modern Times*, Part I, Cambridge, 1921, pp. 460–1.

ising', but hopelessly wedded to the concept of *laissez-faire*.[2] In Mexico the situation was different, since silver mining, still in a prosperous phase, continued to be the basis of the regional economy. Moreover, the indigenous Mexican Indian population, which had begun to increase again in the last century of colonial domination, was starting to exert pressure on the latifundian structure, based on the ownership of large estates and the exploitation of indigenous communities. The element of social unrest thus introduced into the independence struggle remained, and marked the country's evolution for more than a century. Thus two distinct movements, which were to govern Latin America's subsequent evolution, are discernible in the struggles for independence: on the one hand we find the rise of a European-influenced bourgeoisie that sought to wipe out by decree the pre-Columbian and colonial past and to integrate the different regions into the expanding flow of international trade; on the other, the emergence of forces tending to challenge the domination of the colonial regime and seeking to integrate the native masses into the political and social framework, in an attempt to create a distinctive and independent cultural personality. The first of these movements dominated the greater part of the nineteenth century but, as we shall see further on, it was only in the latter half of that century that it finally bore fruit. The second movement entered the foreground in the present century which, for Latin America, began with the Mexican Revolution.

Formation of nation-states

In nearly all of Latin America the building of nation-states proved a formidable task. The liberal bourgeoisies who had led or supported the independence movements in Buenos Aires and Caracas were in no position to organise systems of political control capable of replacing those of the former metropolis. As we have seen, the colonies had been evolving in the direction of regional autonomy. In the absence of significant new economic links, political localism tended to prevail. In the North, where

---

[2] A conspicuous representative of this liberal current is the Liberator, Simón Bolívar, who issued decrees in 1824 and 1825 from Trujillo and Cuzco, dissolving the native communities, establishing private ownership of land by peasants, and ordering the 'so-called Indians' who were owners of the lands in their possession 'to sell them or dispose of them in any way they deemed fit'. These measures were not implemented at the time but clearly reflect the European-influenced outlook of the leaders of the wars of independence. For relevant comment see Arturo Urquidi Morales, 'Las Comunidades Indígenas y su Perspectiva Histórica' in *Les Problèmes Agraires des Amériques Latines*, Paris, 1967.

the growth pole of the mining industry remained comparatively vigorous and where a tradition of administrative centralism antedated the Spanish conquest, the political unity of what had been New Spain was preserved. In the South the captaincies of Venezuela and Chile became independent political units, New Granada split up into Colombia and Ecuador, the vast Viceroyalty of New Castile gave rise to Peru, and the recently created Viceroyalty of the Rio de la Plata broke up, giving rise to the present-day republics of Argentina, Uruguay, Paraguay and Bolivia.

Once the ties with the metropolis had been severed, power tended to shift to the landowning class. The structuring of the new states was conditioned by two factors: the absence of genuine interdependence between the landowners, who joined forces or submitted to whoever succeeded in the power struggle; and the action of the urban bourgeoisie, who maintained contact with the outside world and explored every possibility of expanding external trade. This second group was gradually joined by parts of the rural sector. Thus, as opportunities for different types of export lines arose, the urban group tended to consolidate itself and at the same time to become attracted to rural interests, creating the conditions for building up an effective power system. In countries such as Mexico, Peru and Bolivia, where mining dominated the economy, control of this activity was enough to define the power of the State although there was hardly any connexion between this power and the vast majority of the population organised on the estates. Nonetheless, no regional landowner was powerful enough to challenge the authority of the State, control of which was the main objective of the political struggles. In regions with an agricultural economy, the consolidation of state power was dependent on the opening up of new export lines which, by favouring one region, enabled it to dominate the others. In Colombia, where none of the regions had managed to achieve a sufficiently solid economic base to become dominant, there were civil wars, lasting until the end of the nineteenth century. In Argentina, the privileged position of the port of Buenos Aires enabled the coastal region to impose itself as the centre of a national power system, after a number of civil wars.[3]

We have seen that events in Europe, which isolated Spain from her colonies, hastened the wars of independence, led by the local bourgeoisies which had emerged in the areas benefiting from the diversification of trade in the last century of the colonial era. Mexico is a case apart, in

[3] For an account of the role of the 'unifying autocracy' in the formation of the nation-state in Argentina see Gino Germani, *Política y Sociedad en una Época de Transición*, Buenos Aires, 1962.

the sense that its isolation from the metropolis had more far-reaching consequences, setting in motion a process that challened the social order itself, giving another dimension to the power struggle and creating a situation of social instability which was to be aggravated by the Reform movement and the prolonged dictatorship of Porfirio Díaz, and which was at the root of the Mexican Revolution at the beginning of the present century. We have also noted the part played by the English in breaking the trade monopoly and creating Europe-orientated urban interests. It must be pointed out, however, that English penetration, in the first decades of the nineteenth century, contributed to the disruption of the existing social and economic order rather than to the consolidation of the emerging nation-states. The English were essentially involved in organising an import trade: numerous English import houses were founded, responsible for the wide distribution of English-manufactured goods, which changed consumption habits and led to the disruption of local artisan activities. The influx of imported goods forced many countries to depreciate their foreign exchange rates, and governments had to apply for foreign loans to ease the balance of payments situation. On the other hand, the commercial houses importing British goods were able to accumulate liquid reserves and establish powerful financial agencies.

The local bourgeoisies, who had connexions with English import interests, had to face the problem of an inadequate external payments capacity. External indebtedness and the recurrent balance of payments crises created fiscal and foreign exchange problems which were met by issuing inconvertible paper currency, entailing the deterioration of the domestic and foreign purchasing power of the national currencies. The urban population, hardest-hit by the periodic price increases, were at times driven to open revolt. The export drive that this situation demanded led local bourgeoisies to turn to the interior for exportable products and to foreign countries for potential markets. However, during the first half of the nineteenth century external markets were limited and access to them proved difficult. This was largely because the Industrial Revolution, in this early phase, displayed two features that had a negative effect on the Latin American countries: the concentration in England, a country with colonies of her own able to supply her with primary products, particularly tropical commodities; and the key role of the cotton textile industry, for which the raw material could be produced on a large scale in the United States, using slave labour. The shorter distance involved was also a direct advantage in an age when maritime transport was precarious.

By and large, the Latin American countries experienced great difficulty in opening up new lines of trade in the three or four decades following the wars of independence. Apart from precious metals, hides and skins, no other export managed to find favourable market conditions. Although cotton consumption in England had risen from two thousand to a quarter of a million tons, cotton prices had tumbled and it was difficult to compete with growers in the southern United States. Moreover, the prices of sugar and other tropical commodities had fallen steeply after the end of the Napoleonic Wars. It has been argued that expansion of exports was handicapped by the political instability that prevailed in almost all the Latin American countries. But it can be argued that the causal direction was opposite: the difficulties encountered in finding foreign outlets for their export lines left the urban groups, who had led the independence struggles, in no position to organise a stable power system. An interesting exception to this rule – and the exception proves the rule – is the case of Chile. This country, an autonomous captaincy in colonial days, was distinguished by the fact that it had been neither an exporting centre for precious metals (its silver output was relatively small) nor a region exporting agricultural and livestock products to foreign markets. In fact, Chile was an agricultural and cattle-raising region focusing on the Peruvian growth pole. Unlike other commercial bourgeoisies, established through the contraband trade and under strong English influence, Chilean export interests were integrated with the region's agricultural and livestock interests, and had emerged within the legal framework of the monopoly organised by the metropolis. As a result, the Chilean ruling class was not subject to major internal conflict and managed to build up a stable power system in the decade following the wars of independence. In 1833 the *Portales* Constitution formalised a representative oligarchic power system, which remained stable until the late nineteenth century. On the other hand, Chile was able to take advantage of particularly favourable conditions for her foreign trade. First, she had the nucleus of a mining economy based on silver and copper, which expanded during this period. In the second place, she produced a surplus of temperate agricultural commodities, notably wheat, which gave her a distinct advantage in the Pacific zone at the time when gold was discovered in California and Australia.[4] Thus, for a brief but crucial period, Chile became a strategic food supplier to the West Coast of the United States. To what extent Chile's stable political

---

[4] For an outline of the evolution of the Chilean economy in the nineteenth century see Aníbal Pinto Santa Cruz, *Chile, un Caso de Desarrollo Frustrado*, Santiago de Chile, 1962.

structure enabled her to take advantage of the favourable foreign market conditions, or whether these conditions made it possible to consolidate the emergent political structure, is a matter of secondary importance. Obviously there was some interaction between these two factors. But one cannot ignore the fact that Chile's experience in relation to foreign market conditions constitutes a special case. No other Latin American country in the Pacific zone could match Chile's agricultural potential and export 'knowhow' in this particular sector. On the other hand, given the transportation difficulties of the time, no Atlantic country, Latin American or otherwise, offered any serious competition.

The Brazilian situation during this period also displays distinctive features worth analysing for a better understanding of the political structures on which the Latin American States are based. In Brazil, unlike in the regions occupied by the Spaniards, agricultural activities and the export of surplus produce were the Colony's *raison d'être*. The Portuguese monopolised commercial activities, preventing the emergence of a local bourgeoisie with foreign trade connexions. In the gold- and diamond-producing region the metropolis exercised an even stricter control over relations with the exterior. Meanwhile, this same region, which offered a ready market for pack animals, saw the rise and consolidation of a class of cattlemen and mule traders with connexions in various parts of the country. Large convoys of mules were brought from Rio Grande do Sul to São Paulo, where the bustling livestock fairs attracted dealers who supplied the mining regions through the network they maintained with the coastal area. After independence, foreign trade interests either remained in the hands of the Portuguese, protected by the continuity of the Crown, or were taken over by Englishmen. There was thus little change in the sugar region where the old structures were maintained under the more direct control of English interests. Significant changes occurred in the south, where the mining economy had been on the decline since the end of the eighteenth century. The reduction in gold output to a third or a quarter of the quantity formerly produced at a time when administrative expenses were rising sharply as a result of the transfer of the Court and the subsequent establishment of independent government, provoked an overall imbalance in the economy. This was countered by contracting foreign loans and issuing paper currency which rapidly depreciated.

Inflation bred dissatisfaction in the urban zones and centrifugal forces began to manifest themselves in several regions in the form of revolts and separatist movements. Nonetheless, the development of coffee production, whose possibilities became apparent as early as the 1840s, permitted the formation of the nucleus which was to become the basis of the new power structure. The men responsible for establishing the connexion between the mining areas and the coastal zone played a major role in setting up a coffee economy in the Paraíba Valley, from which it spread to the São Paulo highlands half a century later. Thus, coffee developed outside the latifundian structures established earlier, through the initiative of individuals with a mercantile outlook. Consequently the economic activity that was to be the mainstay of the Brazilian State in its formative phase and throughout its period of consolidation was from the outset an agricultural-export activity. As in the case of Chile, planters and merchants came to have joint interests and presented a perfectly united front. The traditional *latifundio*, with its mainly subsistence economy, was destined to have a marginal place in the power system that took shape in Brazil. Nonetheless, since the new export agriculture was also modelled on the large unit, it achieved a basic solidarity with the established *latifundios*. The latter were thus able to retain control of local power in their respective regions while leaving hegemonic control of national power to the new interests.[5]

[5] For a synthesis of Latin American history in the independence period see Victor L. Tapié, *Histoire de l'Amérique Latine au XIXe Siècle*, Paris, 1945. The book includes detailed bibliographies. For general bibliographies consult Jaime Vicens Vives, *Bibliografía Histórica de Espana y Hispanoamérica*, Barcelona, 1953. See also Robert A. Humphreys, *Latin American History: a Guide to the Literature in English*, London, 1960. The revised second edition of Jacques Lambert's *Amérique Latine: Structures Sociales et Institutions Politiques*, Paris, 1968, is also a valuable bibliographical source. See also Tulio Halperín Donghi, *História Contemporanea de América Latina*. Madrid, 1969 and the basic work *La História Economica en América Latina*, a collection of papers presented at the first symposium on Latin American economic history held in 1970 under the auspices of the Latin American Social Sciences Council, Consejo Latino-americano de Ciencias Sociales, Mexico, 1972.

4 The transformation of international trade in the second half of the nineteenth century and its impact on Latin America

International division of labour

During the first half of the nineteenth century, the Industrial Revolution was essentially an English phenomenon. For this reason the structural evolution of the English economy provides the key to the radical changes which took place during this period in the world economy as a whole. The economists who witnessed the beginnings of these changes, and interpreted them from the English viewpoint, immediately realised that it was in England's interests to become a vast factory, opening its doors to primary products from all over the world. In fact, industrial activity, violating the law of diminishing returns, signified unprecedented qualitative change.

In economies in which technology had made little or no progress – based essentially on agricultural activity – it was evident that there were limits to the degree to which the relative proportions of the productive factors employed could be altered. Beyond a certain point, the output obtained per unit of agricultural land necessarily tended to decrease, regardless of the amount of labour added, which meant that availability of land governed the use of the other factors. Industrial activity made it possible to break this barrier, since growth itself, by creating the possibility of further specialisation in labour and equipment (greater division of labour, additional and more complex machinery), became the source of increased productivity, which meant increasing returns. In such circumstances, even if prices of imported agricultural products remained stable and were the same as those of home-produced goods, it would still be to the advantage of a country like England, where land was scarce, to be able to pay for them with industrial products. On the other hand, once England had established an important industrial nucleus and consolidated its advantage over other countries, it would not be difficult to demonstrate that, in terms of the principle of comparative advantage, considered from the static point of view, it would be in the interests of other countries to buy industrial products from England and pay for them with raw materials. However, despite the enormous advantages it represented for England (since it implied nothing less than the concentration in this country of those activities in which rapid technological progress was being made), this development *model* met with resistance on the part of agricultural interests, and its acceptance was much slower than is generally supposed. Throughout the first half of the nineteenth century, English agriculture continued to enjoy effective protection through an adjustable tariff mechanism which permitted customs barriers to be automatically raised whenever world prices fell below a certain critical point. However, faced with the growing power of the industrial bourgeoisie, resistance gradually broke down and, between 1846 and 1849, England eliminated barriers to external trade without expecting other countries to follow suit.

The complete victory of free trade ideas in some ways marked the end of the first phase of the Industrial Revolution. During this phase a dynamic nucleus was formed and consolidated in England, which was to lead, in the second half of the nineteenth century, to the establishment of a system of international division of labour of world-wide scope. Of decisive importance in the transition from the first to the second phase of the Industrial Revolution was the application to the transport sector of technology originally developed in connexion with manufacturing industries. Railroads made possible the rapid integration of the domestic markets in European countries, while the mechanisation of maritime transport brought about radical changes in the conditions of international trade. The propeller was invented around 1840, and in the course of the following decade the introduction of iron hulls, reducing the resistance of water, permitted an increase in the size of vessels. From then on, the total world tonnage of the merchant marine was to increase with extraordinary speed: from 6.7 million tons in 1840 it rose to 12.8 million in 1860, and to 43 million in 1913. The impact on long-distance freight charges was dramatic, and in many cases ocean freight rates were cut by as much as 70–90 per cent. The consequent fall in the prices of raw materials, particularly of cotton, reinforced England's competitive position. By pursuing a policy of free trade and substantially reducing her own agricultural activities, England was able to extract the maximum advantage from the fall in raw material prices brought about by the cut in shipping costs. In this way, English manufacturers managed to 'internalise' the external economies resulting from the technological revolution in transport. It should be recalled that in the first few decades of the second half of the nineteenth century, two-thirds of the manufactures circulating in the world market were made in England.

The century between the Napoleonic Wars and the First World War witnessed the shaping of a world economic system based on the international division of labour. The economic activities of a growing proportion of mankind became interdependent elements of an integrated complex. The new pattern of the world economy displayed some notable features. The first was the rise in the economic growth rate of many of the countries involved in the system. This applied not only to countries which specialised in activities benefiting from rapid technical progress, but also to those making use of their natural resources within the framework of geographical specialisation. This phenomenon had far-reaching historical consequences. Up to this time, growth rates had been irregular and, even when they showed a long-term upward trend, were too weak to imply really significant changes in standards of living within the lifetime of a single generation. It seemed natural, therefore, to assume, as did the mercantilists, that the enrichment of one community inevitably meant the impoverishment of another. With the Industrial Revolution, the accelerated output of goods and services made it possible to double a community's purchasing power in the course of a single generation.

The second significant change was the dramatic rise in the rates of population increase brought about by urbanisation, improvements in public services and the rise in real incomes. Immediately afterwards, striking advances in the application of public health measures greatly improved life-expectancies. Expectation of a longer life and the possibility of seeing it dramatically altered produced a new outlook, based on the realisation that the horizon of possibilities open to mankind could be vastly extended on both individual and social planes. The great collective movements, which in the past had had a religious or military inspiration, became increasingly orientated towards understanding and mastering the physical world and reshaping social structures.

The third noteworthy characteristic is the creation and rapid expansion of a fund of transmittable technical knowledge related to the forms of production.[1] In the pre-industrial age, production techniques were the result of the gradual accumulation of empirical knowledge, handed down from generation to generation through apprenticeship in the skilled trades. Productive activity gave rise to further productive activity, just as one generation gives birth to the next. With the growing importance of an equipment industry based on advanced technology, the

---

[1]   Simon Kuznets, *Modern Economic Growth*, p. 286.

situation was radically altered. Transmission of techniques took the form of a straightforward commercial transaction, and it became possible to transform an entire productive sector at a hitherto undreamed-of speed. By creating a transport equipment industry, England set in motion a process that was to transform the means of transport throughout the world. Further, by providing adequate financing for this industry, it created a capital exporting mechanism which was to be a decisive factor in shaping the world economic system since it encouraged the emergence of new forms of hegemony outside the traditional framework of colonial inplants.

The result of the interplay of these factors was the growth and integration of the world economy in the nineteenth century and the intensification of international specialisation. World trade expanded rapidly: its growth rate was far higher than that of the domestic products of the nations that took the lead in bringing about the transformation of the world economy. The value of world trade, which was no more than 1.5 billion dollars in the 1820s, rose to 3.5 billion in the 1840s and to 40 billion just before the outbreak of the First World War. This growth was reflected in the growing 'internationalisation' of the industrialised economies and more particularly of the British economy. Thus, Great Britain's external trade coefficient,[2] which was 8.5 per cent in the period 1805–19, rose to 29.4 per cent in the period 1910–13. Generally speaking, the external trade coefficient rose in all the European countries that started industrialising in this period. The same phenomenon occurred in countries exporting primary products – the case of the Latin American countries – where exports were developed at the expense of subsistence economic activities. This did not happen, however, in countries whose development was essentially an expansion of the European economic frontier, i.e. countries such as the United States,[3] Canada, Australia and

[2] The coefficient of external trade is defined as the ratio between the average value of imports and exports and the domestic product. For historical data see C. P. Kindleberger, *Foreign Trade and the National Economy*, Yale University Press, 1962, p. 180.

[3] The reference to the United States is restricted to the expansion of its agricultural frontier, particularly in the cereal-growing region. By the time the American provinces gained their independence, they already had a nucleus of manufacturing activities, including iron and steel works and shipbuilding. During the Napoleonic Wars, the United States benefited considerably from her position as a neutral country and became the possessor of the world's second largest merchant fleet, consisting entirely of vessels built in her own shipyards. Modern textile industries were established at the beginning of the nineteenth century and by the 1820s a textile machinery industry had already been set up. On the other hand, the marked increase in cotton exports produced on the basis of slave labour made it possible to maintain a high

New Zealand, whose development was dependent on an inflow of European labour and capital. Development in these countries, when it took the form of incorporating new territories, was an extension of the European economic space, whose natural resource base, including arable soils, was being enriched. Diminishing returns were avoided by increasing the supply of good agricultural land. Thus, Britain could curtail agricultural production while prices of agricultural products could be reduced thanks to the incorporation of land in the temperate zones of America and Oceania. The economy that developed in these new areas was specialised from the start, that is, it had a high coefficient of external trade and a high level of productivity and income. These conditions made it possible to attract the European immigrants on whose labour these developing areas depended. The result was that when they entered the world economy they already had effective domestic markets for industrial products and a labour force equipped for industrial activity, a circumstance which accounts for their early industrialisation. Since the newly established industries competed with imported manufactures, the external trade coefficient, which was high to begin with, showed a tendency to decline or level off, rather than following the upward trend noted in the first two cases.

In summary, the following features of the formative process of the world economic system are worth emphasising, because of their significance in shaping international relations:

(a) the existence of a nucleus which achieved a considerable advance in the process of capital accumulation, concentrating a large proportion of industrial activity, practically all centred on the production of equipment; this nucleus was also the financial centre for world exports of capital goods, controlled the transport infrastructure in international trade and was the major import market for primary products.

(b) the emergence of the system of international division of labour under the hegemony of this growth pole; the stimulus to geographical specialisation favoured rapid settlement of vast empty spaces in tem-

level of imports, benefiting regions of the country which were in the process of industrialising. The great expansion of agriculture in the Mid-West was supported by the markets provided by the commercial-industrial Eastern region and the region of specialised agriculture in the South. It was the interconnexion of these three dynamic poles – the industrial-commercial complex of the East, the agricultural exporting South and the food producing Mid-West – that gave the US economic system its extraordinary dynamism. Nonetheless, the expansion of the US agricultural frontier, creating large exportable surpluses, had the same stimulating effect on the European economy as the settlement of other empty spaces in the temperate latitudes outside Europe.

perate zones and the reorientation of commodity production in other areas specialising in the export of primary products.

(*c*) the creation of a network for transmitting technical progress as a subsidiary of the international division of labour; this network facilitated the export of capital and at the same time promoted the spread of final consumer goods emerging at the centre of the system with the advance of accumulation and technology; since production of capital goods was concentrated in the centre described above, new production techniques also remained geographically concentrated, benefiting those activities in which the dominant economy already had experience or in which it had more direct interest. Hence the evolution of technology was conditioned by the system of international division of labour that emerged with the Industrial Revolution.[4]

Typology of economies exporting raw materials

The Latin American countries began to enter the channels of expanding international trade in the 1840s. The primary product-exporting economies involved in this process can be divided into three types: (*a*) economies exporting temperate agricultural commodities; (*b*) economies exporting tropical agricultural commodities; (*c*) economies exporting mineral products. In each case, foreign trade helped to shape a distinctive economic structure whose characteristic features should be borne in mind when studying its subsequent evolution.

The first type is represented essentially by Argentina and Uruguay. In this case, exportable agricultural production was based on the extensive use of land and was destined to compete with the domestic production of countries undergoing rapid industrialisation. Extensive use of good agricultural land made it possible to achieve high profitability from the start. On the other hand, the very extensiveness of the agriculture practised and the sheer volume of freight involved necessitated the creation of a widespread transportation network which indirectly led to the rapid unification of the domestic market, focusing on the major ports of shipment. These countries display the characteristics of regions referred to earlier as constituting an expanding frontier of the industrialising European economy. This frontier, to which European agricultural techniques were transplanted in the early stages, soon became an important centre

---

[4] For the relation between development and international trade in the nineteenth century see Ragnar Nurkse, 'Trade Theory and Development Policy', in H. S. Ellis (ed.), *Economic Development for Latin America*, London, 1961.

for developing new agricultural techniques of its own. Both the techniques of farming vast open spaces and of large-scale transportation, storage and shipment of cereals originated in the United States. In sum, the countries in this group, precisely because they competed with the domestic production of countries at a more advanced stage of development and with regions of recent European settlement enjoying a high standard of living, were from the start integrated into a productive sector of the world economy characterised by continuing technological advance. Throughout the phase of expansion in their foreign trade, these countries achieved high rates of growth.

The second type, represented by countries exporting tropical agricultural products, involves more than half the Latin American population. It includes Brazil, Colombia, Ecuador, Central America and the Caribbean, as well as large regions of Mexico and Venezuela. Countries in this group entered international trade in competition with colonial areas and the slave-holding region of the United States. Sugar and tobacco remained typically colonial products until the last years of the nineteenth century. It was the rapid expansion of world demand for coffee and cacao from the mid-nineteenth century that enabled tropical commodities to play a dynamic role in integrating the Latin American economy into world trade during the period under consideration. The direct impact of the structural changes in the British economy was much less, since the British market continued to be abundantly supplied by colonial regions where labour was plentiful and wages were low. The role of dynamic centre fell to the United States and, to a lesser extent, to the European countries. On the whole, tropical commodities were of little significance as a factor in development, although they did involve the opening up of large areas for settlement. On the one hand, their prices continued to be influenced by the low wages prevailing in colonial regions, which had long been traditional tropical commodity producers. On the other, they did not usually require the creation of a complex infrastructure; in many regions traditional means of transport continued to be used. Finally, since they were produced in areas lacking the capacity to develop new techniques for themselves, tropical products tended to remain within the framework of the traditional economies. Nonetheless, in certain regions tropical export agriculture did manage to play an important role in development. The most notable instance is probably that of the coffee region of São Paulo, in Brazil. Here the physical and chemical qualities of the soil permitted extensive coffee planting. The relatively high productivity of labour, the vast size of the area planted and the use of European immigrants who demanded monetary wages, favoured the creation of a modern infrastructure and the emergence of a domestic market. The special nature of this case becomes evident when we recall that at the end of the nineteenth century the São Paulo highlands supplied two-thirds of the total world coffee output.

The third type of economy, represented by countries exporting mineral products, includes Mexico, Chile, Peru and Bolivia. Venezuela entered this group in the 1930s as an exporter of petroleum. The lowering of freight rates for long-distance transport and the rapid expansion of the mechanical industries, by creating an international market for industrial metals, brought about a radical change in Latin American mining. In the first place, precious metals, notably silver, rapidly lost their importance. Secondly, small-scale mining operations of the artisan or quasi-artisan type were gradually replaced by large-scale production controlled by foreign capital and administered from abroad. The considerable rise in the world demand for non-ferrous metals coincided with major technical advances in production methods which permitted or required the concentration of production in large units. This process of concentration carried out initially in the major producing country – the United States – soon spread to other areas, where local producers were marginalised by American organisations with heavy financial backing and the technical 'knowhow' required to handle low-grade ores. Thus, the development of the export mining industry entailed not only denationalisation but the establishment of a productive sector which, given its marked technical advance and high capital intensity, tended to become isolated and to behave as a separate economic system, or rather, as part of the economic system in which the decision centre controlling the production unit belonged. Foreign control of a highly capitalised activity, employing a small labour force, meant that the major share of the flow of income generated by this activity was deflected from the domestic economy. In these circumstances its value as a factor for inducing direct change in the domestic economy was practically nil. Moreover, since the infrastructure created to serve export mining industries was generally highly specialised, the resultant external economies were minimal or non-existent for the economic system as a whole. Finally, since this type of mining activity used inputs of industrial origin acquired outside the country and created a limited flow of wage income, it made no significant contribution to the creation of domestic markets. Its potential as a dynamic factor became evident only when the State intervened, obliging mining companies to acquire part of their inputs locally and collecting, in the form of tax revenue, a significant share of the flow of income traditionally remitted abroad.

5 Reorientation of the international economy in the present century

Export expansion phase

The three decades preceding the First World War were a period of rapid economic development and some social change in Latin America as a whole: in Mexico, where the Porfirio Díaz administration created the conditions for a large inflow of foreign capital directed mainly into mineral production; in Chile, whose victory in the War of the Pacific against Bolivia and Peru enabled her to monopolise the sources of nitrate; in Cuba, where, even before independence was attained in 1898, the country's increasing integration into the United States market had brought about a dramatic expansion in sugar production; in Brazil, where the spread of coffee over the São Paulo highlands and the influx of European immigrants hastened the collapse of the slave economy; finally, in Argentina, where economy and society underwent drastic changes under the impact of the great wave of immigration and the penetration of substantial foreign capital.

A closer look at the three largest countries reveals the importance of the changes that occurred during this period. In Mexico, the population increased from 9.4 million in 1877 to 15.2 million in 1910. In the last of the nearly three decades of the Porfirio Díaz administration (1900–10), the annual average growth rate of the real per capita product was 3.1 per cent. During this decade the production of minerals and petroleum, the country's basic export sector, grew at an annual rate of 7.2 per cent, that is, twice as fast as manufacturing production and nearly three times as fast as agricultural production.[1] In Brazil, the population increased from 10.1 million in 1872 to 17.3 million in 1900. In the last decade of the nineteenth century, the rate of population increase in São Paulo was

[1] For basic data see Daniel Cosio Villegas, *História Moderna de México*, VII, *El Porfiriato: Vida Económica*, Mexico, 1965. See also Leopoldo M. Sólis, 'Hacia un Análisis General a Largo Plazo del Desarrollo Económico de México' in El Colégio de México, *Demografia y Economía*, I, no. 1, Mexico, 1967.

over 5 per cent a year, while for the country as a whole it was under 2 per cent. Nearly all the 610,000 immigrants entering Brazil during this decade went to the State of São Paulo. Between 1880 and 1910, the total length of railways increased from 3.4 to 21.3 thousand kilometres. Coffee exports, which were around 4 million 60-kilogram bags in 1880, rose to almost 10 million in 1900 and to over 16 million on the eve of the First World War, a total seldom surpassed in later years. In the same period, exports of cacao rose from 6,000 to 40,000 tons, and rubber exports from 7,000 to 40,000 tons.[2] However, it was in Argentina that the changes brought about in this phase were most marked. Between the periods 1890–1904 and 1910–14, Argentina's population doubled, increasing from 3.6 to 7.2 million; the country's railway network was extended from 12.7 to 31.1 thousand kilometres; cereal exports rose from 1,038,000 to 5,294,000 tons, and exports of frozen meat rose from 27,000 to 376,000 tons.[3]

In sum, during the period under consideration, Latin America became an important contributor to world trade and a key source of raw materials for the industrialised countries. In 1913, the Latin American share in world commodity exports was as follows: cereals – 17.9 per cent; livestock products – 11.5 per cent; coffee, cocoa and tea – 62.1 per cent; sugar – 37.6 per cent; fruit and vegetables – 14.2 per cent; vegetable fibers – 6.3 per cent; rubber, furs, hides and leathers – 25.1 per cent.[4]

New trends in the international economy

After the First World War there were important changes in the long-term trends of the international economy. These changes were accentuated by the 1929 crisis. In the first place, there was a reversal of the upward trend in the external trade coefficient of the industrialised countries. In Britain, for instance, it fell from around 30 per cent (for the period 1910–13) to 25 per cent in 1927–9 and to 17 per cent in the 1930s. In the United States, Germany, France and Japan, the coefficient levelled off in the 1920s and declined in the 1930s.[5] This downward trend shifted

[2] Cf. Instituto Brasileiro de Geografia e Estatística, *Anuário Estatístico do Brasil, Quadros Retrospectivos, 1939–40.*

[3] See Aldo Ferrer, *La Economía Argentina*, Mexico, 1963, 2nd ed., revised, Mexico, 1974 (translated by Marjorie M. Urquidi, *The Argentine Economy*, Berkeley, University of California Press, 1967). See also Roberto Cortés Conde, 'Problemas del Crecimiento Industrial (1870–1914)', Torcuato di Tella, Gino Germani and Jorge Graciarena (ed.), *Argentina, Sociedad de Masas*, Buenos Aires, 1965.

[4] Basic data from P. L. Yates, *Forty Years of Foreign Trade*, London, 1959.

[5] Cf. C. P. Kindleberger, *Foreign Trade and the National Economy.*

again only after the Second World War, this time within a new international economic framework in which the central feature of world trade had become the exchange of manufactured products between industrialised countries.

In the second place, there was a persistent deterioration in world market prices of primary products. This tendency, already discernible in the preceding period, became more pronounced after 1913. To the short-term inelasticity of supply of primary commodities and the structural rigidity of countries specialising in primary production for export, was added the effect of technological progress as a factor responsible for this downward trend in world prices of raw materials. After the First World War, synthetic nitrates progressively displaced Chilean nitrates; synthetic fibres and synthetic rubber appeared shortly afterwards. Greater efficiency in the industrial use of mineral products was to have a similar effect.

The third tendency worth noting is linked to the steady change in the composition of world trade; this tendency became apparent only after the Second World War. In the three decades preceding World War I, the quantum of world trade in primary products increased at just about the same rate as the trade in manufactures. In the two decades following, as a result of the sharp rise in petroleum exports and the protectionism prevailing in the industrialised countries, the quantum of exports of primary products increased more than that of exports of manufactures. However, the most significant shifts in trend have occurred only since the 1950s. As Table 5.1 indicates, the situation in 1953 was already quite different from that of 1913 with regard to the share of foodstuffs and manufactures in the composition of world trade.[6]

The relative decline in natural fibres and the rise in petroleum are the main changes that took place in the period indicated. It was from the 1950s onwards that the new trends, which were to radically alter the

TABLE 5.1   *World trade composition*

	1913	1953
	% of total	
Foodstuffs	29	23
Agricultural raw materials	21	14
Minerals	13	20
Manufactures	37	43

[6] Cf. P. L. Yates, *Forty Years of Foreign Trade*.

composition of world trade in the course of a decade, became apparent. Between 1953 and 1967, the annual rate of growth of world exports of foodstuffs was 3.5 per cent, that of other primary products (excluding fuel) was also 3.5 per cent, of fuel, 7 per cent, of chemical products 15 per cent, and of other manufactures 8.5 per cent. As a result of these trends, exchanges between industrialised countries have become of growing significance in world trade. Thus, in 1966, the total exports of developed countries with a market economy amounted to 139 billion dollars, of which 106 billion were accounted for by their exports to each other.[7]

If we compare the overall pattern of development of the world economy in the half-century following the end of the First World War with the half-century preceding it, significant differences become immediately apparent, particularly from the point of view of the underdeveloped countries. The earlier period was marked by the emergence of a system of international division of labour under the hegemony of the group of countries which had begun to industrialise during the first half of the nineteenth century. This system permitted the concentration in certain areas of production activities which benefited most from technological progress, as well as the fuller and more rational utilisation of abundant resources (labour and land) in other areas. The increased overall activity of an expanding world economy was accompanied by the establishment or accentuation of interdependence between its various parts. If we look more closely at this process, it becomes immediately apparent that it involved two forms of development. On the one hand, we have the development of industrial centres based on technological progress and a rapid accumulation of capital. This type of development entailed increasingly complicated production processes, which required both a change in the relative quantities of productive factors, with more capital per unit of labour, and a change in their quality, more particularly a progressive improvement in the human factor. On the other hand, we have the development of the so-called 'periphery', or outpost areas, induced by changes in overall demand and effected through the external sector. This second type of development was nearly always extensive in character; that is, it made it possible to increase the economic productivity of available factors without requiring significant changes in the forms of production. Thus, the substitution of a subsistence crop such as maize by an export crop such as coffee brought about an increase in

---

[7] For the basic data, see UN *Yearbook of International Trade Statistics, 1964,* and *Monthly Bulletin of Statistics, Dec. 1967* and *July 1968.*

overall output while requiring no major changes in production techniques. In other instances – the case of mining production – this peripheral development took the form of assimilating modern techniques and increasing the input of capital in a production sector strictly geared to exports and lacking the capacity to transmit its growth to the economy as a whole. In either case, peripheral development had little capacity to transform traditional techniques of production. Nevertheless, by requiring the modernisation of infrastructures and of part of the State apparatus, it set in motion an historical process which opened up important new possibilities.

The 1929 crisis and its impact on Latin America

In the period which began with the First World War and assumed marked characteristics with the 1929 crisis, the traditional system of international division of labour played a progressively less important role. International demand for primary products lost its dynamism as a reflexion of the structural evolution that had taken place in the industrialised countries. Full realisation of the nature and magnitude of the problem and of its repercussions on the international economy was delayed by the Great Depression. The extent and severity of the depression highlighted the general features of the economic situation and obscured the structural factors. It took time to perceive that the very magnitude of the crisis already reflected the important changes that were taking place in the world economy. The quantum of world exports fell by 25 per cent between 1929 and 1933, and the general level of export prices by 30 per cent, entailing a fall of over 50 per cent in the total value of world trade. Moreover, the change in the flow of international capital greatly aggravated the situation of countries exporting primary products. Britain, the United States and France, which had together exported an annual average of 3,300 million dollars in the form of short- and long-term capital in the period 1928–30, became net importers of 1,600 million dollars, on yearly average, in the period 1931–2. Britain, who in the period 1925–9 had paid for 22 per cent of her imports out of the income earned on British capital abroad, raised this proportion to 37 per cent in the period 1930–4. In Latin America, the crisis assumed catastrophic proportions, precisely because it was one of the underdeveloped regions which had been most closely integrated into the international division of labour. The entire monetary sector of the Latin American economy was geared to external trade. In Mexico nearly 30 per cent of the country's reproducible capital was controlled by foreign

TABLE 5.2 *Latin America: Evolution of external trade*
(% *variation from annual average for 1925–9*)

	Quantum of exports	Terms of trade	Capacity to import
1930–4	−8.8	−24.3	−31.3
1935–9	−2.4	−10.8	−12.9

SOURCE: ECLA, *Economic Survey of Latin America, 1949.*

groups, and in Argentina more than 40 per cent. The situation in the other countries was much the same. The external debt and its servicing conditioned not only the behaviour of the balance of payments but also that of public finance and the monetary system. Throughout the decade following the crisis, the capacity to import was severely curtailed, not so much as a result of the decline of the quantum of exports but mainly as a reflexion of the adverse trend in the terms of trade, as Table 5.2 clearly indicates.

Taking into account the population increase, the capacity to import declined by 37 per cent in the period 1930–4 relatively to the pre-crisis period, and by 27 per cent in the subsequent five-year period. The impact of the crisis was felt most violently in the public sector because of its dependence on revenue from foreign trade and also as a reflexion of the financial significance of the external public debt. With the exception of Argentina, all the Latin American countries suspended debt-service payments for more or less lengthy periods, which made it even more difficult to obtain foreign capital to pay for badly needed imports of equipment.

Although the whole region was hard hit, the consequences of the 1929 crisis varied in accordance with the degree of the country's integration into the system of international division of labour and the nature of this integration. Countries such as Argentina, exporting temperate-zone food products, were *relatively* less severely affected, in the first place because demand for these products has a low income elasticity, particularly in countries with high living levels and, secondly, because the supply of these commodities, nearly all annual crops, is relatively elastic, since it is possible to reduce the crop areas from one year to the next. Finally, since these products compete with surpluses produced in developed countries, markets are relatively better organised.

In the case of tropical products, demand is also relatively inelastic in terms of income. But, given the inelasticity of supply in the case of perennial crops, any decline in demand provokes catastrophic falls in prices in the absence of any possibility of financing surpluses and with-drawing them from the market. In the case of mineral products, we have a different picture: the curtailment of industrial production in the importing countries led to the liquidation of stocks and the collapse of production in the exporting countries. The fall in the volume of exports tended to be considerable. The external trade statistics of Argentina, Brazil, Chile and Mexico for the decade following the crisis illustrate the different forms of reaction in dependent economies. Given the extreme inelasticity of coffee production and other tropical commodities, Brazil attempted to offset the fall in commodity prices by increasing the quantum of exports, which rose by 10 per cent in the 1930–4 period, relatively to the period 1925–9. Argentina reduced exports by 8 per cent, Chile by 33 per cent and Mexico by 25 per cent. The deterioration in Brazil's terms of trade was twice as severe as in Argentina's, but not very different from that in Chile and Mexico. The hardest-hit countries were the mineral exporters, affected both by the fall in prices and the reduction in the quantum of exports. The countries in the least vulnerable position were those exporting commodities with annual crop cycles, whose production structure was more flexible. In the following five-year period (1935–9) Brazil continued to force the external markets, making a concerted effort to dispose of her enormous output of coffee, since the accumulation of stocks was proving a heavy financial burden.

TABLE 5.3   *External trade indicators for selected Latin American countries (% variation from annual average for 1925–9)*

	Quantum of exports	Terms of trade	Capacity to import	Quantum of imports
Argentina				
1930–4	−8	−20	−27	−32
1935–9	−11	0	−11	−23
Brazil				
1930–4	+10	−40	−35	−48
1935–9	+52	−55	−32	−27
Chile				
1930–4	−33	−38	−58	−60
1935–9	−2	−41	−42	−50
Mexico				
1930–4	−25	−43	−55	−45
1935–9	−11	−36	−39	−26

SOURCE: ECLA, *Economic Survey of Latin America, 1949.*

This effort was completely defeated by the deterioration in the terms of trade. In Argentina, the reduction in the quantum of exports was accompanied by a significant improvement in the terms of trade. The Chilean economy, more closely integrated into the system of international division of labour than any of the other three economies mentioned, was easily the most severely affected. Its behaviour during this decade revealed the extreme vulnerability of primary-exporter economies within the framework of the international division of labour established in the nineteenth century.

6 Some indicators of the degree of development reached in Latin America

Economic indicators

Whereas the period extending from the Wars of Independence to the 1870s was one of stagnation in nearly all the countries of the region, in the century that followed, the Latin American economies underwent relatively intense development, although the pattern varied from country to country. In the first half of the century – during which development was induced largely through the expansion of raw material exports – the regions with temperate climates and abundant empty lands received a large inflow of immigrants and capital from Europe. In these regions, economic development was particularly intense during this first phase and was accompanied by a precocious urbanisation process and other social changes. The essentially rural old society, in which political power was monopolised by a small minority of landowners, was rapidly transformed as large urban centres came into being, with the growing participation of the middle social strata. The southern region of the South American continent – Argentina, Uruguay and, to a lesser extent, Chile and the southern areas of Brazil – which had received an influx of European immigrants, became rapidly urbanised and the agricultural economy became entirely monetarised. An elastic food supply and the relatively high wage rates demanded by the European immigrants contributed to the establishment of much higher living standards than those prevailing in the areas settled much earlier.

Today, the living conditions of the Latin American population as a whole are basically an outcome of the social structures that emerged during their first phase of modern development – from about 1870 to 1914 – and of the intensity of this development from that period up to the present time. In fact, living conditions in the various areas of the region were probably not very different in the mid-nineteenth century. With the expansion of production for export, the evolution of social structures was conditioned by certain factors such as the relative importance of the existing subsistence economy, the recently incorporated European contingent and the degree to which manpower was absorbed by the monetary sector.

A comparison between the two phases of coffee expansion in Brazil reveals the significance of these factors. In the first phase, involving the occupation of lands in the State of Rio and the southern part of the State of Minas Gerais, expansion was based on the abundant manpower available in the latter State as a result of the decline in gold and diamond production in an earlier period. The abundance of labour permitted the expansion of coffee to proceed within the framework of the traditional plantation, in which the monetary flow was minimal and the level of real wages extremely low. In the second phase, during which coffee planting spread to the São Paulo highlands, the shortage of labour played a key role. The government sponsored and financed a large inflow of European immigrants, stipulating from the outset that wages were to be paid in money, and that living conditions should be sufficiently attractive to appeal to prospective immigrants from southern Europe. These social changes account for the more rapid pace of urbanisation in the São Paulo highlands, the formation of a domestic market nucleus in this region, and its subsequent development. If the standard of living of the people in the São Paulo highlands failed to keep pace with the region's productivity in the period that followed, this was due to the overall pattern of the Brazilian economy, whose integration, in the present century, made it possible for the surplus manpower in the less-developed regions to condition the wages paid in the more-developed regions.

In Argentina, the manpower shortage and the intensity of development in the phase of expanding exports made it possible to create social conditions which placed Argentina, along with Uruguay, in an exceptional position among Latin American countries.[1] In the industrialisation phase Argentina failed to achieve as high a growth rate as Mexico or Brazil. Nonetheless, since industrialisation has not produced a change in the pattern of income distribution or led to a significant absorption of surplus manpower, Argentina and Uruguay have continued to be the only Latin American countries in which development has brought about an effective improvement in the living conditions of the bulk of the population.

[1] In the period preceding the First World War, nominal wages (in convertible currency) in Argentina were higher than in the industrial countries of Western Europe. Cf. Alejandro Bunje, *Riqueza y Renta de la Argentina*, Buenos Aires, 1917.

TABLE 6.1 *Latin America in the world economy*

| | Capitalist economies | | | | |
	Developed	Underdeveloped (total)	Latin America	Socialist economies	World
1. Gross domestic product (weighting in 1963)					
(a) Share (world = 100)	61	12	4	27	100
(b) Average annual growth rate 1950–69 (%)	4.7	5.0	5.2	8.0[a]	5.5
Per capita	3.5	2.5	2.4	6.4[a]	3.5
2. Exports (current values)					
(a) Average annual growth rate 1948–70 (%)	8.6	5.3	3.8	10.5	8.0
(b) Share of group in world exports					
1938	65	25	7	10	100
1948	63	30	11	6	100
1960	67	21	7	12	100
1970	72	17	5	11	100

[a] Excluding the Asian Socialist countries.
SOURCE: ECLA, *Economic Survey of Latin America, 1971*, Part I, Table 2.

Latin America accounts for nearly 7.7 per cent of the world population and at present contributes about 4 per cent to the overall world product and 5 per cent to world trade. Its per capita income is one-third lower than the world average, but about twice that of the so-called Third World countries.

The Latin American average obviously conceals wide disparities between the different countries. Thus, Argentina's per capita income approximates the average for European countries, whereas that of Haiti is below the African average. Haiti's per capita income is only 11 per

TABLE 6.2 *Latin America: annual growth rates of the gross domestic product*

	Annual growth rates[a]		1972 (in dollars at 1970 prices)	
	1950–60	1960–70	Total (in millions)	Per capita
Argentina	3.0	4.2	26,223	1,096
Bolivia	0.4	5.6	1,109	214
Brazil	6.8	6.0	45,548	464
Colombia	4.6	6.2	8,447	376
Costa Rica	7.1	6.8	1,079	572
Chile	3.9	4.4	8,610	945
Dominican Republic	5.7	3.8	1,821	422
Ecuador	4.9	5.3	2,006	308
El Salvador	4.7	5.8	1,121	306
Guatemala	3.8	5.2	2,140	415
Haiti	1.9	0.6	485	111
Honduras	3.4	5.5	772	289
Mexico	5.8	7.1	37,233	709
Nicaragua	5.3	7.3	942	488
Panama	4.8	8.1	1,222	803
Paraguay	2.4	4.6	655	272
Peru	5.3	4.9	6,838	503
Uruguay	2.1	1.2	2,397	810
Venezuela	7.6	5.8	12,257	1,116
Latin America (excluding Cuba)	5.0	5.6	160,903	591

[a]Average GDP at factor cost and in 1960 prices.
SOURCES: ECLA, *Economic Survey of Latin America, 1971* and IDB, *Annual Report, 1973.*

cent of that of Argentina, representing a far greater difference than that between the Latin American average and the per capita income of the United States. Besides Argentina, the other countries with incomes per capita well above the regional mean are Venezuela, Chile and Uruguay. Mexico and Panama, whose relative positions improved substantially in the 1960s are also above the average. Brazil's per capita income is one-quarter below the regional mean and Colombia's one-third.

Social indicators

Indicators related to nutritional conditions, health, education, housing and other aspects of social development confirm Latin America's inter-mediate position between developed-economy countries and the Third World average. In addition, they confirm the region's extreme hetero-geneity and reveal certain specific characteristics of Latin American societies in the phase of industrialization.

The average availability of calories and proteins (animal proteins in particular) is above the world average. This signifies that there is an even greater disparity between Latin American levels and those pre-vailing in the underdeveloped countries as a whole. Nevertheless, for most of the region, this availability is below the minimum levels estab-lished by the United Nations Food and Agriculture Organization (FAO). These levels vary from 2,200 to 2,600 calories and 32 to 44 grams of pro-tein, depending on the age structure of the population and other factors. It should be noted that the national averages shown in column IV of Table 6.3 are subject to two qualifications: in the first place, they are estimates of food *availability*, as established by the FAO. Survey after survey has shown that these figures over-estimate effective food *consumption*. It has been established that in Brazil, for example, the daily per capita intake of calories is not more than 2,340, a level 19 per cent below the figure derived from the 'national food balance sheets' prepared by the FAO.[2] Secondly, these averages conceal wide disparities among social groups, stemming from the pattern of income distribution. It has been estimated that in a typical Latin American country with an average daily per capita intake of 2,600 calories (an adequate level by international dietary stan-dards) the daily per capita intake of the low-income half of the popula-tion is seldom as much as 2,000 calories.[3] Surveys carried out in Bolivia

---

[2] Cf. ECLA, *América Latina y la Estrategia Internacional de Desarrollo: Primera Evalua-cion Regional*, Santiago, 1973, Part I, p. 56.

[3] FAO, *Prospects for Agriculture*, United Nations, 1972, vol. I, ch. 5.

TABLE 6.3   *Latin America: indicators of social conditions*

	I	II	III	IV	V	VI
Argentina	68.2	521	56	3,036	92.9	67.9
Bolivia	46.8	2,174	24	1,997	49.1	8.4
Brazil	61.4	1,918	52	2,816	66.7	31.4
Colombia	60.2	2,341	61	2,103	47.7	14.4
Costa Rica	68.2	1,804	78	2,344	61.3	37.4
Cuba	72.3	1,123	74	2,688	63.1	–
Chile	64.4	1,803	66	2,562	65.7	67.5
Dominican Republic	57.8	2,247	38	2,143	48.5	9.7
Ecuador	59.6	2,928	34	1,993	46.5	16.1
El Salvador	57.8	5,101	43	1,873	46.0	10.2
Guatemala	52.9	4,498	38	1,972	49.7	29.4
Haiti	47.5	15,750	10	1,896	46.5	1.0
Honduras	53.5	4,085	36	2,042	52.3	4.8
Mexico	63.2	1,726	57	2,660	67.1	20.9
Nicaragua	52.9	2,014	50	2,314	61.4	14.9
Panama	66.5	1,616	74	2,429	65.4	34.3
Paraguay	61.6	1,811	16	2,760	74.7	3.6
Peru	55.7	1,917	39	2,341	60.8	27.8
Uruguay	70.1	1,032	77	3,105	110.6	–
Venezuela	64.7	1,115	80	2,359	59.9	22.9

I   Life expectancy at birth.
II   Number of inhabitants per physician in 1968–71.
III   Percentage of population with drinking-water facilities, 1971.
IV   Availability of calories per capita per day, 1970.
V   Availability of proteins per capita per day (grams), 1970.
VI   Percentage of economically active population covered by social security, 1969.
SOURCE: ECLA, *Economic Survey of Latin America, 1973*, Part III, Tables 185 and 187.

and Ecuador have shown that the food consumption of the low-income half of the population is below 1,500 calories. In El Salvador, only 20 per cent of the population had calorie intakes above the basic nutritional requirements; in 1970, the average daily per capita intake of the low-income half of the population was only 1,326 calories and 30.7 grams of protein. It can be said, without exaggeration, that in the mid-1970s more than 150 million people in Latin America are inadequately nourished, both in qualitative and quantitative terms.

A feature of nutritional inadequacy which has been attracting attention in recent years, because of its serious social implications, is the food intake of children under 5 years of age. Sample surveys carried out between 1965 and 1970 in 13 countries of the region have shown that the proportion of malnourished children (body weight 10 per cent or more below the mean) was high in all cases and in some cases was as high as 80 per cent of the sample child population. In five countries, one-fifth of the children included in the sample suffered from severe malnutrition (body weight 25 per cent or more below the mean).[4] These figures are particularly disturbing because the damaging effects of malnutrition in the early stages of an individual's physical growth are extremely difficult to remedy at a later stage. Attention has been drawn not only to the permanent reduction in working capacity but also to the possibility of irreparable brain damage caused by the lack of protective foods in the diet during early infancy.

Education indicators show that there has been a marked decline in illiteracy in practically all the countries of the region for which recent statistical information is available. In one group of countries (Argentina, Uruguay, Chile, Costa Rica and Cuba) illiteracy has been reduced to levels similar to those of Western European countries. In a second group of countries (Mexico, Venezuela and Panama) the proportion of illiterates in the population 15 years of age and older is around one-fifth. In El Salvador and Nicaragua more than 40 per cent of the population is still illiterate. In these two countries, and in Brazil (where one-third of the population 15 years of age and older was illiterate in 1970) the absolute number of illiterates is still increasing despite the rise in literacy rates.[5]

The figures in Table 6.4 indicate a remarkable expansion of secondary and higher education in the region. In 1972, the number of students enrolled in secondary schools was 11 million, reflecting an annual accumulated growth rate of 10.3 per cent since 1960. The number of students enrolled in universities, colleges and other institutes of higher education, was 2 million, indicating an annual growth rate of 12 per cent since 1960.

[4] Pan-American Health Organization, *Proyecciones Quadrienales, Ministerios de Salud*, 1972–75.

[5] In Brazil, the proportion of the total illiterate population at 15 years of age and over fell from 50.5 per cent in 1950 to 39.4 per cent in 1960 and 33 per cent in 1970; however, in the same period, the *number* of illiterates rose from 15.3 million to 15.8 and 17.9 million. Cf. Organisation of American States, *América en Cifras, 1972, Situación Cultural*, p. 5.

TABLE 6.4 *Latin America: educational levels and performance*

	Primary I	Secondary II	Higher III	Percentage increase in enrolments 1960–70		
				Primary	Secondary	Higher
Argentina (1972)	95.0[a]	40.5	17.5	19.7	73.0	51.9
Bolivia (1971)	84.6	16.0	7.8	89.8	69.7	100.8
Brazil (1971)	76.2	35.6	6.6	71.3	247.0	486.6
Colombia (1968)	62.7	20.5	3.5	61.7[b]	141.5[b]	181.5[b]
Costa Rica (1972)	101.6	37.8	12.5	75.8	171.1	225.5
Cuba (1970)	103.8[b]	26.8[b]	4.2[b]	51.3	109.1	51.3
Chile (1972)	102.0[c]	49.4[de]	9.2[e]	74.1[f]	32.2[f]	230.2
Dominican Rep. (1970)	89.3	19.4	4.6[g]	51.5	125.6	379.4[g]
Ecuador (1969)	86.7	26.5	6.9	63.7	190.2	239.4
El Salvador (1970)	76.1	19.6	1.5	65.3	155.6	241.7[g]
Guatemala (1970)	49.9	10.9	3.7	70.3	172.9	219.2
Haiti (1968)	31.0	4.2	0.3	27.1[b]	75.4[b]	—
Honduras (1970)	76.6[b]	12.7	1.5[b]	83.8[b]	161.8	105.9[b]
Mexico (1970)	94.4	24.1	6.1	89.3	209.3	215.8
Nicaragua (1971)	74.0	19.5	5.4	97.2	350.9	571.4
Panama (1970)	93.5	43.0	6.3	57.8	101.3	95.0
Paraguay (1970)	92.6	17.6	3.4	40.6	126.8	114.7[b]
Peru (1970)	104.1	39.8	11.0	88.7	240.0	314.2
Uruguay (1970)	95.8	60.8	8.7[b]	10.5	87.4	21.4[b]
Venezuela (1971)	83.4	38.6	11.2	44.7	181.6	286.8

[a] 6–13 years. [b] 1968. [c] 7–15 years. [d] 16–19 years. [e] 1971. [f] Since compulsory education was extended to 7 years of schooling in 1966 and 8 years in 1967, secondary education was reduced to 5 and 4 years respectively.
I   Enrolment in primary education as a percentage of the population aged 7–13 years.
II   Enrolment in secondary education as a percentage of the population aged 14–19 years.
III   Enrolment in higher education as a percentage of the population aged 20–24 years.
SOURCE: ECLA, *Economic Survey of Latin America, 1973*, Part III, Table 187.

The proportion of students in the relevant age group enrolled in colleges and universities is already higher in many Latin American countries than the average in Western European countries. Still more significant is the fact that this proportion is increasing rapidly even in countries which have not yet managed to achieve universal primary education. In the Dominican Republic, for example, where the number of illiterates increased from 569,000 to 846,000 between 1960 and 1970, enrolments in primary schools increased only 51.5 per cent during the decade, compared with an increase of 379 per cent in higher education enrolments. In Brazil the situation is even more serious: in 1971, the proportion of children with no access to schooling was almost one-quarter, whereas in the Dominican Republic this proportion had been reduced to one-tenth in the previous year.

Since nearly all Latin American countries are already making a considerable financial effort in the field of education – many spend well over the 4 per cent of GNP recommended by UNESCO – the current tendency to divert an increasing share of resources into secondary and higher education must give cause for concern. All the more so since primary education continues to be inadequate not only in quantity (although this is no longer generally applicable throughout the region) but principally in quality. Even in Argentina, only 50 per cent of the children enrolled in school complete primary education, as compared with 93 per cent in the United States. In representative countries of the region, like Brazil and Colombia, the corresponding proportion is only one-fifth. Moreover, there is considerable disparity between urban and rural primary schooling. In the rural areas, not only is the quality of education relatively inferior, but the average number of years of schooling is very much shorter. In Costa Rica, where 50 per cent of pupils are in the last year of primary school, in rural areas the proportion is only 38 per cent.[6] In Bolivia, only 1 in 5 pupils completed primary schooling, but in rural areas the corresponding figure is 1 in 20.

Using data on Chile for reference purposes, it can be estimated that the average cost of educating a university student is 15 times as great as that of educating a primary school pupil.[7] Since the growth of secondary and higher education in Latin America is related to the tactics used by the middle-strata of society to move upward socially and improve their relative positions in income distribution, which is geared to graduate

[6] Cf. *América en Cifras*, cit. Table 501–40.
[7] Cf. Universidad de Chile, Oficina de Planificación, *Antecedentes e Informaciones*, no. 4, August 1973.

qualifications rather than technical competence, the question arises whether educational systems are not helping to reinforce increasingly inequitable social systems. We will come back to this point in considering the patterns of income distribution and social stratification.

The analysis of social indicators, taken as a whole, shows that in countries where the growth of the product from the mid-nineteenth century was effected in conditions characterised by a manpower shortage – Argentina, Uruguay and, to a lesser extent, Chile – the gains from development have been fairly widespread. Comparison between Venezuela and Argentina is illustrative in this respect. Measured in dollars of comparable purchasing power, the per capita incomes of the two countries are almost the same. Nonetheless, nutrition levels in Venezuela are close to the Latin American average, whereas in Argentina they are well above and reach Western European standards.

III. THE TRADITIONAL STRUCTURAL PATTERN

7 Characteristics of agrarian structures

Large estates and social organisation

In Latin America, agrarian structures are not only an element of the production system but also the basic feature of the entire social organisation. We have seen, in chapter 2, that both in the economies whose point of departure was export agriculture and in those initially organised around mining production, the large estate tended to become the basic element of social organisation. From the outset, the principle governing grants of land was that grantees should have the necessary means to exploit their lands in order to produce a surplus which could be converted into cash and partially transferred to the Crown. After independence, several countries sought to modify this principle by promoting *colonisation* schemes under which lands were granted as family holdings to settler families who undertook to work the land themselves. This policy was nearly always bound up with the encouragement of European immigration and achieved some success in Southern Brazil, Argentina and Chile.

The family farm system made headway in regions which remained relatively isolated and were characterised by the prevalence of recent settlement of European origin. Thus, in the southern regions of Brazil, where there was no profitable export crop, the pioneer European 'colonies' were forced to turn to a subsistence economy, producing marginal surpluses for sale in the home market, particularly in the rapidly expanding coffee areas. Given the abundance of land and the farming techniques which settlers brought from Europe, subsistence levels were relatively high, although the economy had a low coefficient of integration into markets. In the phase that followed, stimulated by the growth of the home market, these regions developed within a social framework which offered much greater scope for social mobility than that of other areas in the country.

Consolidation of the family farm system in regions where agricultural expansion was based on production for export required conditions which

68

did not exist in Latin America. The highly specialised nature of export agriculture meant that it was subject to a high degree of natural risk: a a bad harvest could give rise to an irreversible process of indebtedness. On the other hand, since world prices were subject to wide fluctuations, the financial risks were equally considerable. Survival thus depended mainly on financial capacity which nearly always increased more than proportionally with the size of the enterprise. But the problem is not confined to its microeconomic aspects. Other factors, relating to broader questions of economic structure, may be decisive in determining the pre-dominant type of agricultural organisation. Thus, the growing impor-tance of cattle-raising, and the possibility of cutting production costs in cereal farming by using the land in rotation with grazing, favoured the development of extensive farming in Argentina. Control of land remained in the hands of financially powerful groups who speculated in land and invested in cattle, leaving agricultural production to be organised, wherever possible, on rented lands. The experience of the American Mid-West, where powerful groups controlling marketing clashed with small farmers, revealed the importance of the broad factors determining the structure of the economic framework in conditioning the methods of production. The development of transport systems had enabled railroad companies to introduce a differential tariff policy, which permitted a reduction in the overall cost of transporting cereals and facilitated their regular flow, so enhancing their competitive position in the world market. However, this policy tended to centralise all tertiary activities in Chicago, transforming the interior into little more than a zone of agricultural production. The reaction of the local populace, voiced in the demand for a change in the rail tariff policy and leading to the enactment of State laws in matters normally coming within Federal jurisdiction, must be regarded as a virtual revolution in which social values prevailed over economic criteria. Had the Federal Government come down on the side of the interests vested in Chicago, backed not only by the written law but by economic arguments which were, at that time, irrefutable, the social framework which permitted the consolidation of the system of family holdings would probably have evolved very differently.

The type of agrarian structure which had prevailed in Latin America since colonial times, and which provided the framework for the region's social pattern, is characterised, as we have seen, by the dual pattern of *latifundio* – Indian community and *latifundio–minifundio*. Since the indigenous communities were simply transformed into instruments of social control, becoming from the economic viewpoint a constellation of *minifundios*, it is in the type of relationship established between *latifundio* and *minifundio* that we must seek the characteristic features of the region's agrarian structure. The *latifundio* system had its origin in the fact that large grants of land were originally distributed among a small number of persons who came to control, limit and block access to the ownership of land. Control was made easier by the fact that the best lands were those able to reap the external economies resulting from public investments in infrastructure. Anyone lacking the financial means to buy land and either unwilling or unable to find work on the large estate had to establish himself on lands with poorer quality soil or badly situated from the economic viewpoint, becoming of necessity a *minifundista*.

While the basic features of the institutional framework are part of the colonial inheritance, the appropriation of a large proportion of Latin American land and its conversion into large estates is a feature of the nineteenth century.[1] In Argentina, for example, private appropriation of the Pampas region accompanied the territorial occupation which took place in the course of that century. By 1840, fewer than 300 people had appropriated 8.6 million hectares of land which was to become the object of an extraordinary boom in the second half of the century. If we bear in mind that the average area of these *estancias* was 30,000 hectares, we can understand why the big landowning class was to become so significant a factor in the country's subsequent history even though it was one of the most recently formed in Latin America. The policy of handing over large areas of the public domain to a favoured few continued during the last stage of the War against the Indians in 1879–83. By the following decade the value of these lands had already increased considerably.[2] The Argentine situation is, of course, an extreme case of vast empty spaces, thinly occupied by nomadic tribes of Indians against whom settlers waged a war of destruction. The occupation of the São Paulo highlands, scene of the spectacular spread of coffee-growing at the end of the last century, offers some similarities with this model of a rapid advance of the frontier of settlement across a practically empty space.[3] Even in densely populated regions, however, there was a considerable expansion of the large estate in the nineteenth century, a clear indication of the essentially capitalist nature of the Latin American estate.[4] In Mexico, the growth of the *hacienda* as the basic institution in the organisation of agricultural pro-

[1] Cf. Ignácio Sotelo, *Sociología de América Latina*, cit., pp. 68–78.

[2] Cf. Aldo Ferrer, *La Economía Argentina*, cit. pp. 61–3 and Carlos F. Díaz Alejandro, *Essays on the Economic History of the Argentine Republic*, pp. 35–40.

[3] Cf. Pierre Monbeig, *Pionniers et Planteurs de São Paulo*, Paris, 1952, pp. 116–20.

[4] Cf. Rodolfo Stavenhagen, *Sept Thèses Erronées sur l'Amerique Latine*, Paris, 1973, p. 130.

duction took place in the second half of that century, under the influence of the spread of Liberal ideas. The *Lerdo Law* of 1856 and the Federal Constitution of 1857 were inspired by the belief that the communal lands were an obstacle to progress since they hindered the creation of a land market. The Church lands and the lands of the Indian communities were released from mortmain, facilitating their subsequent alienation. From the 1880s, transfer of communal land (*suertes* or *terrenos de común reparti-miento*) to private ownership was intensified, as was the alienation of other public land. Under a Law passed in 1894, any piece of land to which the occupant had no legal title could be considered 'uncultivated' (*terreno baldío*) and could be bought by anyone prepared to pay the cash price. Between 1881 and 1889, 14 per cent of the country's arable land had come into the possession of 29 companies or individuals; in 1894 more than 20 per cent was in the hands of 50 owners; and on the eve of the Revolution in 1910, families representing less than 1 per cent of the population owned or controlled approximately 85 per cent of the farm-land.[5] In Peru, the phase of intense concentration of landownership is even more recent.[6] Control of ownership of the land, as a means of extracting a surplus from the Indian masses, was consolidated in Peru from the first century of Spanish occupation, and the Peruvian land-owning class was one of the oldest established in Latin America.[7] In the phase of large-scale concentration of landownership consequent upon the entry of Peruvian agricultural products into the world market, the old rural aristocracy was largely replaced by newcomers with commercial links abroad.

Control of land use in many parts of Latin America was a social technique used by a minority to impose a rigid discipline of work on populations living in extreme misery. In many areas, the average daily per capita food intake of rural communities is only 1,500 or even 1,200 calories, which signifies that part of the population must be going with-out the basic essential to make it possible for the other part to put in a full working day. Even in such conditions, however, a surplus is ex-

[5] Cf. Charles C. Cumberland, 'The Díaz Régime as Background for the Revolution' in *History of Latin American Civilization*, cit. vol. II, pp. 290–93.

[6] For a case study of extreme concentration of ownership of the land on the Peruvian coast which took place between the close of the last century and the opening of this one *see* Peter Klaren, *La Formación de las Haciendas Azucareras y los Orígenes del APRA*, Lima, 1970, pp. 19–41. *See also* François Chevalier, 'La Expansion de la Gran Propriedade en el Alto Peru en el Siglo XX' in *Comunidades*, Madrid, May – August, 1968.

[7] Cf. Robert G. Keith, 'Origen del sistema de Hacienda', in *La Hacienda, la Comunidad y el Campesino en el Peru*, Lima, 1970.

tracted from these communities, in one form or another, ranging from one-quarter to one-third of what they produce. The current form of extracting this surplus is to combine subsistence farming with commercial agriculture. Small plots of land are ceded to families to cultivate for their own subsistence needs. In each region the tenant of a small plot of land (nearly always of poor quality) living within the boundaries of the large estate has been given a local name: *huasipunguero* in Ecuador, *conuquero* in Venezuela, *yanacona* in Peru, *inquilino* in Chile, *morador* in Brazil.

This subsistence economy is combined with a second type of activity, organised along commercial lines, either in lands set aside for this purpose, or in the family plots; in some cases the tenant – labourer contributes his labour free for a certain number of days, in other he contributes part of the cash crop. In this way he pays an indirect rent, which is nearly always high, for the land he uses to grow his subsistence crops.

This type of organisation makes it possible to extract a relatively large surplus from a labour force with extremely low productivity. Moreover, the natural and financial risks involved in all agricultural production are shared by the workers. This type of organisation also makes it possible to invest in agriculture regardless of its low profitability in terms of the cash return. The families working a subsistence plot on the large estate can be employed, in return for a supplementary wage, to open up new lands, to build access roads, to plant permanent crops or to carry out other capital improvements. This explains why the large estates can constantly incorporate new lands although, by and large, they utilise only a fraction of the lands appropriated earlier.

The role of the *minifundista* in the Latin America agrarian structure is extraordinarily complex and requires close scrutiny if the essence of the land-tenure problem is to be understood. A *minifundista* is a small-holder working a plot of land which is either too small to occupy him fully or which, while providing full employment, does not provide sufficient income to meet his needs (given the standards prevailing in the region) whether because of the poor quality of the soil or because of the rent he is required to pay, in one form or another, for the use of the land. The case of the *minifundista* who pays no rent for the use of the land but is nevertheless unable to obtain the minimum level of income, is applicable to regions where land is scarce or extremely impoverished and where there are no alternative employment opportunities. This situation exists in Haiti and in certain sub-regions of Central America and the Andean highlands but is in no way representative of the region. Generally speaking, the condition of the *minifundista* is a consequence of his obligation to produce a surplus for the benefit of another social group. In other words, even when he lives at bare subsistence level or below, the *minifundista* has no savings to invest. The accumulation process takes place on a level very different from that of the *minifundista*'s decision-making level and does not revert in his favour. The vast bulk of the *minifundistas* constitutes a population in search of work, used by commercial agriculture in whatever form it finds most convenient. Some *minifundistas* are integrated regularly into the permanent labour system as is the case of those whose plots are within the boundaries of a large estate. Others work as hired labourers in areas where new lands are being brought under cultivation or being prepared for livestock production.

In Latin America as a whole, the *minifundistas* make up approximately one-half of the agricultural labour force; the other half is made up of full-time or part-time wage earners. However, the overall agrarian structure is defined by the specific conditions of *minifundismo*, since these determine the effective costs of labour and hence the relative value of the surplus extracted from agriculture. *Minifundismo* makes it possible for commercial agriculture to draw on a plentiful supply of cheap labour while remaining free of responsibility for the creation of permanent employment for the bulk of the rural population.

In the humid tropical regions, which concentrate a substantial proportion of Latin America's rural population, *minifundismo* is far less a question of the size of plots than of the agricultural techniques to which the farmer has access. Using primitive farming methods and with declining soil fertility, the farmer is obliged to practise a form of itinerant agriculture known as *shifting cultivation*. With this form of farming, preparation of the land by the 'burn and slash' method, cultivation of crops for a year or two, and subsequent abandonment of the clearing to permit the growth of a new cover of brush and weeds which will regenerate the soil after an interval of some ten years, is still the typical sequence in many parts of the tropical and semi-tropical regions of Latin America.[8] For a man to establish settlement of any permanence in this type of region, within the framework of the family unit, he would need to have access to levels of capital investment and technique incompatible with the level of income he could obtain. Since opportunities for permanent employment as wage earners in commercial agriculture are strictly limited, the only alternative open to many rural workers is part-time labour, combined with the cultivation of small plots of land on the large estate, or hired migrant labour in lands being prepared for farming. In some cases, the virgin lands already belong to a large estate; in others,

[8] Cf. R. F. Walters, *Shifting Cultivation in Latin America*, FAO, 1971.

they are public land. Frequently, however, the public land is appropriated by latifundists once it has been cleared by the migrant labourers and made ready for farming. In any event, the wages and living conditions of the independent migrant workers determine the cost of the labour of those who remain behind, including that of the wage workers. The migrant rural worker who limits his activities to subsistence farming has the lowest status, from the point of view of income, in the minifundist hierarchy. It is common, however, for these farmers to plant cash crops in the recently cleared land, where soil fertility may be high even though not sustained. The isolation in which these small farmers find themselves, with the difficulties of transport and the inadequate means of communication in the new areas of agricultural settlement, puts them completely at the mercy of commercial agents to whom they frequently become heavily indebted. The middleman is often the large landowner himself who is preparing to take over the land once it has been brought under cultivation; in other cases the same function is fulfilled by local traders and small businessmen or representatives of the big commercial firms. It should be noted that the situation of the *minifundista* is not simply a consequence of his co-existence with the *latifundista*: where the large estate is absent, other structures emerge which accomplish the same ends, namely the extraction of a surplus from the *minifundista* in the form of labour, and the maintenance of a reserve of manpower to be used wherever the large estate may come to be established.

Latifundio–minifundio pattern and under-utilisation of resources

Until recently, the structure of agriculture in the Latin American countries was relatively uniform. With the exception of Mexico, where the most significant period of land reform was in the 1930s, the countries of the region entered the 1950s with structures evolved in the colonial period. Between 1952 and the beginning of the 1970s, four more countries carried out land reform programmes: Bolivia, Cuba, Chile and Peru. Although these reforms destroyed the large estate as the basic institution of the agrarian structure, they did not entirely succeed in significantly changing the living conditions of the rural masses, as we shall see in a later chapter. The structures analysed below provide the framework for the evolution of Latin American society over many centuries; they continue to be representative of the majority of Latin American countries and their basic features continue to prevail in most of the countries which have already carried out land reform programmes.

The most characteristic feature of these structures is the bipolar

TABLE 7.1 *Minifundios and latifundios in the agrarian structure of selected Latin American countries, 1950–60*

	Minifundios		Latifundios	
	% of farms	% of occupied land	% of farms	% of occupied land
Argentina	43.2	3.4	0.8	36.9
Brazil	22.5	0.5	4.7	59.5
Colombia	64.0	4.9	1.3	49.5
Chile	36.9	0.2	6.9	81.3
Ecuador	89.9	16.6	0.4	45.1
Guatemala	88.4	14.3	0.1	40.8
Peru	88.0	7.4	1.1	82.4

SOURCE: CIDA. (Translator's note: The Inter-American Committee for Agricultural Development (CIDA) carried out studies of land tenure and development in seven countries of Latin America: Argentina, Brazil, Chile, Colombia, Ecuador, Guatemala and Peru. These studies were published by the Pan American Union, Washington, D.C. under the title *'Tenencia de la Tierra Desarrollo Socio-Económico del Sector Agrícola'*, from 1965–66.)

pattern of large estates and small-holdings. This *latifundio–minifundio* polarity is clearly evident from the figures shown in Table 7.1.

The definition of *minifundio* used by the Inter-American Committee for Agricultural Development (CIDA) embodies an economic and a social criterion: it is taken to mean a plot of land which is too small to provide full employment for one family (2 man-years) and cannot yield an income sufficient to sustain a standard of living considered to be the adequate minimum for the region concerned. A *latifundio* is defined as an estate employing more than twelve workers in a permanent capacity.[9] It should be pointed out that the minifundio is more widespread in countries with dense indigenous populations – Ecuador, Guatemala and Peru. The average size of the *latifundios* in Argentina is 270 times that of the *minifundios*; in Guatemala the *latifundio* may be as much as 1,732 times the size of the *minifundio* as can be seen from Table 7.2. In countries where indigenous populations are crowded on to constantly shrinking areas of impoverished land, the so-called *'microfundio'* or *'microfinca'* is the main form of landholding. The 74,300 *microfincas* in Guatemala yield an average income only one-third of that provided by its *minifundios* and about one-thousandth of the average income provided by its *latifundios*.

[9] See Solon L. Barraclough and Arthur L. Domike, 'La Estructura Agrária en Siete Paises de América Latina', *El Trimestre Económico*, April–June 1966.

TABLE 7.2 *Latifundio–minifundio*
ratios[a] in selected Latin
American countries,
1950–60.

	area	income
Argentina	270	66
Brazil	546	61
Colombia	491	36
Chile	1,549	72
Ecuador	618	165
Guatemala	1,732	399

[a] Average land area of a *latifundio* as a
multiple of the average land area of a
minifundio and income per *latifundio*
(gross value of agricultural output per
farm unit) as a multiple of income per
minifundio [translator].
SOURCE: CIDA Studies.

Apart from the *latifundios* and *minifundios*, Latin American agriculture is carried on in family farms and medium-sized farms. Family farms
provide work for two to four people, medium-sized or 'multi-family'
farms employ four to twelve workers. In Argentina, Brazil and Colombia,
these intermediate forms of farm organisation account for 60 per cent or
more of the total agricultural output. (See Table 7.3).

In Chile, the only one of the countries included in Table 7.3 which has
carried out an agrarian reform programme, the *latifundio* traditionally
occupied a major position both as a form of land tenure and as a form of
organising production and providing a source of employment. The average
size of the Chilean *latifundio* was more than 1,500 times that of the *minifundio*, but its average income was only 72 times greater. If we relate the
average size of the *latifundio* to that of the *minifundio*, we find that the
concentration ratio in Chile is three times as high as in Brazil and
Colombia and five times as high as in Argentina. On the other hand, if
we relate average incomes of *latifundios* and *minifundios*, we find that the
Chilean ratio is only 10 per cent higher than the Argentine and Brazilian
ratios and 50 per cent higher than the Colombian ratio. The figures shown
in Table 7.4 enable us to compare the degree of efficiency in the utilisation
of resources by the various types of farm. The data for the *minifundios*
are taken as the base. From these figures, the extreme under-utilisation
of the land held by latifundios is clearly evident. In Chile, the value of
output per unit of land in the *latifundios* was 20 times lower than in the

TABLE 7.3 *Agrarian structure indicators in selected Latin American countries 1950–60*

	Mini-fundios	Family farms	Medium sized farms	Lati-fundios
Argentina				
% of total farmland	3	46	15	36
% value of agricultural product	12	47	26	15
% of labour employed	30	49	15	6
Brazil				
% of total farmland	10.5	6	34	60
% value of agricultural product	3	18	43	36
% of labour employed	11	26	42	21
Chile				
% of total farmland	10.2	8	13	79
% value of agricultural product	4	16	23	57
% of labour employed	13	28	21	38
Colombia				
% of total farmland	5	25	25	45
% value of agricultural product	21	45	19	15
% of labour employed	58	31	7	4
Guatemala				
% of total farmland	14	13	32	41
% value of agricultural product	30	13	36	21
% of labour employed	68	13	12	7

SOURCE: CIDA studies.

minifundios. In Argentina and Brazil it is around 10 times lower. It should be borne in mind, however, that the *latifundios* include lands of different types and hence they use only a fraction of their total areas. The index of yield per unit of land actually under cultivation is thus more significant. And on this measure of productivity too, the efficiency of the *latifundios* is low, not only in relation to the *minifundios* but also in relation to the medium-sized family farms. The figures for the output per worker are equally interesting. The high labour productivity of the

TABLE 7.4 *Farm efficiency indicators (index: minifundios = 100), 1950–60*

	Value of yield per hectate of		
			Value of yield
		Area under	per agricultural
Country and type of farm	Farmland	cultivation	worker
Argentina			
Family farms	30	50	250
Medium-sized farms	50	62	470
Latifundios	12	49	620
Brazil			
Family farms	59	80	290
Medium-sized farms	24	53	420
Latifundios	11	42	690
Colombia			
Family farms	48	90	418
Medium-sized farms	19	84	753
Latifundios	9	80	995
Chile			
Family farms	14	32	170
Medium-sized farms	12	25	310
Latifundios	5	21	440
Guatemala			
Family farms	56	80	220
Medium-sized farms	54	122	670
Latifundios	25	83	710

SOURCE: CIDA Studies.

latifundios is largely the result of the extensive way in which the land is used, bearing in mind that the land used for farming is of good quality since it is selected from among the abundant lands available on the large estates.

A sample survey carried out in eleven different regions of Brazil provides data which enable us to complete the picture outlined above, revealing other aspects of the typical Latin American agrarian structure.[10] Table 7.5 offers a comparison of the Brazilian *latifundio* with the

[10] For basic data and a detailed analysis of the Brazilian case, see Inter-American Committee for Agricultural Development, *Posse e Uso da Terra e Desenvolvimento Sócio-Económico do Sétor Agrícola: Pan American Union, Brasil*, Washington, 1966.

TABLE 7.5 *Brazil: Investment per farm in relation to class of farm tenure*

Class of farm tenure	Average size	Investment per farm (excluding cattle)	Crop land per farm	Investment per hectare of crop land
Family farms	100	100	100	100
Latifundios	3,160	1,100	1,150	100

SOURCE: CIDA Studies.

family farms. For the *latifundio*, with an average area 31.6 times larger than that of the family farm, investment per unit of crop land was similar to that on family farms. The *latifundio* is thus not justified by a greater propensity to invest, if we exclude the investment represented by the lands left idle. If we compare the figures given for Brazil in the two tables above, we see that although investment per unit of crop land is the same for the *latifundio* and the family farm, the value of the *latifundio's* output per unit of crop land is only half that of the family farm, whereas its labour productivity is twice as high. This is obviously accounted for by the fact that the *latifundios* adopt extensive farming methods and invest in labour-saving equipment which reduces the creation of employment and helps to keep wage rates low. In theory, the same amount of investment could produce twice the output on the family farms creating almost twice as much employment. Thus, investment in the *latifundios* is directed towards raising labour productivity, while large tracts of land are left idle. On the other hand, the productivity of labour is extremely low in the *minifundios* because the land must be more intensively worked in view of the small size of the plot. Since the productivity of labour is three times higher on the family farm than in the *minifundio*, and the investment yield per unit of crop land is twice as high on the family farm as in the *latifundio*, it seems obvious that a simple reorganisation of Brazil's agricultural structure would result in a substantial increase in the productivity of the factors employed. The present agrarian structure in Brazil does not act as a complete brake on the increase of production because there is still an abundant supply of land.[11] But growth through the spread of *latifundios* condemns tracts of land to lie idle, thus raising transport costs and failing to create enough employment opportunities in the expanding areas at a time when there is increasing pressure on the land in the *minifundio* areas. Between 1950 and 1960 the

[11] Cf. C. Furtado, 'A Estrutura Agrária no Subdesenvolvimento Brasileiro' in *Análise do 'Modelo' Brasileiro*, Rio, 1972, pp. 91–122.

average size of the Brazilian *minifundio* decreased from 2.6 to 2.4 hectares.

In the Latin American countries where the settlement of new land advanced more rapidly than in Brazil, the obstacles to development imposed by the agrarian structure were obvious sooner, setting in motion the land-reform process analysed in chapter 23.

8 Distribution and utilisation of the social income

Pattern of demand in underdeveloped structures

The way in which the social product is distributed among the members of the community is doubtedly one of the most significant features of the economic structure. This aspect is particularly important in the case of underdeveloped economies. The preponderance of exogenous factors, such as the external demand for a few primary products subject to short-run fluctuations in price, as well as the considerable disparity between the remuneration of factors of production and their opportunity costs in productive use, both in the export sector and in the sectors most affected by modern technology, tend to compartmentalise economic decisions, giving rise to demand schedules with characteristic discontinuities, each segment displaying different behaviour patterns or trends. Thus, in a given phase of expansion of the domestic product, one group of consumers may show a rapid advance in purchasing power while another remains stationary; or one group, benefiting from a rise in the real income of its members, may *diversify* its demand schedule through the inclusion of higher quality goods, while another grows horizontally, that is, through the addition of new members to the group without any change in the demand schedule of existing members. Traditional economic analysis blurred the perception of these problems, based as it was on assumptions of homogeneous factors and of an identical technological horizon for all decision-making agents related to production. For an understanding of the problems of underdevelopment we must start with different hypotheses, such as the absence of a unified labour market in the production of the same good, and the simultaneity of diverse production functions, according to the level of the economic structure on which the productive agent operates. Study of the demand schedule provides an understanding of the very basis of the underdevelopment problem insofar as underdevelopment signifies the non-integration of productive activities.

The existence of a structural surplus of labour is the most evident symptom of the high concentration of income and discontinuity at the demand level found in Latin American countries. The basic problem, however, is the failure to absorb this labour surplus, which tends to be perpetuated in spite of the rapid acceleration of the capital accumulation process which takes place in the phase of industrialisation. Studies of external dependency relations, which have helped to clarify relations between the form of resource allocation, the consumption patterns adopted and the orientation of the technology incorporated into productive processes, have shed new light on this complex problem.

There can be little doubt that the considerable disparities in the productivity of labour found both in the region as a whole and within individual countries, are an immediate cause of the concentration of income. Around one-third of the active Latin American population continues to be employed in activities considered 'primitive' because of the technology they use. The average productivity of labour in activities considered 'modern' is 4.3 times higher than in productive activities as a whole; in agriculture the ratio is 1 to 7 and in commerce 1 to 3. The average income generated by a worker in craft production is less than 5 per cent of the average income generated by a worker in 'modern' manufacturing[1]. But the basic problem is to account for the extremely uneven diffusion of technical progress which is concomitant with the reproduction in poor countries of consumption patterns and production systems found at much more advanced stages of development.

Comparative analysis of the situation in selected countries

In Latin America, studies of income distribution are very recent. Income distribution curves have been established for a limited number of countries but systematic research into the non-economic factors responsible for the particular shape of the individual curves and their variations in time is still at an early stage. Table 8.1 reproduces data on income distribution for the three most highly populated countries.

Argentina has the least uneven distribution pattern, easily explicable by the fact that there is less disparity here between the living standards of urban and rural populations. Comparing the income distribution curve for Argentina with the curves established for the more highly industrialised countries, we see that the significant difference is the relatively

---

[1] Data referring to the late 1960s, published in Anibal Pinto and Armando Di Filippo, 'Notas Sobre la Estrategia de la Distribución y la Redistribución del Ingreso en América Latina', *El Trimestre Económico*, April–June, 1974.

TABLE 8.1 *Income distribution in selected countries in the mid 1960s*

	Argentina[a]	Brazil[b]	Mexico[a]
Lowest decile	2.9	2.8	1.5
2nd	4.1	3.2	2.1
3rd	4.8	4.0	3.1
4th	5.5	4.4	3.8
5th	6.1	5.4	4.9
6th	7.1	6.4	6.0
7th	8.0	7.7	8.1
8th	9.6	9.8	12.0
9th	12.9	14.8	.17.0
10th	39.1	41.5	41.5
Top 5 per cent	29.4	31.0	29.0
Top 1 per cent	14.5	19.0	12.0

[a] Households. [b] Individual earners.
SOURCE: ECLA, *Estudio sobre la Distribución del Ingreso en América Latina*, UN, 1967.

greater weight of the higher income groups. In England, for instance, the richest 10 per cent account for 30 per cent, and in the United States for 31 per cent, of the total income, whereas in Argentina this decile accounts for as much as 39.1 per cent of the total. The 50 per cent with the lowest incomes account for 25 per cent of the total income in England, and in the United States for 23 per cent, whereas in Argentina their share is 23 per cent, i.e. the same as in the United States. The concentration of income in the upper part of the curve found in the case of Argentina, is most probably related to the relative weight carried by the pattern of land ownership in this country, the greater prevalence of monopolies in the industrial sector and the high level of overall protection for industrial activities in relation to imports.

The most significant difference between Argentina, on the one hand, and Brazil and Mexico on the other is that in Argentina the standard of living of the 20 per cent of the population in the lower income brackets is more than three times as high as that of the corresponding group in Brazil and Mexico and, in the case of Brazil, it is higher than that of the national mean. In other terms, the poorest fifth of the Argentine population has an average income of 300 dollars, in 1960 purchasing power, whereas the income of the poorest half of the Brazilian and Mexican populations averages around 150 dollars, which means that this section of the population is only marginally integrated into the money economy. The half of the Argentine population ranked between the third and seventh deciles constitutes a fairly homogeneous group – the difference between the two deciles being 60 per cent – and has a relatively high standard of living, corresponding to 63 per cent of the national average. In Brazil, the half of the population ranked between the third and seventh deciles has an average income corresponding to 56 per cent of the national average, and the difference between the two extremes is 90 per cent.

The particular conditions under which Argentine agriculture developed, offering relatively high wages in order to attract European manpower whose access to ownership of the land was severely restricted, doubtless account for differences which still persist at present, although the disparities between the per capita income in Argentina and that of the other two countries, particularly Mexico, have been substantially reduced in the course of the last few decades. Average labour productivity in the Argentine agrarian sector is only 17 per cent lower than in the domestic economy as a whole. In Brazil, it is 50 per cent below the national average and in Mexico two-thirds lower. Heavy population pressure on the land, which characterises the Mexican *Mesa Central*, accounts in part for this figure. In this region, where the population is organised in rural communities, land reform freed the rural worker from paying an open or disguised rent for his land, but also helped to reduce the mobility of labour. On the other hand, the development of farming in other regions benefiting from substantial public investments prevented prices of agricultural products from rising in the more crowded areas.

Since data on income distribution in Mexico are more readily available than for the other Latin American countries, they provide a basis for a more detailed analysis of the way in which gains from development are distributed in an underdeveloped economy.[2] Of all the countries in the region, Mexico undoubtedly holds the record for steady growth of the national product over the last three decades. Between 1940 and 1950 the accumulated rate of growth of the per capita product was 3.9 per cent a year, and in the decade following it was 2.7 per cent. During this period there were significant changes in the country's economic structure. In 1940, agriculture accounted for 24.3 per cent of the gross domestic product and manufacturing for 18 per cent; in 1950, the share of agriculture had declined to 22.5 per cent, while manufacturing had increased its

[2] Cf. Ifigenia N. de Navarrette, *La Distribución del Ingreso en el Desarrollo Económico de México*, Mexico, 1960.

share to 20.5 per cent; in 1960 these percentages had changed to 18.9 per cent and 23 per cent respectively.

The figures for the decade 1940–50 show that the average annual wage increased by 30 per cent in real terms, rising from 266 to 355 dollars at 1950 prices. However, a more detailed analysis of these figures shows that the average non-agricultural wage fell from 550 to 517 dollars, and the average agricultural wage from 95 to 85 dollars, corresponding to a decline of 6 per cent in the first case and 11 per cent in the second. Thus the average wage increased by only 33 per cent in a decade when average productivity increased by 44 per cent; but even more significantly, the rise in the average wage was simply the result of the transfer of labour from lower-wage sectors to sectors paying higher wages. The existence of a manpower surplus and the growth of the population exerted sufficient pressure on the labour market to bring about a decline in wage rates in both the rural areas and the towns. This transfer of income at the expense of wage-earners was facilitated by the inflationary process that occurred during this period. Differences between living conditions in the rural areas and the towns are so considerable that even under conditions of an overall decline in real wage rates there may be a marked increase in the overall consumption of wage-earners as a result of changes in the occupational structure.

The changes that took place between 1950 and 1963–4 are shown in Table 8.2.

TABLE 8.2   *Mexico: Income distribution in selected years*

	1950	1956–7	1963–4
Lowest decile	2.7	1.7	1.5
2nd	3.4	2.7	2.1
3rd	3.8	3.1	3.1
4th	4.4	3.8	3.8
5th	4.8	4.3	4.9
6th	5.5	5.6	6.0
7th	7.0	7.4	8.1
8th	8.6	10.0	12.0
9th	10.8	14.7	17.0
10th	49.0	46.7	41.5
Top 5 per cent	40.0	36.5	29.0
Top 1 per cent	23.0	16.0	12.0

SOURCE: ECLA, *Estudio sobre la Distribución del Ingreso en América Latina*, 1967.

These figures reveal other important aspects of the structural evolution of the Mexican economy. Four population groups can be clearly distinguished. The first group, composed of the 40 per cent of the population in the lowest income brackets, continues to be totally excluded from the benefits of development. The share of national income accruing to this group, which includes the bulk of the rural population and the poorest urban groups, was reduced from 14.3 to 10.5 per cent, showing that the average real income of this section of the population remained stationary. The second group, composed of the 30 per cent of the population ranked between the fifth and seventh deciles, increased its average income at a rate 10 per cent above the national average. Since income per capita increased by around 47 per cent in the period under consideration, it can be inferred that the average real income of this section of the population must have increased by slightly more than 60 per cent. The third group, comprising the population ranked in the eighth and ninth deciles and representing the skilled artisans and the middle brackets in general, increased its share from 19.4 to 29 per cent of the total income. The average income of this group, which had been equal to the national average in 1950, exceeded this average by 45 per cent in 1963–4, showing that this section of the population had practically doubled its standard of living. Finally, the fourth group, composed of the upper middle class and higher-income brackets – i.e. the top decile – decreased its share from 49 per cent to 41.5 per cent of the total income. A more detailed examination of the figures for this last group reveals that significant changes had taken place within the group. The first half, composed of the middle-income brackets and small entrepreneurs (including farmers using modern agricultural techniques), increased its average income at a faster rate than the national average, the rise in its real income averaging more than 80 per cent. The share of national income accruing to the 40 per cent ranking immediately above this subgroup, and including the upper income brackets, remained unchanged, which means that the rise in average real incomes was identical to the rise in national per capita income. Finally, the top 10 per cent – corresponding to only 1 per cent of the country's population – consisting of the top income brackets, decreased its share of the national income from 23 to 12 per cent, which signifies a decline in average real income.

The data analysed above reveal the importance of institutional factors in determining the pattern of income distribution in underdeveloped structures in the process of modernisation. The existence of a manpower surplus concentrated in the rural sector is the most important single factor. A quarter of a century of rapid development, which enabled

Mexico to more than double its per capita income, has not prevented stagnation and even decline in the living conditions of a large section of the population, representing certainly not less than one-third of the total. The second determining factor seems to be the growing organisation of the urban groups. From the fifth decile upwards, all groups have increased their share of the social product, which indicates that urban wage-earners have enjoyed greater participation in the benefits of development than they did in the 1940–50 period. The third salient feature is the upward social mobility of the higher income brackets: the average real income accruing to the ninth decile rose by 135 per cent in the period after 1950. Finally, it seems clear that fiscal policy has had a strong influence in breaking down income concentration in the top group. The 20 per cent with the highest incomes, accounting for 59.8 per cent of the national income in 1950, reduced their share to 58.5 per cent in 1963–4. Moreover, there has been a considerable change in the distribution pattern within this top group, largely in favour of the middle-class groups.

Data on income distribution in Brazil, derived from censuses taken in 1960 and 1970 confirm the trend towards a concentration of income, concomitant with the acceleration of growth, already noted in the case of Mexico.

As in Mexico, the growth of average productivity in Brazil benefited only a minority of the population. The stagnation of the per capita income of the 40 per cent at the lowest income level leaves no doubt that wages declined in both the rural and urban sectors, since the differential in favour of the urban areas is considerable and there was a significant

TABLE 8.3   *Income distribution in Brazil*

Percentage of population (starting with lowest income level)	Percentage of income		Per capita income in 1960 dollars	
	1960	1970	1960	1970
40	11.2	9.0	84	90
40	34.2	27.8	257	278
15	27.0	27.0	540	720
5	27.4	36.3	1,645	2,940

SOURCE: Original data from 1960 and 1970 censuses.

transfer of manpower from the country to the towns. In fact, according to official data, the minimum wage was reduced by 13 per cent in Rio de Janeiro and São Paulo in the decade under review, whereas the average productivity of labour in the country as a whole (including agricultural activities) increased by 33 per cent. But whereas in Mexico the proportion of income received by the second 40 per cent of the lower income group increased from 26 to 31 per cent in the same period, the share of total income of the corresponding group in Brazil declined from 34.3 to 27.8 per cent.

Taking the 80 per cent of the population in the low income levels as a whole, we find that in Brazil the average income of this group increased during the period under consideration from 171 to 180 dollars; given the margin of error which must be allowed for in this type of calculation, the difference cannot be considered insignificant. On the other hand, the average income of the 15 per cent of the population comprising the next group increased 33 per cent, which exactly matches the national average. Thus, concentration of income took the form of a transfer of income from the poorest 80 per cent to the wealthiest 5 per cent of the population. In fact, the personal income of the top 5 per cent was increased, on average, by 1,300 dollars, whereas that of the group comprising the poorest 80 per cent increased, on average, by only 13 dollars.

The experience of Brazil in recent years is, of course, an extreme case, which must be considered in the context of a deliberate policy to reduce real wages while providing fiscal and financial incentives to increase the consumption of the high-income groups. Nevertheless, it simply highlights a situation which is undoubtedly characteristic of the majority of countries in the region. With the exception of Argentina, Uruguay and Cuba, in all the Latin American countries there are sizeable proportions of the population (between 20 and 40 per cent of the total) whose living conditions are determined by the level of productivity in the so-called 'primitive' sector: subsistence agriculture and artisan manufacturing or small-scale production. A large share of the income of this population never enters the monetary circuit and is hardly affected by the growth of average national productivity. If this group is discounted, the remaining 10 to 30 per cent with incomes below the national average and the 20 to 30 per cent receiving more than the national average (a group comprising 30 to 60 per cent of the population) have a share of total income well below the corresponding figures for the developed capitalist countries. In fact, the second group (the 30 per cent below and the 30 per cent above the mean) receives an income equal to half the national per capita income, whereas in the developed countries the corresponding group has an income close to the national averages for the country concerned. The gap between the upper-income brackets and the national average widens dramatically in the top three distribution deciles. In some cases, as in Brazil, for example, incomes begin to rise rapidly only in the eighth decile.

As a result of this form of distribution, the average income of the 20 per cent in the upper brackets is about two and a half times the national average while that of the top 5 per cent is almost 6.6 times as high. This means that in a country with an average national income of 500 dollars, the 5 per cent at the top of the scale receive an average income of 3,300 dollars, giving this group access to the living standards of the wealthy countries. If the income distribution pattern of a country with a per capita income of 500 dollars were similar to that in the developed countries, where per capita incomes are three or four times that amount, there would be no domestic market for a wide range of durable consumer goods, in particular motor cars. Thus, it would seem less reasonable to conclude that the distribution of income reflects wide disparities in productivity levels between sectors and the uneven spread of technology than to affirm the opposite. The adoption of a particular life-style implies a particular income distribution pattern and conditions the diffusion of technical progress.

Comparison of the income distribution patterns in three countries differing in size and in the degree of industrialisation, and with different coefficients of external trade, but with a similar level of per capita income – Chile, Mexico and Venezuela – shows that the curves are remarkably similar.[3] The average income of the poorest 20 per cent of the population was 18 per cent of the national average in Chile and Mexico and 15 per cent in Venezuela. The per capita income of the wealthiest 5 per cent was 6.1 times the national average in Chile, 5.8 times in Mexico and 5.3 times in Venezuela. Moreover, the average income of the 60 per cent comprising the 30 per cent below and the 30 per cent above the mean, was 63 per cent of the national per capita income in Chile and Mexico and 65 per cent in Venezuela. If we compare the average for these three countries, which is representative of Latin America as a whole, with the income distribution curve for a capitalist

[3] Per capita income in 1965 (in dollars at 1960 prices) was 480 in Chile, 475 in Mexico and 530 in Venezuela. For the relevant data see ECLA, *Economic Bulletin for Latin America*, nos. 1–2, 1973, p. 37.

country with a homogeneous structure, such as Norway, we find the following results:

	Chile, Mexico, Venezuela (a)	Norway (b)	(b)/(a)
Per capita income	100	200	2.0
Poorest 20 per cent	100	250	2.5
60 per cent approximating the mean	100	280	2.8
15 per cent below the top	100	160	1.6
Top 5 per cent	100	100	1.0

The biggest difference in income levels is found in the group comprising the 60 per cent approximating the mean. Whereas in Norway the income of the top 5 per cent is a little over three times as high as the average for that group, in the three Latin American countries it is about nine times as high. This is why the effects of disparities in productivity levels (2 to 1) fail to make themselves felt in the consumption patterns of the privileged minority comprising the 5 per cent of the population with top incomes.

Collection and utilisation of income by the State

The action of the State affects the flow of income accruing to the community in a number of ways. Part of this income is transferred from the private recipient to the State and the structure of the tax system may be an important factor in determining the final pattern of demand. On the other hand, the way in which the government uses the resources it appropriates operates in the final analysis as a mechanism for redistributing income in favour of one or another group. The data available for Latin America do not permit us to undertake a detailed analysis. However, the available statistical information does provide an overall picture. In its study *The Economic Development of Latin America in the Post-War Period*,[4] the Economic Commission for Latin America outlined a scheme exemplifying the utilisation of personal income in the region as a whole. Since the data for Venezuela and Mexico – countries in which income is particularly highly concentrated – carried considerable weight in the preparation of this scheme and since data for Argentina were not available at the time, the figures must be taken as representing the Latin American mode rather than the Latin American average. For the purpose

---

[4] ECLA, *The Economic Development of Latin America in the Post-War Period*, 1964.

of constructing this representative model, the population was grouped into four categories. Group I, comprising 50 per cent of the total, whose average yearly income was taken as the base of 100, included the mass of rural workers and small artisans. Group II, comprising 45 per cent of the total, with an average yearly income 3.3 times higher, included the mass of urban wage-earners. Group III, comprising 3 per cent of the total, with an average yearly income 15 times higher than the base, included those in the higher income brackets and small entrepreneurs. Finally, Group IV, comprising 2 per cent of the population, with an average yearly income 30 times higher than the base, included the big landowners and entrepreneurs. Table 8.4 shows how these groups used their personal incomes.

Given the existing structure of the tax system, with its broad emphasis on indirect taxation, the proportion of personal income contributed to the State by the mass of urban wage-earners was equal to that of the small minority earning high incomes, who spend 6.5 times as much on consumption per head. The upper middle class, whose consumption spending per capita is four times that of the urban wage-earners, pays out relatively less in taxes. This is explained by the ease with which direct taxes can be avoided, particularly in the case of professionally earned income. Group II has a low savings coefficient, not so much because of a high propensity to consume – which, given its low income, would be normal – but because the tax burden weighs more heavily on this group. The propensity to consume appears to be higher for Group III, whose status requires competitive spending on 'prestige' forms of consumption.

The funds collected by the State are used to finance investments and collective forms of consumption which benefit the various sectors of the population in different ways. The figures given in Table 8.5 show how the State allocates its resources among the four groups indicated.

Group I, composed of the poorest half of the population, whose con-

TABLE 8.4 *Allocation of personal income*

	Taxes and social insurance contributions	Savings	Consumption	Total
		% figures		
Group I	13.0	− 3.0	90.0	100
II	20.0	3.5	76.5	100
III	16.5	9.5	74.0	100
IV	21.0	21.0	58.0	100
Total population	18.4	6.6	75.0	100

TABLE 8.5 *Allocation of public expenditure*

	Total	I	II (% of GDP)	III	IV
A. taxes	15.2	1.7	8.4	1.9	3.2
B. Government services					
Education	1.8	0.2	1.1	0.3	0.2
Health	1.2	0.7	0.5	0	0
Other	2.4	0.8	1.6	0	0
Total	5.4	1.7	3.2	0.3	0.2
A minus B	9.8	0	5.2	1.6	3.0

sumption is hardly diversified and only marginally enters the monetary flows, receives services from the State corresponding to only 1.7 per cent of the product, i.e. a sum practically equal to the total it pays out in taxes. It should be noted that the State's expenditure on education is the same for this half of the population as for the wealthiest 2 per cent of the population. Group II receives services from the State corresponding to 3.2 per cent of the product but contributes 8.4 per cent in taxes. Thus, this group contributes more than half the funds made available to the State mainly for allocation to investment. Since public investment is largely intended to create external economies for private investment and since the latter is in the hands of the 2 per cent minority whose savings represent a significant proportion of its income, it may be deduced that both in the way it finances its expenditures and in the way it allocates its resources, the action of the State serves not only to consolidate the existing pattern of wealth and income distribution but to foster an even more concentrated form of distribution.

9 Monetary and foreign exchange systems

Failure to adjust to the rules of the gold standard

In an earlier chapter it was pointed out that the world economic crisis of 1929 dramatically revealed structural changes that had been taking place in the world economy for some time. Among such changes we must mention the tapering off in world demand for most primary products. The crisis emphasised the magnitude of the 'external vulnerability' of economies specialising in the production of raw materials, among which the Latin American economies were prominent.

The financial movements involved in the system of international division of labour, based on so-called comparative advantage, were regulated by the Gold Exchange Standard, which assumed the definition of all currencies in terms of their gold value, free convertibility on the basis of a fixed rate of exchange (at least in so far as foreign transactions were concerned) and the free transfer of funds on the basis of 'foreign exchange reserves' held by the monetary authorities of each country. In countries with a diversified economy, characterised by some degree of substitutability between imports and home-produced goods, any sharp fall in exports due to external factors could be offset, to some extent, by an increase in domestic supply. Proper management of monetary reserves and foreign credit, in conjunction with a judicious policy of domestic expansion, could be sufficient to divert productive activity towards new types of export and towards the satisfaction of domestic demand formerly supplied by imports. In other words, the mechanisms of the Gold Exchange Standard could be adjusted to offset its more serious internal depressive effects without completely abandoning its rules. In economies specialising in the export of raw materials, however, the problem took a different form because of the rigidity of supply in the export sector and the incompressibility of demand for imports.[1]

[1] Cf. C. Furtado, *Teoria e Política do Desenvolvimento Econômico*, São Paulo, 1967, particularly chapter 20, 'A Tendècia ao Desequilibrio Externo'. See also Victor L. Urquidi, *Viabilidad Económica de América Latina*, Mexico, 1962, chapter 3, 'Los Embrollos Monetários y Financieros'.

Latin American countries were characterised at the time by relatively high import coefficients. The share of imports in the domestic supply of manufactured goods was never less than one-third of the total and in some cases more than two-thirds. However, these figures reveal only one aspect of the real situation. In most of the countries, a large proportion of the product was excluded from the monetary flow, which suggests that if we take into account only the monetary sector of the economy, the import coefficient was in fact much higher. On the other hand, domestically produced goods could not be substituted for imports in the short or medium term, even if they could in the long run. Consequently, a temporary reduction in exports tended to provoke a serious internal depression unless the country had sufficient monetary reserves to tide it over a transition period during which it would attempt to recover its former export levels in traditional or other lines of export. In other words, the situation required an extremely able compensatory policy and careful orientation of investments in the export sector to make sure that this sector achieved the flexibility which the sector producing for the home market lacked. One need only remember the wide fluctuations in world prices of primary products and the long gestation period of the cash crops involved to realise that an economy with a high import coefficient specialising in exports of one or two primary products would find it difficult to submit to the discipline of the Gold Standard. This would have required not only large monetary reserves – which would have meant freezing a considerable proportion of domestic savings – but also a policy of controlling the level of domestic activity, which was not feasible in countries lacking a developed capital market and a sufficiently flexible fiscal system.

Moreover, the problem was not confined to the short-run instability of world prices of primary products – a consequence of climatic factors and the structural inflexibility of supply in underdeveloped countries. No less serious was the disruption of markets during world-wide depressions, when Latin American countries found it impossible to take counter-action by reorientating their exports. Cyclical crises entailed not only falls in the value of exports but also flights of capital, which precipitated the liquidation of monetary reserves, with a subsequent loss of credit abroad. The situation was particularly serious in view of the heavy external debts accumulated by Latin American countries in the course of the nineteenth century. Whatever the origin of these debts – wars during the phase of consolidating the nation-states, speculation by groups dominating the state apparatus, or investments in infrastructure, mainly in railroads and ports – it is certain that temporary payments difficulties led to the negotiation of fresh loans and burdensome refinancing arrangements, making external debt service one of the major items of expenditure in public budgets.

Given the sharp fall in the value of exports and the extent to which government revenues depended on the export trade, it is understandable that, faced with a major crisis, Latin American countries should have begun almost automatically to finance part of their public expenditures by expanding the money supply. This led to immediate expansion of imports, precipitating liquidation of the monetary reserves and the devaluation of the exchange rate. In fact, anticipatory measures, reflecting falls in prices of raw materials in the major importing markets, were enough to spark off capital flights and devaluations of the exchange rate. The strains of devaluation forced governments to make greater financial efforts to meet debt service claims at precisely the time when public receipts were declining. A deficit in the public sector was thus inevitable and monetary expansion to finance the deficit became a relentless necessity. In practice, the domestic effects of the external crisis were attenuated by the simple fact that rules of the Gold Standard were not obeyed, or were jettisoned at the first sound of the alarm bell. During the lulls, governments created 'stabilisation' or 'equalisation' funds for the purpose of intervening in the exchange market in an attempt to stabilise it. But these experiments all ended in a return to inconvertibility or floating exchange rates which made it possible to penalise capital flights when crises occurred.

Experience proved that the system of floating exchange rates allowed the Latin American countries to protect themselves more easily against the impact of cyclical crises and generally against contractions in the capacity to import, inasmuch as the inflexibility of the productive structure tended to be partially offset by adjustments in the price structure. The consequent changes in income distribution were for a long time absorbed without creating major social tensions. After a time, however, and particularly in some countries, the emergence of a more clearly defined social structure provided an outlet for these social tensions and increasingly serious inflationary processes were set in motion.

The sudden and periodic monetary devaluations provoked by the cyclical crises in the Latin American economies had a number of consequences. Since devaluations coincided with falling export prices, they offset the decrease in the money income of the export sector, transferring a substantial proportion of the loss in real income to the economy as a whole, through the relative rise in import prices. In countries whose exports provided a substantial proportion of the world supply of certain commodities – as was the case with Brazilian coffee, which accounted for over half the world supply – this mechanism could aggravate the downward trend in world market prices. In most cases, however, the consequences were strictly internal, taking the form of a 'socialisation of losses' or of a mechanism for defending the export sector. In the phase that followed, an upward shift in external demand could lead to partial revaluation of the currency at the exchange level, the export sector thus restoring to the community as a whole part of the income it had appropriated during the depression. The flexibility of the price structure made it possible to cushion the impact of the external crisis and preserve the export sector's capacity to recover. But there can be no doubt that it also tended to open the way to a long-term deterioration in the terms of trade, inasmuch as it increased the price-inelasticity of the world market supply of primary products.

The creation of central banks

In the textbooks of the classic age of the Gold Standard, Latin American monetary systems, with their floating exchange rates and chronic non-accelerating inflation, were regarded as aberrant phenomena, comparable to the movement of the satellites of the planet Mars. A few descriptive studies published in Europe[2] drew attention to these peculiarities. But the theoretical assumptions of the time made it difficult to see in these features anything beyond the consequences of political instability and the absence of adequate institutions equipped to handle monetary systems properly. It was in this spirit that important international financial groups, intent on maintaining the regularity of external debt service payments and interested in the transfer of dividends on the substantial direct investments beginning to be made in the region after the First World War, pressed Latin American governments to reform their monetary systems, offering technical assistance for this purpose. This ushered in the phase of reforms in the issue systems and the creation of central banks.

Under the guidance of British and United States advisers, central banks were established in one Latin American country after another from 1925 onwards.[3] These banks, designed to function within the framework

---

[2] Chilean inflation was the subject of two monographs published before the First World War, one written by Benjamin Subercaseaux and published in France, the other by Alfred Wagman, published in Germany.

[3] Uruguay, whose central bank was created in 1896, was the only country in the region with a centralised system of monetary authorities before the First World War. Mexico's central bank – the Banco de México – was founded in 1925, without the aid of the Anglo-American missions referred to.

of the Gold Exchange Standard, were to have a monopoly of note issue, determine the bank rate, undertake open-market operations and act as 'lenders of last resort', that is, rediscount bills held by the commercial banks. It is not very likely that members of the technical missions imagined that the creation of a central bank would suffice to conjure up money and capital markets. What they essentially had in mind was the regulation of a government's discretionary powers of currency issue. It was hoped, in this way, to put an end to the chronic budgetary deficits which were thought to be the root cause of inflationary pressures. Since control of the central bank was to be jointly in the hands of the private banks and the business community in general, political pressure would be minimised. The government would have to finance its expenditures from legitimate resources by collecting taxes or turning to the capital market. The power to issue legal tender would be controlled by the level of gold and convertible foreign exchange reserves held and rediscount operations would be limited to short-term commercial and agricultural paper.

Since the central banks lacked the requirements necessary to control interest rates by the classical means (attracting funds from abroad whenever necessary) and, on the other hand, since the commercial banks in the region were relatively conservative, the monetary reforms of the 1920s were in practice reduced to an attempt to control the power of note issue. The rigidity introduced into the monetary system by these reforms helped to aggravate the consequences of the 1929 crisis. Monetary reserves were more rapidly exhausted and capital flights were penalised far less. The public-sector deficit – which could not have been avoided without paralysing the state machine – tended to be financed by issuing government bonds to be rediscounted by the central banks.

The Central Bank of Argentina, created in 1935, was the first to depart from the conventional blueprint based implicitly on the working of the Gold Exchange Standard and to incorporate novel features in its statutes. It could intervene in the exchange market on behalf of the government and, under the supervision of the treasury, could engage in operations with government securities to provide short-term finance for State deficits. Experience had shown that these practices were needed and they were introduced in more than one country. What was new was the acceptance of the existing situation as the basis for the creation of a central banking system, which meant acknowledging the shortcomings and artificiality of the orthodox approach. However, because it incorporated the accumulated experience of years of effort to adapt to fluctuations in the foreign trade sector, the new system was at the time regarded as an extraordinary innovation.[4]

Experiments in monetary and foreign exchange policy and the influence of the IMF

In the absence of a sufficiently developed capital market and given the failure to control the process of currency issue – by using the rediscount mechanism the central bank could go on bolstering the total supply of money and credit – the main weapon of monetary policy in Latin America tended to be control of the reserves held by deposit banks. While the main aim of classical reserves policy was to assure the financial solvency of the commercial banks, Latin American practice gave rise to complicated reserves policies, which took into account not only the basic resources held by the commercial banks but also the expected increase in these resources. These policies were carried out by the central banks with the specific aim of controlling the total supply of money and credit. Another significant innovation was the creation of a second line of reserves for the banking system – in point of fact, deposits held with the central bank – consisting of government securities offering interest rates far below the current bank rate.

Another field in which the Latin American experience has been extremely varied since the 1929 crisis is that of intervention in foreign exchange operations. In view of the severity of the Great Depression and the inflexibility of the fiscal systems, some countries began to manipulate their exchange rates in order to prevent the currency devaluation from aggravating the effects of a fall in export prices or sparking off an excessive rise in the prices of certain products such as fuels and wheat. In the past, sudden devaluation had been a mechanism for redistributing income, which operated in favour of certain groups. The purpose of manipulating the exchange rates was to control this mechanism so that

---

[4] The Banco Central de Argentina was created with British technical assistance. Raúl Predisch, who was the Executive Director of the Argentine Central Bank from its foundation up to 1943, inspired by the empiricism with which the Bank of England had traditionally conducted its affairs, departed from the rigid patterns imposed on the newly created central banks. It should also be borne in mind that at that time Argentina already possessed a relatively developed capital market. During the 1938 crisis, Prebisch took masterly action to counter depressive domestic effects and the Argentine Central Bank was thenceforth regarded as a model in the region. For the Latin American experience in this field, see Miguel S. Wionczek, 'Central Banking', in Claudio Veliz (ed.), *Latin America and the Caribbean: A Handbook*, and Frank Tamagna, *Central Banking in Latin America*, Mexico, 1965.

devaluation would not unduly favour some groups while penalising others. The next step was to orientate the manipulation of exchange rates in order to build up reserve funds to absorb inflationary pressures. Finally, there was a move in the direction of using differential rates to direct the pattern of investments. The simple fact that capital formation is relatively more dependent on the capacity to import than on the level of aggregate expenditure means that devaluation will act as a curb on investment unless corrective measures are adopted by providing disguised subsidies in the form of multiple exchange rates.

In the last two decades, the influence of the International Monetary Fund (IMF) has made itself increasingly felt in Latin America. Innovations and experiments in the field of monetary and foreign exchange policies have not ceased completely but, as balance of payments difficulties become more serious, with a growing dependence on short- and medium-term foreign loans to finance deficits, the IMF blueprint has been more widely accepted. Under IMF regulations, exchange rates are fixed in terms of US dollars. Balance of payments equilibrium presupposes internal stability, that is, the absence of uncontrollable inflationary pressures. The use of fiscal and monetary instruments to maintain this internal stability is the recommended IMF weapon. Since the fiscal structure in underdeveloped countries is not very flexible and, in many respects, totally inadequate, the responsibility falls mainly on monetary policy, i.e. on the control of credit. Thus we return by a different path to the conclusions underlying the policies of the orthodox central banks established in the 1920s. Where structural factors give rise to constant pressure on the balance of payments, monetary policy must create a permanent depression in order to keep the economy in equilibrium. The problem will be reconsidered when we come to analyse the pattern of Latin American inflation.

---

10 The industrialisation process
1: The initial phase

Industrialisation induced by expansion of exports

In countries specialising in primary production for export, that is, countries in which productivity was raised in response to the expanding world demand for raw materials, the change in the structure of production particularly the process of industrialisation, is characterised by a number of distinctive features which constitute one of the most interesting aspects of the economic theory of underdevelopment. The rise in productivity and the consequent increase in the purchasing power of the population led to diversification in the pattern of overall demand involving also a more than proportionate rise in the demand for manufactured products. It has been observed that in countries with a per capita income level below 500 US dollars there is a high income-elasticity of demand for manufactured goods, the coefficient value being between 1.3 and 1.5. Hence any rise in the population's purchasing power will mean not only diversification of demand but diversification in a particular direction, requiring a more than proportionate increase in the supply of manufactures. Since specialisation in primary exports (almost invariably only one or two products) concentrates resources in a few lines of production, the evolution of the productive structure will be the inverse of that of the demand schedule. Thus, rapid growth of an export monoculture may be accompanied by an increase in imports of food, expansion of an export mining sector may lead to the substitution of imported manufactured goods for local artisan products destined for the home market, etc. Considering the process as a whole, it becomes apparent that rising productivity is accompanied by a simplification in the supply structure of home-produced goods and diversification in the overall composition of demand.

In the Latin American countries, the process outlined above was the starting point for industrialisation. Specialised production permitted a rise in productivity and income, facilitating the formation of a domestic market nucleus for manufactured products and the creation of an infrastructure. Whereas the classical industrialisation experience was the result of innovations in productive processes which, by cutting prices, made possible substitution of craft manufactures and the creation of a home market, in the Latin American case the market was created as a result of the rise in productivity brought about by export specialisation and was at first supplied by imports. In this case, the competitor to be displaced by industrialisation was not the artisan of low productivity but the highly efficient producer operating through the world market. None the less, growth of the domestic market was an inevitable accompaniment of export expansion. When the home market reached a certain size, a protectionist policy was enough to spark off an industrial upsurge, particularly since industrial investment could take advantage of the external economies provided by the existing infrastructure.

The embryonic home market's capacity to induce industrialisation was, of course, dependent on a number of circumstances varying from one country to another. Where the export nucleus consisted of mining activities, the labour force directly absorbed was strictly limited; moreover, in such cases the capital was almost always predominantly foreign. There was thus little possibility of creating an adequate domestic market. The degree of concentration of land ownership and the relative size of the manpower surplus also played an important role in shaping the final pattern of demand, since both factors affected the distribution of income. A high concentration of income meant that consumption of luxury goods would tend to predominate and, in the case of manufactured luxuries, that they would have to be imported. The size of the manpower surplus affected the creation of the domestic market nucleus even more than the system of land tenure. Given the abundance of land, the shortage of manpower led to intensive use of labour and extensive use of land, making it possible to reconcile concentration of income with relatively high wage rates. Under these conditions – and they fit the case of Argentina and Uruguay – concentration of income did not inhibit the growth of a large domestic market for manufactured products.

In sum, the transition towards an industrial economy depended on a number of factors, the most salient being:

(*a*) the nature of the export activity: this determined the relative amount of manpower to be absorbed by the expanding high-productivity sector;

(*b*) the type of infrastructure required by the export activity: temperate agriculture creating an extensive transportation network; tropical agriculture, concentrated in smaller areas and often in mountainous regions, being able to make do with a more modest infrastructure; mining production requiring a specialised infrastructure, in most cases scarcely producing external economies for other economic activities;

(c) ownership of the investments made in the export economy: foreign ownership reducing the proportion of the flow of income generated by the expanding sector that remained in the country; given the greater prevalence of foreign ownership in the export mining economies, their negative aspects were aggravated;

(d) the wage rates prevailing in the export sector during the initial phase, these being dependent largely on the relative size of the manpower surplus;

(e) the absolute size of the export sector, in most cases reflecting the country's geographical area and population size.

Argentina offers the perfect example of a country in which a primary-product export economy gave rise to the rapid growth of a sizeable domestic market for manufactured goods, providing the basis for the emergence, with hardly any transitional phase, of an industrialisation process. The unprecedented growth of the population as a result of immigration, rapid urbanisation and the extensive infrastructure required by the type of export produced, provided a combination of circumstances that proved exceptionally favourable to industrialisation. The relatively high level of wages obtaining in the initial phase of expansion, and the population's advanced integration into the market economy are equally important factors in accounting for the impetus given to industrialisation in this country even before the First World War. We find a diametrically opposite example in the case of Bolivia which, despite its important export sector, took no steps towards industrialisation.[1] In this second case, the export mining sector absorbed an insignificant fraction of the country's labour force at low wage rates, while the infrastructure created for the mining economy was of little importance to the country's other economic activities. In sum, the export sector followed the structural economic pattern prevailing in the traditional sectors and the bulk of the labour force was excluded from the benefits of gains in productivity.

In the group of countries exporting tropical agricultural products,

---

[1] Bolivia's population at the time of Independence certainly exceeded that of Argentina. According to census data, Bolivia's population increased by only 60 per cent between 1831 and 1900, whereas in Argentina the population increased by 130 per cent between 1869 and 1895. Between 1900 and 1950, the Bolivian population grew from 1,696,400 to 3,019,000 while the Argentinian population grew from 3,954,911 to 15,897,127 between 1895 and 1947.

Brazil enjoyed the set of conditions most favourable for the transition to industrialisation. In contrast with Colombia and Central America, coffee was produced in the São Paulo highlands with extensive farming methods under conditions favouring the creation of an important transportation network. Moreover, with the shortage of manpower in this region,[2] wage rates had to be high enough to attract settlers from other regions, particularly from Europe. On the other hand, given the abundant supply of foodstuffs, produced in the region itself or in the southern areas of European settlement, which had accompanied the expansion of the coffee frontier or taken place in an earlier period, the capacity to import was not absorbed by food imports. Finally, exceptionally favourable conditions for the installation of hydro-electric power plants meant that the region could benefit from the electric energy available at extremely low rates from the start of industrialisation.

Of the countries exporting both agricultural and mineral products, Mexico deserves special attention because of the distinctive features of its early industrial development. The new phase of development of the export mining industry, based on the expansion of world demand for industrial metals, was centred in the northern part of the country. This once more raised the problem of connecting these areas with the central region, where the Mexican population was most concentrated. Historical experience provided a severe warning on the consequences of non-integration: the isolation of the northern areas undergoing rapid settlement had led to the loss of Texas and California. On the other hand, an agricultural export activity of great importance at the time was situated in the far south, in the Yucatán Peninsula, which was the centre of henequen production. Convinced that the country's survival depended on its integration, the Mexican government promoted the establishment of a transportation network and eliminated the internal customs barriers that had traditionally fragmented the national market. Physical barriers, which made it difficult for foreign products entering the country by sea to reach the central plateau, had encouraged the

[2] The mobility of the rural labour force in Brazil was hampered by the slave system which lasted until 1888 and, later, by restrictions on population movements imposed by local authorities at the behest of the large estate owners. The population increase in the State of Ceará, stimulated by the penetration of cotton and the great drought of 1877, led to the first significant migrations in the Northeastern region. At first migration was directed towards the Amazon region where rubber production was undergoing rapid expansion in the last two decades of the nineteenth century and the first two decades of the twentieth. C. Furtado, *Formação Económico do Brasil*, chapters 21 to 24.

establishment of a complex of textile industries since the first half of the nineteenth century. However, internal tariff barriers had inhibited their development, permitting the survival of local weaving, one of the oldest traditional crafts of the Mexican people. The integration of the domestic market brought about by the building of railroads and the elimination of local tariff barriers led to the rapid expansion of this manufacturing nucleus. Thus, the first phase of Mexican industrialisation is closer to the classic model than those of Argentina and Brazil: based on local artisan production displaced by the introduction of new techniques, the industrial products serve markets previously satisfied largely by the supply of local craft manufactures. It is important to bear this aspect in mind when considering Mexico's subsequent evolution. The nature of exports – mainly mineral products – and the abundance of manpower, which made it possible to keep wages at extremely low levels, could have hampered the country's development. There was a strong likelihood that, as the capacity to export grew, increasing quantities of foreign manufactured goods would enter the country, ruining the local craft industries without creating alternative forms of employment for the population. This problem hardly arose in countries such as Argentina and Brazil, with their relatively sparse populations, supplied by imported manufactures. In Mexico, a relatively dense population was traditionally supplied by local artisan production, whose displacement by imports would have been all the more serious as the expanding export sector's capacity to absorb labour was limited.

Like Chile, Mexico benefited from a protectionist policy in the first half of the nineteenth century, that is, before liberal ideology had come to be widely accepted. Unlike Chile, however, the country went through a phase of great political instability accompanied by economic stagnation or retrogression. But this did not prevent the emergence of a nucleus of manufacturing activity, which was to be of decisive importance in the period that has come to be known as the 'Porfiriato',[3] an era of political stability and expanding export activities. In fact, despite the predominance of liberal ideas in this period, the industrial nucleus managed to consolidate itself and expand under the stimulus provided by the integration of the domestic market promoted by the government and the natural protection afforded by the concentration of population in the central plateau.

[3] From the name of Porfirio Diáz, the dictator who ruled Mexico from 1876 to 1910. The term *Porfiriato* appears in the monumental work edited by Cosío Villegas, *História Moderna de México*, of which vol. VII, *El Porfiriato: Vida Económica*, was published in Mexico in 1965.

Differences between the Argentine and Mexican cases

Mexico and Argentina, the two Latin American countries to attain a significant degree of industrialisation before the First World War, represent totally different historical experiences. In the case of Mexico, industrialisation began in the period before the rapid expansion of exports in the second half of the nineteenth century and was fostered by the existence of a market previously supplied by local craft manufactures. Whereas in Argentina export activities were directly responsible for the rise in the purchasing power of large sections of the population, in Mexico the flow of income directly generated by exports was strictly limited. Nevertheless, expansion of the foreign trade sector created conditions for the establishment of an infrastructure which unified the home market to the advantage of an existing manufacturing nucleus. Around 1900–5, the industrial sector in Argentina already contributed 18 per cent to the domestic product, and in Mexico it contributed 14 per cent.[4] In both cases, the dynamic centre of economic development during this period was the expanding export sector. In other words, development was a reflexion of the national economy's integration into the system of international division of labour. However, while in Argentina the expansion of exports led to the vigorous growth of the home market, which in turn induced industrialisation, in Mexico the home market grew much more slowly. In Argentina infrastructure investments were a product of the nature and location of the export activity. In Mexico, the creation of an infrastructure was largely a reflexion of the government's unification policy designed to counteract the centrifugal forces at work in the country, which had been aggravated by long civil wars and the presence of a powerful neighbour openly professing an imperialist doctrine.

One further point must be made. In countries exporting primary products, the initial phase of industrialisation was influenced by the nature of the products exported, inasmuch as the processing of such products, whether for export or for meeting home market requirements, constituted an industrial activity. Thus, the processing of agricultural and livestock products for both export and home markets was the original nucleus of modern Argentine industry, and the processing of minerals was an important sector of Mexican industry. This explains how Mexico gained the metallurgical experience that was to play a key role in

[4] Earlier statistics of industrial production and the industrial sector's contribution to the gross domestic product in Latin American countries can be found in ECLA, *El Proceso de Industrialización en América Latina, Anexo Estadístico,* 1966.

the country's industrial development, particularly in the later period when the export sector was hit by the world crisis. Finally, it should be recalled that, although both countries were under the influence of liberal ideas during the phase of growth stimulated by a dynamic export sector, State action in Mexico could not ignore the existence of an industrial nucleus dating from an earlier period, since its displacement would entail social repercussions exacerbated by the export sector's limited capacity to absorb manpower. The problem was complicated still further by the fact that the penetration of capitalist forms of production in the agricultural sector was causing widespread population shifts. Whereas Argentine development was accompanied by a rise in the population's overall standard of living, in Mexico there was increasing marginalisation of large groups of the population and an aggravation of social tensions that exploded in the revolutionary phase that convulsed the country from 1910 onwards. In the next phase of industrialisation, when more far-reaching action by the government became indispensable, the Mexican State showed a greater aptitude for action in the industrial field, which would be diffficult to explain if we did not take into account the experience of the previous period.

11 The industrialisation process
2: Import substitution

Intrinsic limitations of the first phase of industrialisation

The industrialisation process that had started in some Latin American countries was profoundly affected by the 1929 crisis. This does not mean that the crisis represents a watershed between a period of prosperity and a period of depression. Indeed, some countries had already shown symptoms of a decline in the export sector in the period immediately preceding the crisis. In Brazil, for instance, there had been recurrent crises of overproduction in coffee since before the First World War, and rubber had lost its privileged position in world trade in the 1920s. In Chile, the nitrate crisis sparked off by competition from the synthetic product had been a burden on the country's economy for more than a decade. Nonetheless, with the exception of Brazil, in all the region's most economically significant countries the quantum of exports was 50 to 100 per cent higher in the 1925–9 period than in the first decade of the century. It was in relation to the nature of the industrialisation process that the 1929 crisis constituted a landmark. Until then, the development of the industrial sector had been a reflexion of export expansion; from then on, industrialisation was induced largely through the structural tensions provoked by the decline or inadequate growth of the export sector. The exception to this rule is represented by countries that were to experience a phase of vigorous export growth in a later period: Venezuela, Peru and the Central American countries.

In the countries in process of industrialisation, the industrial sector's contribution to the product in 1929 was as shown on p. 108.[1]

Before considering the features of the new phase in industrialization, the following question must be tackled: what possibilities were there

---

[1] The basic data on industrial production trends and the share of the industrial sector and imports in GDP are taken from ECLA, *El Proceso de Industrialización en América Latina, Anexo Estadístico.*

for industrialisation in Latin America within the framework that prevailed before 1929? In other words: to what extent did the sudden disruption of world trade frustrate an industrialisation process already making rapid headway?

	Industrial sector as % of GDP
Argentina	22.8
Mexico	14.2
Brazil	11.7
Chile	7.9
Colombia	6.2

Detailed study of the data available for Argentina, Brazil and Mexico indicates that the industrialisation process stimulated by the expansion of exports was already showing clear symptoms of exhaustion before the 1929 crisis. Thus, structural changes in the Argentine economy had been of little significance since 1910. In that year, industrial output contributed 20 per cent to the gross domestic product, a proportion that remained virtually unchanged until 1920. In 1925 it rose to 24.6 per cent, but declined to 22.8 per cent in 1929. This structural immutability coincided with the vigorous growth of the Argentine economy. In the course of the two decades mentioned, the volume of industrial output increased by 120 per cent and the quantum of exports by 140 per cent. In Mexico, the coefficient of industrialisation (share of industrial output in gross domestic product) began to decline in the first decade of the twentieth century, before the revolutionary period. In the period 1900–10, the average yearly rate of growth of the gross domestic product was 4.2 per cent, whereas that of industrial output was only 3.6 per cent. In Brazil, where the industrialisation process lagged behind that of the other two countries, the index of industrial output rose by 150 per cent between 1914 and 1922, but between the latter year and 1929 it remained practically stationary.

To grasp the intrinsic limitations of this initial phase of industrialisation in the Latin American countries, some of its basic features should be borne in mind. It consisted essentially of the establishment of a nucleus of industries producing non-durable consumer goods – textiles, leather goods, processed foodstuffs, clothing – which had become a feasible proposition as a result of the increased income made available for consumption with the expansion of exports. Moreover, the urbanisation process that was taking place at the same time, created new demands in the building sector, opening up prospects for manufacturing building materials, which largely replaced the traditional materials produced by local craftsmen. But these industries – non-durable consumer goods and building materials – had little power to generate sustained growth. In the case of consumer goods of a non-durable nature, the vigorous upward trend in the growth curve in the early stages was due simply to the fact that they were replacing goods hitherto imported. Thus, the output of textiles in Brazil increased from 22 million metres in 1882 to 242 million in 1905 and 470 million in 1915.[2] After 1915, however, the growth of the textile industry was extremely weak since import substitution had exhausted its possibilities and the growth of the export sector had slowed down or levelled off.

Given an elastic supply of labour – even when largely recruited abroad, as in the case of Argentina – the growth of the industrial sector took place under conditions of steady wage rates as in the case of the expansion of the export sector in an economy with a sizeable subsistence sector. Increased industrial output was due largely to the addition of new units of production similar to those already in existence, and was dependent on imported equipment. There was no question of creating a system of industrial production by steadily diversifying production. What was involved was simply the addition of similar units in certain sectors of industrial activity. The labour force absorbed, benefiting from a wage rate above the national average, provided reinforcement for the domestic market in the same way that growth of the export sector, by absorbing part of the surplus manpower, contributed to the expansion of the home market. Thus there was no essential difference between industrial expansion in this initial phase and the growth of export agriculture. The main difference was that the latter, dependent on overseas demand, acted as an exogenous variable, whereas investment in the industrial sector was dependent on the growth of a market created by the expansion of exports. In fact, the export sector acted as a multiplier of employment in the industrial sector. The industrial sector could overcome this dependence only if it became sufficiently diversified to generate its own demand. In other words, it required the establishment of machine-making and other industries whose output could be absorbed by the industrial sector itself and by other productive activities. But the facilities available abroad for financing investments in infrastructure and even industrial investments were tied to the acquisition of equipment and technology in foreign centres. Financial dependence

[2] For data on the evolution of the Brazilian cotton textile industry see Stanley J. Stein, *The Brazilian Cotton Manufacture: Textile Enterprise in an Underdeveloped Area, 1850–1950*, Harvard Univ. Press, 1957.

made it necessary to buy equipment from foreign suppliers, with the result that industrial activity was limited to the processing of local raw materials or to the finishing of imported semi-manufactured consumer goods, the equipment used being invariably purchased abroad. With an industrial complex geared to the processing of consumer goods, there was little need to assimilate modern technology. The only technical assistance given to existing industries was the replacement of worn-out equipment, which could be handled by agents acting for the import houses. This apparent initial advantage turned out to be negative in the next phase, since industries could be established without the emergence of a genuine industrial outlook, which presupposes not only the encouragement of managerial skills but the training of skilled personnel equipped with a thorough knowledge of technical processes.

Structural changes induced by the crisis of the export sector

The sudden collapse of the capacity to import, the contraction of the export sector and the ensuing fall in export profits, the blocking of international channels of finance, all provoked by the 1929 crisis, profoundly altered the course of development of the Latin American economies, particularly of those that had already begun to industrialise. The contraction of the export sector led to two types of reaction, depending on the degree of diversification attained by the economy concerned: (*a*) factors of production were shifted back into the pre-capitalist sector – subsistence agriculture and craft manufactures – as the money economy shrank; (*b*) the industrial sector geared to the home market was expanded in an effort to replace, wholly or in part, goods previously purchased abroad. The second case constitutes what has been called the import-substitution process, defined as the increase in the share of industrial output destined for the home market (*E*) in the gross domestic product (*P*) under conditions in which the share of imports (*M*) in the product is on the decline. In terms of growth rates we have:

$$\frac{1}{E} \cdot \frac{dE}{dt} > \frac{1}{P} \cdot \frac{dP}{dt} > \frac{1}{M} \cdot \frac{dM}{dt}. \tag{1}$$

To measure the extent of import substitution (*SM*) the following formula may be applied:

$$SM = \frac{M_{t-1}}{P_{t-1}} - \frac{M_t}{P_t}. \tag{2}$$

TABLE 11.1   *Evolution of import coefficient in selected countries*
             (imports as % of GDP)

	Argentina	Mexico	Brazil	Chile	Colombia
1929	17.8	14.2	11.3	31.2	18.0
1937	13.0	8.5	6.9	13.8	12.9
1947	11.7	10.6	8.7	12.6	13.8
1957	5.9	8.2	6.1	10.1	8.9

The evolution of the import coefficient from 1929 onwards in the Latin American countries with the longest-established industries is indicated in Table 11.1. Estimates are based on GDP and imports series, both at constant prices, taking 1960 as the base year.

In the decade following the crisis, there was a substantial decline in the import coefficient in all the countries mentioned and in the case of Chile it fell dramatically. Of the countries included in the table, Chile is the only one in which the domestic product had not recovered its 1929 level in absolute terms by 1937. The extremely high degree of its integration into the pattern of world trade – for a country exporting raw materials – and its dependence on imports of food products which would be difficult to replace (tropical commodities and sugar, for instance) made Chile not only the country most violently affected by the crisis but also the one in which the import-substitution process faced the greatest obstacles. The reduction in the import coefficient was made possible by the more than proportional growth of the industrial sector, i.e. the increase in the industrialisation coefficient. Table 11.2 shows the evolution of the industrialisation coefficient based on the GDP and industrial output series, calculated in 1960 prices.

Chile shows the most significant rise in the industrialisation coefficient in the course of the 1930s. Even so, the rise in industrial output would not be sufficient to account for the considerable decline observed in this

TABLE 11.2   *Evolution of industrialisation coefficient in selected countries*
             (industrial output as % of GDP)

	Argentina	Mexico	Brazil	Chile	Colombia
1929	22.8	14.2	11.7	7.9	6.2
1937	25.6	16.7	13.1	11.3	7.5
1947	31.1	19.8	17.3	17.3	11.5
1957	32.4	21.7	23.1	19.7	16.2

TABLE 11.3   *Evolution of import substitution in selected countries*

	1929–37	1937–47	1947–57	1929–57
Argentina	4.8	1.3	5.8	11.9
Mexico	5.7	−2.1	2.4	6.0
Brazil	4.4	−1.8	2.6	5.2
Chile	17.4	1.2	2.5	21.1
Colombia	5.1	−0.9	4.9	9.1

country's import coefficient, which also reflects import substitution in the agricultural sector, a substantial reduction of investments and their reorientation with a view to cutting down on their import content. By applying formula (2) and on the basis of the data presented above, we can measure the intensity of the substitution process in different periods.

If we exclude Chile, the substitution process proceeded at the same rate of intensity in the four remaining countries during the first period under consideration. In the following decade, which was influenced by the recovery of raw materials in world trade in the immediate post-war period, the substitution process lost momentum or even suffered a setback in countries registering the lowest import coefficient, i.e. Brazil and Mexico. In the period after 1947 the substitution process went ahead once more, but with diminished intensity. It is interesting to note that in Argentina, which provides the exception to the rule, industrialisation lagged behind in the period under consideration. Given the particular circumstances of each country and the fact that they were all at different stages of industrialisation, it would be wrong to expect any clear positive correlation between the rate of substitution and the growth of industrial output. None the less, if we compare the data for the two countries with the most similar degrees of development – Brazil and Mexico – we find they follow a clearly parallel trend in their substitution and industrialisation processes in the three decades considered.

TABLE 11.4   *Intensity of industrialisation process in selected countries (per cent)*

	1929–37	1937–47	1947–57	1929–57
Argentina	23	73	50	220
Mexico	46	86	98	407
Brazil	42	82	123	475
Chile	16	9	58	100
Colombia	90	110	130	830

Table 11.4 indicates the percentage increases in industrial output in the periods under consideration.

We have already referred to the special features of the Chilean case. Being a mineral-exporting country, Chile's industrial activity was partly integrated with the export sector whether through the processing of ores or the development of by-products. As a result of the sharp decline in these activities during the 1930s, the overall index does not reflect the substitution process that really took place in the manufacturing sector. For example, between 1929 and 1937 the output of cotton textiles was more than quadrupled, that of clothing more than doubled and that of paper more than tripled. However, the impossibility of curtailing food imports and the need to increase imports of fuels and raw materials, such as cotton, in a phase when the import capacity had been reduced by one half, account for the slow rate of Chilean industrialisation in the 1930s. It was no doubt partly as a result of these difficulties that the country became aware of the urgent need for State action, designed to introduce changes into the economic structure and to foster the development of the industrialisation process. The creation of the Corporación de Fomento de la Producción (CORFO) in 1939, a government agency that was to provide a model for other Latin American countries ten years later, was the point of departure for the second phase of Chile's industrial development. CORFO was responsible for devising and carrying out an electrification plan, for creating the basis for petroleum production and refining, for establishing a modern steelworks at Huachipato, for developing sugar beet production and fostering the paper industry and for several other initiatives in the industrial field. Chile is thus less a case of industrialisation based on spontaneous import substitution than of industrialisation fostered by State action designed to surmount the obstacles to the country's economic development created by the disruption of the foreign trade sector.

In the case of Colombia, the fact that industrial development was still at an early stage in 1929 permitted the two phases of the industrialisation process in some ways to overlap. The nature of the export sector, dominated by coffee grown mostly on family holdings, fostered the growth of the home market, leading to the establishment of non-durable consumer goods industries as early as the 1920s. The crisis, acting as an additional protection mechanism, speeded up this process. An elastic domestic supply of foodstuffs, agricultural raw materials and fuel was another favourable factor. None the less, Colombia's industrialisation coefficient in 1947 still lagged behind the coefficient registered in Argentina, Mexico and Brazil in 1929. It was in the latter three countries that the import-substitution process revealed its full potential as a factor for stimulating industrialisation.

The 1929 crisis, by initially taking the form of a contraction in the capacity to import, provoked exchange depreciations in these countries, which unleashed the inflationary processes mentioned in earlier chapters. Both these factors (exchange depreciation and inflation) had the effect of raising the profitability of the industrial nucleus geared to the domestic market. The process can be clearly observed in the case of the Brazilian textile industry, which had undergone remarkable expansion before the First World War and continued to increase its productive capacity in the 1920s. Between 1915 and 1929, the number of spindles in operation increased from 1.5 to 2.7 million and the number of looms from 51,000 to 80,000, an increase reflected in the creation of a relatively large margin of idle capacity.[3] As indicated in the preceding chapter, once the first phase of import substitution had run its course, the expansion of this sector became dependent on the growth of overall demand which, in the period that came to an end with the crisis, was closely bound up with the performance of the export sector. The existence of unused capacity in the Brazilian textile industry, and the fact that the industry was only very marginally dependent on imported raw materials, enabled it to expand its output rapidly in the period that followed. Thus, between 1929 and 1932 output increased by one-third, and between 1929 and 1939 by two-thirds. This vigorous growth is accounted for by the fact that certain sectors of the market, formerly supplied by imports – particularly of better-quality articles – were now supplied by domestically produced goods. A second factor was the enlargement of the existing market brought about by industrial expansion itself, which raised the level of overall demand. We see here the twin aspects of the substitution process. On the one hand, domestic production improves its competitive position and supplies a wider section of the market; this becomes possible because the level of money demand remains constant while relative prices of imports rise, and because domestic supply has a certain degree of elasticity – otherwise marginal costs would rise, offsetting the favourable effect for the domestic product of the price increase in imports. On the other hand, the development of industrial production creates an additional flow of income which enlarges the domestic market.

[3] In the latter half of the twenties, Brazilian textile manufacturers conducted a vigorous campaign aimed at persuading the government to prohibit imports of equipment. This clearly indicates the impasse reached at the end of the stage in which the growth of the industrial sector failed to effect any significant structural changes in the economy.

Import substitution took place only in countries that had already completed the initial stage of industrialisation, i.e. countries that already possessed a significant nucleus of non-durable consumer goods industries. By and large, these industries could make more intensive use of equipment and plant by introducing one or more extra shifts. This made it possible to increase output without further fixed capital investment, that is, without importing additional equipment. In conjunction with this elasticity of supply, the other essential condition for embarking on import substitution is the expansion of money income, which should be sufficient to offset the depressive effects of the contraction in export activities at the level of employment. This additional condition was more easily met in countries with a perennial cash crop, such as Brazil, where the government began to buy up coffee stocks, financing this operation with credits provided by the monetary authorities. Where these conditions were met, industrial production expanded rapidly and its profitability increased even faster. Bearing in mind the acute depression of the export sector, it is easy to understand why not only available financial resources but entrepreneurial capacity should have been attracted by industrial activities.

The increase in the output of manufactured non-durable consumer goods that took place at the beginning of the import-substitution process was matched by a rising demand for intermediate products and equipment in general. Given the limited import capacity, costs of industrial inputs tended to rise, opening up new sectors to investment. In countries with considerable metallurgical experience, such as Mexico, or in those where the government's action in promoting basic industries had proved most effective, the import-substitution process was able to continue and extend its range. Comparison of the Argentine, Brazilian and Mexican experiences illustrates this point. In Argentina, a considerable effort was made, during the 1930s, to maintain the country's credit-worthiness abroad. This required a policy of domestic restraint. Production of import substitutes in the agricultural sector – cotton and other agricultural raw materials – was encouraged, and industrialisation was orientated towards the manufacture of non-durable consumer goods. The concern to defend the level of domestic activity during phases of cyclical depression involved favouring industries with a less elastic demand, i.e. the non-durable consumer goods industries. It was assumed that the demand for consumer durables and equipment could be more easily curtailed as a means of coping with the sharp decline in the country's capacity to import. In other words, Argentina's chief concern was to adapt itself to the unstable conditions prevailing in the world market for raw materials. Mexico's position differed in certain fundamental aspects. In contrast with Argentina, the export sector was controlled by foreigners in the 1920s, which tended to clarify the demarcation line between the interests of the Mexican State and those of the exporting groups. In the 1920s and early 1930s, the Mexican State was already preparing the ground for far-reaching action in the economic sector, with the creation of the central bank, a government development bank (*Nacional Financiera*) and the Federal Electricity Commission. The expropriation of the petroleum industry in the late 1930s marks the culmination of the crisis between the Mexican State and the powerful foreign groups controlling the country's export activities. Brazil's position was somewhere between that of Argentina and Mexico. In contrast with Argentina, where the exporting interests managed to strengthen their position in the State through the military coup of 1930, in Brazil the position of exporting interests was weakened.[4] However, there was nothing like the dichotomy noted in the Mexican case. The Vargas government, notwithstanding the defeat of the counter-revolution backed by traditionalist groups in 1932, pursued a policy of compromise with the coffee growers, buying up surplus coffee stocks even when these mostly had to be destroyed. Nonetheless, the acuteness of the crisis in Brazil made it extremely difficult to foster any illusion that the export sector could be restored to its former role. Thus, during the 1930s, the Brazilian government tried to unify the home market by eliminating the surviving trade barriers between States; it created the National Steel Company, which was responsible for building the steel plant at Volta

---

[4] The 1929 crisis had far-reaching political repercussions in most Latin American countries, in many instances triggering off military takeovers and popular uprisings. However, these political disturbances did not always mean the same thing. In Argentina, for instance, the Unión Cívica Radical, a party essentially representing the middle classes and particularly the urban middle class, had been in power since the 1916 election; the 1929 crisis, by creating the conditions that led to the military *putsch* of 1930, smoothed the path for the restoration to power of conservative groups, bringing together interests connected with foreign trade, land speculation and stock-raising. A different process occurred in Brazil: with the 1930 revolution, more in the nature of a popular uprising than a military takeover, the coffee oligarchy was ousted from power under pressure from peripheral groups in the Northeast and the South (Vargas was Governor of the State of Rio Grande do Sul). Since the urban middle class was less influential than in Argentina, the displacement of the oligarchy led the Vargas government to move less in the direction of a formal democracy – as was the case in Argentina under the Unión Cívica Radical – than towards an enlightened authoritarianism.

Redonda, and it promoted the training of industrial workers on a nationwide scale.

In the post-war period, the industrialisation process in these three countries came to depend far more on State action designed to concentrate investment in the basic sectors, on the temporary recovery of the export sector and on the introduction of foreign capital and technology, than on import substitution. However, it was still regarded as import substitution since industrial production was strictly geared to domestic demands and took over markets formerly supplied, albeit on a small scale, by imports. Strictly speaking, new markets were created by the expansion of overall demand that accompanies industrialisation. Since these economies reproduced forms of consumption that already existed in other countries, the supply of a particular commodity was bolstered by imports in the initial stage although this stage tended to become increasingly brief.

In the four countries under consideration – Argentina, Mexico, Brazil and Chile – industrialisation induced by import substitution is strictly a phenomenon of the 1930s and the war period, that is, the period when the decline in the capacity to import permitted the intensive use of an industrial nucleus formed in an earlier period. The fact that industrialisation in these countries was intensified during the depression of the external sector is a clear indication that the process could have started sooner if these countries had had the benefit of appropriate policies. In other words, advance beyond the first stage of industrialisation required economic measures designed to change the structure of the industrial nucleus, and in default of such measures at the appropriate time, the industrial sectors found themselves in a relatively depressed situation. By creating the conditions for an intensive use of the productive capacity already installed, and by broadening the demand for intermediate products and equipment, the crisis made it clear that the industrialisation process could only move one stage further if it extended its range. State action, leading to the creation of basic industries, was to open up a third stage in the process of industrialisation in Latin America.

12 Imbalances created by import-substituting industrialisation: structural inflation

Development as a consequence of structural change

The countries specialising in primary production for export, within the framework of the system of international division of labour that developed in the nineteenth century, created economic structures with a highly inflationary bias. We have seen that cyclical crises in these countries entailed not only a fall in the quantum of exports but also deterioration in the terms of trade, flights of capital and obstruction of foreign credit lines. Thus there was a more accentuated and more rapid reduction in the capacity to import than in the flow of the money income generated internally by the export sector, creating pressures on the balance of payments which could not be eased simply by mobilising gold and exchange reserves. The immediate alternative was a devaluation of currency, bringing about an expansion in the export sector's money income, an increase in the tax revenue derived from exports and a rise in the prices of imported goods. Inflation was thus a consequence of the economic system's effort to adapt itself to a combination of external pressures. Since it was not feasible to defend the currency by manipulating interest rates and mobilising gold and exchange reserves, and since the short-term capital movements aggravated the critical state of the balance of payments on current account, it was natural that flexible exchange-rate systems should have come to prevail. The disadvantage of these systems is that they make speculation easier and thus accentuate the tendency to instability.

Industrialisation based on import substitution started a new inflationary cycle in Latin America, which differed from the classical regional disequilibria engendered by the effort to adapt to pronounced fluctuations in the income of the export sector. We have seen that one of the requisites for starting the substitution process after the contraction in the capacity to import, was an expansion of money income. Although

118

this expansion was in part absorbed by the increase in production destined for the home market – and without this increase substitution could
not have taken place – it sparked off a number of structural tensions
which were translated into an inflationary process. The study of structural tensions is one of the most interesting aspects of recent Latin
American development and its understanding was furthered only when
the traditional theoretical framework for approaching inflation problems
was called in question.

Considered simply in its broadest aspects, the problem can be stated
as follows: structural economic change is inherent in any process of
development and takes the form of sudden or gradual changes in the
demand schedule and in the composition of supply. In fact, the study of
development can be regarded as the identification and anticipation of
such changes and of the interaction and possible causal relations between
them. It is as though the development process were a chain of interdependent situations in which certain situations, while dependent on
those preceding them, also possess the germinative capacity to modify
the trends that have already emerged. To say that development consists
of structural change is practically a tautology. What matters is to identify
the changes that condition further changes, the agents responsible for
the decisions that engender these changes and the elements – situations
or agents – that offer the greatest resistance to change. The degree of
development depends on the effectiveness of the strategic decision centres
and the flexibility of structures. The agents whose decisions are capable
of provoking cumulative processes and hence of bringing about structural change act both on the supply side and on the demand side. In
fact, there is a process of circular causation in which increased productivity and diversified demand are mutually reinforcing. How rapidly the
agents will respond to the new situations will depend on the relative
flexibility of the economic structure.

In the classical model of Latin American development – integration
into the system of international division of labour – the dynamic
sector, which was the supply of primary products hardly interacted
with domestic demand. Expansion of the export sector led to a rise in
domestic income and diversification of a section of demand, indirectly
provoking the growth and diversification of imports. Since imported
goods were precisely those for which demand was most income-elastic,
there could be no cumulative interaction between supply and demand
in the direction of broadening any initial impulse to growth. On the
other hand, as the export sector was limited to a few export products,
it could not of itself offer many possibilities for innovation. Thus,

neither the expansion of demand nor the growth of the export sector required structural changes of major significance. It can be said, therefore, that the development model in question was one that did not require much structural flexibility, or rather that it was compatible with structures having little capacity for change. In fact, by allowing development to proceed with the minimum of change, the export model that prevailed in Latin America created a climate of resistance to change on the social plane. By failing to make the ruling classes realise that structural change was an essential ingredient in development, it contributed towards the emergence of attitudes that were to become obstacles to the region's development in the period that followed.

Focuses of basic inflationary pressures

The significance of the observations made in the preceding paragraphs becomes apparent when we remember that industrialisation with a declining import coefficient, i.e. import-substituting industrialisation, is a form of development requiring rapid changes in economic structures. Imports, which had given flexibility to overall supply in the preceding period, enabling it to respond promptly to the evolution of the demand schedule, were now in relative or absolute decline and consisted increasingly of industrial inputs, that is, products for which demand could not be curtailed. In fact, imports now became the instrument to use in changing the production structure developed in connexion with the home market. Development had thus passed from the stage in which it took the form of changes in the composition of demand (and in the composition of imports) to a stage in which it could proceed only if the supply structure was rapidly transformed. Let us imagine a concrete situation. In response to tensions in the export sector, textile production is intensified by working extra shifts in order to replace imports. The level of overall income rises and with it the demand for a whole range of consumer goods. In some cases, domestic supply can respond immediately, even though indirectly and only in part, by setting in motion substitution processes. Pressure to increase imports of intermediate products and equipment will make itself felt, reducing the capacity to import consumer goods. There will be significant changes in relative prices and important transfers of income, reflecting the structural tensions needed to change the supply structure, or rather to restore a balance between supply and demand. The time needed to bring about this balance largely reflects the structural flexibility of the country's system of production, taking into account the degree of differentiation it had achieved in the preceding period.

Structural tensions and the ensuing inflation were conditioned by local circumstances in each country. However, certain factors made their influence felt throughout the region, albeit in different degrees, and this makes it possible to attempt an overall interpretation of the inflation that accompanied import-substituting industrialisation in the Latin American countries. Among these factors, which should be considered as focuses of *basic inflationary pressures*, the following should be singled out:

(a) *The inelasticity of supply of agricultural products.* If Latin American agricultural structures had adapted to the growing demand for a few export commodities, they had failed to accommodate rising domestic demand. In fact, there was a substantial difference in the pattern of response. In the case of export agriculture we have a rigid system, almost invariably based on cultivation of a single crop, in which increased output is achieved by extensive farming methods, absorbing factors formerly employed in subsistence agriculture with a low economic productivity, even though the production techniques used are not essentially different. Production for the home market required a highly diversified output with the capacity to accommodate changes in demand since it competed with the surpluses produced by the subsistence sector, which varied greatly from year to year in accordance with climatic factors. Extensive growth alone in the case of production destined for the home market, would lead to increasingly marginal prices, since the land brought under cultivation had to be further and further away from the markets, or of poor quality. Given the rapid growth of the population employed in urban areas, a corresponding increase in agricultural productivity was required if output were to keep pace with rising demand. Unlike traditional export agriculture, whose growth could be extensive, agriculture producing for the home market had to develop by raising its technological level. Failure to do so resulted in a relative shortage of agricultural products in the urban areas, with a consequent rise in prices. As in the Ricardian model, the rise in agricultural prices was translated into an increase in the income accruing to landowners, thus consolidating the power of traditionalist groups and reducing the capacity of the supply structure to adapt itself to the new demand schedule.

(b) *Inadequacy of the infrastructure.* Transport and other basic services, originally geared to the needs of a few homogeneous export products, often displayed a considerable degree of inadequacy in relation to the requirements of the new production structure. Both in relation to agriculture, expanding into new areas, and in relation to industry, largely dependent on raw material supplies from the interior and requiring access to different areas of the country for domestic outlets for its products, the existing infrastructure revealed serious inadequacies. The problem was, of course, more serious in some countries than in others, but it arose in all of them to a significant degree. The existing network of warehouses and silos proved similarly inadequate in relation to production destined for home consumption. The financial infrastructure also called for considerable adaptation. The financing of homogeneous products of a standard type and with an assured demand in the great international centres is a relatively simple operation compared with the financing of a highly diversified agricultural production handicapped by precarious storage conditions. A substantial part of the investment made by Latin American governments in the last three decades was directed into the rehabilitation and improvement of transport systems and other public utilities.

(c) *Short-term inadequacy of labour.* Although there was an abundant supply of labour in most of the Latin American countries, the labour force lacked skills suited to the demands of industrial activities. In many instances, even a tradition of artisan industries was lacking, and the labour force had to move straight from technically backward agriculture to the factories. Even more important was the lack of an entrepreneurial tradition. With the exception of countries benefiting from recent European immigration, there was little entrepreneurial experience in the industrial sector. We have already remarked that the traditional export economy did not favour the development of a capacity for innovation. Apart from foreigners, the initial nucleus of industrial entrepreneurs was formed by national elements with experience in enterprises importing manufactured goods – almost invariably controlled by foreign groups. Given its isolation from the traditional ruling class and the professional middle class, this nucleus tended to grow slowly, constituting one of the main reasons for the lack of structural flexibility.

(d) *The inadequacy of fiscal systems.* We have seen that fiscal revenue was essentially dependent on foreign trade, particularly on imports. When this source of revenue was curtailed, a shift to an excise tax was tried, involving high collection costs. The regressive nature of this tax made it inelastic in relation to the rising level of domestic income. The income tax imposed in Argentina in the 1930s played no more than a complementary role. By and large, tax structures are extremely regressive and inelastic to the growth of income generated by activities connected with the home market. Thus, the State's capacity for collecting taxes involved heavier outlays and became more inelastic at a time when there was an increasing demand for investment of public funds. Since the possibilities of external financing had been sharply curtailed or had ceased to exist in the fifteen years following the 1929 crisis, and as there were no domestic financial markets to absorb public bond issues, governments throughout Latin America came to depend, to a greater or lesser extent, on credits from the banking system, with an automatic rediscount to finance investment or even to cover part of current expenditure. Fiscal systems were only gradually brought up to date to cope with the new responsibilities assumed by governments and the new forms of economy that were emerging. Thus, the public sector itself became a factor in structural rigidity, even in areas where the government was seeking other means to promote development.

(*e*) *Increased financial commitments.* Given the fact that investment was being made under conditions of balance of payments difficulties, or even of a declining capacity to import, the costs of equipment (almost entirely imported) tended to rise in relative terms. The savings ratio therefore had to rise proportionally in order to keep pace with the real rate of investment. Enterprises had to take on additional financial investments and this became a factor exerting pressure for a rise in the price level.

The relative importance of the factors indicated varied from one country to another and, in the same country, from one period to another. Only when development was deliberately fostered did structural tensions become fully manifest. Thus, in the thirties, when the capacity to import was curtailed and money income expanded, investment shifted to industry, causing a minimum of tension in Argentina and a maximum in Chile. In the case of Argentina, export surpluses found an alternative market through the expansion of urban employment. In Chile, not only was there no possibility of domestic absorption of exportable production but the domestic supply of agricultural products proved extremely rigid. However, in the subsequent period, Argentine agriculture also became a focus of structural tension. Once the stage of extensive expansion in the region producing cereals and livestock had been exhausted, agriculture found itself competing with other sectors of production in a market with a relatively inelastic labour supply, and it became imperative to raise its technical level and increase capital inputs if economic structures were to retain the flexibility they had shown in earlier periods. In default of this development in depth of the agricultural sector, the supply of agricultural and livestock products tended to become inelastic and the home market began to compete with exports, aggravating the basic problem of the inadequacy of the country's capacity to import.

Structural tensions were often aggravated by the government policies pursued. In Brazil, for instance, the government continued its policy of buying up unsold coffee surpluses (which it proceeded to destroy in large quantities) even during the war years when the adverse trade balance and the budgetary deficit (Brazil had entered the war and partial mobilisation was taking place) gave rise to inflationary pressures. In Argentina, towards the end of the 1940s and in the early 1950s, the government's over-emphasis on industrial investment reduced the profitability of the agricultural sector, whose rigidity had already become manifest as the main focus of structural tension. By and large, by seeking to intensify investment, governments aggravated inflationary tensions. The achievement of a rate of growth that would make it possible to absorb the increase in the population of working age and to satisfy the expectations of groups that already had attained modern standards of living, turned into a difficult obstacle race for which the ruling groups and the administrative apparatus were ill equipped. The faster the pace aimed for, the more difficult, *ceteris paribus*, became the obstacles.

Circumstantial factors and propagation mechanisms

In a structuralist analysis of inflation, attention is initially directed towards the focuses from which so-called basic inflationary pressures spread. These are the points in the economic structure that offer most resistance to the changes required by development.[1] The *basic* pressures

---

[1] On the structuralist theory of inflation, the basic works are: Juan Noyola Vazquez, 'El Desarrollo Económico y la Inflación en México y Otros Paises Latinoamericanos', *Investigación Económica*, XVI, 4, Mexico, 1956; ECLA, *El Desequilibrio Externo en el Desarrollo Económico Latinoamericano: El Caso de México*, 1957; C. Furtado, 'The External Disequilibrium in the Underdeveloped Economies', *The Indian Journal of Economics*, April 1958; Ozvaldo Sunkel, 'La Inflación Chilena – Un Enfoque Heterodoxo', *El Trimestre Económico*, Oct.–Dec. 1958; Aníbal Pinto Santa Cruz, 'Estabilidad y Desarrollo', *El Trimestre Económico*, Jan.–Mar. 1960; Julio Oliveira, 'La Teoria no Monetaria de la Inflación', *El Trimestre Económico*, Jan–Mar. 1960; Raúl Prebisch, 'El Falso Dilema entre Desarrollo Económico y Estabilidad Monetaria', *Boletín Económico de América Latina*, March 1961; Dudley Seers, 'Inflación y Crecimiento: Resumen de la Experiencia Latinoamericana', *Boletín Económico de América Latina*, Feb. 1962. For an overall survey, see Joseph Grunwald, 'The Structuralist School on Price Stabilization and Economic Development: the Chilean Case' in A. Hirschman (ed.), *Latin American Issues*, New York, 1961; Rosa Olivia Villa Martinez, *Inflación y Desarrollo: el Enfoque Estructuralista*, thesis for the Universidad Nacional Autónoma de México, 1966. See also Werner Baer, 'The Inflation Controversy in Latin America: a Survey', *Latin American Research Review*, II, 2, 1967.

act together with other factors which may be as much *circumstantial* as engendered by the inflationary process itself. Cicumstantial factors often spark off a new inflationary wave. They could as easily be of an economic nature – a sharp rise or fall in export prices – as non-economic: the loss of a coffee crop through frost, a shortage of food supplies after a drought, government action of the kind instanced above. In fact, the inflationary process always starts with the action of some agent whose operations frustrate what may be called 'conventional expectations'. Thus a rise in export prices, by providing additional public revenue, may prompt the government to launch a public works programme, changing conditions in the labour market, increasing urban employment, raising the demand for agricultural surpluses, provoking sudden shifts in the composition of imports, etc. In this way, a numper of expectations will be frustrated, causing resistance to the changes required in the allocation of resources. Once set in motion, the inflationary process tends to create situations that react upon the initial impulse and increase its inflationary impact. Thus the rise in money costs provoked by the inflation has repercussions on the export sector, reducing its competitive capacity abroad. The consequences may be a reduction in exports – which will affect the capacity to import and aggravate the inflation – or an exchange devaluation with a consequent rise in the price level of imported industrial inputs, which cannot but aggravate the inflation. Another example of a derived factor which becomes an autonomous multiplier of inflationary pressures is the behaviour of public services: cuts in utility rates may act as disincentives to investment in public facilities, increasing the structural rigidity of the economic system as a whole, or they may require compensatory public subsidies aggravating one of the focuses of basic inflationary pressure.

The most rigid points in the economic structure act like a barrier damming up the accumulated potential energy of a constantly rising level of water. In some circumstances, this energy can be diverted and the economic system will continue to operate as though it did not exist. It is far more likely, however, that the pressure will spread and affect other points of the economic structure, the course taken being dependent on the *propagation mechanisms* that it uses. Thus, the power to propagate the inflationary potential inherent in the need to finance a deficit in the public sector will depend on the method of financing adopted. A rise in agricultural prices will be reflected in falling real wages for the urban sectors or rising costs for the industrial activities dependent on agricultural inputs, transferring the pressure to other sectors. The speed at which inflationary pressures are propagated reflects the varying ability of the different social groups to defend their share in the social income and the effectiveness with which public and private sectors defend their respective positions in the process of appropriating available resources.

The *decision centres* able to intervene in the propagation of inflationary pressures are mainly those that intervene in credit, exchange and wage policies and in the method of financing deficits in the public sector. In other words, inflationary pressure tends to be propagated through the various monetary channels that constitute its *propagation mechanisms*. Since these channels offer some resistance, the inflationary pressure may be partially absorbed. Thus, the credit system is not completely elastic, the decline in real wages may be gradual, the balance of payments deficit may be refinanced abroad, etc. If pressure is prolonged, however, or suddenly accentuated, the channels will offer decreasing resistance and may even come to act as automatic propagation mechanisms.

The difficulty in understanding the true nature of the inflationary processes that accompanied Latin America's development policies in the phase when the export sector lost its dynamism arose from the emphasis given to the propagation mechanisms. This led to the prevalence of the view that inflation reflected the poor functioning of money flows. Thus, the banking system's exaggeratedly lenient attitude towards the private sector or towards budgetary deficit abuses was blamed for the excess of demand over supply—and a *demand inflation* was diagnosed; in other instances, government complaisance was blamed for excessive wage increases and the existence of a *cost inflation* was recorded. There can be no question that both siuations have occurred repeatedly in many Latin American countries in the course of the last decades, particularly in the immediate post-war years. However, they were nearly always *responses* to more deep-seated pressures, or rather they reflected an adaptation effort within the framework of a more complex process, whose main ingredients were structural inflexibility and the determination to press ahead with a development policy.

Significant cases

Mexico, one of the industrially most advanced Latin American countries, was the only case in which inflationary pressures were completely controlled until the beginning of the 1970s when inflation acquired new characteristics, affecting the capitalist economies as a whole. Since 1954, the last time the Mexican peso was devalued against the dollar, the level of prices in the country has remained relatively stable, the increase being fairly close to that observed in the United States. To explain this singular situation, we must take into account several factors. First, there is a one-party political system which guarantees strict continuity in control of the Executive Power and subordinates the functions of the Legislative Power.[2] Since the trade union system is closely integrated into the government party, the likelihood of friction between those responsible for administering wages policy and trade union leaders is eliminated. On the other hand, the possibility that the export sector will exert strong pressure on the government to compensate for a fall in market prices abroad is practically ruled out. The propagation mechanisms are thus subject to control, which explains why changes in income distribution can be effected without altering the level of prices. Furthermore, the weakness of certain social groups creates conditions for a particular type of structural adaptation, and there have been times when the growth of the domestic product has been accompanied by a fall in the average real wages of these groups. But these considerations are not in themselves sufficient to explain the Mexican experience. An important aspect of this experience must be found in the greatly increased structural economic flexibility brought about by the social changes following the revolution and the determination shown by successive governments over the last decades to promote the country's industrial development. Control of the petroleum industry not only created an important source of investment funds but also made it possible to carry out a policy of keeping down fuel prices, with favourable effects on industrial costs. Finally, the modernisation of the agricultural sector, involving large-scale irrigation works in the north and the introduction of improved cultivation techniques in the *Mesa Central*, eliminated one of the focuses of inflationary pressure most difficult to control. It should be added that the remarkable expansion of tourism has considerably eased Mexico's capacity to import. Thus, greater structural flexibility and stricter control of the propagation mechanisms created the conditions for achieving the monetary stability referred to above.

Both in Chile and in Argentina the situation is in many respects the opposite of that of Mexico. The power system reflects a compromise between powerfully structured groups and the propagation mechanisms are consequently in no position to resist inflationary pressures. In Argentina, the chronic inadequacy of the capacity to import, the failure to

[2] An analysis of the present power structures in Mexico is given in Pablo Gonzalez Casanova, *La Democracia en México*, Mexico, 1965. See also Daniel Casio Villegas, *El Sistema Politico Mexicano*, Mexico, 1972.

modernise agriculture and stock-raising, the intrinsic weakness of the State when faced with prolonged social tensions, the lack of a long-term industrialisation policy – all this in a precociously modernised country where popular expectations are constantly rising – have combined to produce one of the most complex inflationary processes on record.

The behaviour of the Brazilian inflation also displays individual features worth mentioning. In the decade following the Second World War, inflation played an important role in accelerating the country's development. The sharp rise in coffee prices after 1949, and in other export products after the Korean war, was reflected in the familiar favourable effects produced on the levels of income in both private and public sectors. Nevertheless, given the structural inflexibility of the export sector, infrastructure, skilled labour market etc., the inflationary process dating from the war period tended to be aggravated. In order to curb any further propagation of inflationary impulses while at the same time defending coffee prices on the world market, the government maintained a stable exchange rate. As the domestic level of prices rose, there was a marked shift in income from the foreign trade sector (particularly the coffee sector) to the import sector. In this way, relative prices of imported equipment declined considerably, greatly increasing the profitability of the industrial sector. What was involved was a change in income distribution within the private sector, to the benefit of the most dynamic groups, giving rise to the extraordinary industrial growth of the 1950s. New investment in the coffee sector, already overburdened by structural surpluses, was discouraged, and diversification of the industrial sector was stepped up. With the introduction of an auction system for foreign exchange in 1954,[3] a substantial proportion of the increment in the export sector's income, which was being gradually absorbed by the industrial sector, was appropriated by the government, making it possible to reduce the inflationary potential created in the public sector largely as a result of heavy investment in infrastructure.

Since the mid-1950s, the Brazilian inflation has come more and more to resemble the Argentine–Chilean model which has also been reproduced, in an acute form, in Uruguay. The propagation mechanisms are increasingly prompt to operate and the secondary focuses–created by the inflation itself–begin to act in increasingly autonomous ways. Banks

[3]   The exchange reform introduced by Minister Osvaldo Aranha in 1954 established five categories of imported goods in accordance with their degree of *essentialness*. Since only a small amount of foreign exchange was made available for the category of goods considered less essential, quotations at exchange auctions for this category of imports rose, the consequent 'profit' reverting to the public coffers.

which benefited from the effects of interest regulations in respect of holders of small and medium savings, and from the cheap money available through the re-discount mechanism tended to hold privileged positions. Firms reduced their own liquidity as much as possible and came to rely entirely on the banking system for their working capital. In consequence, the economic system became extremely sensitive to changes in credit policy. Any attempt to curb inflation by curtailing credit would cripple financially weak firms without affecting those who had connexions with the banks or were in a position to negotiate short-term loans abroad. Credit restrictions could thus paralyse certain businesses – not necessarily the least efficient – and raise money costs of others as a result of their increased financial commitments. This is why the anti-inflationary policies prescribed by the International Monetary Fund, and followed by Chile towards the end of the 1950s and by Argentina and Brazil in the following decade, have provoked recessions in economic activity without achieving relative stability in the level of prices.

At a certain point, as we shall see in detail in a later chapter, structural inflexibilities begin to act not only as focuses of inflationary pressure but as a brake on development. At that stage, any development effort tends to be translated into acute inflationary pressures, which can be absorbed only by applying policies directly designed to induce structural change. In sum, the problem of controlling inflation tended to become part and parcel of development policy, inasmuch as it had not proved feasible to achieve stability outside the framework of a concerted effort to promote structural reform.

Since 1964, Brazil's economic and social policy has assumed characteristics which bring it closer to the Mexican experience in regard to the control of inflation. A combination of interrelated measures, carried out by an authoritarian government, restored a certain degree of elasticity to the cost structure and inflation took the form, in part, of a cumulative concentration of income. With State control of trade unions and arbitrary fixing of wages by the government, one of the primary mechanisms for the propogation of inflationary pressures was eliminated at the expense of the low-income wage-earners. On the other hand, a series of measures was introduced to defend the real value of financial assets (held by persons and companies) against inflationary erosion. These measures stimulated the development of the capital market and strengthened the position of financial intermediaries. In this way, the redistributive effects of inflation were channelled in favour of the middle- and high-income groups, while certain focuses of inflationary pressure, in particular the fiscal deficit, were eliminated. Nevertheless, the rigidity of the agricultural sector has persisted, as has the inability of the system to raise the rate of savings.[4]

The effort to accelerate economic growth after 1968 reopened the problem of finding additional resources in terms reminiscent of the past and once more the solution found was external indebtedness and inflation. Following the period of rapid acceleration and slackening of inflation, in the first half of the 1960s, there has been a resumption of the inflationary pace of the 1950s since 1968: an increase in the index of consumer prices of around 20 to 25 per cent a year. The intensification of inflation since 1974 is a consequence of the current world economic situation which affects all countries of the region.

[4] Cf. Andrea Maneschi, *Aspectos Quantitivos do Sétor Publico de Brasil de 1939 a 1970*, São Paulo, 1970; Maria da Conceição Tavares, *Da Substituição de Importações ao Capitalismo Financeiro*, Rio de Janeiro, 1972; and C. Furtado, *Análise do 'Modelo' Brasileiro*, Rio de Janeiro, 1972.

V. REORIENTATION OF DEVELOPMENT IN THE RECENT PERIOD

13 Evolution of macro economic structures

Diversity in behaviour patterns

A comparative analysis of overall development trends in the post-war period reveals wide differences in the stages at which the Latin American countries find themselves, and at the same time makes it possible to establish the broad outline of a representative model for the regional economy. For the purpose of this analysis we have used data covering the period starting in 1950 for the countries of greatest relative economic importance in the region:[1] Argentina, Brazil, Chile, Colombia, Mexico, Peru and Venezuela. All these countries have experienced significant structural economic change during the period under review, as can be seen from the figures given in Tables 13.1 and 13.2. In all of them, the agricultural sector's share in the gross domestic product has decreased: between 1950 and 1970 it declined from 18.7 to 13.8 per cent in Argentina; from 22.5 to 12.2 per cent in Mexico; from 39.8 to 29.7 per cent in Colombia and from 27.4 to 19.1 per cent in Peru. By contrast, manufacturing increased considerably in every one of these countries. In Brazil, the share of the manufacturing sector in GDP was slightly over half that of the agricultural sector in 1950; two decades later it was 36 per cent more than that of agriculture. In Argentina the share of manufacturing in GDP is two and a half times that of agriculture and in Mexico it is nearly double the figure for agriculture. Of the seven countries considered, Colombia is the only one in which agriculture

[1] Cuba, with a population similar in size to those of Chile and Venezuela and ranking fourth in regional per capita income for 1960 (after Argentina, Uruguay and Venezuela), is among the countries of greatest relative economic importance in Latin America. However, owing to the lack of data on this country, particularly data that can be compared with those available for the seven countries considered, the Cuban economy cannot be dealt with in an overall survey of the regional economy during the last decade. Cuba is thus excluded from the data on Latin America unless otherwise stated. The Cuban economy will be separately analysed in chapter 24.

TABLE 13.1   Structural evolution of GDP in selected countries at factor cost in dollars at 1960 prices (% of GDP)

	Agriculture	Mining industry	Manufacturing	Building	Basic services[a]	Other services	Total
Argentina							
1950	18.7	0.7	28.9	4.9	9.4	37.4	100
1955	19.6	0.8	29.9	3.9	9.5	36.3	100
1960	16.9	1.4	31.4	4.1	9.4	37.8	100
1965	16.0	1.4	33.9	3.1	9.5	36.1	100
1970	13.8	1.7	35.3	4.4	9.5	35.0	100
Brazil							
1950	31.3	0.3	16.5	1.1	7.1	43.7	100
1955	31.0	0.3	18.9	1.1	7.6	41.2	100
1960	28.3	0.5	23.4	1.2	8.6	38.0	100
1965	23.7	0.7	22.0	1.0	9.4	43.5	100
1970	19.1	0.8	25.3	1.2	10.5	43.3	100
Mexico							
1950	22.5	5.7	20.6	3.1	5.8	42.3	100
1955	20.2	4.4	21.0	4.6	6.3	43.5	100
1960	17.4	4.3	23.0	5.0	6.1	44.2	100
1965	14.8	4.4	21.5	4.2	4.3	50.9	100
1970	12.2	4.5	23.6	4.8	4.9	50.0	100

Chile

1950	12.5	7.2	16.7	2.3	7.9	53.4	100
1955	12.8	6.9	18.8	3.1	8.7	49.7	100
1960	12.2	7.0	18.7	2.8	8.1	51.1	100
1965	10.2	9.8	25.4	4.8	12.0	37.9	100
1970	9.8	10.3	25.2	4.2	21.0	38.5	100

Colombia

1950	39.8	3.6	14.2	3.2	5.9	34.3	100
1955	35.2	3.5	15.4	4.5	7.6	33.8	100
1960	34.6	4.0	17.0	3.7	7.3	33.4	100
1965	31.1	3.8	18.0	3.3	8.3	35.5	100
1970	29.7	3.1	18.6	3.4	8.7	35.5	100

Peru

1950	27.4	5.4	14.6	3.5	4.7	44.4	100
1955	23.8	6.4	16.6	4.5	5.5	43.2	100
1960	22.9	9.0	17.7	3.2	5.5	41.7	100
1965	20.2	7.0	20.3	4.2	5.8	48.3	100
1970	19.1	6.5	22.6	3.7	5.8	48.1	100

Venezuela

1950	8.5	26.1	9.6	4.6	6.3	44.9	100
1955	7.3	27.0	9.4	5.0	6.0	45.3	100
1960	7.2	27.3	10.7	3.9	5.2	45.7	100
1965	6.5	23.3	11.5	2.5	5.5	50.7	100
1970	6.9	19.8	12.2	2.5	6.9	51.7	100

a Electricity, gas, water, transport and communications.
SOURCE: ECLA, on the basis of figures taken from *Economic Survey of Latin America, 1963, 1965, and 1973*.

TABLE 13.2 *Structure and growth of the GDP in the post-war period (average annual growth rates in percentages)*

	Argentina	Brazil	Mexico	Chile	Colombia	Peru	Venezuela
Agriculture							
1950–5	4.1	5.0	5.8	3.5	2.7	2.2	5.9
1955–60	− 0.4	3.7	3.0	1.0	3.5	3.8	6.1
1960–5	2.1	6.9	3.9	2.6	3.0	5.9	6.6
1965–70	1.1	3.0	2.7	3.0	4.8	2.4	5.4
Mining industry							
1950–5	7.8	6.6	4.7	− 2.9	4.3	8.8	8.7
1955–60	14.3	14.9	6.1	11.0	6.8	11.9	6.6
1960–5	7.8	11.1	4.2	4.0	4.4	2.6	3.7
1965–70	9.0	10.6	7.2	4.9	1.5	2.2	1.0
Manufacturing industry							
1950–5	3.8	8.1	6.6	5.4	6.9	7.8	11.6
1955–60	3.8	10.3	8.1	2.6	6.1 .	6.1	9.1
1960–5	4.1	4.9	8.0	6.4	5.9	7.4	9.4
1965–70	5.0	10.3	8.8	3.6	6.4	5.8	5.6
Building							
1950–5	1.5	6.4	6.4	3.9	12.4	10.7	10.6
1955–60	4.3	7.2	8.1	1.4	− 6.2	− 2.0	1.1
1960–5	2.0	2.8	5.9	4.6	1.9	13.5	7.9
1965–70	11.7	10.7	9.8	0.7	12.3	9.7	3.7
Basic services							
1950–5	6.2	4.4	9.6	6.0	9.6	—	18.0
1955–60	12.0	10.8	6.5	3.5	11.7	—	18.1
1960–5	9.9	9.7	10.0	7.4	9.2	—	12.0
1965–70	4.6	9.8	9.7	3.8	6.8	3.6	8.9
Total GDP							
1950–5	3.0	5.7	6.1	3.1	5.1	5.3	8.7
1955–60	3.2	5.9	6.1	3.6	4.0	4.8	6.5
1960–5	3.5	4.2	5.9	5.1	4.4	6.1	5.0
1965–70	4.1	7.1	6.4	4.1	5.8	3.4	4.7
GDP per capita							
1950–5	0.8	2.9	3.1	0.9	2.3	3.1	4.7
1955–60	1.4	2.9	3.1	1.2	1.0	2.2	2.6
1960–5	2.0	1.1	2.8	2.7	1.1	3.0	1.5
1965–70	2.7	4.6	3.7	1.6	2.6	0.7	1.1

SOURCE: ECLA, as for Table 13.1.

maintained its position as the leading sector in the generation of the GDP in 1970. In the countries with important mining sectors (Venezuela and Chile) agriculture had experienced a relative decline in an earlier phase.

The period under consideration was one of relatively rapid economic growth in the region. With the exception of Argentina and Chile, the other countries included in Table 13.2 registered average annual rates of growth of the product of 5 per cent or more during the two decades analysed. In three countries – Brazil, Mexico and Venezuela – the GDP grew by 6 per cent or more. From the figures in Tables 13.1 and 13.2, considered together, we can identify three types of behaviour pattern:

(*a*) countries with a high import coefficient and hence with the structural flexibility derived from an open external sector. These countries show the characteristics of the classic Latin American model of 'outward-directed' development, with an import-substitution process partly prompted by government action and partly due to the initiative of international corporations seeking to defend their position in local markets by taking anticipatory action. This is the case of Venezuela and Peru. In these two countries this development model entered a critical stage in the 1960s, with a consequent decline in the rate of growth.

(*b*) countries whose import coefficient underwent a long period of decline but whose industrialisation has gained sufficient momentum to sustain development. This is the case of Brazil and Mexico. Colombia falls midway between this group and the first. Its import coefficient remains relatively high but its export sector lacks the capacity to provide a dynamic impulse for the economy.

(*c*) countries that have experienced a sharp fall in the import coefficient and have considerably expanded their industrial production, but in which the industrialisation process has lost momentum. This is the case of Argentina and Chile. The average annual percentage growth rate of the industrial sector in the fifties was 3.8 in Argentina and 4.0 in Chile, as against 9.9 in Venezuela, 9.2 in Brazil, 7.4 in Mexico, 7.0 in Peru and 6.5 in Colombia.

Taking the period as a whole, a number of general observations may be made. The first is the change in the behaviour of the external sector. Exports have expanded only where there has been a deliberate export-promotion policy. The export sector's traditional forms of extensive growth in response to expanding external demand have given way to other forms of growth based on the realisation that an inadequate capacity to import is a serious obstacle to development. In Chile, for instance, recovery in the growth of exports was the outcome of a deliberate policy designed to regain the country's share in the world copper market. Similarly, the record increase in Peru's fisheries exports is the result of a combination of deliberate measures rather than a simple response to an expanding external market. In Argentina, a considerable effort has been made since the second half of the 1950s to reduce the relative prices of agricultural inputs, in order to raise the profitability of the export sector. In recent years, all the countries have made efforts, in one way or another, to promote 'non-traditional' exports, providing generous subsidies for export sales of manufacturers.

The second point is that industrialisation of what we have called the first phase – directly induced by the growth of the export sector – has tended to proceed side by side with import-substituting industrialisation, that is, industrialisation engendered by an inadequate capacity to import. Countries with a low level of industrialisation in 1950 – an industrialisation coefficient of less than 15 per cent – sought to intensify the industrialisation process independently of the behaviour of the export sector. Venezuela, in the first half of the 1950s, is the last example of a Latin American country in which the domestic product grew considerably without a corresponding increase in the share of the industrial sector. In fact, Venezuela's industrial sector was expanding, but massive investment in the petroleum sector, whose inputs at that time were wholly imported, meant that the structure of the production system showed no appreciable change. In Peru, a country in which the import coefficient rose steadily throughout the entire period – from 12 per cent to 26 per cent between 1950 and 1970 – the rapid growth of the industrial sector was matched by a steady structural transformation as indicated by the evolution of the coefficient of industrialisation which rose from 14.6 to 22.6 per cent.

Thirdly, it should be noted that the rise in productivity and income and the structural changes brought about by industrial development were not reflected in any significant changes in the rates of saving. The figures in Table 13.3 show that there were no substantial changes in savings rates in any of the countries considered, if we exclude Venezuela and Peru where the role played by foreign groups controlling highly profitable export activities led to a substantial outflow of resources. In Brazil and Mexico, the rate of saving remained stable despite the manifest concentration of income that took place in the 1960s. With the exception of Argentina, in all the countries included in the Table, and in the region as a whole, the share of domestic savings in investment expenditure declined. However, the foreign contribution was of decisive im-

TABLE 13.3   *Indicators of capital formation (in percentages)*

	Domestic savings/ GDP		Domestic savings/ investment		Public investment/ total investment	
	1960/61	1970/71	1960/71	1970/71	1960/61	1969/70
Argentina	19.8	22.0	90.4	95.8	24.5	40.7
Brazil	16.6	16.7	90.6	89.0	39.2	52.c
Mexico	17.9	18.6	92.4	89.6	34.3	34.7
Chile	12.4	13.9	68.4	86.5	38.0	55.9
Colombia	19.0	16.5	90.1	84.3	16.7	34.4
Peru	22.2	17.9	99.9	100.6	16.6	21.2
Venezuela	26.0	17.5	153.5	101.8	39.0	34.9
Latin America	17.9	17.7	93.5	89.9	29.1	36.3

SOURCE: ECLA, *América Latina y la Estrategia Internacional de Desarrollo: Primera Evaluación Regional*, Santiago, 1973, Part 1, pp. 98 and 100.

portance only in the case of Chile, in the first half of the decade. In five of the countries considered, there was an appreciable relative increase in public investment. Since the rate of saving remained relatively stable, it would seem that the growing participation of the public sector in the formation of capital was an endeavour to offset the decline in savings in the private sector. In Brazil and Chile, for example, the state was already responsible, by the end of the 1960s, for more than half the investment financing.

Finally, it should be noted that structural changes in the region's production systems have given rise to growing disparities in relative sectoral productivities, that is, to increasing technological heterogeneity and widening disparities in standards of remuneration for labour, or both. In all the countries included in Table 13.4, with the exception of Argentina, the gap between the economic productivity of the secondary sector (industry and basic services) and that of agriculture has widened during the period under consideration. If we exclude Venezuela, where the petroleum sector weighs heavily in the figures, in 1960, the scissors of disparities in productivity, ranged between 1.3:1 (Argentina) and 4.9:1 (Mexico). In 1970 the level of disparity in Argentina was practically the same but in Mexico it had risen to 5.7:1. In Chile, the productivity ratio in favour of the secondary sector rose from 3.3:1 to 3.9:1 and in Peru from 3.1:1 to 3.8:1. The decline of the favourable differential for the tertiary sector found, for example, in Argentina, is less

TABLE 13.4   *Sectoral productivity rankings (national averages = 100)*

	1960			1970		
	A	B	C	A	B	C
Argentina	91.1	122.1	84.4	97.4	133.8	70.7
Brazil	42.3	147.4	177.4	42.7	155.8	145.5
Mexico	30.6	151.6	209.9	27.1	155.4	172.9
Chile	45.0	149.4	174.4	41.0	159.7	157.3
Colombia	70.7	131.8	123.1	71.6	148.7	102.3
Peru	46.2	142.7	176.1	39.4	150.8	153.2
Venezuela	21.1	198.7	108.3	29.3	170.2	99.4

A: Agriculture.
B: Manufacturing, building, mining, basic services.
C: Other services.
SOURCE: ECLA, *Tendencias y Estructuras de la Económia Latinoaméricana*, Santiago, 1971, Table 15.

a reflection of a process of homogenisation in the system as a whole than of heterogeneity in the services sector, attributable to the migration of under-employed manpower from the rural to the urban areas.

Anticipation and the loss of effectiveness of the substitution process

If we compare the industrialisation process in countries such as Colombia, Peru and Venezuela with the experience of countries whose industrial development began at the end of the last century – Argentina, Mexico and Brazil – we find certain significant differences. We have already referred to the fact that in the latter group of countries, periods when there was a boom in exports, as in the 1920s, were reflected in a slackening of industrial development. This did not occur in the case of the first three countries mentioned: in the first half of the 1950s, industrial output in Venezuela grew at a rate unequalled in the region up to that time, while the country's coefficient of imports remained above 30 per cent (see Table 13.5). In Peru, the rate of growth of industrial output remained above 7 per cent between 1950 and 1965, a period during which the coefficient of imports more than doubled. This would appear to confirm the observation made above with respect to the second group of countries that the industrialisation associated with the crisis of the foreign trade sector corresponded to existing possibilities that had not been explored in an earlier period.

In the 1950s a clearer perception of the problem enabled countries in

TABLE 13.5 *Evolution of the coefficient of imports*

	1950	1955	1960	1965	1970
Argentina	7.3	5.4	11.3	9.3	9.6
Brazil	7.3	5.4	7.4	4.1	6.6
Mexico	8.0	7.4	12.3	10.0	11.6
Chile	9.0	9.3	16.8	13.6	18.1
Colombia	11.4	13.7	15.6	12.1	14.8
Peru	11.9	12.9	21.1	26.1	25.6
Venezuela	35.4	34.2	20.0	13.6	16.6
Latin America	9.9	9.4	10.9	8.9	10.3

SOURCE: ECLA, *The Process of Industrial Development in Latin America* (Statistical Annex), Santiago, 1965, Table I–2; *América Latina y la Estrategia Internacional de Desarrollo*, cit. p. 140.

the first group – the five Central American countries were to repeat this experience later as a result of their integration efforts – to *anticipate* their industrialisation process, not only by taking appropriate protectionist measures but by orientating investments in infrastructure so as to favour industrialisation and even by providing direct incentives to industry. It is significant, for instance, that in the mid-1950s government initiative in all three countries (Colombia, Peru and Venezuela) was responsible for sponsoring the installation of basic industries, including steel manufacturing. It should be pointed out that this industrialisation was carried out with the notable participation of international groups and has brought about integration with the import sector. Industrialisation seemed to proceed as if it were directed less towards the creation of an integrated system of production than towards the extension of the import sector, whose turnover increased as it extended its activities to encompass complementary local manufacturing industries. The experience of the sixties made it clear that these countries would not find it easy to reconcile the industrialisation process with a reduction in the coefficient of exports below relatively high levels, given the considerable cost in foreign exchange (patented inputs, royalties, technical assistance, remittance of dividends) of industrial activity. Contraction of the export coefficient to less than 15 per cent appears to create serious obstacles to development, a situation that seems to have arisen before the manufacturing sector managed to increase its share in the domestic product to 20 per cent. Among the countries whose industrialisation began earlier, Argentina, Mexico and Brazil have managed to continue their industrialisation with an export coefficient of less than 10 per cent. Nevertheless, the Chilean experience had already demonstrated the difficulties of continuing to develop with a coefficient of exports below 15 per cent, which seems to indicate that the overall size of the market also acts as a restrictive factor. Thus, taking into account the foreign control of industrial investment, which implies a high content of imported inputs, and the size of the domestic markets concerned, it can be deduced that import-substituting industrialisation is relatively ineffective as a factor for bringing about structural change in countries where this type of industrial development began only in the 1950s.

14 Agricultural sector

Agricultural production

The structural features of Latin American agriculture, described in detail in chapter 7, largely account for the behaviour of this sector in recent years. By and large we find a pattern of extensive farming, that is, agriculture geared to a utilisation of land and labour involving limited capital outlays. Moreover, the emphasis is on production of a few commodities, mainly those destined for export, enjoying a privileged position and monopolising available credit facilities and infrastructure. It is with this background in mind that we must analyse the evolution of the agricultural sector over the past few decades, a period characterised by the weakening of external demand and the expansion of the domestic market. The population explosion, rapid urbanisation and the rise in purchasing power of part of the population failed to elicit the required response from the Latin American agricultural sector, since prevailing systems of extensive agriculture were no longer adequate methods for coping with the situation.

The figures given in Table 14.1 show that agriculture and livestock production did not always keep pace with population growth. It should be added that these figures underestimate the insufficiency of supply since as a result of rapid urbanisation, demand for agricultural surpluses has grown much more rapidly than the population. Even if we assume that the food consumption patterns of the population that has emigrated from the countryside to the towns have remained the same, we would still have to consider the much higher wastage coefficient involved in transporting food, particularly in countries with a tropical climate, because of the inadequacy of means of transport and lack of warehousing, etc. The figures in Table 14.1 indicate that in the period 1950–65 Chile was the only one of the countries included in which agricultural production grew less than the population. In the mid-1960s,

TABLE 14.1   *Growth of agricultural production and population in selected countries (% annual growth rates)*

	Agricultural production 1950–65	1969–70/ 1964–5	Population
Argentina	2.2	2.8	1.8
Brazil	4.2	3.2	3.0
Colombia	3.0	3.7	2.8
Chile	2.0	1.7	2.5
Mexico	6.4	2.3	3.2
Peru	3.2	2.4	2.6
Venezuela	5.5	5.6	3.8

SOURCE: ECLA, *El Segundo Decenio de las Naciones Unidas para el Desarrollo*; *El Desarrollo Agricola de la América Latina*; and *América Latina y la Estrategia Internacional de Desarrollo*.

however, Peru and Mexico joined Chile in this respect. It should be added that in Venezuela, at the beginning of the 1970s, half the food consumed was imported.

Increases in agricultural production depend not only on the extension of the area under cultivation but also on improvements in yield per unit of land used. It is significant that the expansion of Latin American agriculture continues to depend more on the incorporation of new lands than on increased yields. The figures for the region as a whole show that 57.4 per cent of the overall rise in agricultural production between the years 1960 and 1971 is attributable to the increase in the area under cultivation, whereas in Western Europe and North America the increase in production was due entirely to the rise in yield, which in the case of cereals, was double that of Latin America. For the production of oil-seeds, the rise in the unit yield was 1.9 per cent in Latin America, 3.3 per cent in North America and 3.9 per cent in Europe.[1]

A comparative analysis shows that there were wide differences between the countries of the region, as regards both production trends and the levels of yield obtained. These differences are clearly illustrated by the figures given in Table 14.2. In Argentina the improvement in

[1] For an overall survey of the problem and comparative data for other regions see ECLA, *Economic Survey of Latin America, 1966*, Part IV: Agriculture: Present Situation and Trends; see also Interamerican Development Bank, Montague Yudelman (ed.), *Agricultural Development in Latin America: Current Status and Prospects*, 1966, and ECLA/FAO/IDB, *El Uso de Fertilizantes en América Latina*, 1966.

TABLE 14.2 *Average yields of key crops in selected countries (100 kg per hectare)*

	Wheat				Maize				Rice				Cotton (fibre)			
	1948–52	1958–62	1964–5	1969–70	1948–52	1958–62	1964–5	1969–70	1948–52	1958–62	1964–5	1969–70	1948–52	1958–62	1964–5	1969–70
Argentina	11.5	12.8	17.1	13.0	14.8	18.2	19.2	23.3	30.5	33.2	37.3	39.9[a]	2.4	2.2	2.6	3.1
Brazil	7.4	6.0	6.9	9.6	12.4	12.9	12.7	14.2	15.7	16.6	15.8	14.2	1.5	1.7	1.7	1.8[a]
Colombia	7.2	9.0	8.8	–	10.7	13.3	9.1	–	20.4	20.0	18.0	27.9	2.2	4.3	4.3	5.1
Chile	11.9	13.4	15.4	17.7	13.8	20.4	32.6	32.3	29.0	26.5	25.0	30.4[a]	–	–	–	–
Mexico	8.8	16.0	20.7	28.5	7.5	9.0	11.5	12.1	18.0	21.7	24.0	25.4	3.3	5.4	7.7	7.9
Peru	9.2	9.9	9.6	9.5	14.3	13.3	16.4	16.0[a]	38.5	38.5	39.0	40.5[a]	5.0	5.4	5.9	5.6[a]
Venezuela	4.7	6.0	5.4	4.4	11.4	11.3	11.0	11.3	11.4	15.2	18.7	19.0	2.8	2.1	2.6	3.1

[a] 1969.

SOURCE: ECLA, *Economic Survey of Latin America, 1966,* and Instituto Interamericano de Estadística, *América en Cifras,* 1972.

yields was significant in some cases but varied considerably. In Venezuela, where yields are extremely low, there was an improvement only in the case of rice. In Mexico there was a spectacular rise in wheat and cotton yields, but only moderate improvement in the yields of rice and maize, which is significant in view of the fact that maize is the staple food of the Mexican population. In Brazil, Colombia and Peru yields remained generally at a standstill. The case of Brazil is particularly serious, since not only did yields fail to show any improvement but overall yield per hectare was one of the lowest in the region.

The level of yield obtained by Mexico for wheat is higher than in the United States and Canada and compares favourably with the European average, which is around 2 tons. In the case of maize, the yield obtained by Chile is close to the European average but lower than that of the United States, which is around 4 tons. It should be pointed out, however, that the Chilean yield is more than double the Latin American average. In the case of rice, Argentina and Peru obtained yields approximating the European and US averages. On the other hand, in Brazil, accounting for over three-quarters of overall rice production, the average yield was only about one-third of the European and US averages. Average cotton yields were very high in Mexico and Peru, where cotton is grown on irrigated land, and also improved significantly in Colombia.

Trends in agricultural yield are determined by the number of factors, whose relative importance varies from country to country. Among these factors must be mentioned the existence of an open agricultural frontier, that is, of land available for extending crop areas, the agrarian structure's capacity to raise the technical level of production, financial and technical support from the government and the intensity of the growth of demand for agricultural products. It seems obvious that in Mexico the land reform programme, the most significant part of which was carried out in the 1930s, and the determined efforts made by the government to invest in the agricultural infrastructure and promote an increase in the domestic supply of fertilisers, created a combination of circumstances favouring development of agricultural production. The Mexican experience is particularly striking since this country's basic natural resources were traditionally regarded in Latin America as being rather unfavourable to agricultural development. Between 1948–52 and 1969–70, the average yield of wheat more than trebled, the cotton yield more than doubled and maize and rice yields increased by 60 and 40 per cent respectively. However, the level of yield obtained for maize, which is the staple food of the population, continued to be a little over a quarter of the average obtained in the United States. Expansion of the irrigated area was mainly for the benefit of export crops. In Venezuela, expansion of production can be ascribed primarily to the incorporation of new lands and substantial State aid.

One of the principal factors responsible for raising agricultural yields is the use of fertilisers. This factor, in conjunction with the use of improved varieties of seed and pest control, is responsible for the remarkable rise in agricultural yields achieved in the developed countries over the last two decades. Fertiliser consumption in Latin America rose from about 500,000 tons of nutrients in 1950 to about 3 million in 1964. The present average consumption, however, is still well below that for the developed countries as a whole. The increase in fertiliser consumption was particularly marked in Brazil during the late 1960s and early 1970s, reflecting the renewed expansion of sugar-cane production and the rapid development of soya bean cultivation – commodities for which world market conditions were extremely favourable – as well as the considerable increase in the cultivated area under wheat, which was extended from 562,000 hectares in 1967–8 to 1,861,000 hectares in 1970–1. Thus, the increase in fertiliser consumption in Brazil was due mainly to the relative growth of the area under crops requiring greater quantities of plant nutrients, which explains why crop yields for the principal commodities remained virtually at a standstill.

The low consumption of fertilisers in Argentina is due to their scanty use in the pampas region, where cereal production is concentrated. A combination of circumstances – the semi-extensive nature of cereal growing, the possibility of rotation with livestock production and the natural fertility of the soils – makes it possible to attain relatively high levels of profitability without the use of fertilisers and does not favour development of a tradition of fertiliser use. In fact, in most countries the tendency is to concentrate the use of fertilisers on a few crops, generally those for which credit is available and an organised marketing system exists. Even in Mexico, where relative prices of fertilisers are lower than in any other country of the region, fertilisers are used for only 18 per cent of the area under maize, whereas the figure rises to 84 per cent in the case of cotton.

The comparatively slow progress of farm mechanisation in the region is largely attributable to the relative abundance of manpower that still characterises Latin American agriculture. Nevertheless, precisely because agricultural expansion continues to take the form of bringing new land under cultivation, mechanisation has helped to increase output in certain countries. Moreover, the rainfall pattern in certain areas limits the time available for the preparation of the soil, making a certain degree of mechanisation an indispensable prerequisite for the proper use of the land. Table 14.4 gives figures for the region's tractor inventory.

TABLE 14.3 *Fertiliser (nitrogen, phosphorus and potassium) consumption in selected countries (annual averages in thousands of tons of plant nutrients)*

	1957–9	1964	1971
Argentina	15.9	48.5	86.9
Brazil	227.8	255.5	957.9
Colombia	61.0	94.8	177.0
Chile	55.4	120.1	158.5
Mexico	131.4	300.5	594.4
Peru	62.6	91.9	119.0
Venezuela	11.6	32.0	69.4

SOURCE: ECLA/FAO/IDB, *El Uso de Fertilizantes en América Latina*, 1966; ECLA *La Estrategia International de Desarrollo*, cit., p. 126.

The highest degree of relative mechanisation is found in Chile and the lowest in Brazil. It should be pointed out that even in countries where extensive farming is practised, such as Canada and Australia, the level of mechanisation of agriculture is well above that of the most advanced countries of Latin America.

TABLE 14.4 *Tractors used in farming in selected countries (thousands of units)*

	1957	1961–5	1971
Argentina	70.0	139.0	180.0
Brazil	57.9[a]	70.1	99.4
Colombia	–	24.3	27.9
Chile	15.0	–	30.5
Peru	–	–	12.3
Mexico	–	64.8	92.0
Venezuela	–	13.1	19.2

[a] 1955.

SOURCE: *Instituto Interamericano de Estadística, América en Cifras*, 1965, ECLA, *Economic Survey of Latin America*, 1966, and *América Latina, y la Estrategia International de Desarrollo*, cit., p. 128.

Livestock farming

Even more than agriculture, livestock production trends reveal the difficulties facing the region in raising the technical level of its rural activities. Table 14.5 gives figures for the increase in the principal species of livestock in selected countries.

In the case of pigs, inventories expanded significantly in Brazil and considerably in Mexico. In the case of sheep there was stagnation or even decline in the inventories of the region's major wool-producing countries, Argentina and Uruguay. Cattle stocks in Argentina, Chile, Peru, Uruguay and Venezuela remained stationary or grew less than the population. In Brazil and Colombia the increase was around 3 per cent per annum which is equal to the rate of demographic expansion. Only in Mexico was the growth of cattle herds of real significance. Thus the growth of cattle herds in the region generally only matched that of the population. Considering that the income-elasticity of demand for meat is relatively high, it must be concluded that meat consumption was confined to an increasingly restricted group of the population.

The expansion of livestock production in the region continues to be based almost entirely on the opening up of new lands, which provide natural pastures, often simply by burning the forest cover. The pastures cleared in this way can support only a low density of animal population, and, since the lands tend to be increasingly distant from urban centres, which raises the costs of fattening and transporting the animals, stock-farming yields decline. Consequently, the meat production statistics available indicate that it lags behind the increase in herds. With the exception of Argentina, Uruguay and Southern Brazil, the economic yield of Latin American livestock production is extremely low. The calving rate ranges from 40 per cent to 60 per cent, whereas in the United States the rate is 85 per cent. This is due to the fact that cows calve every two years instead of every twelve months, as they would do if properly fed. Moreover, the slaughtering rate, that is, the ratio of animals slaughtered annually to total stock, is also extremely low and in some countries slightly below 10 per cent. Finally, average carcass weights are relatively low. Consequently, not only is there a slow increase in herds, but the number of animals that can be slaughtered without affecting the growth of the herd is relatively small, and the meat yield per animal slaughtered is relatively low. Thus, if Argentina and Uruguay are excluded, meat production per head of stock in the region averages 22 kg against 52 kg in Australia and 77 kg in the United States. Argentina, where meat yield per animal slaughtered averages 54 kg, occupies

TABLE 14.5 Growth of stocks of cattle, sheep and pigs in selected countries (millions of head)

	Cattle			Sheep			Pigs		
	1955–6	1964–5	1969–70	1955–6	1964–5	1969–70	1955–6	1964–5	1969–70
Argentina	46.9	44.5	47.8[a]	44.5	48.3	—	4.0	3.6	4.1[a]
Brazil	65.2	87.3	95.2[a]	18.0	22.0	24.5[a]	40.0	56.8	64.5[a]
Colombia	12.5	14.3	19.1[a]	1.1	1.5	—	1.7	1.8	—
Chile	2.9	2.8	2.9	6.4	6.6	6.7	0.9	1.0	1.1
Mexico	16.7	32.0	38.0	5.1	6.2	9.2	6.5	9.4	18.0
Peru	3.5	3.7	4.1	16.7	14.8	8.6	1.3	2.0	1.1[a]
Uruguay	7.4	8.6	8.5	23.9	22.0	22.0	0.3	0.4	0.4
Venezuela	6.3	6.1	8.4	—	—	—	2.3	3.5	1.6

[a] 1969.

SOURCE: ECLA, *Economic Survey of Latin America, 1966*, and Instituto Interamericano de Estadística. *America en Citras*, 1972.

TABLE 14.6 *Agricultural production (principal commodities) in major producing countries (in thousands of tons)*

	1956–7	1960–1	1964–5	1969–70
Wheat				
Argentina	7,100	4,200	10,100	5,625
Mexico	1,243	1,190	2,134	2,218
Chile	892	1,123	1,276	1,307[a]
Brazil	855	713	614	1,515[a]
Colombia	110	145	85	–
Peru	123	153	161	145
Rice				
Brazil	4,072	5,392	6,691	6,943
Colombia	300	450	576	675
Peru	246	328	332	444[a]
Mexico	235	327	274	377
Argentina	193	149	268	407[a]
Venezuela	47	72	166	235
Maize				
Brazil	6,095	6,886	10,760	14,037
Mexico	5,460	5,415	7,760	8,748
Argentina	1,958	2,744	6,900	9,580
Colombia	802	715	741	–
Venezuela	287	398	498	690
Peru	235	246	569	590[a]
Potatoes				
Argentina	1,311	2,072	2,488	2,147
Brazil	1,003	1,113	1,264	1,539
Peru	1,013	1,146	1,533	1,856[a]
Beans				
Brazil	1,585	1,745	2,121	2,252
Mexico	432	723	892	917
Chile	86	91	89	66[a]
Soya beans				
Brazil	122	271	475	1,260
Mexico	—	22	69	273
Colombia	—	19	49	85
Coffee				
Brazil	979	1,797	2,887	2,147
Colombia	365	462	480	585[a]
Mexico	124	124	145	179[a]
El Salvador	95	103	114	113[a]

149

TABLE 14.6   (*Continued*)

	1956–7	1960–1	1964–5	1969–70
Cocoa				
Brazil	161	178	154	219
Ecuador	26	44	47	48[a]
Mexico	14	24	31	30
Dominican Rep.	33	35	38	37
Venezuela	23	19	20	19
Sugar cane				
Brazil	43,976	56,927	71,126	83,180
Mexico	14,597	19,167	28,973	32,067
Argentina	9,874	9,650	12,530	9,700[a]
Peru	7,033	8,663	8,103	6,882[a]
Colombia	14,480	14,569	13,418	14,550[a]
Bananas				
Brazil	4,481	5,127	6,867	9,569
Ecuador	1,953	2,075	2,651	5,388
Oranges				
Brazil	1,576	1,918	2,354	3,233
Mexico	625	766	855	979
Argentina	610	717	568	862
Cotton (lint)				
Brazil	400	536	622	758
Mexico	426	470	566	387
Peru	115	130	133	91[a]
Argentina	105	124	119	126
Linseed				
Argentina	620	562	815	617
Uruguay	72	67	64	81[a]
Sunflower seed				
Argentina	625	585	757	1,160
Uruguay	79	57	80	65[a]

[a] 1969.

SOURCE:Instituto Interamericano de Estadistica, *América en Cifras*, 1965, 1972.

an exceptional position in the Latin American livestock production record, due to the high quality of its pastures, even in the case of natural pasturelands. Nevertheless, unlike other countries where new lands continue to be reclaimed for livestock-farming, livestock production in Argentina can only be expanded by taking over crop lands or improving existing pastures as well as cattle raising and fattening techniques.

Even more than in the case of agriculture, whose expansion in many areas still reflects simply the growth of the rural population, the development of Latin American livestock-farming is now essentially dependent on the improvement of its technical levels. The extensive forms of growth which have hitherto characterised it are no longer sufficient for production to keep pace with the region's population growth, and still less to meet the growing demand consequent upon the rise in per capita income. It is more than likely that in many countries beef will be replaced by other sources of animal protein, particularly poultry and fish. None the less, except for Argentina and Uruguay, indices of meat consumption and of animal proteins in general are extremely low, which signifies that there must be an increase in the meat supply if meat consumption is not to be restricted to an increasingly small proportion of the population. This increase could easily be achieved by raising the technical level of livestock-farming, particularly if there were improvements in nutrition and greater attention to animal health problems. Given the fact that the region possesses extremely favourable conditions for the development of livestock-farming, and that the supply of meat has fallen off at a time when demand has been expanding, it becomes evident that Latin American economies, particularly in the case of the agrarian sector, display little aptitude for the assimilation of technical progress.

15 Industrial sector

Structure of Latin American industry

The manufacturing industry, which contributed around 26 per cent to the region's gross domestic product at the beginning of the 1970s and employed around 17 per cent of its active population, is the key factor responsible for the structural changes that have taken place in the post-war period. With regard to the region as a whole, the average annual growth rate of manufacturing for the period 1950–60 was 6 per cent and, in the 1960s, 6.9 per cent. In the second half of the sixties and the first three years of the seventies, it rose to 8.7 per cent. Nevertheless, Latin America's relative position in world industrial output has remained stationary at around 3.4 per cent. In terms of population growth, there was a decline in the Latin American position: world industrial output per capita grew at an annual rate of 4.7 per cent between 1960 and 1970 whereas the annual rate of increase for Latin America was 3.8 per cent.

TABLE 15.1   *Recent evolution of manufacturing production in selected countries (average annual growth rates)*

	1955–60	1960–5	1965–70	1970–3
Argentina	3.7	6.2	5.0	7.0
Brazil	10.3	3.7	10.3	13.7
Colombia	6.1	5.6	6.3	9.2
Chile	3.2	7.3	3.3	3.8
Mexico	8.1	9.4	8.9	6.8
Peru	6.1	8.9	5.8	7.7
Venezuela	7.7	9.0	4.4	7.9

SOURCE: ECLA, *Economic Survey of Latin America*, 1967, and *El Proceso de Industrializacíon en América Latina en los Primeros Años del Segundo Decenio para el Desarrollo*, 1974.

TABLE 15.2   *Structure of production in the manufacturing sector (percentages)*

	1960			1971		
	A	B	C	A	B	C
Argentina	44.5	26.8	28.7	33.9	31.9	34.2
Brazil	41.2	29.4	29.4	30.3	32.7	37.0
Mexico	53.7	35.5	10.8	47.6	38.4	14.0
Colombia	63.4	27.2	9.4	58.8	29.1	12.1
Chile	61.2	29.1	9.7	57.8	33.2	9.0
Peru	63.6	28.7	7.7	60.3	28.0	11.7
Venezuela	63.5	29.4	7.1	49.9	40.6	9.6
Latin America	56.5	26.1	14.4	50.8	30.0	19.2

A: Industries mainly producing non-durable consumer goods: food, beverages, textiles, clothing, footwear, furniture, printing, other.
B: Industries mainly producing intermediate goods: paper, rubber, chemicals, petroleum and coal products, non-metallic minerals, basic metallurgy.
C: Industries mainly producing capital goods and consumer durables: metal-working, electrical equipment, transportation, machinery and equipment.
SOURCE: ECLA, *El Proceso de Industrialización en América Latina en los Primeros Años del Segundo Decenio para el Desarrollo*, Santiago, 1974.

From the point of view of its degree of structural diversification, the manufacturing sector varied a great deal from one Latin American country to another. In countries in which manufacturing has been contributing at least one-fifth to the domestic product since 1960, more than half the total industrial output is accounted for by the intermediate goods and engineering industries. Because they play a key role in bringing about structural economic change, these industries have been described as 'dynamic' industries.[1] In Argentina and Brazil, this group of industries contributed two-thirds or more of total manufacturing output in 1971. The figures in Table 15.2 show that in these two countries the equipment and durable consumer goods industries (Group C) occupied a relative position well above that found in the industrial rankings for the other countries. Mexico's position is less a reflection of relative backwardness in the engineering industry than of the low degree of integration in the durable consumer goods industry, particularly motor vehicles. In countries at the intermediate stage of industrial develop-

[1] Term used by the Technical Secretariat of the United Nations Economic Commission for Latin America (ECLA).

ment – Chile, Colombia, Peru and Venezuela, the food industry contributed around one-quarter of the industrial output and textiles around one-sixth. In the remaining countries, all at an early stage of industrialisation, the food and related industries contributed more than 40 per cent to the total industrial product, while the textile and allied industries contributed around 20 per cent. These figures clearly show that industrialisation in the region starts with the simple processing of agricultural products for food, with textile activities marking the transition to modern industry. Once beyond the first stage, the relative importance of the textile sector tends to decline more rapidly than that of the food sector, while the manufacturing sector becomes more complex, with a more than proportional growth of industries whose market is the industrial sector itself. In the group of so-called 'dynamic' industries, the first to develop are the pulp and paper and rubber products industries. Where favourable conditions exist, petroleum refineries may be installed before the chemical sector is developed. This explains why industries in Group B grew considerably in Venezuela. However, it is the metal and engineering industries that define the structure of the industrialisation process at its most advanced stage. In countries in the initial stage of industrialisation this group of industries accounts for 2 to 4 per cent of total industrial output, whereas in those at the intermediate stage this share rises to 18.2 per cent, and in the countries with a more advanced industrial structure it accounts for more than 25 per cent.

The more rapid growth of Latin America's industrial production in the 1960s, particularly in the second half of the decade, is attributable to the combined action of a number of factors:

(a) the dynamic external economies reaped in the countries with a more advanced industrial structure;

(b) the growth of intra-regional trade within the framework of the Central American Common Market, the Latin American Free Trade Association, and the Andean Group; and

(c) the policy of promoting manufacturing exports by providing tax and credit incentives.

With regard to the last two factors listed, it should be noted that the share of exports in industrial production rose from 0.7 to 2.7 per cent in the period considered. In Mexico, this share rose to 4.5 per cent in 1971 and in Brazil to 3.4 per cent (see Table 15.3). Special legislation permitted the development of a new industrial sector, strictly geared to exports, in the frontier area of Northern Mexico.

TABLE 15.3 *Manufacturing exports and their share in industrial production*

	Value of manufacturing exports in millions of dollars (f.o.b.)		Growth rates annual averages		Share in industrial production		
	1960	1971	1960/70	1969/71	1960	1965	1971
Argentina	44.3	257.9	18.7	8.4	0.5	0.8	1.6
Brazil	28.4	582.8	31.0	63.8	0.4	1.3	3.4
Mexico	79.6	494.2	16.6	28.0	1.7	2.4	4.5
Colombia	6.9	80.0	28.0	16.7	0.3	0.9	1.5
Chile	25.2	42.4	7.8	9.4	1.5	0.9	1.5
Peru	3.6	13.0	15.2	10.0	0.3	0.3	0.5
Venezuela	3.1	31.3	26.0	2.4	0.1	0.4	0.5
Latin America	246.9	1,888.4	20.5	24.5	0.7	1.3	2.7

SOURCE: ECLA, *Notas Sobre la Economía y el Desarrollo de América Latina*, 16 June 1973.

Textile industry

The textile industry merits special attention not only because of its present relative importance but because of its role as a new source of exports. Since Latin America is currently a leading exporter of natural fibres, it is favourably placed for participating in the world market for textile products as the highly industrialised countries realise the advantages to be gained from a greater decentralisation of manufacturing activities on a worldwide scale. Given the limited extent to which the textile industry can be integrated with other industries and the fact that it does not significantly benefit from economies of scale, it offers considerable possibilities for export development, even in less industrially developed countries.

The production capacity of Latin America's textile industry increased by 1.5 million spindles between 1955 and 1963, one-third of which were installed in Brazil, one-fifth in Mexico and another fifth in Argentina. The most notable increase, however, was recorded in Colombia.[2]

During the period under review, i.e. between 1955 and 1963, the capacity of the Indian textile industry increased from 11.9 to 14.7 million

[2] For a survey of Latin America's textile industry at the end of the 1960s, see ECLA, *La Industria Textil en América Latina, XII: Informe Regional*, UN, 1968.

TABLE 15.4   *Installed capacity in the
cotton textile industry
(millions of spindles)*

	1955	1963
Brazil	3.4	3.9
Mexico	1.1	1.4
Argentina	0.7	1.0
Colombia	0.4	0.6
Others	1.0	1.2

SOURCE: ECLA, *La Industria Textil en América
Latina*, 1968.

spindles, that of Pakistan from 1.4 to 2.4 million and that of Egypt from
0.6 to 1.3 million. The growth of Latin America's production capacity,
although relatively slow, was not always accompanied by a corresponding
increase in output, an indication that demand was very sluggish. Per
capita consumption for the region as a whole is relatively low – 4.0 kg
annually as against 9.7 kg in Western Europe and 16.3 kg in the United
States – and its growth rate has been abnormally sluggish at around 0.6
per cent annually. This figure is one of the indicators that the living levels
of the bulk of the Latin American population have hardly been affected
by the economic growth of recent years.

In Peru and Venezuela, particularly in the latter country, growth
largely reflects the progress of the import-substitution process. In the
other countries, however, locally manufactured goods have for some time
satisfied more than 95 per cent of the domestic market requirements.

TABLE 15.5   *Recent evolution of textile production in
selected countries (index: 1963 = 100)*

	1956	1960	1963	1970
Argentina	131	134	148	–
Brazil	70	94	88	99[b]
Colombia	65	84	103	103[c]
Chile	73[a]	75	108	117
Mexico	76	91	123	137[b]
Peru	76	94	122	–
Venezuela	38	72	117	122

[a] 1957; [b] 1969; [c] 1968.
SOURCE: ECLA, *La Industria Textil en América Latina*,
1968, and *América en Cifras*, 1974.

TABLE 15.6 *Modernity indices for the cotton textile industry*

	Spindles				Looms		
	Modern	Modern-isable	Obsolete	Total	Auto-matic	Mech-anical	Total
Argentina	83	12	5	100	67	33	100
Brazil	21	42	37	100	25	75	100
Colombia	91	8	1	100	99	1	100
Chile	81	19	–	100	83	17	100
Mexico	66	5	29	100	52	48	100
Peru	31	18	51	100	70	30	100
Venezuela	98	–	2	100	91	9	100

SOURCE: ECLA, *La Industria Textil en América Latina*, 1968.

Latin America's textile machinery inventory, despite large-scale recent replacements, still includes a good deal of obsolete machinery and equipment, mainly because of the relative age of the Brazilian and, to a lesser extent, the Mexican industries. With regard to spindles, 44 per cent of the 8.1 million cotton spindles installed are modern, 30 per cent can be modernised and 26 per cent are obsolete; in the artificial and synthetic fibre sector, 88 per cent of the spindles installed are modern, and in the wool sector only 37 per cent are up to date. As regards looms, the automatic looms in operation represent 20 per cent of the installed capacity for wool, 33 per cent for man-made fibres and 44 per cent for cotton.[3] Table 15.6 indicates the disparities between various countries.

Brazil excluded, Latin America's cotton textile industry is reasonably up to date, and in the case of Colombia modernity indices are exceptionally high. The latter country has the highest indices not only for modernity of equipment, but also for productivity of both labour and equipment.

Chemical industries

The chemical industries now constitute a production sector ranking with the textile industry in order of importance for Latin America as a whole and contributing about 15 per cent to the total value of manufacturing output. Moreover, in contrast with the performance of the textile sector, it has registered one of the highest sectoral growth rates although in

---

[3] Data refer to the situation in the mid-1960s. Since then, only in Mexico has there been significant investment in the textile industry.

the larger countries the import-substitution process is in its final stages. Between 1968 and 1972 the average annual growth rate was 9.3 per cent, which is below the growth rates for only two industries: non-metallic minerals (10.2) and metal products/machinery (12.6) Nevertheless, the total value of Latin America's chemical production was only 50 per cent of that of West Germany and 80 per cent of that of France, in the mid-1960s.[4] In 1964 Brazil accounted for 38.6 per cent of the region's chemical output, Mexico for 22.7 per cent and Argentina for 19.1 per cent. Latin America's chemical production at that time supplied around three-quarters of the domestic market requirements, a share which did not increase significantly in the subsequent period, particularly in Argentina and Brazil where local production already supplied more than 80 per cent of the market at the end of the previous decade. It must be concluded, then, that the present structure of the region's chemical industry, in which tensoactive agents and bleaches play a major role, is less a reflexion of inadequate development in this particular manufacturing sector than of the degree of diversification of the industrial system as a whole. In the region's most industrially developed countries, import substitution has apparently reached saturation point, which seems to be around 80 per cent of the domestic supply in the three countries with the largest domestic markets and about 60 per cent in those with medium-size markets. Table 15.7 gives the figures for selected products in Latin America' chemical production.

Pulp and paper industries

The paper and cellulose industry has made rapid progress in recent years not only under the stimulus of import substitution but mainly to keep pace with rapidly expanding demand. Between 1960 and 1965 total paper consumption increased from 2.4 to 3.5 million tons, while consumption of paperboard rose from 1.1 to 1.9 million tons. Domestic production supplied three-quarters of the region's market requirements. As regards newsprint, however, a very different situation obtained, with imports from outside the region accounting for four-fiths of total consumption. Chile is in a special position since it produces an exportable surplus of newsprint and the quantity available for export has been expanding. Domestic production of newsprint covers 40 per cent of the total demand in Brazil, 20 per cent in Mexico and 7 per cent in Argentina. The other countries are totally dependent on imports for their newsprint requirements.

[1] A survey of the region's chemical industry is given in ECLA, *La Industria Quimica Latinoamericana en 1962–4*, UN, 1966.

TABLE 15.7 *Production sectors of the chemical industry*
(*thousands of tons*)

	1964	1972
sulphuric acid (100% H_2SO_4)		
Argentina	151	188[d]
Brazil	300	421[b]
Colombia	15	42[b]
Chile	178	374[c]
Mexico	433	1,518
Peru	47	62[a]
Venezuela	51	82[c]
caustic soda (Na OH)		
Argentina	63.0	123
Brazil	103.0	158
Colombia	16.1	73
Mexico	100.0	169
sodium carbonate (Na_2CO_3)		
Brazil	76.2	106[b]
Colombia	8.8	52[b]
Mexico	106.0	347

[a]1968   [b]1969   [c]1970   [d]1971
SOURCE: Instituto Interamericana de Estadística, *América en Cifras*, 1974

Chile, where a notable reforestation project based on conifers has been carried out over the last twenty-five years, has considerable potential for the expansion of its paper and cellulose industry. The substantial investments still being made in the Chilean industry will boost exports intended to supply the regional market, particularly the Argentine market. In the other countries of the region, expansion of the industry is dependent either on a reforestation policy based on fairly fast-growing trees, whether conifers or another species, or on the utilisation of hardwoods and other raw materials such as bagasse. On the whole, the technical problems posed by the utilisation of local raw materials are being studied and possible solutions are being explored.

Steel

Latin America's iron and steel industry currently comprises 14 integrated plants and 35 small semi-integrated mills. More than 95 per cent of the total output, which amounted to 15 million tons of ingot steel in 1972, was produced by the integrated steelworks. The establishment of steel

TABLE 15.8 *Paper production in selected countries (thousands of tons)*

	Newsprint			Writing paper			Other paper			Paperboard		
	1957	1964	1970	1957	1964	1970	1957	1964	1970	1957	1964	1970
Argentina	20	12	3	65	84	123	125	189	335	104	127	182
Brazil	49	119	126	107	149	231	218	251	412^{ab}	106	139	330
Colombia	–	–	–	–	–	40^a	25	60	145^b	12	55	–
Chile	20	77	120	15	30	46^a	23	38	95^b	1	20	–
Mexico	–	16	40	62	110	133^a	104	257	554^{ab}	170	175	–
Peru	–	–	–	–	6	11^a	17	32	95^{ab}	12	29	–
Venezuela	–	–	–	–	11	25^a	7	62	195^{ab}	–	62	–

^{a}1969. ^{b}Includes paperboard.

SOURCE: Instituto Interamericano de Estadística, *América en Cifras*, 1974.

industries, mainly during the post-war years, marks a vital stage in the transition of the Latin American economies towards the industrial age. Since the establishment of steel industries was essentially due to State action, direct or indirect, one wonders what would have happened if the State had taken the initiative a quarter of a century earlier. In fact, Latin America did have a fairly long tradition of steelmaking, particularly in countries with abundant supplies of high-grade iron ores. In Mexico, the first years of the century witnessed the installation of a coke-fired blast furnace at Monterrey, with a daily capacity of 350 tons; in Chile, the charcoal-fired furnace at Corral came into operation before the First World War, and in Brazil the Belgo Mineira Company had been operating fairly large charcoal-fired furnaces since the twenties. Nevertheless, it was not until the forties that concrete steps were taken to establish a modern steel industry in the region. Thus, in Mexico, a second blast furnace with a daily capacity of 600 tons was installed in 1942 by the company already operating in Monterrey. In 1944, Mexico's second integrated mill, specialising in flat products, came into operation at Monclova, and in 1946 the Hojalata y Laminas steel company started operations in Mexico. This enterprise was to become well known for its innovations in the technological field with the introduction of a gas-fired iron-ore reduction mill, doing away with the need for a blast furnace and making it possible to reduce the economic size of the plant. In Brazil the Volta Redonda steelworks, an integrated plant comprising a blast furnace with a daily capacity of 1,000 tons and rolling mills for sections and flat products, came into operation in 1946. In Chile, the integrated plant at Huachipato started production in 1950 with a blast furnace whose capacity was expanded to 800 tons a day. In Colombia the Paz del Rio plant began to operate in 1954; in Peru the Chimbote mill started in 1958; in Argentina the San Nicolas plant started in 1960 and in Venezuela the Orinoco plant started in 1962.[5]

Table 15.9 gives figures for the evolution of production over the last decade.

The ores currently exploited in Latin America have a very high iron content. It is only in Argentina and Colombia that ores are exploited with an iron content ranging from 47 to 53 per cent. The output of coal suitable for coking is, however, insufficient in Argentina, Brazil and Chile. Inadequate local supplies of raw materials, and the size of the markets for which the output of individual producers is destined, are the two chief factors conditioning the development of Latin America's steel industry. In some instances coke has been partly replaced by petroleum,

[5] ECLA, *El Proceso de Industrialización en América Latina*, cit. vol. I.

TABLE 15.9   *Steel ingot production in selected countries (thousands of tons).*

	1958	1965	1972
Argentina	244	1,368	2,103
Brazil	1,362	2,983	6,520
Colombia	149	242	276
Chile	348	477	641
Mexico	1,038	2,043	4,364
Peru	20	81	–
Venezuela	40	625	924[a]

[a] 1971.

SOURCES: Instituto Interamericano de Estadística, *América en Cifras*, 1965, 1972, 1974.

gas or pulverised coal, making it possible to effect substantial economies in the consumption of coke per unit of pig iron. Where abundant hydro-electric power is available at a low opportunity cost, as in the case of Venezuela, the steel industry utilises electric energy. With ores of low phosphorus content, production of sponge iron by direct reduction methods makes it possible substantially to reduce the economic size of the operating unit.

The greatest stumbling block to the achievement of competitive prices for the region's steel products is the size of rolling mills for flat products, with respect to which economies of scale assume considerable significance. In fact, the investment required per ton/year for manufacturing flat rolled products drops from 484 dollars to 199 dollars when the scale of production is raised from 100,000 to one million tons.[6] For medium and small-sized countries this problem can be solved only within the framework of a regionally planned expansion of the steel industry.

In view of the industry's inevitable concentration in a few countries and the problems relating to the size of market for certain production lines, imports continue to play a leading role in supplying the region's steel requirements. In Brazil, Mexico and Chile imports account for less than one-quarter of the total supply of steel products; in Argentina the share of imports is about 40 per cent, and in the remaining countries imports continue to be the main source of supply. Chile exports sizeable quantities of steel to neighbouring countries and Mexico has become a regular exporter of certain types of rolled products. At the beginning of the 1970s, Brazil and Venezuela – countries with large reserves of iron

[6] ECLA, *Las Economias de Escala en Plantas Siderurgicas*, UN, 1967.

ore, began to implement plans for a considerable expansion of steel production, part of which is destined for the world market.

Engineering industries

The development of the engineering industries is, in some ways, the crowning point of any industrialisation process. While the term is far too broad, embracing establishments as diverse as maintenance and repair shops for industrial or domestic equipment, foundries or heavy forges and factories manufacturing highly complex machinery and equipment, the relative importance of this sector in industrial production is a clear indicator of an economic system's capacity for transforming itself. Given the key role of the engineering industries in transmitting technological progress to the different sectors of productive activity, the attainment of a degree of self-sufficiency in these industries implies the ability to regulate the diffusion of such progress. Their role is similar to that of imports in the underdeveloped countries, whose access to innovations in forms of production is largely dependent on imported manufactures, so that a relative decline in their capacity to import tends to increase structural rigidity. In fact, in the case of the Latin American countries, a sizeable volume of imports now consists of products manufactured by the metal-transforming and engineering industries with a growing share made up of industrial equipment.

In most countries of the region the engineering industry still consists largely of factories manufacturing consumer goods, assembly plants utilising imported parts and components, and maintenance and repair shops. Nevertheless, in the industrially more advanced countries the manufacturing of machinery and transport equipment has made good progress in recent years, and now ranks as the leading sector in the group of engineering industries. In Argentina and Brazil the machine tool industry had already made significant strides by the 1950s. In 1960 Brazil's output of machine tools was 13,000 tons, providing the market with 50 different types and about 150 models. In the period 1957–61 domestic output covered 40 per cent of the country's requirements. In 1960 there were 205,000 machine tools operating in the country, 55 per cent of them of less than ten years' standing.[7] In Argentina the output of machine tools in 1961 amounted to 10,500 tons, and in 1963 the number of machine tools operating in the country totalled 172,000, of which 55 per cent were less than ten years old.[8]

[7] ECLA, *Las Máquinas-herramientas en el Brasil*, UN, 1962.
[8] ECLA, *Las Máquinas-herramientas en la Argentina*, UN, 1966.

TABLE 15.10   *Motor vehicle production and assembly*
(thousands of units)

	1966	1972	Degree of integration[b]
Argentina	179.4	254.2	A
Brazil	224.6	613.5	A
Colombia	1.3	–	C
Chile	7.1	26.4	C
Mexico	117.9	232.3	B
Peru	13.2	21.8	C
Venezuela	57.6	61.0[a]	C

[a] Proportion of nationally manufactured parts to the unit weight of the vehicles.

[b] 1970.

A: more than 90 per cent; B: between 31 and 60 per cent; C: up to 30 per cent.

SOURCE: Instituto Interamericano de Estadística, *América en Cifras, 1974.*

A survey of the equipment required for the expansion of five important groups of industries – (a) petroleum, natural gas and petrochemicals, (b) generation and transmission of electric energy, (c) steel, (d) ship-building, (e) pulp and paper – indicated that Argentina's engineering industry is currently in a position to produce almost three-quarters of its total needs. A similar study was carried out for Brazil and indicated that the local engineering industry could satisfy 90 per cent of the equipment needs of the electrical energy generation sector, 77 per cent of the steel industry's, 66 per cent of the cement industry's and a similar percentage of the needs of the petroleum-refining and petrochemical sectors.[9]

However, the most notable progress in any branch of the engineering industry has undoubtedly been the growth of motor vehicle production. This activity, established before the outbreak of the Second World War in the form of local assembly plants, became a matter of growing concern to a number of countries as a result of the ever-increasing weight of motor vehicle imports in their balances of payments. The rapid expansion of demand, both for utility and passenger vehicles, led to the establishment of quantitative import restrictions with the result that domestic prices tended to be three or four times higher than on the international market. This situation made the production of motor vehicles an attractive proposition, even for relatively small-size factories. The favourable

[9] ECLA, *El Proceso de Industrialización en América Latina,* II.

conditions of the market and the ample incentives offered by governments led to a proliferation of enterprises in Brazil and Argentina, countries with relatively large markets and particularly severe balance of payments difficulties. The relatively small size factories and the underutilisation of their capacity brought the industry into financial difficulties once the demand, curtailed by the import shortages of the preceding ten years, had been satisfied. The industry subsequently remodelled its structure, cutting down on the number of enterprises, all of which are, in fact, subsidiaries of international corporations. After 1968, Brazil's production of passenger vehicles expanded rapidly and in 1972 output was 2.2 times greater than in 1968, as a result of the availability of credit facilities for consumers, the effective expansion of the home market and, more recently, the growth of exports.

Petroleum production and refining

The Latin American petroleum industry comprises two essentially different sectors: on the one hand, there is the output of Venezuela, accounting for more than two-thirds of the total and destined basically for export; on the other, the output of the other producer countries, destined mainly for their own home markets, although Bolivia and Ecuador have growing exportable surpluses. Production for export (Venezuela, Bolivia and Ecuador) is controlled by international consortia, while production for home markets is entirely or predominantly controlled by national enterprises financed from public funds. Heavy investments were made in the petroleum industry during the 1960s, both for drilling operations and for installing refineries. The number of wells drilled in Argentina rose from 284 in 1955 to 712 in 1966 and in Brazil from 73 to 331 over the same period. Bolivia and Ecuador also registered a marked increase in drillings between 1955 and 1961.[10] Output of crude in the latter country doubled between 1965 and 1972 while in Bolivia it increased fivefold and in Brazil it doubled.

Of the countries included in Table 15.11, Brazil and Chile are the only ones still dependent on imports for a substantial proportion of their crude petroleum requirements. The share of imports in Brazil's domestic supply declined in the first half of the sixties but began to increase again in the latter half and accounted for 73.6 per cent of the total in 1972. In Chile, there was a similar trend but the increase in the share of imports was attributable to a decline in output rather than to a substantial increase in consumption. In 1972, imports accounted for 66.8

[10] ECLA, *Economic Survey of Latin America, 1967*, Part II.

TABLE 15.11 *Crude petroleum production in selected countries (thousands of cubic metres)*

	1958	1965	1972
Argentina	5,668	15,625	25,067
Bolivia	546	534	2,538
Brazil	3,009	5,460	10,068
Colombia	7,457	11,141	11,390
Chile	885	2,020	1,615
Ecuador	494	453	4,620
Mexico	16,000	21,008	29,158
Peru	2,978	3,661	–
Venezuela	151,160	201,533	188,000

SOURCES: Instituto Interamericano de Estadística, *América en Cifras*, 1965 and 1974.

per cent of total supply in Chile, 29.1 per cent in Peru, 6.3 per cent in Argentina and 4.5 per cent in Mexico.[11]

Refining expanded even faster than output, as can be seen from Table 15.12. With the exception of Venezuela, which consumes a fraction of its refinery output, the output of Latin America's refineries is destined

TABLE 15.12 *Crude petroleum refined in Latin America (thousands of cubic metres)*

	1955	1960	1965	1972
Argentina	9,537	13,629	19,495	29,604
Bolivia	338	359	512	827
Brazil	4,089	10,412	17,841	38,009
Colombia	2,248	4,221	5,325	9,008
Chile	753	1,727	2,746	5,700
Ecuador	319	674	873	1,356
Mexico	13,028	17,028	21,444	30,524
Peru	2,356	2,637	3,300	5,476
Uruguay	1,302	1,508	1,867	1,899
Venezuela	31,140	51,339	68,210	65,475

SOURCES: ECLA, *Economic Survey of Latin America*, 1967 and *La América Latina y los problemas actuales de la Energía*, 1974.

[11] ECLA, *La América Latina y los Problemos de la Energia*, 1974. Table 9.

for the local markets. Mexico imports a certain amount of by-products to supply outlying areas near the United States frontier, and in turn exports a certain quantity of petroleum products. Apart from Venezuela and Ecuador, whose refineries are all owned by international companies, the refineries in the remaining Latin American countries are operated by national companies, most of which are State-owned.

Electric energy

Electric power generation in Latin America grew at an average annual rate of 9.5 per cent between 1950 and 1960 and 9.6 per cent between 1960 and 1965. For the world economy as a whole, the corresponding growth rates for these two periods were 8.4 and 7.8 per cent respectively. In recent years electric power consumption has increased even more rapidly: between 1967 and 1973 the annual growth rate was 11 per cent while regional consumption increased from 58.6 million kWh in 1958 to 196.7 million in 1973.[12] The increase reflects the relative growth of the industrial sector in the Latin American economy, as well as population expansion and rapid urbanisation. Nevertheless, considering that, despite the regional economy's low degree of industrialisation, 55 per cent of the electric energy generated is destined for industrial consumption – as against 50 per cent in the United States and 65 per cent in Europe – levels of per capita consumption are still very low.

The electric energy sector in the Latin American countries was traditionally controlled by large international companies whose headquarters were mostly in the United States. For various reasons, both internal and external, investments by these companies grew very slowly during the period between the 1929 crisis and the end of the Second World War. Thus, most of the Latin American countries – nearly all affected by energy supply shortages in the immediate post-war years – were faced with the problem of creating institutions capable of mobilising the substantial resources needed to expand electric energy generation and transmission capacity. The new resources came almost exclusively from public funds through taxes levied specifically for this purpose or from international financing agencies such as the World Bank and, later, the Interamerican Development Bank.

Despite the considerable increase in generation of electric energy over the last few years, the inadequate supply has been a permanent

[12] ECLA, *Los Nuevos Precios del Petroleo y la Industria Electrica en América Latina*, 1974.

TABLE 15.13 *Electric energy generation in selected countries (millions of kWh)*

	1957	1965	1973
Argentina	9,418[a]	14,700	26,700
Brazil	16,963	30,128	65,800
Colombia	2,850	6,000	11,600
Chile	4,188	6,131	8,400
Mexico	8,463	17,769	38,660
Peru	1,792	3,808	77,140
Venezuela	—	8,171	15,800

a 1958.
SOURCES: Instituto Interamericano de Estadística, *América en Cifras, 1965,* and ECLA, *Economic Survey of Latin America, 1966* and *1967.*

stumbling block to industrial development in many countries, particularly in Argentina. In the region as a whole, the share of industry in electric energy consumption rose from 30 per cent in 1958 to 44 per cent in 1973. It should be noted, however, that a considerable proportion of the regional population, including urban population, has no electricity. In the mid-1960s, 14 per cent of the population in Argentina was without electricity, in Chile 24 per cent, in Brazil 26 per cent, in Mexico 59 per cent and in Peru 61 per cent.

Of the total installed capacity in Latin America, which rose to 51 million kW in 1973, about one-half (26 million kW) was thermal. Of the 26 million kW of installed hydroelectric capacity in the region, 12.8 million kW is installed in Brazil, 3.9 in Mexico, and 2 kW in Colombia. The most rapid progress over the last two decades has been made in the hydroelectric sector, reflected in the expansion of existing central power stations and the growing interconnexion of networks. This development is making it possible to link up various areas in interconnected systems, integrating thermal and hydroelectric units and raising the load factor. From the projects currently under way it can be predicted that power from hydroelectric sources will account for an even larger share of the region's energy supply in the next few years, with an increase in the average size of power stations and interconnexions between areas with different hydrographic systems. Existing programmes for the installation of central power stations (see Table 15.14) provide for an increase of around 50 million kW by 1980. Of this total, 23.3 million kW will be

TABLE 15.14 *Programmes for the installation of central power stations (thousands of kW)*

	Installed capacity in 1973		New installations (1974–80)			
	Hydro-electric	Thermal	Hydro-electric	Thermal	Nuclear	Total
Argentina	1,335	7,135	6,680	1,765	920	9,365
Brazil	12,835	3,080	14,000	1,499	625	16,124
Mexico	3,930	5,270	3,300	6,067	1,340	10,707
Colombia	2,005	1,140	1,654	792	–	2,446
Chile	1,270	1,175	820	650	–	1,470
Peru	1,290	920	1,965	216	–	2,181
Venezuela	1,243	2,400	1,290	2,200	–	3,490
Latin America	25,400	25,978	32,349	15,116	2,885	50,350

SOURCE: ECLA, *Los Nuevos Precios del Petroleo y la Indústria Eléctria en América Latina,* 1974.

hydroelectric power, 6.7 million being installed in Argentina, 14 million in Brazil, 3.3 million in Mexico, 2 million in Peru, 1.7 million in Colombia and 1.3 million in Venezuela. The 'economically feasible' hydroelectric potential – estimated at 20 per cent of the 'technically feasible' potential – permitted a thirty-fold increase in the generation of hydroelectric energy in 1973, in the region as a whole. Given the sharp rise in the price of petroleum in that year, the feasibility margin has increased considerably.

16 Inadequate growth and the reorientation of development

Overall regional trends

During the last two decades, the economy of the Latin American countries, taken as a whole, has experienced a marked expansion and has undergone structural changes of real significance. Measured in 1960 prices, the region's gross product, which had barely exceeded 40 billion dollars in 1950, rose to more than 135 billion in 1970. Output of ingot steel, which was just over 1 million tons in 1950, was more than 15 million in 1970. Nevertheless, despite these and similar indicators that could be taken into account, it would be wrong to assume that the regional economy had achieved the combination of conditions needed for development to become self-sustaining. On the contrary: the figures show that the pace of growth of the regional economy has not even been sufficient to maintain the region's relative position in the world economy. In the two decades under consideration, the annual rate of growth of the world economy was 5.5 per cent, while that of Latin America was 5.2 per cent. In terms of population growth, however, the difference is greater, since the world growth rate was 3.5 per cent and the Latin American rate only 2.4 per cent. Data for the region as a whole show that the growth rate of the gross domestic product declined in the 1960s in relation to the preceding decade: in the period 1960–2 to 1966–8, the average growth rate of the per capita product was 1.8 per cent, whereas, in the period 1950 to 1960–2, it had been 2.5 per cent. After 1968, however, there was a change in trend and in the five years from 1968 to 1973, the annual average growth rate of the per capita product was 3 per cent.

Present trends can be more readily understood if it is borne in mind that the Latin American economies do not constitute a *system* and that the overall figures are strongly influenced by trends in the region's three major national economies – Brazil, Mexico and Argentina – which together account for over two-thirds of the regional product. However, it must also be borne in mind that the national economies have been developing along certain common lines and for this reason the evolution of the more advanced economies in some ways prefigures the evolution of those in earlier stages of development. Thus, the structural evolution of economies that experienced in the post-war period a phase of growth under the impulse of expanding exports – such as bananas, in the case of Ecuador, cotton in Central America or fish-meal in Peru – was a repetition of a pattern that had already become familiar in the region, as was that of the countries that started import substitution during the recent period.

While making no attempt to establish a model of development based on a series of precisely defined stages for the region's economies, which would imply that the experience of the less-developed countries can be anticipated, one must recognise that the *present* performance of these economies can be fitted into a given number of *types*. In certain countries an extremely favourable set of circumstances for a given *type* – the agricultural commodity exporter, the mineral product exporter or the import substitute – made it possible to sustain development over a relatively prolonged period. In others, conditions were less favourable and the period of development of a given type was correspondingly shorter. The overall development curve for the region represents the aggregate of national curves whose behaviour reflects the dynamic of a given number of types operating under a variety of conditions. The slackening of growth can manifest itself in economies corresponding to various types, and the movement of the overall curve will be accentuated or attenuated according to whether the processes occur simultaneously or not. On the other hand, the recovery in growth can be the result of the emergence of new types. In effect, the uptrend in economic expansion that began in 1968, is linked to a broadening of State action, whether through the deliberate attempt to extend the home market – or at least the home market made up of certain groups of consumers – or through the redirection of production for export, albeit at high social cost.

We have already seen how development induced by the growth of exports of primary products had made industrialisation possible. However, given the conditions prevailing in the world market for primary products between the early 1950s and the late 1960s, reflected in the persistent downward trend of relative commodity prices, it was widely held that the region's development would become increasingly dependent on the industrialisation process. That the pace of growth should have weakened in a number of countries during the 1960s seemed to indicate that industrialisation had failed to become sufficiently broad or had to contend with greater obstacles than initially foreseen. The problem that arises, then, is to determine whether Latin America's industrialisation suffers from intrinsic limitations or whether it was inadequately directed from the outset. This problem will be considered in the light of the experience of the now most industrially advanced countries: Argentina and Brazil. In Argentina, the growth rate of the industrial product was presistently below the regional average in the two decades under consideration. In Brazil, while the growth rate of the industrial product fluctuated widely, there was a steady determination to continue the country's industrial development.

Case of Argentina

Having achieved a high degree of urbanisation while still at the stage of export-led development, and having established a relatively high level of average wages in agriculture to attract European immigrants, Argentina stands in a class of its own in the Latin American context. However, because of the country's relative importance, the Argentine experience constitutes a significant aspect of the region's recent evolution. The industrialisation process in the 1940s and early 1950s took place under strong protection with subsidies for the importation of industrial inputs. The consequences were twofold: (a) an increase in the marginal efficiency of investment in the final consumer goods industries, and (b) a change in the internal terms of trade which moved against the agricultural sector. The tendency was thus in the direction of horizontal expansion of the industrial sector, which continued to be largely dependent on imported inputs. This meant the creation of a growing short-term *incompressibility* of imports at a time when there was a growth in the demand for imported products as a result of expansion in the industrial sector. Underlining the aspect that concerns us here, it can be said that the growth of the industrial sector proceeded less in the direction of creating an integrated system than in that of reinforcing the industrial structure that had emerged in an earlier stage and continued to be vertically integrated with imports. This integration, did, of course, evolve in the direction of a greater participation for domestic production, which meant that the items still imported became increasingly essential. Since imports of intermediate products and equipment enjoyed a substantial foreign exchange subsidy, the price structure operated against the integration of the industrial system. The level of economic activity became more dependent, in the short term, on the fluctuations of the capacity to import than it had been when the bulk of imports consisted of final consumer goods. The fears underlying Argentine economic policy in the second half of the 1930s and early 1940s, when anticyclical preoccupations prevailed, were thus confirmed. On the other hand, the unfavourable evolution of the internal terms of trade had discouraged investment in the rural sector, the country's traditional source of exports. Furthermore, the stagnation of petroleum production in the 1940s and 1950s created additional pressures on the declining capacity to import.

In sum, two processes were simultaneously at work in Argentina: the excessive horizontalisation of industrial growth and the discouragement to investment in the export sector. There has been a tendency to emphasise one or other aspect of the problem according to the intellectual approach of the analyst.[1] There can be no question that the second process would, in any event, have tended to reduce the productivity of investment and increase the instability of the economic system. But it is no less true that if industrialisation had broadened its base sooner, its capacity to bring about overall structural economic change would have been far greater and it is even possible that it would have come to have a favourable impact on the export sector itself, by reducing its relative input prices. It must be pointed out that Argentine industrialisation could only have gained in depth after the 1940s if it had followed a policy based on a diagnosis taking into account the long-term trends of international trade. In effect, industrialisation implied the absorption of manpower from the agricultural sector, which meant a relatively high level of wages. If industrial investments had been channelled towards projects with longer maturation periods and greater capital intensity, the profitability of the industrial sector would have been lower and accumulation less rapid. Given the relative shortage of manpower in the second half of the forties, reflected in the pressure for a rise in real wages, it must be admitted that a more balanced expansion of industry would have called for the active financial support of the government, together with simultaneous investments in the agricultural sector aimed at releasing labour. In practice, policies followed the line of least resistance, which consisted of an expansionary wage policy and a concentration of industrial investments in activities with the fastest capital turnover. This resulted in the inadequacy that characterised both the social overhead facilities and the capacity to import in the mid-fifties. Since then, the main objective of

---

[1] See, as an example of the first tendency, Aldo Ferrer, *La Economía Argentina*, and, as an example of the second, Carlos F. Diaz-Alejandro, 'An Interpretation of Argentine Economic Growth since 1930', *Journal of Development Studies*, Oct. 1966 and Jan. 1967.

Argentine economic policy has been the recovery of the capacity to import, whether by improving the terms of trade of the rural sector, by reorientating credits towards agriculture or by promoting exports of manufactured goods. In the 1960s, the volume of exports grew at an annual rate of 3.7 per cent, compared with a growth rate of 2 per cent in the previous decade. If we take into account the effects of the terms of trade, the purchasing power of exports increased, during the sixties, at a rate of 4.2 per cent compared with the decline of minus 1.5 per cent annually registered in the previous decade. As a result of this expansion in the export sector, which permitted the stabilisation of the coefficient of imports at around 10 per cent, and of the parallel effort to broaden the base of the industrial system, particularly during the period 1959–62, the rate of growth of industrial production rose to 4.6 per cent in the 1960s, compared with the rate of 3.8 per cent in the previous decade. The intensification of industrial production at the beginning of the 1970s (at a yearly average of 7 per cent between 1970 and 1973) is in part due to the policy of export promotion. Manufactured exports more than trebled between 1970 and 1973, and in the latter year their value rose to 725 million dollars, representing 23 per cent of the total value of exports.

Case of Brazil

The Brazilian experience of industrialisation, while more recent than that of Argentina, is more interesting because of the greater representativeness of Brazil's economic structures in the region as a whole. In contrast with Argentina, industrialisation in Brazil proceeded under conditions of a totally elastic labour supply (a similar situation to that now obtaining in practically all the other countries of the region). On the other hand, Brazil had become aware of the need to broaden the bases of its industrial system as early as the 1930s and had recognised that the government must assume the responsibility for carrying out this task. It is significant that, in the midst of the difficulties of the Second World War, the Brazilian government succeeded in providing the country with a modern steel industry.[2] A preliminary plan for public investments in infrastructure (the SALTE plan) was launched in the immediate post-war

---

[2] The Brazilian government's Steel Plan was framed just before the outbreak of the war. The steelworks at Volta Redonda were constructed during the war years with funds provided by the Export–Import Bank and equipment bought in the United States; this was possible only because of the political understanding between the Vargas Administration and President Roosevelt. The plant came into operation in 1946.

period. The Banco Nacional de Desenvolvimento Economico (National Bank for Economic Development), established in 1952, was responsible for allocating substantial resources to the basic industries and to the construction of an infrastructure. Petrobras, created shortly afterwards, provided resources for the production, refining and shipping of petroleum. In sum, Brazil's industrialisation was supported by a broad base which permitted the achievement of high rates of growth after the 1950s.

By the beginning of the 1960s, domestic output accounted for about 90 per cent of the total supply of industrial products available on the Brazilian market. In the case of consumer durables, domestic production covered more than 95 per cent of the total domestic supply, in the case of intermediate industrial goods about 90 per cent and in the case of capital goods about 80 per cent. Industrialisation had thus made considerable progress towards the creation of an industrial system with a degree of diversification comparable to that of the highly industrialised economies. Mention should also be made of the import-substitution process in the petroleum sector, which started in the second half of the 1950s when petroleum imports accounted for nearly one-fifth of the total value of Brazilian imports. Since then, the value of these imports has been stabilised as a result of the rapid expansion of refining in the first instance, followed by a steady increase in the output of crude. By the early years of the sixties, when the structural diversification of industry was nearing completion and the industrial system was largely in a position to create its own means of expansion, the balance of payments threat constituted by the rapid increase in petroleum imports seemed to have been contained. Notwithstanding these favourable conditions, the growth rate of the industrial sector began to show a sharply downward trend, falling from an average annual rate of 10.8 per cent for the period 1956–62 to a rate of 4.8 per cent for the period 1963–8. In the first period it was around 60 per cent higher than the growth rate of the gross domestic product, whereas in the second it was only 20 per cent higher.

This loss of dynamism in Brazilian development was accompanied by mounting inflationary pressures and an aggravation of social tensions with serious repercussions on the political plane. Furthermore, the radical change in policy since 1964 – the containment of inflationary pressures having become the main objective of government action in the economic and financial sphere – had secondary repercussions, to the point that the level of industrial production declined by 5 per cent in 1965, with an even more marked decline in manufacturing output. It would be by no means easy to demonstrate that social and political factors were of only secondary importance in the decline of the growth rate discernible in

Brazil after 1962. On the other hand, it would be even more difficult to demonstrate that these factors were the prime or principal cause of this decline. Closer examination of the data shows that exports tended to grow much faster than imports. Between 1959–60 and 1965–6 the export coefficient rose, while the import coefficient declined. Thus, it seems evident that the factors responsible for the deceleration in Brazil's economy derived far more from a failure on the demand side than from shortcomings on the supply side.

It has already been pointed out that import-substituting industrialisation is essentially characterised by the fact that demand precedes industrial investment, which means that the demand schedule is defined before industrialisation gains momentum. New investments are consequently orientated towards an existing demand structure, established in the period preceding industrial investment. In a country where the structural manpower surplus was practically absorbed in the pre-industrial period – as in the case of Argentina – the problem is not of major importance. However, in countries with a large labour surplus, that is, where there are wide differences between the living levels of the bulk of the population and the middle and upper classes, the composition of demand assumes particular significance, since the market for manufactured consumer goods consists of two distinct sectors only precariously articulated with one another. Since the manpower surplus continues to exert downward pressure on wages, there is little or no change in the standards of consumption of the mass of the population, and the market for general consumer goods grows simply by the addition of new elements moving from conditions of underemployment or disguised unemployment into productive employment. Meanwhile, in the second section of the market, comprising a mere fraction – less than 5 per cent – of the total population, real income rises, and consumption is diversified along the lines of the new patterns emerging in the more-developed countries. Since technical progress tends to increase the capital coefficient per employee and per unit of additional output, the structural situation outlined above is even further aggravated. The slower absorption of manpower contributes to the growing structural labour surplus. Thus the social distribution of benefits deriving from the spread of technical progress will be hampered by this very progress. Growth of the industrial sector will therefore be supported by two separate markets functioning in practically watertight compartments. The first, composed of the bulk of the population, grows horizontally only and is negatively influenced by technical progress. The second expands dynamically but, given its small size, this very dynamism, reflected in the greater diversification of demand, will limit its real size. Economies of scale, one of the most significant indications of the assimilation of technical progress, cannot be realised to full advantage.

In the Brazilian case, we find that between 1955 and 1965 the productivity of the labour force employed in the manufacturing sector rose at an annual rate of 5.2 per cent, whereas the annual rate of increase in real wages in this sector was 1.3 per cent.[3] Thus, even in the sector with the highest rise in productivity, real wages increased less than the per capita income of the population as a whole, that is, less than average productivity. It must be concluded, therefore, that development was accompanied by a decline in the share of total income accruing to wage-earners, particularly if we exclude from this share the earnings of the middle-income groups. On the other hand, there is statistical evidence of the existence of large margins of idle capacity in practically all branches of Brazilian manufacturing, particularly in the capital goods sector during the period under consideration. Data for 1965 show that when operating only one shift the capital goods industries used just over 50 per cent of existing capacity.[4]

Fluctuations in the rate of growth seem to have had little repercussion on the process of capital formation since they reflect mainly the degree of utilisation of productive capacity. Between 1964–7 and 1968–9, the product–capital ratio (measuring the degree of utilisation of productive capacity) practically doubled, whereas the rate of investment grew only very slightly. Since this cannot be attributed to lack of effective demand, in an economy subject to permanent inflationary pressure, it must be recognised that the economic system failed to generate a *type of demand* corresponding to the supply structure.

The successive waves of industrial expansion in Brazil after the Second World War can only be explained if we take into account the role of the State which not only subsidised investment but broadened certain sectors of demand. By operating differential rates of exchange and providing credit at negative rates of interest, the State made it attractive to invest in industries which were to under-utilise the installed capacity. Thus, during a first stage in the post-war period, government action was directed mainly towards increasing the marginal efficiency of investment, which permitted the extension of the import-substitution process to sectors in which the size of the market was acknowledged to be small.

[3] For the basic data see ECLA and Banco Nacional de Desenvolvimento Economico, *A Evolução Recente da Economia Brasileira*, Rio de Janeiro, 1967.

[4] Cf. Werner Baer and Andrea Maneschi, *Import-substitution, Stagnation and Structural Change: an Interpretation of the Brazilian Case* (mimeograph), 1968.

Since such investment failed to create direct or indirect employment which could bring about any significant broadening of domestic demand, industrialisation began to lose momentum as the import-substitution process became exhausted.

After 1968 there was a substantial change in the strategy of the Brazilian government: protection to industry was reduced in order to facilitate income concentration by excluding the financially or economically weaker groups and resources were mobilised to broaden demand in sectors with an under-utilised capacity, that is sectors producing for the restricted market made up of the high-income minority. In these circumstances, acceleration of the growth rate necessarily entailed a high concentration of income and consumption.[5] It should be added that the extension of demand was complemented by a policy of promoting exports of manufactured products.

The Brazilian experience takes on great significance for Latin America when we consider that it has taken place in the country with the region's largest population, an extremely favourable endowment of basic natural resources and an entrepreneurial class whose dynamism is widely recognised.

Since the industrialisation of countries such as Colombia and Venezuela is currently proceeding within a framework not very different from that of Brazil, – both these countries face the problem of a large structural surplus of manpower – it would come as no surprise if similar phenomena, involving a slackening of industrialisation were reproduced in the near future, particularly since the home markets are much smaller than in Brazil. It should be noted, however, that Brazil's strategy in the second half of the sixties does not seem viable for smaller countries since the concentration of income is a necessary requirement for the dynamisation of an industrial system with a high degree of diversification but is not enough on its own. The dynamic growth of Colombia's manufactured exports, and Venezuela's new industrial strategy, which aims to concentrate investment in basic industries geared to the export market, indicate that attempts are being made to circumvent the difficulties encountered by Brazil in the preceding decade in the context of international specialisation. In some countries, awareness of these problems has prompted efforts to bring about structural change with a reorientation of the development process.

[5] Cf. C. Furtado, *Análise do 'Modelo' Brasileiro*, Rio de Janeiro, 1972.

17 Traditional forms of external dependence

Corrective policies: aims and instruments

The system of international division of labour, which enabled Latin American countries to initiate their development in the nineteenth century, created asymmetrical relations that were reflected in the close dependence of countries exporting raw materials on the industrialised centres. The development of international economic relations involved not only increased trade between the various nations but also the creation of 'poles of command' controlling financial flows, orientating international transfers of capital, financing strategic stocks of exportable products, intervening in the formation of prices, etc. Expansion of the exportable surplus in a Latin American country depended, almost always, on infrastructural investments financed by foreign capital made available when the increment in production entering the world market matched expectations in the world economy's decision centres. What was involved was thus a form of dependence consequent upon the very structure of the world economy. By making economic decisions little more than an automatic operation involving the transfer of price mechanisms from the microeconomy to the level of international relations, liberal ideology diverted attention from this problem and hindered perception of its consequences for the national economies on the domestic plane.

Reference has been made in earlier chapters to some of these consequences. So long as primary exports continued to play a role in these countries similar to that of investments in the industrialised countries, the instability of raw material prices was bound to have far-reaching internal effects. Administration of the monetary system and public finances became extremely difficult and the operations of the gold standard proved a heavy burden on account of the volume of foreign exchange reserves required and the fluctuations in the level of domestic economic activities implied. The prevailing economic doctrine made it even more difficult to find a way out since, far from helping to solve these problems, it in some ways obscured the perception of their more important aspects. Orthodox concepts were only gradually abandoned, at first thanks to empiricists in search of solutions to isolated problems and, since the forties, under the influence of economists trying to understand the specific nature of international relations involving primary-exporting economies.[1]

As they came to realise the dependent situation inherent in their integration into the international economy, Latin American countries made several attempts to counter the negative effects of this dependence. On the one hand, they sought to reduce what has come to be called the 'external vulnerability' of their economies by taking steps to control foreign economic and financial relations; on the other, they sought to increase the internal integration of these economies by reducing their dependence on the international system of division of labour. The first line of policy was designed mainly to control real and financial flows in order to reduce the domestic propagation of external imbalance. The second sought to prevent outflows of resources generated within the country and to channel investments towards home market expansion. A line of policy nearly always envisaged more than one aim or, with one particular end in view, attained several others. Hence it is easier to identify a policy through the instrument used, which, as a rule, involved exchange, fiscal or trade control measures.

Exchange control, which tended to be widely adopted in Latin American countries from the 1930s onwards, was designed mainly to reduce external vulnerability. Disturbances resulting from short-term capital movements were traditionally recognised; the disturbances tended to become more serious with the build-up of inflationary pressures in the context of pegged rates of exchange. An expected devaluation provoked massive flights of capital while the devaluation itself entailed sudden movements in the opposite direction. Exchange control was not, how-

---

[1] The Executive Secretariat of ECLA, under the guidance of Argentine economist Raúl Prebisch, played a decisive role in furthering the effort to break with orthodox concepts and gain greater insight into the region's economic problems. In a study prepared for the ECLA conference held in 1949, and subsequently published in the March 1961 issue of the Economic Bulletin for Latin America as 'The Economic Development of Latin America and its principal problems', Prebisch made an original contribution to the study of the problems of external dependence and the role of import-substituting industrialisation in the context of regional development. This study had an immediate and marked influence on Latin American economic thinking. It should be added that diagnosis of underdevelopment problems in Latin America is bound up with awareness of the phenomenon of external dependence and has been based on original studies carried out by Latin American economists within the framework of the work undertaken by United Nations research teams that included members from various countries in the region.

ever, restricted to capital movements. In many countries it acted as a mechanism for rationing a suddenly reduced capacity to import, making it possible to defend the level of domestic economic activity. Exchange control in the form of multiple exchange rates was used by some countries to modify income distribution, obtain resources for the State, and intervene in the orientation of investments.

Various types of fiscal policy have been used in the region in an effort to reduce their external dependence. In this field, the experience of mineral exporting countries becomes extremely significant. When production of non-ferrous metals and petroleum is controlled by international consortia, local productive factors generally receive only a small share of the flow of income generated by the exportable product. On the other hand, technological progress tends to reduce the proportion of labour while wages account for a mere fraction of total production costs. Furthermore, it is in the interests of international producing companies to purchase virtually all intermediate products abroad, within the framework of a buying policy designed to supply production units located in several different countries. In the case of petroleum companies, it is common practice to try to limit local expenditures, including wage payments, to the amount received in local currency from sales of fuel in the market of the country in question. Up to the 1930s the existence of 'enclave' mineral-exporting sectors, operating in total isolation from the country granting the concession, with a different level of prices and a separate balance of payments, was a situation that prevailed throughout Latin America. Chile played a pioneer role in this respect, with a policy aimed at *internalising* the costs of the big copper-producing companies. Through a combination of exchange and fiscal measures, the Chilean government managed to retain in the country a growing share of the foreign exchange earned on exports by the major copper companies. In 1928–9 only 17 per cent of these earnings returned to the country. By the end of the 1930s this proportion had more than doubled and the upward trend continued in the post-war period, as we shall see further on.

Petroleum policy in Venezuela

Venezuela's policy in the petroleum sector is an interesting example of the use of a fiscal instrument to cope with a situation of acute external dependence. The development of the Venezuelan oil industry was carried out under the terms of the extremely liberal 1922 law. As the result of subsequent developments in petroleum technology, the industry cut its labour costs and became more and more detached from the economy of the country. The new fiscal policy introduced in 1946 modified this trend and opened up enormous possibilities for the country. Under the new regulations, oil companies operating in Venezuela paid a royalty per unit of output, a standard income tax and a surtax, the latter having been introduced in 1944. The royalty corresponded to $16\frac{2}{3}$ per cent on the value of crude, based on Texan quotations. Taxes could be paid either in money or in petroleum, which enabled the State to develop a national oil-refining industry and to participate directly in exports. The Venezuelan government was extremely cautious in its use of this prerogative but fiscal legislation left the possibility open. Income tax was substantially increased in 1946, and in 1948 a further tax was introduced, establishing the principle that profits from the petroleum industry were to be divided on a fifty-fifty basis between the Venezuelan State and the foreign producer companies. This principle was later adopted by all Third World countries in which oil is exploited by foreign companies. Finally, in 1958, changes in income tax legislation increased the State's share of the industry's gross profits to 60 per cent. The scope of this policy was all the greater because the extraordinary rise in productivity tended to reduce the industry's importance as a source of employment. Between 1948 and 1963, output increased from 490 million barrels to 1,186 million, while the number of workers employed declined from 55,170 to 33,742. Output per worker rose from 8,877 barrels to 35,178. Although average wages rose substantially, the total spent on wages increased by only 49 per cent while output went up by 142 per cent. Between 1950 and 1962, the companies increased their outgoings on labour by 70 per cent, and on the purchase of locally produced goods and services by 110 per cent, while in the same period the amount paid out in taxes to the State increased by 220 per cent. In 1962, tax receipts amounted to twice the total paid out by the oil companies in wages and other local expenditures. Thus, despite the rise in productivity – reflected in the greater share of foreign capital in the income generated by petroleum production – the share of total value returned to the country increased from 55 per cent in 1950 to 66 per cent in 1962.

In the second half of the sixties, Venezuela's petroleum policy was used both to increase the State's share of the producer companies' profits and to defend petroleum prices in the international market. The system of 'posted prices' introduced in 1967, provided the basis for assessing the taxable income of the oil companies. Posted prices were to be effective for a period of five years and were to be increased gradually in order to stabilise government receipts from taxation and royalties. A law passed in 1970 authorised an increase in taxes and royalties paid by concessionaires. The State's share of the profits of the major operating company (a subsidiary of Standard Oil of New Jersey) increased from 74 per cent in 1969 to 81 per cent in 1971. In addition, the State was empowered to establish posted prices unilaterally and after 1972 the assessment of the operating companies' income was based on posted prices rather than on prices actually *received*. These measures created the conditions for the State to assume complete control over petroleum export prices, a step that was to be taken in 1973 within the framework of the joint action agreed upon with other members of the Organization of Petroleum Exporting Countries (OPEC).

Coffee policy in Brazil

The coffee policy followed by the Brazilian government since the beginning of the present century is a notable example of action through trade measures designed to lessen dependence on the outside world. The fact that at the turn of the century Brazil's coffee exports provided four-fifths of the total supply available on the world market meant that any fluctuations in the Brazilian crop had a marked impact on prices. Thus the value of Brazilian coffee exports could suddenly be halved because a bumper crop was forecast, or rise sharply because a frost had occurred. Consequently, the strategic position for the coffee economy became the regulation of stocks. Brazil's position was in some ways like that of the United States in the world cotton market about the middle of the last century. But there was one important difference: in the latter case the American monopoly faced the English monopsony, since the textile industry was then concentrated in England. Prices were not subject to violent fluctuations but the financially more powerful monopsonist was always in the dominant position.

Realising their own strength – which had been used against them as a result of their failure to seize its advantages – Brazilian coffee planters outlined a policy for stabilising supply at a meeting held in 1906 in Taubaté, a city in the State of São Paulo. Surpluses were to be withdrawn from the market and financed through loans negotiated abroad. Servicing of the debt contracted would be covered by a tax levied in gold on every bag of coffee exported. At first this policy encountered resistance from Brazil's international creditors, led by the House of Rothschild, but it was carried through with the support of German and North

American financial groups and its initial success soon made it a highly attractive financial proposition.[2] However, its very success was to become the source of its later weakness. Brazil was anticipating by half a century the attempts to organise international markets that have been made in the last decade through commodity agreements. Acting in isolation, Brazil had to assume the entire responsibility for financing the costs of the operation, creating a privileged position for other producers. Coffee came to stand out among tropical commodities for the exceptional stability of its prices at a profitable level. It was only natural, therefore, that production and supply in other countries should tend to rise, which meant that in order to maintain the price stabilisation policy Brazil had to accept a steady decline in her share of the world market. Nor was this the only difficulty. The policy outlined in Taubaté envisaged action on the part of the State governments designed to discourage the rapid expansion of coffee planting which was absolutely necessary, since coffee occupied a privileged position among the country's exportable commodities. This essential feature of policy was neglected and the surpluses to be withheld began to pile up alarmingly. Thus in 1929 production totalled 28.9 million bags while exports amounted to only 14.3 million. It has been estimated that in this same year, investments in coffee stocks amounted to 10 per cent of the domestic product. The catastrophic slump in prices following the world crisis – in twelve months prices tumbled from 22.5 cents a pound to 8 cents – did not affect output, which continued to increase until 1933, as the result of new plantings undertaken in the latter half of the twenties when prices were attractive. As we have seen in a previous chapter, in the absence of external financing, surpluses began to be financed by means of credit expansion which would provoke inflation but would also cushion the domestic impact of the crisis. World market conditions and the growing output of competitor countries ruled out the possibility of finding outlets for the enormous coffee stocks which had continued to accumulate throughout the thirties. Apart from the heavy costs involved in retention, the existence of these stocks was affecting world market prices, which led the Brazilian government to opt for the destruction of part of the surplus as the only feasible solution. Consequently, almost 80 million bags – about 1.3 times the world production in 1970–1 were destroyed (see Table 17.1). Coffee prices were to recover their pre-1929 level in real terms only towards the end of the forties. The upward trend in

[2] Cf. Celso Furtado, *Formação Econômica do Brasil*, for a detailed discussion of Brazilian coffee policy.

TABLE 17.1 *Destruction of coffee by the Brazilian government*

Years	Number of 60-kg bags
1931	2,825,784
1932	9,329,633
1933	13,687,012
1934	8,265,791
1935	1,693,112
1936	3,731,154
1937	17,196,428
1938	8,004,000
1939	3,519,8/4
1940	2,816,063
1941	3,422,835
1942	2,312,805
1943	1,274,318
1944	135,444
After 1944[a]	1,300,000
Total	79,514,253

[a] Coffee donated to various firms for conversion into oil and feedstuffs.
SOURCE: Ruy Miller Paiva and others, *Sétor Agrícola do Brasil*, São Paulo, 1973.

prices after 1949, accentuated by the Korean war, led to a new wave of planting in Brazil, mainly in the virgin lands of North Parana. In 1961, the total number of coffee trees was around 3.9 billion with a production capacity of 36 million bags, while total demand in that year was 26 million bags (18 million for export and 6 million for domestic consumption).[3] As a result of the activities of the Executive Group for the Rationalisation of Coffee Growing (GERCA), established in that same year, 1.4 billion trees were uprooted and yields in the surviving plantings were improved. On the other hand, a concerted effort was made to persuade other producers to organise supply, leading in 1962 to the establishment of the International Coffee Organisation to administer the first world coffee agreement, under the provisions of which producers and consumers co-operate in regulating the international marketing of coffee.

[3] Ruy Miller Paiva, and others, *Sétor Agricola do Brasil*, São Paulo, 1973. pp. 155–6.

Argentina's export control policy

Argentine foreign trade policy between 1946 and 1955, carried out through the Institute for the Promotion of Foreign Trade (IAPI), is a pioneer example of the attempt made in Latin America to bring exports under the control of the State. The system of multiple exchange rates operated in this country since the 1930s enabled the government to freeze a considerable proportion of the export sector's income during the war years, which made it possible to cushion the inflationary pressure created by the balance of trade surplus. On the other hand, the revenues thus obtained permitted the financing of export surpluses resulting from the bumper crops of 1944 and 1946. To prevent supply fluctuations from having an adverse effect on world market prices at a time when there was a marked insufficiency of supply, IAPI was established with a monopoly over exports. In this way, domestic market prices and export prices could be separately fixed, while at the same time the marketing of the exportable surplus could be undertaken in accordance with an overall strategy designed to maximise the income of the country's export sector. The way in which this policy was applied had a number of consequences whose interpretation has been the subject of heated debate in Argentina. Given the marked improvement in the external terms of trade – which improved by 41 per cent between 1943 and 1946 – the IAPI was able to begin its career by absorbing a substantial share of the increment in the income accruing to the export sector without causing any reduction in the latter's profitability. In fact, between the years indicated the internal terms of trade for the agricultural sector, which constitute an indicator of this sector's profitability vis-à-vis the other sectors of the country's economy, improved by 25 per cent. Between 1946 and 1948 the external terms of trade continued to improve – the index rose by 18.4 per cent – while the internal terms of trade for the agricultural and livestock sector deteriorated, declining practically to their 1943 level. The agricultural and livestock sector thus lost the relative advantage it had gained between 1943 and 1946, a loss that occurred precisely when the expanding economy was making it possible to raise investment. To what extent this decline in relative profitability was responsible for the fall in investment in the agricultural and livestock sector is not easy to determine. But agricultural output fell after 1949. The effects of the deterioration in the internal terms of trade and the decline in the volume of production combined to produce a substantial reduction in the real income of the agricultural and livestock sector. After 1950 government policy was revised and the IAPI began to pay producers prices above those it could obtain in the international markets.

Since the Institute's losses were covered by the expansion of credit, its policy became a focus of inflationary pressure during a phase of serious tensions provoked by the marked deterioration in the country's external terms of trade, whose index was practically halved between 1945 and 1952. Agricultural and livestock production responded favourably to the change in policy, and the average level of output between 1953 and 1958 was 25 per cent above that for the 1943–8 period. However, exportable surpluses did not regain their former levels in view of the substantial growth of domestic demand. After 1955 the Argentine government gradually re-established a liberal exchange policy, using credit support to continue its efforts to promote the recovery of the agricultural and livestock sector, although the results were not very different from those achieved in 1953 and 1954. There can be no doubt that the IAPI had proved as effectual in deflecting resources from the agricultural and livestock sector as in re-allocating them to its own advantage (see Table 17.2).

Petroleum policy in Mexico

The policy followed by Mexico in the petroleum field also illustrates a number of problems that face the countries of the region in their attempt to counter foreign domination of their economies. In the opinion of authorities such as Jesús Silva Herzog,[4] the Mexican government did not reach its decision to expropriate the oil companies as part of any pre-meditated plan. The 1917 constitution established the principle of public ownership of the subsoil resources, but shortly afterwards the concessions granted earlier were all ratified. In fact, Mexican output expanded rapidly in the years following the First World War, reaching a peak in 1921 when it accounted for one-quarter of the world's production of oil. Production levels stayed high but began to show a downward trend in the mid-twenties. It is possible that one of the reasons for this decline was the predatory form of exploitation that characterised the early stages. However, the main reason why Mexico lost ground probably lay in the expansion of Venezuelan production, which in 1928 was already out-stripping Mexican output. The great productivity of the Venezuelan oil industry was reflected in the fall in world prices, which became more marked after 1930 owing to the economic crisis. It is interesting to note that Venezuelan output declined only slightly during the depression, rising in 1935 to levels above that for 1929. In the same period Mexican

---

[4] Cf. Jesús Silva Herzog, *História de la Expropriación de las Empresas Petroleras*, Mexico, 1964.

TABLE 17.2	*Argentina: external and internal terms of trade, and indices of agricultural and industrial product*

	External terms of trade	Internal terms of trade	Index of	
			Agricultural product	Industrial product
1943	83.5	97.0	100.0	100.0
1944	84.6	87.2	126.9	120.8
1945	87.7	101.6	104.0	113.2
1946	120.3	122.6	180.7	130.7
1947	143.8	106.5	154.0	151.1
1948	141.7	100.9	157.7	158.2
1949	117.8	91.3	126.0	157.4
1950	100.0	100.0	108.8	152.4
1951	109.5	111.3	122.6	150.7
1952	75.2	113.2	99.6	137.4
1953	100.0	128.2	173.9	130.3
1954	90.0	111.3	148.7	147.4
1955	88.0	104.0	152.4	167.1
1956	76.0	116.0	155.3	154.8
1957	72.5	125.1	177.7	157.6
1958	76.6	130.2	202.9	165.6
1959	81.0	147.3	196.2	145.6
1960	84.5	145.3	188.9	155.4

Note: The internal terms of trade reflect changes in agricultural prices to the producer in terms of prices of industrial goods on the home market.
SOURCE: Data given in Javier Villanueva, *The Inflationary Process in Argentina, 1943–60* (mimeographed), Buenos Aires, 1964.

production declined steeply, falling in 1932–3 to one-half the 1927 output and less than one-fifth of the levels attained in the first half of the twenties (see Table 17.3). There had been no new drillings in Mexico since 1927 and the foreign oil companies' determination to cut back on production was having serious repercussions on the social plane. It was these social tensions that brought the companies into conflict with the Mexican government, leading them to the extreme of ignoring a Supreme Court decision, which left the executive power with no alternative but to expropriate their properties.

In 1937, the year before expropriation, oil accounted for one-fifth of the Mexican export total and about half the output was already destined for the home market. Between 1937 and 1938 exports were practically

TABLE 17.3 *Petroleum production in Mexico and Venezuela*

	Mexico	Venezuela	Petroleum prices in the United States (dollars per barrel)
	(in thousands of cu. metres)		
1920	24,971	73	3.40
1921	30,747	230	1.70
1922	28,979	355	1.80
1923	23,781	688	1.45
1924	22,206	1,451	1.45
1925	18,365	3,169	1.65
1926	14,375	5,669	1.95
1927	10,194	9,606	1.30
1928	7,973	16,845	1.20
1929	7,105	21,634	1.25
1930	6,285	21,502	1.15
1931	5,253	18,581	0.60
1932	5,216	18,560	0.80
1933	5,406	18,792	0.60
1934	6,069	21,668	0.95
1935	6,398	23,612	0.95
1936	6,523	24,586	1.05
1937	7,457	29,533	1.20
1938	6,122	29,896	1.15
1939	6,820	32,518	0.95
⋮	⋮	⋮	⋮
1946	7,900	61,763	1.25

SOURCE: ECLA, *Economic Survey of Latin America, 1949.*

halved, although production declined by less than 20 per cent. The production level for 1937, amounting to 47 million barrels, was only surpassed in 1946 when output rose to 50 million barrels. Thereafter, exploratory activities were intensified and Mexico managed to incorporate new producing areas. Output kept pace with the rapid growth of domestic consumption and in 1970 amounted to 178 million barrels. There can be no doubt that expropriation was a serious challenge to the country, since failure to organise the exploitation of oil as a national industry would have undermined the Mexican State's authority to such an extent that it would have had great difficulty in implementing its agrarian reform programme. Because it called for the formation of a pool of skilled technical and executive personnel and provided the State with

substantial resources for investment, the oil industry came to play a key
role in the rapid industrialisation occurring after the 1940s. Petroleos
Mexicanos (PEMEX), the comany set up by the State to take over the
expropriated properties of the foreign oil companies, is at present one
of the largest operating in Latin America.

Copper policy in Chile

Relations between the Chilean State and the big enterprises engaged in
exploiting the country's copper resources provide an equally striking
instance of a prolonged effort to integrate into the national economy one
of its vitally important sectors, traditionally under foreign control.
Copper production in Chile grew strongly after the First World War,
rising to 321,000 tons in 1929. This growth was essentially due to the
operations of United States companies which had relegated the older
national enterprises, established since the previous century, to a completely secondary position. In 1925–9, Chile already contributed 18 per
cent of the world's total copper output, ranking second to the United
States among world producers. On the other hand, copper accounted for
40 per cent of the total value of Chilean exports. The new industry,
employing modern technology, located in isolated regions and paying
extremely light taxes, returned only a small share of the value of production to the host country. In fact, one ton of copper produced by the
small national enterprises represented as much for the country as four
tons produced by the foreign companies.

After the world crisis, the Chilean government made concerted efforts
to 'internalise' the copper industry. Through fiscal and exchange measures the government sought to increase the share of locally-purchased
inputs and to appropriate a growing share of company profits for the
State. These measures made it possible to integrate into the national
economy the flows created by a sector which had hitherto existed as an
'enclave', while at the same time significantly increasing the country's
capacity to import. The first income tax legislation, passed in 1934,
provided for a tax of 18 per cent on the industry's profits. In 1939, when
a development agency (CORFO) was established, the tax was raised to
33 per cent. The subsequent course of events was profoundly marked
by the disturbances in the copper market provoked by the Second
World War and the Korean war. The policy of the United States government, in fixing a relatively low ceiling price on copper during the
Second World War, left the impression in Chile that the country had
suffered serious harm. When the Korean war started and the United

States again tried to impose a wartime price ceiling on copper – in 1950 three American companies operating in Chile signed an agreement with Washington providing for a fixed price on copper effective for the duration of the Korean conflict – there was an immediate outcry in Chile and the government was forced to react by intervening more directly in this sector of the country's economy. An agreement was signed between the two governments in 1951, which provided *inter alia* for one-fifth of production to be disposed of by the Chilean government as it saw fit, thus opening the door to government intervention in the marketing of copper. On the basis of this agreement, the Chilean Central Bank began to buy its 20 per cent quota of copper at the prevailing New York price and to sell it at the highest prices obtainable on the world market. These operations provided the Chilean Treasury with profits amounting to 190 million dollars between 1952 and 1955.

The year 1955 saw the beginning of a new phase in Chilean copper policy. Rising taxes on the one hand and the prospect of an increase in African output on the other led the companies to cut back on their investments in Chile. Chile's share of world copper production, which had been as high as 21 per cent in 1948, had declined to 14 per cent by 1953 and the level of output had remained virtually at a standstill. A new law was passed in May 1955, whose main objective was to ease the tax burden on firms while at the same time simplifying the complicated fiscal system created in the past. The law provided for a fixed tax of 50 per cent on profits and a variable surtax of 25 per cent, to be reduced proportionally as production exceeded the quotas fixed for each firm. In some ways, this legislation represented a reversal in terms of previous developments. The *share* of the total value of copper proceeds returned to the domestic economy (the proportion of foreign exchange retained by the country) fell from 82 per cent in 1950–4 to 78 per cent in 1955 and to a low of 56 per cent in 1959. The value returned in *absolute* terms rose from an annual average of 149 million dollars in 1950–4 to 167 million dollars in 1956–9. The 1955 law created a Copper Department, later to be known as the Chilean Copper Corporation, which was to be the point of departure for systematic action designed to provide a thorough knowledge of all matters concerning the copper industry.

In 1966 a new law was passed redefining Chilean copper policy in an attempt to reconcile the two aims pursued previously: the integration of the industry into the national economy – the principal objective up to 1955 – and the encouragement of its expansion with a view to increasing the country's share in world copper production – the major objective of the policy initiated in 1955. The new policy, known as 'Chileanisation', led the State to participate in the formation of joint stock companies. Thus in 1964–5, the Braden Copper Company became the *Compañia Minera El Teniente S.A.*, in which the Chilean State holds 51 per cent of the stock and the United States group (Kennecott Copper Corporation) 49 per cent. A new company was formed to develop the Exótica deposit, with the State holding 25 per cent of the stock and the Anaconda Group 75 per cent. A third company, in which the State holds 25 per cent of the stock, was established to develop the Rio Blanco deposit. An option was secured on the exploitation of new deposits at present under the control of Anaconda. The agreements with the copper companies included an investment programme involving a total of 587 million dollars, to raise the industry's production capacity to 1,000,000 tons by 1972. The policy thus provided for a system of joint production which would enable the Chilean State to participate increasingly in the decision centres controlling the supply of copper on the world market.

In 1969, the government announced the 'agreed nationalisation' of the Anaconda Group's subsidiaries, one of which controlled the rich Chuquicamata deposit, whose output in that year was 283,000 tons. The State acquired 51 per cent of the company's stock at book value prices and secured an option to buy up the remaining 49 per cent at prices to be established on the basis of the company's profits in the period between the date of purchase of the first 51 per cent and the exercise of its option to buy up the remaining shares.

The 'Chileanisation' policy was really an attempt to interest the large enterprises and international financial centres in the country's effort to increase its copper output in the medium-term. Only in the light of a strategy of this nature can one explain the considerable concessions made to the Kennecott Corporation, which ceded 51 per cent of its stock to the State at a price well above the book value of its total assets. Furthermore, plans for expansion, financed entirely by the State and by government-backed international loans, envisaged the increase of production capacity from 170,000 to 270,000 tons and the increase of refining capacity from 50,000 to 120,000 tons, in the case of the electrolytic refineries, and from 66,000 to 118,000 tons, in the case of furnace smelting. It is estimated that these developments would have quadrupled the real value of the enterprise while at the same time reducing the incidence of the tax burden on the foreign group. The financial effort required of the Chilean State was, of course, considerable, particularly since the cost of buying up the remaining 49 per cent of the Corporation's stock would be affected by the exceptionally high profits reaped as a result of the rise in copper prices (in 1973) and the intensive exploitation of deposits. These negative aspects were accentuated when it became apparent that the expansion programmes were over-optimistic and had been based on inadequate technical studies.

The criticisms levelled against 'Chileanisation' contributed towards the formation of a consensus of opinion in the country, which found expression in the unanimous approval in 1971 of a constitutional reform enabling the Popular Unity Coalition government to carry out immediate and drastic nationalisation of the group of large foreign corporations which had exploited Chilean copper since the beginning of the century. The nationalisation law, which empowered the government to make deductions for 'excess profits' from the indemnities to be paid to the foreign companies, while at the same time providing that the hearing of any claims which might arise from indemnification decisions was outside the competence of the ordinary courts of law, was a daring innovation in a matter of utmost significance for all countries with dependent economies. The political repercussion of this innovation were to affect the Popular Unity government and were not unrelated to its collapse in 1973.[5]

[5] A well-documented study of the 'Chileanisation' policy was published in *Panorama Económico*, Santiago, number 246, July 1969; for a criticism of this policy and background material on the nationalisation of the copper companies in 1971, see Eduardo Novoa Monreal, *La Batalla por el Cobre*, Santiago, 1972.

18 New forms of external dependence

Financial flows

After the Second World War there was a marked change in the evolution of mechanisms for international financial co-operation. During the two decades following the 1929 crisis the amount of foreign investment in Latin America had declined. The capital markets of Europe and the United States had been closed to bonds issued by public or private entities in the region and the bitter experience of the 1930s had made it only too clear that, given the instability of the foreign exchange earnings of countries exporting primary products, the accumulation of a large external debt ruled out any possibility of carrying out rational economic policies in these countries. On the other hand, in the two decades referred to, the development of the region's economies had been financed, in the case of the region's most industrially advanced countries, mostly out of domestic savings. Moreover, a large part of the foreign debt accumulated in the preceding period had been repaid, thanks to the favourable balance of trade of the war years. Besides, the traumatic experiences resulting from the conflicts between foreign-owned enterprises and some of the region's national governments – the expropriation of Mexican oil was only the most spectacular instance – had created a climate that made it difficult to take an objective view of the problems of international financial co-operation.

Two trends emerged in the immediate post-war years. The first was the delimitation of areas closed to the operations of foreign-owned enterprises. The Mexican Constitution was amended in 1938 to reserve to the State all forms of exploiting hydrocarbons. A similar principle was embodied in ordinary legislation passed in Brazil. In Chile and Uruguay the principle of State ownership of the oil industry guided policy from the outset.[1] Even in Venezuela, government policy over the last two decades – with the exception of 1956–7 – has been firmly against the granting of new concessions to foreign enterprises, with the object of bringing the oil industry under State control. Other countries, such as Argentina, have accepted the co-operation of foreign groups in the form of service contracts valid for limited periods. In a less explicit or less coherent form, the same line of policy has prevailed with respect to basic services such as generation of energy and urban and inter-urban transport and communications. In some countries, such as Mexico and Peru, the State has already taken over control of these sectors completely. In others, such as Brazil and Argentina, the State controls the rail transport sector and is steadily extending its control over the electric energy sector in which virtually all new investments have been public.

The second trend was the growing use of international credit agencies as financial intermediaries for the region's national governments. Between 1948 and 1971, the World Bank has made loans to the value of 5.3 billion dollars to private and public enterprises in the region, backed with government guarantee. These loans have been used almost entirely for infrastructure projects, especially electric power and transport. Since these sectors had traditionally been financed from resources obtained abroad, the operations of the World Bank have made it possible to reopen a channel of financial co-operation of major importance to the region in the past. Loans granted by this credit agency represent a considerable advance on the external bond issues formerly floated through banking consortia closely supervised by the traditional finance houses of London and New York, both as regards the cost of the money and the preinvestment study of projects. World Bank requirements, particularly in the early years of its operations, which stipulated not only that investment projects be technically sound but that they conform with the development prospects for the economy concerned, were one of the starting-points for the practice of establishing overall projections and preparing

---

[1] In Uruguay, the oil refining industry is a State monopoly, with half the imports purchased by the State company, ANCAP (Administración Nacional de Combustibles, established in 1931) and half by private foreign companies with marketing interests; there is no local production and the imported crude is processed at the ANCAP refinery, meeting practically all the country's consumption needs. In Chile, the law establishing State monopoly over the petroleum sector was passed in 1927. The Empresa Nacional del Petroleo (ENAP), established in 1950, is responsible for exploration, production and refining. State enterprises with greater or less control over the petroleum sector also exist in the following countries: Argentina (established in 1922), Peru (1934), Bolivia (1936), Colombia (1948), Brazil (1953), Cuba (1959) and Venezuela (1960).

development programmes in the countries of the region. The Inter-american Development Bank, which began operations in 1961, is even more representative of the new trend. Between 1961 and 1974 the Bank authorised loans to a total value of 7.4 billion dollars of which 58 per cent has already been disbursed. Of the total value of these loans, 23 per cent was destined to agriculture and 15 per cent to industry. The Bank has been floating bond issues, on relatively favourable terms, on the US capital market and more recently on the capital markets of Europe and even in the petroleum exporting Latin American countries. The IDB has thus gradually become the financial intermediary for Latin American governments in the world's capital markets, representing an enormous saving for the individual borrowing countries and offering greater security to creditors. On the other hand, the IDB has been collaborating closely with local development banks or similar financial institutions, thus making it possible to extend credit facilities at relatively low cost to medium-size enterprises in the region and even to make lines of credit available to firms exporting locally produced equipment.

The figures in Table 18.1 show that in the 1950s and 1960s Latin America's exports exceeded imports, indicating that, strictly speaking, the region relied only on its own resources for accumulation and consumption. If we exclude Venezuela, however, imports exceeded exports by 3 per cent in both the decades referred to. In the 1950s the country which benefited most from the inflow of real resources was Argentina (imports exceeded exports by 9 per cent) while in the 1960s it was Colombia with an import surplus of 10 per cent. In Venezuela, the export surplus was 36 per cent in the first decade and 51 per cent in the second. An excess of imports over exports may, of course, have a number of very different meanings from a financial viewpoint. It may merely mean the liquidation of assets abroad, particularly of foreign exchange reserves held by Central Banks. In the case of the Latin American countries, however, this excess is a clear indication that the net inflow of capital is higher than the cost of servicing this capital.

It will be seen from the data in Table 18.2 that the net flow of autonomous capital reached an annual average of 832 million dollars in the 1950s. Bearing in mind that the net interest and dividend payments totalled 1,028 million dollars (see Table 18.1) we can understand the need to achieve a favourable balance of trade. Once again, if we exclude Venezuela and Chile, we find that in the fifties, the net inflow of autonomous capital in the other five countries included in the two tables referred to, was higher than the cost of foreign capital. In the sixties, the net inflow of autonomous capital averaged 1,462 million dollars a year

TABLE 18.1 *Current account of the balance of payments (annual averages in millions of dollars)*

	1950–59				1960–69			
	Exports	Imports	Net interest and dividend payments	Balance[a]	Exports	Imports	Net interest and dividend payments	Balance[a]
Argentina	1,106	1,208	− 19	− 127	1,532	1,460	− 103	− 34
Brazil	1,561	1,644	− 135	− 228	1,741	1,755	− 235	− 233
Colombia	612	422	− 30	5	680	750	− 81	− 148
Chile	450	422	− 63	− 34	793	806	− 138	− 144
Mexico	1,108	1,100	− 116	− 110	1,918	1,994	− 355	− 436
Peru	309	348	− 27	− 58	763	750	− 100	− 81
Venezuela	1,956	1,437	− 560	− 89	2,558	1,693	− 651	− 124
Latin America	8,297	7,956	− 1,028	− 750	11,843	11,260	− 1,807	− 1,261
Latin America excluding Venezuela	6,341	6,520	− 468	− 661	9,286	9,567	− 1,156	− 1,385

[a] Including net private transfer payments.

SOURCE: ECLA, *Tendencias y Estructuras de la Economia Latinoamericana B*, Santiago, 1971, Table 18.

TABLE 18.2 *Financing of the deficit in the current balance of payments (annual averages in millions of dollars)*

	Total net financing		Net flow of autonomous capital		Accommodating movements		Errors and omissions	
	1950–9	1960–9	1950–9	1960–9	1950–9	1960–9	1950–9	1960–9
Argentina	127	34	100	88	43	− 44	− 16	− 10
Brazil	228	233	155	301	99	− 30	− 27	− 38
Colombia	− 5	148	32	156	− 1	− 1	− 36	− 8
Chile	40	144	45	148	− 1	− 2	− 2	− 1
Mexico	110	436	147	399	− 37	− 23		− 59
Peru	58	81	61	77	3	18	− 5	− 14
Venezuela	89	− 124	201	− 61	− 16	− 32	− 95	− 30
Latin America	750	1,261	832	1,462	100	− 110	− 182	− 90
Latin America excluding Venezuela	661	1,385	631	1,523	117	− 78	− 87	− 60

SOURCE: As for Table 18.1 (Table 20).

and the cost of foreign capital 1,807 million dollars. Excluding Venezuela, the surplus was 368 million dollars a year. Venezuela emerges as a net exporter of capital because the large foreign-owned companies in the petroleum sector did not even reinvest for depreciation reserves. In the latter decade, the inflow of autonomous capital was once more lower than the cost of servicing foreign capital in Argentina and Peru.

The modest or negligible flow of external resources to Latin America in the period under consideration contrasts with the considerable increase both in the external debt and in direct foreign investment. The figures in Table 18.3 show that the external debt increased 7.4 times between 1950 and 1968 and total direct foreign investment 2.4 times between 1950 and 1969. If we exclude Venezuela, accumulated direct foreign investment rose from 4,752 to 13,316 million dollars, representing an average annual growth of 5.6 per cent, only slightly higher than the growth rate of Latin America's GDP during the same period, which averaged 5.2 per cent a year. The rate of growth of the external debt, however, was twice as high as that of the GDP. Of the countries included in Table 18.3, only in Mexico did direct foreign investment increase more rapidly than the GDP in the two decades referred to.

The data on direct foreign investment relate to the book-keeping value of investment and not to the massive resources effectively controlled by foreign companies. To the extent that these companies cease to operate by preference in public utilities and the extractive industries and enter the manufacturing sector and trade, they gain greater access to local resources which they control in one way or another. The influence of foreign companies is no longer measured in terms of registered foreign-owned capital but in terms of the volume of their sales. Unfortunately, information on sales is more difficult to obtain. Table 18.4 contains data on the increase in the value of sales by American subsidiaries operating in the manufacturing sector in four countries of the region. These data show that in the period 1961 to 1965 the sales of American manufacturing subsidiaries grew 2.4 times faster than industrial output in Argentina and Brazil, 2.3 times faster in Mexico and 1.4 times in Venezuela. They also show that the expansion in the sales of subsidiary companies is much steadier than the pace of growth of the economies in which these subsidiaries operate.

The expansion of subsidiaries is based essentially on locally-obtained resources: depreciation reserves, undistributed profits, bond issues, local bank loans. Available information on American subsidiaries indicates that four-fifths of their expansion in the period 1957–65 was financed from locally-raised resources; resources obtained directly from the

TABLE 18.3 Direct foreign investment and external debt (in millions of dollars)

	Accumulated direct foreign investment				Share of USA				Outstanding external debt					
	1950	1969	1969	1950	1950	1969	1968	1950	1950	1950	1968	1968	1950
Argentina	800	1,892	2.37		44.5	65.8		400	1,478	2,221		5.55
Brazil	1,343	3,661	2.73		48.0	45.0		409	1,824	4,310		10.53
Colombia	423	748	1.76		45.6	91.4		158	377	1,297		8.21
Chile	620	1,022	1.65		87.1	82.8		355	566	1,843		5.19
Mexico	566	3,023	5.34		73.3	54.0		509	1,038	3,048		5.99
Peru	270	1,002	3.71		53.7	70.2		107	268	1,019		9.52
Venezuela	2,630	4,519	1.71		37.8	59.0		–	314	520		–
Latin America	7,382	17,935	2.42		51.1			2,213	6,631	16,432		7.42

SOURCE: As for Table 18.1 (Table 22).

TABLE 18.4   *Growth in sales of North America*
subsidiaries in the manufacturing sector
and in total industrial output

	Annual rates of growth of subsidiary sales		Annual rates of growth of industrial output	
	1957–61	1961–5	1957–61	1961–5
Argentina	23.0	13.7	0.5	5.7
Brazil	8.6	4.7	12.5	2.0
Mexico	6.8	16.9	8.4	7.4
Venezuela	8.8	13.2	8.4	9.4

SOURCE: ECLA, *Economic Survey of Latin America, 1970*,
vol. II, Table 29.

United States covered only 17 per cent of total expenditure. In the case
of manufacturing subsidiaries, the corresponding percentage rose to
22 per cent. It should be added that American subsidiaries remitted 79
per cent of their profits to the parent companies; in the manufacturing
sector the share of profits remitted abroad falls to 57 per cent.[2]

The financial aspect is only one side of the problem. The region's
recent development, particularly where it has taken the form of industrialisation, called for assimilation of modern technology, which had to
be largely imported. Consequently, it is by studying the way in which
the manufacturing sector was organised and how the transfer of modern
technology was effected, that we can grasp the real significance of international co-operation for the region's recent development.

Since Latin American imports consisted largely of manufactures, any
attempt to reduce the import coefficient (the ratio of imports to domestic
product) would have to take the form of industrialisation, that is, a more
than proportional growth of the manufacturing sector. Policies designed
to attain this end took various forms, one being the offering of special
inducements to attract foreign capital to the manufacturing sector. Even
without such incentives, however, the decline in the capacity to import of
countries such as Argentina, Brazil and Mexico meant that industrial
development would have to be intensified and that one of the consequences would be a *loss of markets* for the international groups that had
formerly supplied them. Such groups could safeguard their markets only
by decentralising part of their economic activity, setting up Latin Ameri-

[2] Cf. ECLA, *Economic Survey of Latin America, 1970*, vol. II, Tables 6 and 11.

can subsidiaries to operate local assembly plants or factories manufacturing components of products hitherto imported in their finished state. Two different factors thus converged: the desire of countries in the region to reduce their import coefficient and the concern of international groups to safeguard their traditional position in the markets of these countries.

Access to modern technology

At this point we must consider the following question: would the Latin American countries have registered the high rates of growth characterising their manufacturing sectors in the post-war period if they had not been able to count on the effective co-operation of international groups, primarily North American, with considerable industrial experience and easy access to the sources of financing? There can be no doubt that industrialisation, to be achieved within a relatively short period and on an extremely broad front, meant the setting up of a complex of productive activities, built up over several generations in other countries. Technical personnel with a wide variety of specialised skills had to be found and, given the almost total absence of local laboratories, technological institutes and advisory services, it was necessary to secure outside support to ensure that the many technical and economic problems created by the operation of transplanting an entire industrial system would be solved within a reasonably short space of time. Some form of international co-operation was inevitable since sources of technology were located abroad and access to these was in many cases strictly controlled. Primarily, this co-operation took the form of setting up Latin American subsidiaries of

TABLE 18.5   *United States investments in Latin American manufacturing industries (millions of dollars)*

	1950	1965	1971	Increase 1971/1950
Argentina	161	617	813	5.05
Brazil	285	722	1,409	4.94
Mexico	133	752	1,272	9.56
Chile	29	39	50	1.72
Colombia	25	160	256	10.24
Peru	16	79	92	5.75
Venezuela	24	248	516	21.50
Latin America	780	2,741	4,708	6.04

SOURCES: *Survey of Current Business, October–November 1972* and earlier numbers.

companies that had formerly supplied the market, which were to take over a growing proportion of production activities designed to bridge the the import gap. The new industries were thus largely under foreign control and closely tied to imports. The production units emerging in the process fit into two different complexes: the national complex in which each unit is located, and the economic complex centring on a parent company located abroad. This dual relationship must be kept in mind when considering the behaviour of the unit concerned. The board of directors, for instance, generally includes two types of person: (*a*) those characterised by their legal experience or social prestige and local connexions, recruited in the country of location of the operating unit; (*b*) those with effective control over technical and economic decisions, acting as delegates of the parent company and nearly always citizens of the country in which the parent company is located. Another significant aspect is the control of stock. Although the parent companies are in most cases public joint-stock companies whose shares are bought and sold on the Stock Exchange, the subsidiaries are nearly all private in the sense that 99 per cent of the voting stock is in the hands of the parent company's agents. Expansion is carried out primarily by mobilising local resources without this having any effect on the capital structure of the subsidiary enterprise. The control of key decisions by head office personnel and the fixed capital structure are both results of the concern to preserve the unity of the multinational economic complex controlled by the parent company whose economic rationale is based on the whole rather than on the parts. If a subsidiary operated through some form of joint capital venture, particularly with a group controlled by residents of the host country, the production unit's relations with other units in the same complex would have to follow the same lines as its relations with autonomous enterprises, otherwise the transfers of resources implicit in many transactions between enterprises belonging to the same complex could represent a loss for the parent company. If the rationale of the whole is also to be that of the parts, the latter must be homogeneous, that is, the parts must be integrated into the whole to the same degree.

The behaviour of United States manufacturing subsidiaries in Latin America reveals certain aspects of the new type of external dependence that tends to prevail in the region. Capital held by parent companies rose from 780 million dollars in 1950 to 14.7 billion in 1971, representing an annual growth rate of over 9 per cent. The bulk of this investment went to the three largest countries: Mexico, Brazil and Argentina.

Data show that participation by foreign groups in Latin America's recent development is far less a phenomenon of financial co-operation than one of control over productive activities by groups that had already been supplying the markets with exports. Since they controlled trademarks that had become familiar on the local markets and could more easily mobilise technical resources and domestic and foreign credit, these groups occupied privileged positions on the markets where there was a wave of import substitution. Moreover, foreign enterprises could nearly always count on the exceptional facilities extended by Latin American governments.[3] Several countries have given favourable foreign exchange treatment to enterprises undertaking to manufacture or assemble locally a growing proportion of the finished product, not only with regard to imports of equipment but also for imports of intermediate products or components for local assembly. In other words, the government is providing resources free of charge for the enterprise to establish itself in the country. Once established, undistributed profits, sinking funds and locally raised resources will enable it to press ahead with its expansion plans. During the initial stages the gap created by the shortage of imports in the preceding period provides an opportunity for excessively high profits. Once supply returns to normal, the market tends to be controlled by one or more financially powerful groups, nearly always linked to the international consortia that had traditionally controlled imports. Resources are mobilised abroad by raising loans that are in many cases guaranteed by the local government, which undertakes to provide exchange coverage for remittances of interest and amortisation payments. Finally, patent rights and technical assistance can be as important to the parent company as the dividends remitted to the home country.[4]

Extent of external control of Latin American industry

The quantitative data available are too limited to provide a precise idea of the relative importance of subsidiaries of foreign companies in the manufacturing sector of the Latin American economies. A study of the situation in Mexico at the beginning of the sixties[5] showed that of the

[3] Instruction No. 113, issued by the Brazilian Superintendency of Money and Credit in 1953, established a system which in practice involved discriminating against national companies in favour of foreign companies operating in the country, by granting the latter favourable exchange treatment for imports of equipment. This measure led a number of national companies to join foreign groups so as to have access to favourable exchange treatment.

[4] Between 1955 and 1968, the earnings of North American manufacturing subsidiaries in Latin America from patent rights and technical assistance represented 56 per cent of the profits remitted to parent companies. Cf. ECLA, *Economic Survey of Latin America, 1970*, vol. II, p. 103.

[5] Cf. José Luis Ceceña, *Los Monopolios en México*, Mexico, 1962.

100 major companies operating in the country, 56 were either totally controlled from abroad (39) or had a substantial share of foreign capital (17). Of the remainder, 24 were State-owned enterprises and 20 were private Mexican-owned enterprises. If we take into account the volume of sales invoiced, the participation of the public sector rises to 36 per cent in view of the relative importance of the petroleum sector, which is State-controlled. However, the participation of the national private sector falls to 13.5 per cent, a very marked difference. If the analysis is extended to the 400 largest enterprises, the participation of the foreign group rises to 54 per cent while that of the public sector falls to 25 per cent. Leaving aside the public sector, whose share in manufacturing is small, we find that 77 per cent of the sales invoiced by the 100 largest enterprises is accounted for by groups controlled from abroad. If we consider the 400 largest enterprises, foreign-controlled groups still account for as much as 70 per cent.

Data for 1970 based on the estimated social capital of the 290 largest manufacturing enterprises in Mexico show that foreign enterprises accounted for 45.4 per cent of the total, privately-owned national enterprises for 41.8 per cent and publicly-owned enterprises for 12.8 per cent. Foreign control is particularly striking in the production of non-electrical machinery (87 per cent), electrical machinery and equipment (82 per cent), rubber (80 per cent), transport equipment (70 per cent) and chemicals (57 per cent). In 1973, the participation of privately-owned national enterprises had declined to 38 per cent and that of the foreign-owned enterprises to 43 per cent, while the publicly-owned enterprises had increased their participation to 19 per cent.[6]

A study of the economic power structure, carried out in Brazil,[7] covers 276 consortia whose individual capital in 1962 amounted to one billion cruzeiros and over at 1962 prices. This study, which covered private enterprises only, divided the consortia into two categories. The first included groups with capital totalling 4 billion cruzeiros or more, and the second comprised all the other groups. Of the 55 consortia falling into the first category, 29 were foreign, 2 were mixed companies and 24 were national. A more detailed analysis of the data shows that of the groups with a total capital of 4–10 billion cruzeiros, 19 were national and 19 foreign (including one mixed company), and that of those with a

---

[6] cf. Fernando Fajnzylber and Trinidad Martinez Tarrago, *Las Empresas Transnacionales* (mimeograph), Mexico, 1975, p. 287.

[7] For an outline and analysis of the data on this survey, see the articles of Mauricio Vinhas de Queiroz, Luciano Martins, José Antonio Pessoa de Queiros and Vera Werneck, in *Revista do Instituto de Ciências Sociais*, Rio, Jan.–Dec. 1965.

total capital of over 10 billion cruzeiros, 5 were national and 13 foreign
(also including one mixed company). The 29 foreign groups controlled
234 firms, with an average capital of 1,300 million cruzeiros, while the
24 national groups controlled 506 firms with an average capital of 300
million cruzeiros. Of the 55 largest consortia, 39 operated in the
industrial sector, 23 being foreign. In the consumer durables and capital
goods sectors 26 were operating, of which 16 were foreign and 8 national.
A sample survey carried out among the smaller groups (each with a
total capital of between 1 and 4 billion cruzeiros) showed that of those
operating in the industrial sector 42 per cent were foreign, while more
than half the groups operating in the consumer durables and capital
goods sectors were controlled by foreign groups. An overall survey of
the 276 groups shows that more than half the capital invested in
Brazilian industry is held by foreign groups and that foreign control
increases as we move from the consumer non-durable goods industries
to the consumer durables and capital goods industries, which are precisely those undergoing the most rapid expansion. A survey carried out
in São Paulo[8] indirectly confirms this picture, revealing that the average
age of equipment in factories owned by national groups is considerably
greater than that of the equipment in factories belonging to foreign
groups. A more detailed analysis of the 55 largest Brazilian groups shows
that the majority of the so-called national groups are linked, in one
way or another, to the foreign groups. In fact only 9 of the 55 groups
had no shareholding connexion with foreign interests.[9] In most cases,
part of the capital of the Brazilian group's subsidiaries is held by foreign
groups, an association often unavoidable if the enterprise is to have
access to the 'knowhow' for certain production techniques. A study of
the 50 largest private enterprises, based on the value of their sales,
showed that 31 of these were foreign-owned. Of the 10 largest private
manufacturing enterprises, 9 were foreign, while the value of sales made
by the national enterprise was less than half the average value of the
sales of the foreign companies.[10]

In broad outline, the pattern typical of the region's most industrially
advanced countries is the following: on the one hand we find a group
consisting of a large number of national enterprises, of which the most
important were established in the first quarter of the present century,

[8] See José Carlos Pereira, *Estrutura e Expansão da Indústria em São Paulo*, São Paulo,
     1967.
[9] See the article by Mauricio Vinhas de Queiroz in *Revista do Instituto de Ciências Sociais*,
     Rio, Jan.–Dec. 1965.
[10] Cf. *Brasil em Exame*, September 1974.

in many instances before the First World War. Since these enterprises were established during the phase when the textile, food and building materials (including cement) industries were rapidly expanding, they continue to dominate these sectors. On the other hand, we find a smaller group of enterprises of larger than average size, nearly all established in the second quarter of the century, which are subsidiaries of organisations with headquarters in the major industrialised countries, primarily the United States. This group generally controls production activities that developed in the second phase of industrialisation, particularly the metal-using and engineering industries and the chemical and electrical goods industries. The pharmaceutical industry is in a class of its own. Having achieved considerable development in the first phase of the regional industrialisation process, when it was controlled by national groups, it changed considerably in the period that followed when local laboratories were displaced by competition from new products developed as a result of advances in chemical technology. In this case the industry, revolutionised by technological progress, has been taken over by consortia linked to the large-scale international chemical firms.

To complete the picture, it should be added that the Latin American enterprise is still largely a family concern. Not only is the capital still controlled by one family or by a small group of interrelated families, but management is also in the hands of members of these families, in some cases layered according to the hierarchy of generations within the family. Even where management is staffed by semi-professionals, no clear distinction is made between the ownership of an enterprise and its management. In these circumstances, control of the region's manufacturing activities is being competed for by two types of enterprise, corresponding to two stages in the evolution of capitalism: the family enterprise, in which capital ownership and administration are fused, managers being selected from a limited circle on the basis of kinship ties, family connexions and even age, and the completely institutionalised enterprise, with an independent board of directors, in a position to control shareholders' meetings and with managers selected on the basis of their professional qualifications.

The present situation is, of course, a transitory one. Certain lines of development can be foreseen or have already emerged. Some national groups may evolve towards institutionalisation, a move that could be hastened by State action, whether this takes the form of controlling the penetration of foreign groups or of providing financial support for national groups. National groups may join foreign groups, jeopardising their real autonomy. Foreign groups seek to ensure control over technical, commercial and financial decisions in the areas where they penetrate in order to safeguard the effectiveness of the supranational complex as a whole. Fusion with national groups tends to involve the transformation of locally recruited directors into public relations officers or their co-option onto the boards of the multinational enterprise. A third line of development, feasible only in the case of large undertakings, is the joint production venture, involving participation of the State and international groups. State participation, even when the government holds a minor share of stock, can have a decisive influence on the management of the enterprise. On the other hand, in certain cases the participation of international groups can take the form of service contracts. At the present time these lines of development overlap, the second, i.e. extension of the area controlled by foreign groups, tending on the whole to prevail. Consequently, just as traditional forms of dependence on the outside world were beginning to be overcome, new and more complex forms have emerged, raising problems that are central to the economic policy of the Latin American countries.

19 Towards the restructuring of the international economy

Traditional exports

In studying the long-term trends of the Latin American economies, the single most striking feature is the immutability of the region's export pattern. Apart from a few special cases, we find that despite the considerable changes that have taken place in the production structures of a number of countries, the region's capacity to import is still dependent on exports of a few primary products, which were already being exported before 1929. However, we have seen that the importance of primary products in the pattern of the world economy, and more particularly in the pattern of international trade, has been declining and will tend to decline still further. It is hardly surprising, therefore, that the region's share in world trade should be diminishing, as can be seen from Table 19.1.

The figures in Table 19.1 show that in the period 1948 to 1970, the value of Latin America's exports grew at a rate which was less than half that of the increase in the total value of world trade. The region's participation in world trade, which was 11 per cent in 1948, fell to 7 per cent in 1960 and 5 per cent in 1970, and in the latter year its share of the total was smaller than before the Second World War. In the group of underdeveloped countries, Latin America has also lost ground: the growth rate of the exports of underdeveloped countries taken as a whole was 5.3 per cent in the post-war period, representing a pace of growth 1.4 times more rapid than that of Latin America's exports. The main reason for the loss of ground, in this second case, is the significant expansion of petroleum production in other areas of the Third World. One need only mention that in 1960 Venezuela accounted for more than one-third of the world's petroleum trade, whereas in 1970, its share was less than 10 per cent. The general reason for Latin America's deteriorating trade position is, however, the changing structure of world trade, in which manufactured goods have become of growing importance.

TABLE 19.1 *World trade in the post-war period*

	Period	Developed capitalist countries	Socialist[a] countries	Under-developed countries	Latin America	World
Average annual growth rate of value of exports	1948–70	8.6	10.5	5.3	3.8	8.0
	1969–70	10.1	8.2	7.1	5.6	9.3
	1970–3	14.7	13.8	15.9	12.5	14.7
(a) Primary commodities	1960–70	7.0	9.2	6.1	5.0	6.3
(b) Manufactured products	1960–70	11.4	10.1	13.9	18.1	11.2
Share of region in world exports (per cent)	1938	65	10	25	7	100
	1948	63	6	30	11	100
	1960	67	12	21	7	100
	1970	72	11	17	5	100
Intra-regional trade as percentage of total regional exports	1948	64	44	29	9	—
	1960	70	72	22	8	—
	1970	77	61	19	11	—
Manufactures as percentage of total regional exports	1960	64	56	9	3	51
	1970	72	58	17	9	61
Manufactures as percentage of total world exports	1960	83.9	11.2	3.8	0.4	100
	1970	85.0	10.1	4.9	0.7	100

[a] Excluding Asian countries.

SOURCE: ECLA, *Economic Survey of Latin America, 1971*, Part I, Table 2; *Economic Survey of Latin America, 1973*, Part I, Table 2; and *América Latina y la Estrategia Internacional de Desarrollo, 1973*, Part II, Table 13.

The notable expansion of world trade in the post-war period is attributable mainly to the acceleration in the exchange of manufactured goods among industrialised countries. Econometric studies have shown that in these countries, the elasticity of demand for imports of manufactured goods, in relation to the growth of gross domestic product, is twice that of the demand for imports of raw materials.[1] Thus, the persistence of traditional production structures in Latin America means that the region must continue to lose ground in world trade. This explains why, despite the considerable increase in petroleum sales, the participation of the underdeveloped countries in the imports of developed countries had declined from 31 per cent in 1948 to 24 per cent in 1960 and 18 per cent in 1970.

The second important reason for the decline in Latin America's share of world trade was the deterioration in the region's terms of trade. The figures in Table 19.2 show that the region's terms of trade declined by 23 per cent between the first half of the 1950s and the second half of the

TABLE 19.2   *Latin America: terms of trade and purchasing power of exports (in millions of dollars)*

				Indices 1951–5 = 100	
	1951–5	1966–70	1973	1966–70	1973
Value of exports (annual average)					
(a) Current prices	7,672	12,360	25,925	161	388
(b) 1963 prices	6,131	11,422	14,077	186	229
Terms of trade (1963 = 100)	130	100		77	124
Purchasing power of exports					
(a) In real terms	7,971	11,422	14,077	143	177
(b) Based on terms of trade effective in 1951–55	7,971	14,848	14,753	186	185
(c) Loss sustained as a result of worsening terms of trade	–	– 3,426	– 676	–	–

SOURCE: ECLA, *Economic Survey of Latin America, 1971*, part I, Table 10.

[1] See UNCTAD, *Review of International Trade and Development, 1970*, p. 10.

TABLE 19.3 Latin America: Prices of principal commodity exports

	Average 1948–50		1960		1965		1970		1973	
	A	B	A	B	A	B	A	B	A	B
Sugar[a,c]	4.46	4.29	3.14	2.60	2.12	1.67	3.76	2.55	9.61	5.34
Cocoa[a]	28.8	28.3	26.8	22.2	16.9	13.3	32.3	21.9	61.1	33.0
Coffee[a]	36.5	35.0	36.6	30.4	44.7	35.2	54.6	37.0	66.5	36.9
Wheat[b]	78.5	75.0	61.4	50.9	59.5	46.8	54.7	37.0	137.8	76.5
Cotton[a]	44.4	42.6	26.3	21.8	26.2	20.6	26.6	18.0	51.9	28.8
Wool[a]	133.2	132.2	94.8	78.7	91.8	72.3	70.4	47.7	276.2[d]	153.4
Copper[b]	503	448	678	563	1,289	1,017	1,413	957	1,781	989
Petroleum[b,e]	2.11	2.03	2.12	1.76	1.89	1.49	1.85	1.25	2.26	2.37

[a] Cents per pound.
[b] Dollars per ton.
[c] Open market prices.
[d] Quotations for Australian wool type 64.
[e] Average prices for Venezuelan sales of crude petroleum and petroleum products.

A: Current prices.
B: Current prices deflated by US index of export prices.

SOURCE: ECLA, *Economic Survey of Latin America*, 1973, Part I, Statistical Appendix, Tables B, D, E, F, G, H, I, K.

1960s. The region's worsening position in world trade was due in equal measure to the slower growth of the physical volume of exports and the relative decline in export prices.

It should be noted that in the late sixties and early seventies, there was a change in the downward trend, due initially to the more dynamic performance of manufactured exports and later to the remarkable recovery in the relative prices of commodity exports. The figures in Table 19.1 indicate that the value of Latin American exports increased at a rate of 12.5 per cent a year between 1970 and 1973; if we take into account the improvement in the terms of trade, the rate of increase is 14.5 per cent, which is close to the average annual growth rate of world trade during the same period.

In the 1960s, Latin America's exports of manufactured goods grew at an annual rate of 18.1 per cent and their value increased from 269 to 1,428 million dollars. This expansion was more rapid than the growth of world trade in manufactured products and of manufactured exports by the underdeveloped countries as a group. The upward trend is particularly significant since it became more pronounced towards the end of the decade and continued into the early seventies. Between 1970 and 1973, the value of manufactured exports increased at the rate of 25 per cent; in the latter year, the total value of exports rose to 4,745 million dollars and their share in the export total continued to increase despite the relative improvement in primary commodity export prices during the period under consideration. Since Latin America's manufactured exports represent a negligible proportion of the world total (0.7 per cent in

TABLE 19.4 *Contribution of selected countries to total value of Latin American exports (%)*

	1960	1967	1973
Venezuela	30.1	23.6	18.3
Brazil	16.0	15.3	21.4
Argentina	13.7	13.9	11.4
Mexico	9.6	11.1	14.9
Chile	6.2	8.4	4.7
Peru	5.5	7.1	4.2
Colombia	5.9	4.7	5.1
Other countries	13.0	15.9	20.0

SOURCE: ECLA, *Economic Survey of Latin America, 1967 and 1973.*

1970) there can be no doubt that their rapid expansion in recent years is attributable to factors operating on the supply side. The multiple incentives offered by the more industrially advanced countries and even the policy of large enterprises interested in international integration of their operations, account for these changes in supply conditions.

The figures in Table 19.3 permit a closer analysis of the trend for a deterioration in the terms of trade. The table includes data on eight of the region's principal commodity exports, showing their nominal export prices and these same prices adjusted in relation to the United States index of export prices. Between 1948–50 and 1960, the real prices of seven of these eight commodities declined: by 49 per cent in the case of cotton, 40 per cent in the case of wool and 39 per cent in the case of sugar. The decline in real prices continued into the following decade in the case of six of the commodities listed, although for two of these commodities the 1970 prices were already higher than in 1965. There was a considerable increase in real prices between 1970 and 1973: in the case of wool, for instance, prices more than trebled while prices for sugar, wheat and petroleum practically doubled. Nevertheless, if we compare figures for 1973 with those for 1948–50, the increases are slight, except in the case of copper whose price was lower than in 1965 but double that obtaining in the base period. If we exclude copper, the increase in the real price of six of the remaining seven commodities averaged 12 per cent. In 1973, the real price of cotton was 33 per cent below that obtaining in 1948–50 but 60 per cent above the 1970 price. In sum, despite the considerable increase in nominal prices between 1970 and 1973, the terms of trade of the Latin American countries taken as a whole were 5 per cent lower in 1973 than in 1948–50. However, the recent recovery would appear to be merely temporary: in 1975 the nominal prices of most of the products listed had already declined significantly.

The eight products listed, together with iron ore, beef and fishmeal, accounted for 58.4 per cent of Latin America's exports in 1970; at the beginning of the sixties these products accounted for 60 per cent of the total. Only three of the eleven main primary commodity exports – copper, iron ore and fishmeal – increased their share in the total value of exports during the period under review.

Venezuelan *petroleum*, which accounted for more than half the world's oil exports in the immediate post-war period, has lost a substantial part of its share in the world market as a result of the rapidly increasing supplies of crude oils from the Middle East, North Africa and the Soviet Union. A variety of reasons, such as the remarkable average yield of

Middle Eastern oil wells, their greater proximity to Western Europe and Japan, the greater financial participation of importing European countries in the exploitation of African and Asian oil, helped to account for the decline in Venezuela's share of the world petroleum market, which was reduced to less than one-third by 1960 and to around one-tenth in 1970. To these factors must be added the restrictions on oil imports imposed by the United States, restrictions primarily affecting Venezuela whose sales to that country have remained stationary since the late 1950s. The combined action of these factors accounts for the fact that Venezuelan exports, whose volume had increased by 61 per cent in the 1950s, increased by only 25 per cent in the following decade. At the beginning of the 1970s, the Venezuelan government, in view of the rise in oil prices and the inadequate increase in reserves, placed limitations on production by establishing maximum output levels.

Coffee is exported by fifteen Latin American countries and is the major source of export earnings for a number of these. Whereas in the case of oil, consumption is rapidly increasing and supply is controlled by a small number of large consortia, coffee is dependent on a slow-growing demand (the annual increase in world consumption is estimated at 2.5 per cent) and a supply strongly affected by climatic factors. In the absence of stock control, coffee prices on the world market tend to fluctuate widely in accordance with current crop estimates, particularly in Brazil, which accounts for more than one-third of the world's exportable production. On the other hand, the efforts being made by certain Latin American countries – mainly Brazil and Colombia – to regulate supply, have provided an incentive to production in African countries, a development the more understandable in that these countries, given their relative backwardness, must avail themselves of all possible means of maximising their external payments capacity. Between 1948–52 and 1962–3, African production was multiplied 2.8 times whereas Latin American production increased only 12 per cent. In consequence, Latin America's share of the world coffee market declined from more than four-fifths in the early 1950s to two-thirds in the second half of the 1960s, when relative stability was achieved as a consequence of the International Coffee Agreement signed in 1962. This displacement of the Latin American product occurred not only in Western Europe – where the ex-French colonies have gained a privileged position from their associate membership of the Common Market – but also in the United States, where the soluble coffee industry has given preference to the lower-grade and lower-priced coffees (Robusta) produced in Africa. This situation confronted Brazil with a serious dilemma: whether to place its entire output on the market, provoking a drastic fall in prices which would harm not only its own interests but those of other producing countries, or whether to try to regulate supply, taking into account the slow growth of demand. The second solution involved financing the withholding of stocks and facilitating the progressive penetration of low-grade coffees for which there are highly favourable expansion opportunities in Africa. However, this solution was practically ruled out by the rapid growth of the soluble coffee industry since it would bring about the substitution of the Brazilian product by African Robustas. Brazil attempted to solve this problem by moving towards the establishment of a local industry manufacturing soluble coffee for export on the basis of low-grade green coffees withheld from the export market. The aim is to compete indirectly with low-grade African coffees on the markets of the importing countries. In 1972, during the renegotiation of the International Coffee Agreement, whose membership includes both producers and consumers, producing countries proposed an increase in the indicator prices which provide the basis for adjusting export quotas, to offset the effects of the devaluation of the dollar. The difficulties that arose led the producing countries to take unilateral action for the regulation of supply and the financing of stocks. In addition, the major exporting countries decided to form an international marketing company to free themselves from the pressures of the powerful groups in consuming countries which have traditionally controlled the marketing of coffee.

Apart from petroleum and coffee, which together accounted for 31 per cent of the region's exports in 1971, other products contribute a relatively small share to the total value of exports. The ten agricultural and livestock products ranking next in importance together account for less than one-fifth of the total while the six mineral products ranking below these increased their share from 9.3 per cent in 1961–5 to 13.3 per cent in 1970. With regard to the major temperate-zone commodities – wheat, meat and wool – the decline in the Latin American share of the world market is largely attributable to the reduction in Argentina's exportable surpluses brought about by the slow growth of output and the vigorous increase in domestic consumption. This downward trend became apparent in the 1950s and in the following decade the region failed to recover its former position. Between 1950 and 1960 the region's share in world exports fell from 16 per cent to 9 per cent in the case of wheat, from 27 per cent to 17 per cent in the case of meat and from 19 to 14 per cent in the case of wool. This trend continued into the 1960s, when the physical volume of exports of these three commodities was smaller than in the 1950s.

Cotton, exported mainly by Mexico, Brazil, the Central American countries, Colombia and Peru, has a special position on the world market because of the relative weight carried by exports to the United States. On the one hand, restrictions on US cotton shipments help to maintain prices at relatively stable levels; on the other, strong competition from synthetic fibres discourages any rise in prices above certain levels. Although the growth of demand is relatively slow, Latin American countries have managed to increase their share in world exports from 13 per cent in 1950 to 15 per cent in 1960 and to 20 per cent in 1970–3. The price rise of the early 1970s, after 20 years of depression, was in part due to the relative increase in the cost of synthetic fibres.

Cacao, exported primarily by Brazil, Ecuador and the Dominican Republic, stands out among the world's major agricultural commodities for the relatively intense growth of demand, which has increased at an average annual rate of 4.5 per cent over the last two decades. The region's share of world trade declined from a quarter to a fifth of the total in the 1960s. Like coffee, cocoa, as a commodity produced primarily for export by underdeveloped and hence financially vulnerable countries, is subject to sharp fluctuations in price in accordance with current crop estimates. In 1972, after 16 years of difficult negotiations, 43 exporting and importing countries signed an International Cocoa Agreement drawn up along the lines of the coffee agreement signed a decade earlier. The purpose of the agreement is to stabilise cocoa prices within a price range of 23 to 32 cents per lb. Export quotas were allocated on the basis of maximum production levels since 1964–5 and a buffer stock was established.

Sugar, which figures among the exports of all the countries in the region except Chile and Uruguay, provides a classic example of the enormous gap between the degree of organisation achieved in the local markets and the lack of organisation that still prevails in the world commodity market. Major importers such as the United States and the Soviet Union, who are also major producers, allow access to their own markets on the basis of quotas allocated to privileged clients, a trade carried on outside the world market. The open market, receiving only residual surpluses unable to penetrate preferential markets, is thus subject to sharp fluctuations, and prices tend to be well below those obtaining in the protected domestic markets. The elimination of Cuba from the preferential US market at the beginning of the sixties revealed the great elasticity of the sugar supply available in the Latin American countries as a whole. Thus, the drastic cut in Cuban sugar exports to the United States, which fell from 2.9 to 1.9 million tons between 1959 and 1960, was offset by an increase in the combined exports of Brazil, Mexico, Peru and the Dominican Republic, which rose from 1.9 to 2.9 million tons in the same period. Of this increase 90 per cent was sold on the United States market. Latin America's share in the world sugar trade rose from 43 per cent in 1950 to 49 per cent in the 1960s falling slightly in 1970 to 46 per cent. If we exclude Cuba, whose share of the region's exports was 66 per cent in 1970, Latin America's export sales in that year totalled 3,602 thousand tons. In the early seventies, there was a notable expansion in sales outside the United States market and the free market increased its share from 22 per cent to 53 per cent of the total. This expansion was due entirely to the increase in Brazilian exports, which grew from 1,130,000 to 2,638,000 tons between 1970 and 1972. Sugar sales in the free market were regulated by an agreement which remained in effect from 1969 to 1973. Its renewal encountered obstacles similar to those mentioned in the case of coffee.

Peruvian *fish products* represent the most notable innovation in Latin American exports in the post-war period. Accounting for more than a quarter of Peru's exports, they ranked among the region's ten major export items in the second half of the 1960s. The basis of the industry is provided by the large shoals of *anchoveta* found close to the Peruvian coast almost the whole year round, thanks to the cold waters of the Humboldt Current. Peru had traditionally exploited her *anchoveta* resources through the extraction of *guano*, depositied by the bird populations attracted by the extraordinary abundance of these fish. The fear that the bird migrations might cease was used for many years as an argument against exploiting the shoals directly. When the exceptional richness of these became known, however, a fisheries industry was established, its rapid development providing yet another instance of the speed with which a productive sector tends to grow in Latin America whenever demand conditions are favourable. The output of Peruvian fish-meal rose from 31,000 tons in 1960 to 1,120,000 tons in 1962 and in 1970 reached a peak at 2,253,400 tons, after a record catch of 12,277 thousand tons of *anchoveta*. This spectacular expansion, which has given Peru the leading position in world fisheries production, is accounted for by the simple techniques involved in *anchoveta* fishing: shoals, found close inshore, are encircled by nets, which are drawn tight at the bottom when the circle is complete so that the catch can be pumped aboard the fishing boat. 150 tons or more can be caught at one cast, generally enough to fill the hold. When the fish run freely a medium-sized boat can make two or more trips a day. Onshore, the *anchoveta* is pumped out of the boat and delivered to the plant, where the oil is extracted for use in margarine and other cooking fats and the residue is processed as fish meal, a product with a high protein content used in the preparation of feeding compounds for chickens and pigs. The relatively low cost of protein derived from Peruvian *anchoveta* assures the industry a firm place in the world market. Its expansion has been limited, however, by the availability of fish. The inshore shoals have begun to disappear and yields in the industry have started to decline, calling for greater capital invest-ments and leading to a concentration of enterprises, which has facilitated the penetration of foreign consortia. As in the case of so many other sectors connected with the region's exports, the boom phase of rapid expansion and easy profits has been followed by a phase of crisis and consolidation during which financially stronger foreign groups tend to take over control of the industry while at the same time raising its technical level. The phase of dramatic expansion came to an end in 1964, when Peru already provided 40 per cent of the world's fishmeal supplies.[2]

An abnormal winter in 1972 and the invasion of the warm 'El Niño' current, caused a disastrous decline in the *anchoveta* population: shoals fell from the 20 million tons of normal years to 4 million tons at the beginning of 1970. In order to protect the species, the Peruvian Govern-ment temporarily suspended fishing activities, with the result that the output of fishmeal fell to 4.4 million tons in 1972 and 1.8 million tons in 1973. In 1970, the Government established a State marketing board for fishmeal and fish oil, the Public Enterprise for the Marketing of Fish Meal and Fish Oil (EPCHAP) and in 1973 it set up a State fisheries enterprise – PESCAPERU – with a monopoly over all fishing activities and the fishing industry. This enterprise took over the assets of some 50 private enterprises expropriated in that year. Of the expropriated assets, 37 per cent were owned by foreign groups. In 1973, the fishing industry comprised 97 factories and 1,486 fishing boats and employed 27,000 people.

Mexican *tourism* also deserves mention as one of the few items making up the Latin American capacity to import that has shown a consistently upward-trend in the post-war period. Under this head we include not only the expenditure of tourists proper, i.e. visitors remaining in the country for more than 48 hours, but also the so-called 'frontier trade'. Actually, the latter can scarcely be considered an export since it is not subject to the restrictions imposed on exports to the United States. Re-ceipts accruing to Mexico under the head of tourism, in this broad sense,

[2] See Gerald Ellicot, 'The Fishing Industry of Peru', in Caludio Veliz (ed.), *Latin America and the Caribbean: A Handbook*.

rank after petroleum and coffee as a major factor in generating the region's capacity to import. Moreover, the relative importance of tourist income has been increasing steadily: in 1948–50 it accounted for 3 per cent of the value of Latin American exports; by 1965–7 this proportion had risen to 9 per cent. During this period, the dollar value of Mexican exports was multipled by 2.4 and that of receipts from tourism by 4. In 1967, tourist income totalled 959 million dollars, representing 83 per cent of the value of exports, as against 46 per cent in 1950–3 and 68 per cent in 1960–3. Earnings from tourism have not only grown much faster than Mexican exports but have also proved to be more stable since they are a function of the income available for consumption in the United States whose short-term fluctuations are far less pronounced than fluctuations in US imports, particularly of primary commodities whose price instability is all too well known. Finally, it should be pointed out that Mexico's share in the tourist expenditure of United States citizens showed an upward trend in the post-war period, accentuated by the elimination of Cuba from the tourist circuits and as a result of measures taken by the United States government to curb travel to Europe.

External financial commitments

Up to the early seventies, the capacity to import of the Latin American countries grew, on the whole, in response to the evolution of world demand for primary commodities. In the period between 1951–5 and 1973, the average annual growth rate of the import capacity of the region as a whole, was only 3 per cent, a rate equal to that of population increase. Moreover, the rapid increase in external financial commitments, placed an additional strain on the capacity to import. Thus, whereas in 1950–4, servicing of the external debt absorbed 7.2 per cent of the value of exports of goods and services, in 1965–9 this proportion had risen to 23.8 per cent. In the same period the servicing of private investment rose from 11.3 per cent to 13.2 per cent of the value of exports.[3] The situation tended to deteriorate in the latter half of the sixties as a result of the increase in interest rates in international capital markets. With the rise in the cost of money, the simple renegotiation of loans contracted earlier entailed an increase in financial liabilities. Even the most cautious projections of probable trends in the expansion of exports and new autonomous capital inflows indicate a worsening in the international payments situation. In view of the inadequacy of official financing and the unsatisfactory conditions frequently attached to official loans, the countries

[3] ECLA, *América Latina y la Estrategia Internacional de Desarrollo*, Part II, p. 189.

of the region began to resort increasingly to private loans. By the end of the 1960s, the latter already accounted for 50 per cent of the financial resources entering the region, as compared with 30 per cent for the underdeveloped countries as a whole.[4]

The picture outlined above – which leaves no doubt as to the fact that the region suffers from a growing inadequacy in its capacity to import, with serious repercussions on its development – has highlighted the need for an overall survey of the region's external trade problems.[5] Discussions centring on these problems took place in international organisations, particularly ECLA, making it possible to define certain long-term lines of policy which have provided guidelines for governments in the region in the effort, shared with other underdeveloped countries, to rebuild the international economy. The three United Nations conferences on Trade and Development – the first held in Geneva in 1964, the second in New Delhi in 1968 and the third in Santiago, Chile in 1972 – were largely a consequence of Latin America's realisation of the magnitude of the problem. The limited progress made at these conferences was not altogether unconnected with the fact that, in the other areas of the Third World, structural inadequacy of the capacity to import had not yet become as serious as in most of the Latin American countries.

Towards a global strategy

Significant and irreversible change in international economic relations – capable of bringing about a more equitable distribution of the benefits of technological progress between developed and underdeveloped countries and of creating conditions for accelerating the economic growth of the latter – can be achieved only through a determined and prolonged effort on a number of fronts. The measures most frequently proposed in Latin America relate to the following fronts:[6] (a) international commodity trade, (b) international trade in manufactures, (c) financial flows, (d) international transport, and (e) economic relations between underdeveloped countries. The latter aspect will be considered in the next chapter in the context of the pattern of regional integration.

[4] ECLA, *América Latina y la Estrategia Internacional de Desarrollo*, Part II, p. 189.
[5] For an overall survey of the problem see ECLA, *América Latina y la Política Comercial Internacional*, UN, 1967.
[6] For a formal exposition of the Latin American proposals concerning the reorganisation of the international economy see chiefly the two ECLA documents, *Latin America and the United Nations Conference on Trade and Development*, UN, 1964 and *Latin America and the Second Session of UNCTAD*, UN, 1968; see also, Raúl Prebisch, *Nueva Política Comercial para el Desarrollo*, Mexico, 1964.

Primary commodities are of overriding concern because they are practically the only source, and for some time to come will continue to be the major source, of the region's means of external payment. Given the lack of organisation of the commodity markets, the average annual rate of fluctuations in commodity prices is around 20 per cent which, with the tightness of money on the world markets, makes economic planning impractical. Moreover, in the absence of international regulation of supply, commodity prices are subject to a long-term decline entailing a transfer of income from the exporting countries to the importing countries, as past experience has shown. To deal with these problems, it has been suggested that the product-by-product approach should be adopted, taking into account the particular situation of each country. Some basic guidelines have been proposed:

(1) Setting ceilings on self-sufficiency in the developed countries. Since their domestic output enjoys stable and relatively high levels of prices, it is recommended that protective measures should be designed to guarantee a share of the markets of the developed countries for imports from countries of the Third World. For instance, in European Common Market countries there is already a high degree of self-sufficiency in certain products, e.g. 85 per cent in beef requirements, 66 per cent in the case of cereals (excluding wheat), 97 per cent in that of sugar. If coefficients of self-sufficiency were determined, medium-term forecasts could be made for import requirements which would increase as demand expanded. On the basis of an approximate medium-term forecast of demand, supply could be planned within the framework of an agreement between exporting countries.

(2) Free access to the markets of the developed countries for commodities not produced in the latter. With the elimination of customs duties, discriminatory internal rates and taxes and quantitative administrative restrictions, consumption would rise and substitutes would be discouraged. On the whole, since supply is inelastic in underdeveloped countries, tariffs tend to have a depressive effect on world prices, particularly when substitutes are available. The end result is a transfer of income from the underdeveloped producer country to the government of the developed importing country.

(3) International financing of stocks with a view to regulating commodity supply. This aspect is particularly important in the case of commodities subject to wide fluctuations as the result of climatic factors. The financing of stocks is a heavy financial burden, in many cases beyond the resources of the producer country. Moreover, price stabilisation also benefits consumer countries.

Commodity exports, even if substantially increased, cannot solve the problem of the external-sector bottleneck in the Latin American economies. Access to markets for *manufactured and semi-manufactured goods* is the second most important objective of the effort envisaged in the strategy under consideration. If the underdeveloped countries have lagged behind in the rapid expansion of world trade in the post-war period, this is precisely because their manufactured exports have continued to account for a negligible share of the total. Thus, whereas world trade in manufactured products increased in value by 124 billion dollars between 1960 and 1970, the manufactured exports of the Third World increased only 6.7 billion dollars and those of Latin America 1.2 billion dollars. With a view to changing this situation, a strategy has been devised, based on a *system of preferences* in favour of manufactures and semi-manufactures exported by underdeveloped countries. These preferences are to be (*a*) general, (*b*) non-reciprocal, and (*c*) non-discriminatory. Basically, the aim is to secure free access – elimination of tariff and non-tariff restrictions on imports – to the markets of the developed countries for manufactured and semi-manufactured goods exported by the underdeveloped countries. This would not, however, imply reciprocity. The concession mechanism could take various forms: a list of products to be included in the preferential system could be drawn up; or a list of exceptions could be prepared, or quotas could be allocated for certain products, fixing a ceiling for imports included in the preferential system. The justification for the preferential system is that the increase in exports of manufactures from underdeveloped countries to developed countries automatically entails the expansion of imports of other manufactures in the opposite direction. In fact, whereas any increase in the income of an underdeveloped country not in balance of payments difficulties entails a corresponding increase in the income of the developed countries, the converse does not hold. Moreover, since the new trade pattern would imply a transfer of resources in the developed countries from the traditional industries to those with the most advanced technology, the vanguard sectors would receive the greatest stimulus. This transfer of resources would require, of course, certain structural adjustments, but the transition could be planned and changes could be staggered over a period of time.

The problem of *international financing* is the third front for joint action. We have already mentioned the financing of commodity stocks. Together with this, *compensatory* or *supplementary financing* would be needed to help underdeveloped countries in balance of payments difficulties caused by sharp falls in export prices or a deterioration in the terms of trade. The aim of this type of financing is to prevent the internal propagation of external imbalances, since without this standby development planning becomes impossible. Finally there is the question of long-term financing for specific development projects. The present inadequacy of this type of financing leads underdeveloped countries to make use of high-cost bank credits entailing burdensome amortization conditions.

Lastly, the *shipping front* must be considered. The present organisation of world shipping discriminates against non-traditional products exported by underdeveloped countries, representing an obstacle to the opening up of new lines of trade which is often extremely difficult to overcome.

Many of the proposals included in the strategy outlined above, which was devised by UNCTAD, were put into effect in the late sixties and early seventies. Results have been unimpressive, however, and the progress made is admittedly inadequate. This is the case, for instance, of the *preferential system*, adopted by a large number of industrialised countries. On the other hand, international monetary instability has necessitated the revision of international commodity agreements. Finally, the new approach of the petroleum producing countries and the realisation that reserves of non-renewable resources are being gradually exhausted, have opened up new horizons for the underdeveloped countries and introduced a whole new set of problems. These developments are considered in the final chapter.

20 Integration process in Central America

Institutional framework

As we have seen in earlier chapters, the export of primary products was the starting-point for an initial industrialisation process in many Latin American countries. However, externally induced structural change was dependent on the parallel action of domestic factors such as the relative importance of wage payment flows, the degree of domestic control over export activity, fiscal policy, the existence of a significant volume of recent immigration of European origin, etc. Among such simultaneously acting factors probably none was quite so important as the *size* of the country, if we take this to mean, firstly, the relative population size and, secondly, the natural-resource base. Thus, in the case of the five Central American countries each with a population averaging just over one and a half million inhabitants in 1950, it can be said that the main cause of their relative backwardness was closely related to their small size.

The Central American isthmus, excluding the present territory of Panama – the latter was an integral part of the Viceroyalty of New Granada and remained a province of Colombia until 1903, when it seceded to become, with the help of the United States, the Republic of Panama – was governed in colonial times from the Captaincy of Guatemala and, when it broke away from Spain in 1821, was organised as a Federal Republic.[1] The federation succumbed to centrifugal forces unleashed during the Wars of Independence and broke up into five

---

[1] A year after the break with Spain, i.e. in 1822, the Central American region became part of Mexico. Its independence from the new metropolis was proclaimed a year later when it became first the United Central American Provinces and shortly afterwards the Central American Federation. The Federation fell prey to internal conflicts and was dissolved in 1838. An attempt to establish a Confederation a decade later also failed. In 1885 the Guatemalan dictator, J. R. Barrios, made an attempt, also ending in failure, to unify Central America by force, creating a Republic of Central America.

nation-states seventeen years later. The export economy, based mainly on bananas, coffee and cocoa, linked each of the five countries to the outside world, at first to England and soon afterwards to the United States, rather than to its neighbours. But awareness of past unity was kept alive in the region and it was natural that it should have been frequently thought that the solution of many of the problems of the present required the reconstitution, in some form, of the whole formed in the past. More recently, discussion of development problems allowed this idea to be shifted from the political sphere, where its realisation seemed so remote that it had become little more than a myth, to the economic level. However, it would be difficult to account for the rapid advance of the integration movement over a period of ten years without keeping in mind these historical roots. But, just when the integration process seemed to be reaching the point of no return, the armed conflict between El Salvador and Honduras in July, 1969, paralysed the integration agencies responsible for directing the programme at the highest level, and raised serious doubts as to the future of Central American integration.

The starting-point for the integration movement was a resolution adopted by the five Central American governments at the fourth session of ECLA held in Mexico City in 1951.[2] In this resolution the five governments, represented or advised by economists who had worked together in international agencies, expressed their interest in 'developing agricultural and industrial production and the transportation systems of their respective countries in a form which will promote the integration of their economies and the creation of larger markets through trade, the co-ordination of their development plans and the establishment of enterprises in which all or some of the countries have an interest'. This led to the creation in that same year of the Committee for Economic Co-operation in the Isthmus and the Organisation of Central American States (ODECA). From then on, the Central American integration movement was to advance along two mutually reinforcing fronts: the creation of institutions that could provide the process with continuity, and the progressive liberalisation of trade among the five countries. In the field of co-ordination of national development policies, however, little or no progress was made.

After 1951, a series of bilateral agreements establishing free trade in the specific items listed, were entered into by the following countries:

[2] See the ECLA study 'Contribución a la Política de Integración Económica de América Latina', in ECLA, *Hacia la Integración Acelerada de América Latina*, Mexico, 1966; see also ECLA, *Evolución de la Integración Económica en Centroamérica*, UN, 1966, and *EL Mercado Comun Centroamericano y sus Problemas Recientes*, 1971.

El Salvador–Nicaragua (1951); El Salvador–Guatemala (1951); Costa Rica–El Salvador (1953); Guatemala–Costa Rica (1955); Guatemala–Honduras (1956); El Salvador–Honduras (1957). The multilateral treaty on Central American Free Trade and Economic Integration was signed in 1958, consolidating the lists of duty-free goods established under the earlier agreements and paving the way for complete free trade. The Agreement on the System for Central American Integration Industries was signed at the same time as the General Treaty. This Agreement was the first major step towards the creation of a new productive structure and superseded the limited objective of establishing a free trade area. It provoked strong reactions, particularly from the US government, which held that its purpose was to create State-supported enterprises with exclusive rights to the market. In fact, the system aims to provide a guaranteed regional market for industries – designated 'integration industries' – that are of interest to a number of the Central American countries and require access to the whole, or to a large part of the Central American market for their expansion. The Central American Convention on the Equalisation of Import Tariffs was signed the following year, with a view to co-ordinating policies in this key sector in order to pave the way for a uniform external tariff. Finally, in 1960, the decisive step was taken of transforming the emerging free trade area into a genuine Economic Community. The preferential tariff system was replaced by a general provision establishing immediate free trade for 'all natural products originating in the territories of the contracting parties and goods manufactured therein'. The scope of the articles governing the circulation of goods was extended to include the movement of factors of production, guaranteeing 'the free circulation of persons, goods and capital between their territories ... with no restrictions other than those established by the national law's of the five countries. The new Treaty of Economic Association (later the General Treaty of Central American Integration) was initially signed by Guatemala, El Salvador and Honduras, shorty afterwards by Nicaragua and in 1962 by Costa Rica. In the latter year the five countries signed the Central American Convention on Fiscal Incentives to Industrial Development. Thus, in the course of a decade, the foundations had been laid for the structuring of an economic framework comprising the five national economies, establishing mobility of goods and factors within the union and a common external tariff vis-à-vis the outside world.

The movement was not limited, however, to the liberalisation of economic and financial flows between the five countries. It was accompanied by the creation of several different types of institution, all related to the idea of forming a unified economic space. Thus in 1954 the Central American Institute for Public Administration (ESAPAC) was established, with headquarters in Sao José, Costa Rica, and in the following year the Central American Institute for Industrial Research and Technology (ICAITI), located in Guatemala City. In 1960 the General Treaty gave rise to the Central American Bank for Economic Integration (CABEI), the Central American Economic Council (comprised of the Central American Ministers of Economy), the Executive Council and the Permanent Secretariat for Central American Economic Integration (SIECA). Other regional institutions created within the integration framework were the Monetary Council, composed of central bank directors and in 1967, the Central American School for Textile Training. Lastly, we must mention the concerted effort to improve regional transport and communication links: the construction of a road network was given top priority and a start made on the interconnexion of electricity networks.

Achievements and prospects

The practical achievements of the Central American integration effort, insofar as can be judged from the trade flows, were considerable. The value of intra-area trade, which totalled 33 million dollars in 1960, rose to 299 million in 1970, while its share of total exports rose from 7.6 to 27.3 per cent (see Table 20.1). This remarkable expansion did not affect

TABLE 20.1   *Central America: evolution of exports and intra-area trade (millions of dollars)*

	1960	1963	1965	1968	1970
Traditional exports:					
cotton	36.7	104.6	144.4	122.7	87.1
bananas	66.3	70.1	84.7	136.4	145.9
coffee	212.0	229.8	282.9	270.7	346.7
Total exports to outside world	397.3	524.0	636.2	693	797.1
Intra-area exports	32.7	66.2	136.0	258.3	299.4
Total	430.0	590.2	772.2	951.3	1096.5
% of intra-area exports in total	7.6	11.2	17.6	27.2	27.3

SOURCE: INTAL, *El Processo de Integración en América Latina, 1968–71*, Buenos Aires 1972, Tables 7.2 and 7.3.

traditional lines of export to countries outside the area, since these exports consist of a few commodities with a limited local market and are practically the same for all five countries. In fact, manufactured goods account for the bulk of intra-area trade: their share of the total increased from 45 to 79 per cent between 1960 and 1970. Nevertheless, a slackening in the growth of intra-area trade had become evident even before the 1969 conflict. In the first half of the 1960s its value was multiplied by 4.1; in the latter half by only 2.2.

Analysis of the macroeconomic data shows that the region experienced a marked acceleration of development in the period following the signing of the integration treaty. The growth rate of the domestic product, which averaged 4.5 per cent annually in the 1950s, rose to 5.6 per cent in the following decade (see Tables 20.2 and 20.3). At the same time there was a significant diversification of productive structures, with the indus-

TABLE 20.2 *Central American countries: evolution of GDP since 1950*

	GDP at factor cost[a] (1960)	Average annual growth rates of the gross domestic product (percentages)				
		1950–5	1955–60	1960–5	1965–9	1969–70
Guatemala	971	2.3	5.3	5.3	5.2	5.1
El Salvador	521	4.5	4.8	6.9	4.8	4.3
Honduras	342	2.0	4.7	4.7	6.0	4.0
Nicaragua	344	8.4	2.3	9.1	4.4	4.6
Costa Rica	404	8.3	6.0	6.6	7.1	7.5
Central America	2,584	4.3	4.8	6.2	5.4	5.1

[a] In millions of dollars.

SOURCE: ECLA, *El Mercado Comun Centroamericano y sus Problemas Recientes*, Santiago, 1971.

TABLE 20.3 *Central American countries: growth of GDP per capita*

	1960	1970	Annual rates of growth (percentages)
	(in 1960 dollars)		
Guatemala	257	330	2.5
El Salvador	270	336	2.2
Honduras	203	240	1.7
Nicaragua	250	356	3.6
Costa Rica	368	489	2.9
Central America	257	330	2.5

SOURCE: As for Table 20.1.

trial sector's share in the domestic product rising from 13.2 per cent in 1960 to 17.5 per cent in 1970.

By providing the small Latin American countries with a combined market of approximately the same size as that of Peru, and with a relatively high import coefficient – around 17 per cent in 1960 – the integration process created conditions for starting industrialisation along the same lines as the development experienced in earlier periods by all other countries of the region of similar economic dimensions. The annual growth of manufacturing output, which was 6 per cent between 1950–60, increased to 8.7 per cent between 1960 and 1970, while the share of 'traditional' industries in the value of production declined from 87 per cent in 1960 to 73 per cent in 1967.[3] However, the region's rapid overall growth in the 1960s, cannot be attributed solely to the integration process, since exports to the outside world also experienced a relatively vigorous expansion during this period, permitting a slight rise in the import coefficient even when intra-area trade is not taken into account. If integration was able to proceed fairly smoothly, this was apparently because the region's import capacity vis-à-vis the outside world continued to increase rapidly. The decline in exports to countries outside the area in the latter half of the 1960s had an adverse effect on the growth rate of the region's gross domestic product, which fell from an average of 6.2 per cent in the first half of the decade to 5.3 per cent in the latter half.[4] The experience of the late 1960s has shown that the integration process has failed to reduce the Central American economies' dependence on their traditional exports. A fall in cotton exports or a drop in coffee prices – as in 1967, for instance – had immediate repercussions on the public sector, with a consequent reduction in government-financed investments. Investments linked to integration were not sufficient to offset the depressive effect of the factors indicated. Taxes continued to be extremely low, the share of tax revenues in the regional gross domestic product having increased from 9.4 per cent in 1960 to 10.1 per cent in 1970. Thus, the possibility of compensatory action by the central governments, confronted with a decline in exports to outside countries, continues to be virtually nil, or to depend solely on external borrowing.

Central American industrialisation in the period under consideration is largely attributable to the growth of the traditional export sector and the enlargement of the market consequent upon integration. This enlargement has been based simultaneously on the customs union, the positive

---

[3] Cf. Instituto para la Integración de América Latina (INTAL), *El proceso de integración en América Latina, 1968–71*, Buenos Aires, 1972. Table 7.5.

[4] Cf. *El Mercado Comun Centroamericano y sus Problemas Recientes*, cit., p. 80.

measures taken to create a common infrastructure and the incentives offered to investment projects of regional interest. The process, then, is not one of straightforward import substitution consequent upon tensions in the export sector, which implies growth of the manufacturing sector accompanied by a decline in the import coefficient for industrial products. In some ways, Central American industrialisation is similar to the industrialisation that took place in Argentina and Brazil before 1929. It seems more complex on account of the larger number of enterprises involved and the greater support of the government, as well as the more marked presence of foreign capital and techniques. The degree of industrialisation achieved in the 1960s created the opportunity for the region to move to a second stage, which could have taken the form of the classic Latin American import-substitution model or be based on overall regional development planning. In either case, the region would have moved towards even greater integration of the decision centres on the monetary, foreign exchange and fiscal planes. Meanwhile, transition to this second stage has been interrupted by the 1969 conflict. However, the conflict may have frustrated rapid acceleration of import substitution on the classic Latin American model which, once initiated, has tended to aggravate inequalities between countries and between urban and rural areas. In countries such as Brazil and Mexico, for example, industrialisation based on import-substitution tended to bring about a concentration of income and increase regional disparities. The application of this model to Central America would necessarily create tensions among the five states, jeopardising the progress of the integration programme.

21 LAFTA and the Andean group

Montevideo treaty and its operation

The four southernmost Latin American countries – Argentina, Brazil, Chile and Uruguay – had traditionally carried on a relatively important reciprocal trade in primary products. The bulk of this trade was between Argentina and Brazil, consisting on the part of Argentina mainly of wheat, and on the part of Brazil of tropical products – coffee and cocoa – and timber, an exchange which generally resulted in an adverse balance for Brazil. During the Second World War, difficulties in securing external supplies boosted intra-regional trade. Argentina increased her imports from Brazil and stepped up her trade with other Latin American countries. After 1945, balance of payments difficulties led to an intensification of bilateralism, within the framework of which trade among the southern countries mentioned could continue to develop. In 1950, exchanges between these four countries accounted for 9.2 per cent of their total foreign trade and in 1953 for 12.2 per cent. From the mid-1950s, however, the effort made, under pressure from the International Monetary Fund, to promote trade liberalisation and extend tariff preferences on a multilateral basis, initially in Argentina and Chile and, later, in Brazil, led to a sharp decline in the reciprocal trade of these countries, a problem which caused increasing concern in the region. To some extent, bilateralism had performed the role of protectionism extended over a wider area and, given the characteristics of the national economies concerned, it could reasonably be held that its disappearance would entail a fall in the level of activity. In fact, since these countries could not afford to incur balance of payments deficits in their reciprocal trade if they were to avoid having to settle their accounts in convertible currency, and since short-term financing involved obtaining lines of credit in the major financial centres, serious payments problems arose within the area. This led the countries concerned to seek bilateral equilibrium at lower levels of trade than had prevailed when the trading pattern did not involve multilateral repercussions.

This unsatisfactory state of affairs induced the four countries most concerned – Argentina, Brazil, Chile and Uruguay – to enter into negotiations with a view to devising adequate payments arrangements and recovering their former levels of trade, if possible by creating a free trade area compatible with other international obligations. This movement, albeit modest in its objectives, was speedily reinforced by the line of ideas that had been crystallising within ECLA almost since the setting up of this body in 1948. In fact, in its report for 1949, written by Raúl Prebisch, ECLA had drawn attention to the intrinsic limitations of an industrialisation restricted to isolated national Latin American markets. At that time, the problem had already arisen for the Latin American countries that had advanced beyond the first stages of industrialisation. With each successive shift from light to heavy industry, from non-durable consumer goods industries to durable consumer goods industries and the beginnings of a machinery and equipment industry, the problem of the size of the market became increasingly important. From the mid-1950s, several studies on regional industrialisation and the location of basic industries, as well as explanatory analyses of the low rates of economic growth registered in Argentina and Chile, had highlighted the stumbling block that the small size of the national markets tended to place in the way of the industrialisation process. These views, repeated over and over again at meetings convened by ECLA and other international agencies concerned with the region, had no immediate practical outcome but they helped to create the psychological climate that led to the creation of a free trade area in 1960.[1]

The Treaty of Montevideo, establishing the Latin American Free Trade Association (LAFTA), was signed in February 1960 by the four countries already referred to and by Mexico, Perú and Paraguay. Colombia and Ecuador joined the Association in the following year and Venezuela and Bolivia have subsequently become members. Thus, by 1968, LAFTA encompassed all the South American countries and

---

[1] See the ECLA study, *Contribución a la Política de Integración Económica de América Latina*. Also, Instituto Interamericano de Estudios Jurídicos Internacionales, *Instrumentos Relativos a la Integración Económica en América Latina*, Washington, 1964. For an overall survey see also M. S. Wionczek and others, *Latin American Economic Integration*, Frederick A. Praeger, New York, 1966; Victor L. Urquidi, *Teoría, Realidad y Posibilidad de la ALALC en la Integración Económica Latinoamericana*, Mexico, 1966; José Maria Aragão, 'La Teoría Económica y el Proceso de Integración de América Latina', *Integración*, no. 2, Buenos Aires, 1968, and INTAL, *El Proceso de Integración en América Latina: 1968–71*, cit.

Mexico. The Montevideo Treaty is conceived in the spirit of GATT in two respects: in its objective, which is to liberalise trade within the area rather than to form a customs union, and in its operational procedures, which involve bilateral negotiations on a product-by-product basis and exclude the automatic and linear trade liberalisation schemes characterising the development of the European Free Trade Association and the European Economic Community. This is an important point, since it indicates that the Treaty is a response to the limited problems that have arisen in relation to trade among the southern countries rather than a major step towards the restructuring of economic relations between the countries of the region on a completely new basis.

The Treaty provides for two methods of achieving the liberalisation of trade within the area. The first consists of annual bilateral negotiations with respect to specific products, leading to the granting of concessions which should benefit all members of the Association. Such concessions must be equivalent each year to not less than 8 per cent of the weighted average duties applied by the country concerned to imports from third countries. A total of 3,246 concessions were agreed upon during the first round of negotiations and 4,397 during the second, but since the third annual round the number of additional concessions has been sharply reduced. Between the third and sixth rounds of negotation, the latter held in 1967, a total of 1,831 tariff concessions were made, and between 1968 and 1973, a further 1,572 new concessions were added. The concessions negotiated in these annual rounds form *national schedules*, listing all the tariff reductions granted by each individual country to the remaining members of the Association. However, these national schedules do not constitute a permanently binding obligation, a fact which accounts for the large number of concessions negotiated in the first few rounds. Countries reserve the right to withdraw any concession listed in the national schedule or to limit themselves to broadening the application of concessions granted earlier. The second method of achieving liberalisation consists of transferring items from the national schedules to a *common schedule*, negotiated every three years. The common schedule is irrevocable and products included in it were to be freely traded within the area by 1973.

Since concessions on items listed in the national schedules could later be withdrawn, they could only be of limited significance from the viewpoint of creating new economic activities. Because of this, particular importance was attached from the beginning to the common schedule, to be negotiated every three years and to constitute an additional 25 per cent of the value of the trade carried out among member countries at the end of each three-year period. The first list of products for the common schedule, negotiated in 1964, included 180 products corresponding to 25 per cent of the aggregate value of the trade among members of the Association in the period 1960–2. However, a detailed examination of this common list shows that it consists mainly of primary commodities traditionally traded in the region. The practical scope of this first stage of the common schedule is therefore negligible. The second list of products for the common schedule, drawn up in 1967, proved far more difficult to negotiate, since it was no longer relatively easy to reach agreement on a common list without including a significant number of industrial products or items such as petroleum, which posed particular trade problems. The lengthy and unsuccessful negotiations concerning the second common list, made it clear that the signatories to the Montevideo Treaty did not really have in mind any drastic changes in their traditional trading patterns. This seems to be particularly true in the case of Argentina and Brazil, whose mutual trade continues to constitute the bulk of intra-regional trade. In 1969, the Montevideo Treaty was amended to provide for a reduction in annual concessions, from 8 per cent to 2.9 per cent, and the postponement of the date for the establishment of a free trade area from 1973 to 1980.

In addition to the product-by-product negotiations, the Montevideo Treaty provides for sectoral or 'complementarity' agreements, designed to promote co-ordination at the production level. The idea was to facilitate industrial integration by enabling producers to divide complementary activities among themselves and so gain access to a larger market. In the absence of priority planning by the individual countries, sectoral agreements were left to the initiative of private groups, particularly international groups already operating in the region. Even so, very little progress has been made in this direction. In the first six years of the Treaty's existence, only four complementarity agreements were signed: on data-processing machines (Argentina, Chile and Uruguay), electronic valves (Argentina, Brazil, Mexico, Chile and Uruguay), domestic appliances (Brazil and Uruguay), and certain products of the electronics and electrical communications industries (Brazil and Uruguay). Products included in these agreements represent less than 0.5 per cent of the trade between LAFTA countries. In December 1967 the first complementarity agreement of some importance was signed by all LAFTA countries. It included 125 chemical products, intra-area trade in which amounted to 28 million dollars in that year. Up to 1973, twenty agreements had been signed, but the 'most favoured nation' clause had been deleted and concessions negotiated under these agreements are no longer placed on the common list.

Finally, the Treaty makes allowance for the special position of the relatively less advanced member countries – Bolivia, Ecuador and Paraguay. These countries have to grant only partial reciprocity for the concessions they obtain and may receive concessions that are not extended to the more developed LAFTA countries. Later, LAFTA recognised a difference, for the purpose of discrimination in the concessions made, between the three largest countries – Argentina, Brazil and Mexico – and the medium-sized countries, possessing markets of insufficient size. Uruguay, although one of the countries with the highest per capita income in the region, was included in the group of the less-developed countries on account of its special characteristics.

The practical achievements of LAFTA have been modest. The countries that had traditionally carried on a significant mutual trade recovered and even exceeded their former levels of trade. Other countries, such as Mexico and Colombia, whose intra-area trade had always been insignificant, achieved some export gains. Trade among the group of nine countries that originally formed the Association, i.e. excluding Venezuela and Bolivia, amounted to 635 million US dollars in 1965, as

TABLE 21.1 *Evolution of trade among LAFTA countries (value of exports (f.o.b.) in millions of dollars)*

	1953–5	1959–61	1965	1970
Argentina	205	133	247	366
Brazil	133	86	202	303
Colombia	3	5	20	53
Chile	59	35	56	152
Ecuador	9	7	13	17
Mexico	5	6	44	93
Paraguay	13	9	17	24
Peru	50	37	62	65
Uruguay	29	4	16	29
Total	508	321	671	1102

Note: LAFTA was established by the Montevideo Treaty in 1960. Venezuela joined the Association in 1966 and Bolivia in 1967. The value of Venezuelan and Bolivian exports to other LAFTA countries in 1970 totalled 137 and 20 million dollars respectively.

SOURCE: ECLA, *Elementos para Elaboración de una Política de Desarrollo con Integración para América Latina*, Santiago, 1969; INTAL, *El proceso de Integración en América Latina: 1968–71*, cit.

against 321 million in 1959–61 and 508 million in 1953–5. After 1965, however, trends in intra-area trade began to waver both for the traditional trading partners and for the countries that had entered this trade as a result of the stimulus provided by the Treaty, making it evident that the machinery established by LAFTA had failed to make a significant impact on the regional economies.

In the period 1961–8, intra-area exports increased at the annual rate of 9 per cent and total exports at the rate of 4.9 per cent. The share of intra-area exports in the total was 11.2 per cent in 1968, having practically doubled since 1961, when it was 6 per cent. In fact, however, this increase merely signified that the area's former levels of trade had been recovered, since the share of intra-area exports in the total had averaged 11.7 per cent in 1953–5. Despite the entry of other countries into intra-area trade, the latter level was surpassed only in the early 1970s. If we exclude Venezuela, whose exports consist almost entirely of petroleum, which has never been included in the lists of items for negotiation, it will be seen that Argentina and Brazil continue to account for more than 60 per cent of intra-area exports. In 1961, Argentina contributed 34 per cent of the total and Brazil 30 per cent; in 1972, their relative shares were 33 per cent and 28 per cent respectively. On the import side, however, these two countries accounted for a smaller percentage of the total: in 1972 Brazil's share was 26 per cent and that of Argentina 24 per cent.

New sub-regional orientation

A consequence of the meagre results produced by LAFTA was the attempt to find new avenues for development through the sub-regional approach. This movement was inspired largely by Chile, the country in the region whose limited domestic market most obviously constitutes an obstacle to the progress of the industrialisation process. Realising the problems posed by an integration process involving economies of such widely differing sizes as Brazil, Argentina and Mexico on the one hand and the remaining LAFTA countries on the other, the medium-sized countries sought closer co-operation in an attempt to promote integration at the sub-regional level. Since these countries – Chile, Peru, Colombia and Venezuela – are all linked by the Andean Cordillera, the new association became known as the Andean Group.[2] The designation became

---

[2] Venezuela participated in the preliminary discussions that led to the establishment of the Andean Group but did not sign the Cartagena Agreement, which became the basic instrument of the new sub-regional integration programme. The Agreement

fully justified after the accession of Ecuador and Bolivia. The declared aim of the group is simply to prepare for the integration of Latin America as a whole, but there can be no doubt that it has tended to achieve internal cohesion. The strategy underlying the structuring of the Andean Group is different from that governing the creation of LAFTA. Automatic and irrevocable liberalisation of trade is envisaged, particularly for products not produced in any of the Andean countries at present, simultaneously with harmonisation of tariffs applicable to imports from third countries. In other words, the creation of a customs union is planned. Even before agreements were formalised, the Corporación Andina de Fomento (Andean Development Corporation), with headquarters in Caracas, was set up with responsibility for 'expediting the regional integration process ... through the creation of production and service enterprises and the expansion, modernisation or adaption of existing enterprises'. The new institution, the first entirely Latin American multinational financial agency, gained in importance with the increase in the availability of Venezuelan funds after 1973.

Like the Central American Common Market, the Andean Group is starting from a situation in which trade among member countries is virtually non-existent. Nevertheless, a relatively developed transport infrastructure already exists, since all the Andean countries are interconnected through the shipping lines serving the region's traditional foreign trade. Steps were taken to co-ordinate regional shipping, and a joint air freight line commenced operations. On the other hand, in contrast with the Central American countries in the pre-integration period, the countries of the Andean Group – or, at any rate, the four largest countries in the Group, representing 84 per cent of the 66 million people living in the sub-region – are at a relatively advanced stage of an industrialisation process based on import substitution. However, since the national industrial systems have not yet reached the high degree of internal integration characterising the industries of the 'Big Three' LAFTA countries, there is likely to be less resistance to industrial complementarity between countries.

The integration policy of the Andean Group is based on the following plan of action: the achievement of automatic tariff disarmament; the establishment of a common external tariff for third countries; (these two objectives should be attained by the end of the 1970s); the implementation of co-ordinated planning; the development of a physical infra-

was signed in 1969 by Bolivia, Chile, Colombia, Ecuador and Peru. Venezuela's accession was formalised only in February, 1973, although it had participated from the outset in the Andean Development Corporation.

structure to facilitate integration; the undertaking of a joint financial effort in favour of the relatively less developed member countries; and the application of a common policy for the treatment of foreign capital. Special treatment is envisaged for Bolivia and Ecuador.

One of the most original and pioneering aspects of the Andean Group's integration policy is the common system for the treatment of foreign capital, provided for in Resolution 24 of the Commission of the Cartagena Agreement. This Resolution, which came into effect in July 1971,[3] stipulates the sectors in which participation of foreign capital will be allowed and establishes rules to ensure that all enterprises will be brought under national control within a given period. Thus, enterprises controlled by foreign groups will benefit from the advantages of integration only when they accept national control within the period stipulated in Resolution 24.

Prospects for integrationist movement

The creation of a regional common market is a declared aim of the economic policy pursued by all Latin American governments at the present time. This *idée-force*, which will undoubtedly play a key role in the region's development over the next few decades, has rapidly gained sway in the last few years largely as a reflexion of the realisation that small and isolated countries cannot cope with the growing problems raised by their underdevelopment. However, recent experience has already demonstrated the enormous complexity of the task ahead and the sterility of conventional blueprints for approaching the problem. Straightforward trade liberalisation schemes in the tradition of free trade areas, and even of customs unions, may be meaningful in particular situations, as in the case of the Central American countries, characterised by a similar degree of development and on the point of embarking on the first stage of industrialisation. But for countries already at a relatively advanced stage of industrialisation geared towards the achievement of self-sufficiency – the case of Argentina and Brazil – or countries whose degrees of development are vastly different, such schemes are of little value in themselves. In fact, by creating privileged conditions for international groups in a position to plan their expansion on a region-wide scale, these systems may lead to forms of 'integration' that ignore or tend to undermine the national decision centres. It is now regarded as more or less obvious that the real problem is not simply a matter of liberalising trade but of

---

[3] The complete text of the Resolution is published in *Derecho de la Integración*, Buenos Aires, April 1971.

promoting the progressive creation of a *regional economic system* – a far from easy task in view of the previous orientation of development, the wide discrepancies in present development levels, the risk of aggravating the geographical concentration both of economic activities and development gains, the considerable autonomy with which powerful international consortia controlling not only traditional export activities but also a large proportion of the modern manufacturing sector have hitherto operated in the region, the differences in national policies governing the exploration of natural resources, the ineffectiveness of the nation-states in controlling and orientating economic processes and many other no less important factors.

In sum, the problem is much less the creation of a unified economic framework by means of a progressive mobility of goods and factors of production – which would be feasible only if the national economies had attained a far greater degree of structural homogeneity and achieved similar levels of development – than the reorientation of development on the national plane towards a growing integration of the national economies into a coherent whole. Customs unions and free trade areas are a belated outcome of *laissez-faire* ideology, whereas the type of integration that could benefit the Latin American countries presupposes a considerable advance in planning at national level. The most important decision centres, those that are of a political nature and able to interpret the aspirations of collective groups, will continue to exist on the national plane for a long time to come. It is to be hoped, however, that economic 'integration', at present no more than a development policy instrument of the national governments, will set in motion an evolutionary process involving political structures, a development corresponding to the urgent changes called for in international relations. The need for a more realistic definition of their relations with the great power blocs of the present-day world, particularly with the United States, has led Latin Americans to attach greater value to what they have in common and to move towards the framing of a regional project that will condition socio-political evolution on the national plane in an increasingly perceptible form. To overcome the natural misgivings of countries with a long history of external dependence, this evolution will require a clear definition of development objectives at national level. On the basis of these national objectives, it will be possible to identify those sectors of activity in which there would be undeniable integration benefits from economies of scale, advantages of location or conglomeration phenomena of various orders, that could be shared among all the parties concerned. It is therefore likely that until economic planning becomes an effective policy instrument at national level, the so-called 'integration' movement will continue to make slow progress and disappointments in this field will be frequent.[4]

[4] A vigorous defence of the integration thesis can be found in the proposals to Latin American presidents put forward, in response to a letter from President Frei of Chile, by four former directors of international agencies operating in the region: José Antonio Mayobré (ECLA), Felipe Herrera (IDB), Carlos Sanz de Santamaría (Alliance for Progress) and Raúl Prebisch (Latin American Institute for Economic and Social Planning). This document is included in ECLA, *Hacia la Integración Acelerada de América Latina*. For a different approach to the problem see C. Furtado, *Um Projeto para o Brasil*.

VIII. STRUCTURAL RECONSTRUCTION POLICIES

22 Economic planning experiments

Methodological basis

External vulnerability, a reflexion of fluctuations in the prices of primary commodities on the world market, led several Latin American governments to assume growing responsibilities on the economic plane even before the 1929 crisis. We have seen how the need to regulate coffee supplies obliged the Brazilian government to undertake heavy financial commitments, with far-reaching repercussions on the monetary and fiscal planes, and how these commitments took the form of a compensatory policy in the 1930s, with profound consequences for the subsequent evolution of the national economy. We have also drawn attention to the complex exchange controls practised by Argentina during the decade of the Great Depression in order to cushion the domestic impact of external instability and pointed out the positive form taken by the Chilean reaction during the same period: a greater appropriation of resources generated by the export sector (controlled by foreign groups) and their allocation to strategic sectors, through a state agency specifically established for this purpose, with a view to diversifying productive structures.

By and large, the period extending from the end of the 1929 crisis to the end of the Second World War is characterised by development geared to the national domestic markets which Prebisch would call 'development inwards' as opposed to the 'development outwards' of the preceding period, based on growing participation in the system of international division of labour. After a time, this new development pattern raised the immediate problem of remodelling and broadening infrastructures. Not only was it necessary, in most cases, to rebuild existing transport systems on a completely different basis, but there was also an urgent need to increase the available supply of electric energy. These needs arose at a time when traditional forms of international financial co-operation had practically disappeared. In some countries, such as Argentina and Brazil, governments had to buy foreign-owned railroads and other infra-structural installations, in many cases rendered obsolete by the failure to replace outworn equipment after 1929 and by the reorientation of development.

The need to rebuild and broaden economic infrastructures and the determination to exercise some control over the external sector prompted the first economic programming experiments in the immediate post-war period. These were essentially public works programmes and financing schemes in the transport and electric energy sectors. Domestic financing was obtained, as a rule, by means of taxes on liquid fuel consumption and surcharges on electric energy tariffs. Since the investments to be under-taken required a substantial margin of foreign exchange cover, particu-larly in the case of the energy sector, the problem of their medium-term impact on the balance of payments had to be met. Assessment of the likely impact called for a projection of the capacity to import and of the margin available to meet service payments on the new financial commit-ments involved. At the same time the new credit agencies, particularly the World Bank, began to insist on such prospective analyses, which generally highlighted the severe limitations imposed by the capacity to import on the development prospects of the countries in the region. Theoretical consideration of the problem made it possible to gain a clear-er insight into the nature of the development process taking place in the region, and particularly of the role played by import substitution.

From 1949 onwards, ECLA's overall surveys of regional development laid the groundwork for a better understanding of the nature of external dependence, reflected in the long-term deterioration in the terms of trade, and of the specific characteristics of industrialisation based on import substitution. As a result of these analyses it was no longer possible to accept a working hypothesis based on the possibility of reverting to a situation in which exports of primary products would act as the main driving force in regional development. On the other hand, it became obvious that any attempt to increase the volume of investments would have adverse effects on the balance of payments since capital formation had a high import content and the consumer goods for which demand was most elastic to rises in income were generally imported. If develop-ment at that stage called for a curtailment of the import coefficient, it had to be taken into account that this could not be spontaneously achieved in an orderly way. Hence, the regulation of import substitution clearly required a prospective analysis of the overall development process.

ECLA's ideas on economic programming consequently sprang from a concern to regulate the import-substitution process, which had been the basis of industrialisation and development in the region's largest countries since the external sector crisis.[1] This constituted an entirely new approach in the evolution of ideas on economic planning, since it differed not only from socialist planning – an outcome of the determination to change the overall economic structure and the need to co-ordinate investment decisions in a system involving greatly diminished consumer freedom – but also from planning in Western Europe, for which the starting point was the concern to co-ordinate sectoral programmes or to achieve conditions of full employment for labour.

The methodology worked out by ECLA and later widely adopted in the region, is based on a diagnosis of the national economy in question and on a set of macroeconomic projections established essentially on the basis of hypotheses concerning the evolution of the capital–output ratio and the income elasticities of demand for final products. Recognising that, given its relative *scarcity*, capital is the strategic factor in the development of the region's economies, an attempt is made to measure its productivity in the national economy as a whole and in the different sectors of productive activity.[2] On the basis of the capital–output data and the analysis of inter-industrial relationships, a system of projections can be worked out that makes it possible to forecast the structural inadequacy of the capacity to import, the rate of private domestic savings or of fiscal

[1] The first ECLA study to consider the planning problem explicitly was the essay entitled *Theoretical and Practical Problems of Economic Growth*, presented to the ECLA conference held in May 1951. The last chapter is entitled 'Preliminary discussion on the elements of an economic development programme'. However, this study does not touch on the methodological aspects of programming technique. These were expounded in detail in a study presented to the 1953 Conference entitled *An Introduction to the Technique of Programming*. The full version was circulated only in mimeographed form but a condensed version was published in 1955 as the first volume of a series entitled, *Analyses and Projections of Economic Development*. With the establishment of the ECLA-sponsored Latin American Institute for Economic and Social Planning (ILPES) in 1962, a more systematic study of planning and the publication of a number of works reflecting the theoretical orientation discussed above became possible. See ILPES, *Discusiones sobre Planificación*, Mexico, 1966, Gonzalo Martner, *Planificación y Presupuesto por Programas*, Mexico, 1967, Hector Soza Valderrama, *Planificación del Desarrollo Industrial*, Mexico, 1966. The last two works are based on study courses given at the Institute. For an overall assessment of ECLA ideas see the study prepared by the Technical Secretariat, *La CEPAL y el Análisis del Desarrollo Latinoamericano*, UN, 1968.

[2] The basic hypothesis does not exclude the recognition that skilled manpower, including trained managerial personnel, is an equally scarce factor. It is held, however, that the improvement of the human factor can be achieved only through investment and is thus also dependent on the availability of capital.

revenue in terms of various hypotheses as to the probable growth of the domestic product, the increase in the demand for exports and probable trends in relative export prices as well as in terms of the estimated income elasticities of demand for the major items of consumption. In other words, the technique involves a prospective analysis that makes it possible to define the conditions of internal and external balance, given certain development targets.

Degree of efficacy of the projections

The analyses carried out on the basis of ECLA's programming techniques made it clear, in the mid-1950s, that it was necessary to intensify the industrialisation process in countries such as Brazil and Argentina if their development was to proceed at a reasonable rate. The *Target Programme* carried out in Brazil in the second half of the 1950s was directly inspired by this type of diagnosis.[3] The implementation of this programme enabled Brazil to substantially broaden its industrial system at a time when the export sector was registering adverse trends. The experience also served to expose the serious problems that arise when medium-term programmes are carried out without any effective co-ordination of short-term policies. Aggravation of inflationary pressures and a sizeable external debt were the counterparts of the considerable success achieved in meeting the physical targets set for the industrial sector.

In 1961, through the Charter of Punta del Este,[4] Latin American governments recognised that planning was the fundamental instrument for carrying out the development policy to be pursued in the region. Most countries in the region were experiencing serious balance of payments difficulties at the time, and the mobilisation of external resources was becoming increasingly difficult. Planning was regarded as a means of regulating government action and of giving concrete expression to the

[3] In working out the *Target Programme*, extensive use was made of preliminary studies carried out by an ECLA mission working with the Brazilian National Development Bank, published in 1955 under the title, *Análise e Projeções da Economia Brasileira* and later issued as volume II of the ECLA series, *Analyses and Projections of Economic Development*.

[4] At the Punta del Este conference, which launched the Alliance for Progress – a policy conceived by President Kennedy with a view to creating a climate of better understanding and more effective co-operation between the United States and the Latin American countries – the countries of the region formally declared that within a period of eighteen months they would undertake planned economic policies covering some basic reforms, including tax and agrarian reforms.

need for certain reforms, particularly of the tax system, considered essential to development in view of the growing responsibilities assumed by governments. The plans prepared since then consist of a general diagnosis, a relatively detailed prospective study of the external sector, a set of projections in the form of overall and sectoral targets, a vague statement of the particular social policy goals and an assessment, generally none too precise, of the structural changes required if the targets are to be achieved without causing undue economic imbalances and social tensions. However, the plans establish detailed requirements at the operational level only with regard to public investment schemes and the need to mobilise external resources. In these two sectors there has been a remarkable advance in the formulation of government policies. In the case of public investment, for instance, not only has it been possible to ensure greater compatibility with regard to longer-term objectives, but considerable progress has been made in the techniques of preparing individual projects and controlling financial flows at the implementation stage. From the data given in Table 22.1, the targets established in a number of plans can be compared with the actual economic trends in the countries concerned.

With the exception of Mexico, in the countries included in the Table referred to, exports failed to grow at the target rate established by the planners. Similarly – and Mexico is again the exception – agricultural output grew less than forecast; generally speaking, these two sectors act

TABLE 22.1 *Target (development plan) rates and actual rates of growth in selected countries (percentages of annual growth rates)*

	GDP	Agri-culture	Industry	Imports	Invest-ment	Exports
Columbia						
Plan (1959–64)	5.7	4.1	8.6	7.2	12.9	4.2
Actual rates (1959–64)	4.7	2.2	6.1	10.3	5.4	2.3
Chile						
Plan (1960–5)	4.8	3.7	5.0	6.6	12.0	5.5
Actual rates (1960–5)	4.1	2.0	6.2	7.0	10.1	4.6
Mexico						
Plan (1962–5)	5.4	4.5	6.9	8.8	8.6	4.8
Actual rates (1962–5)	7.3	4.4	10.1	9.3	12.4	5.4
Venezuela						
Plan (1963–6)	7.6	7.9	12.0	2.2	–	4.6
Actual rates (1963–6)	6.0	6.9	9.0	1.7	8.8	1.7

SOURCE: ECLA, *Economic Bulletin for Latin America, October, 1967.*

as independent variables and planners confine themselves to *forecasting* their probable behaviour. In the case of exports, this is because of the uncertainty governing world trade in primary products, particularly when a country is dependent on exports of a few primary commodities, and in the case of the agricultural sector it is because of the rigidity characterising agricultural production in the region which makes it insensitive to the policy instruments used by Latin American governments. In Colombia and Chile, total investment was lower than envisaged, whereas imports expanded more than planners had considered desirable.

Even a cursory examination of the data shows that planning possibilities are greatest when export earnings are most stable and hence easier to forecast. This was the case of Mexico, largely as a result of the growth of tourism and the diversity of Mexican exports. In the case of Venezuela, the relative stability of petroleum prices meant that the flow of income and the capacity to import generated by the petroleum sector were relatively easy to forecast. The failure to meet planning targets indicates the inadequacy of the data available at the time on the policy of the oil companies. In most countries of the region, however, only a substantial progress in organisation of world markets would make it possible to establish reasonable projections for the export sector. In the absence of a minimum of reliability in such projections, or of adequate international arrangements for compensatory financing, planning possibilities, in the framework of the techniques currently employed, will be seriously limited. These limitations will be added to those imposed by the rigidity of the agricultural sector.

The planning experience of the post-war years tested the capacity of the region's governments as agents for regulating economic processes and promoting development. Noteworthy progress was made in the rationalisation of public investment, both through the systematic introduction of medium- and long-term projections and through the use of budget programmes. There was also definite progress in orientation of private industrial investment. The establishment of development banks or similar institutions and the enactment of complex legislation creating development incentives provided governments with the means of influencing private investment decisions or bridging the investment gap, at least in the case of sectors considered strategic for the attainment of the targets established in the plans. Nonetheless, progress in the direction of really effective planning was slow, despite such initial successes as the Brazilian Target Programme and the more rational allocation of public investment in various countries. This slow progress is attributable to three main factors: (*a*) short-term fluctuations in the external sector and the difficulties encountered in increasing the capacity to import, (b) the rigidity of the agricultural sector and (c) the inadequacy of the public sector's mobilisation of resources. We have already referred to the first of these factors, and the second will be considered in greater detail in the next chapter.

Inelasticity of the fiscal sector

As Latin American countries assumed greater responsibility on the economic plane, the need to augment resources channelled through the public sector, whether by increasing tax revenue or by borrowing, became particularly urgent. The adoption of development plans almost necessarily implies a greater effort in the formation of capital, i.e. a rise in the rate of investment, and a more than proportional growth of investments which aim to change the productive structure and have long maturation periods.

The data in Table 22.2 show that in the region as a whole, as well as in the seven economically most important countries, there was an increase in the tax burden, which rose from 14.4 to 17.2 per cent in the course of the 1960s. In Argentina, Mexico and Venezuela, however, this increase was insignificant. In Argentina, the tax burden represented 15 per cent of the gross domestic product in 1969–70, a level below the Latin American average, although the country's per capita income had increased, during the sixties, to more than double the regional average. In Venezuela, whose per capita income in 1969–70 was also double the regional average, the level of taxation in that year was 19.3 per cent, slightly above the regional average of 17.2 per cent. However, if we exclude revenue derived from the exploitation of petroleum, a non-renewable resource, the Venezuelan tax burden was only 4.3 per cent, which is a quarter of the Latin American average. The tax burden in Mexico remained practically unchanged in the 1960s, increasing the dependence of public expenditures on other sources of financing from 46 to 54 per cent in that period. All the capital expenditures and one-third of the current expenditures of the Mexican Government were financed from non-tax resources, mostly domestic and external credits. In Argentina and Chile, too, tax revenues were insufficient to cover current Government expenditures, a situation paralleled in the region as a whole, both at the beginning and end of the decade under review.

To sum up, in Latin America as a whole, and in most of the countries of the region individually, the tax system failed to provide the resources needed to cover the operational costs of government. In the period under

TABLE 22.2 *Indicators of the evolution of public expenditure and taxation*

	Total expenditure/ GDP[a]	Public investment/ GDP	Public investment/ total investment	Tax burden[b]
Argentina				
1960–1	21.4	5.3	24.5	14.2
1969–70	25.2	7.9	40.7	15.0
Brazil				
1960–1	25.3	6.7	39.2	20.1
1969–70	33.3	9.0	52.0	27.0
Colombia				
1960–1	11.2	3.4	16.7	10.4
1969–70	17.3	6.7	34.4	13.4
Chile				
1960–1	29.3	6.8	38.0	16.5
1969–70	34.6	9.0	55.9	21.8
Mexico				
1960–1	16.7	5.7	34.3	9.1
1969–70	21.9	6.8	34.7	10.1
Peru				
1960–1	15.9	3.0	16.6	13.7
1969–70	18.9	3.6	21.2	17.0
Venezuela				
1960–1	22.2	6.7	39.0	18.3
1969–70	24.7	6.7	34.9	19.3
Latin America				
1960–1	20.7	5.6	29.1	14.4
1969–70	25.7	7.3	36.3	17.2

[a] Total expenditure includes current government expenditures and public gross fixed capital investment; GDP at market prices.
[b] Tax revenue as a percentage of GDP at market prices; the data refer to 1960 and 1970.
SOURCE: ECLA, *América Latina y la Estratégia Internacional de Desarrollo: Primèra Evaluación Regional*, Santiago, 1973, Part I, p. 192.

consideration, this inadequacy of the fiscal system worsened, a situation attributable essentially to the regressive nature of the tax burden. In five of the eleven countries included in Table 22.3, indirect taxes increased their share of tax revenues between 1960 and 1970. This dependence on indirect taxation, in economies with highly concentrated income patterns, is reflected in the inelasticity of the fiscal systems. We have already mentioned this rigidity as one of the structural focuses of inflationary pressures. It is also one of the main causes of the tendency to external indebtedness and the slow progress made in the regulation of investments.

TABLE 22.3 *Indicators of the evolution of the tax structure (percentages of total revenue)*

	Direct taxes	Indirect taxes	Taxes on foreign trade
Argentina			
1960	30.6	40.5	28.9
1970	31.6	52.1	16.2
Brazil			
1960	32.2	56.7	11.1
1970	28.5	64.8	6.7
Colombia			
1960	37.3	38.9	23.8
1970	35.2	46.6	18.2
Chile			
1960	22.4	43.3	34.4
1970	23.9	45.8	30.4
Mexico			
1960	37.6	34.5	27.8
1970	51.1	35.7	13.2
Peru			
1960	21.4	43.2	35.4
1970	27.3	42.3	30.4
Venezuela			
1960	10.0	8.2	81.8
1970	14.2	8.2	77.6

SOURCE: As for Table 22.2, p. 206.

23 Agrarian reforms

Roots of the agrarian movements

The economic planning experiments carried out in the Latin American countries, despite their modest aims, served to pinpoint the major obstacles hampering the region's development. By establishing targets and identifying the agents on whose decisions their attainment depended, the development planners initiated discussion of the motives guiding these agents and the means that would have to be mobilised in order to intervene in the behaviour of the policy-makers. It soon became apparent that projecting the expansion of an economic system simply by means of extrapolating rates of growth was limited in scope, and that planning based on the traditional behaviour patterns of the agents involved could not guarantee the attainment of even modest targets. What we needed was a study in depth of the structural elements delimiting the range of options open to the decision-making agents so that the factors hindering the development process could be properly identified. Thus the framework of analysis was imperceptibly broadened as the relevant agents were gradually more clearly identified and observed in their own context. Greater knowledge of the real structures was gradually built up and in many cases this involved going beyond the conventional framework of economic analysis.

The structuralist approach to the development process tended to stress the importance of agrarian problems which, until quite recently, had earned scant attention from economists whose interest had been focused on the study of industrialisation. On the basis of the classical European experience, it had been implicitly held that the expansion of the industrial sector would bring about changes in the traditional structures. But as obstacles to industrialisation increased and the industrialisation process proved itself less effective than expected as a factor for inducing structural change, a completely new approach began to emerge. Field studies of existing agrarian structures, such as those mentioned in chapter 7, were carried out in several countries and at the same time there was a more systematic analysis of the historical evolution of the land system and of recent changes in agrarian structure. The major agrarian reforms, as the most relevant attempts to change economic and social structures in the region, were studied with particular interest and as a result of these investigations, there was a clearer understanding of the relationship between production systems and sociopolitical organisation.

The basic unit of the present-day organisation of agricultural production in Latin America is the large landed estate: the *hacienda*, in the strict sense,[1] originally devoted to stock farming or agricultural production for local consumption, or the *plantation*, originally devoted to production for export. As we have already seen, the large estate reflected a decentralisation of the power system: the estate owner had the means needed to organise the population in a production system capable of yielding a surplus for local use or for export. The *hacienda* was not, however, established in a vacuum. In the most important regions of Spanish America – Mexico and the Andean Highlands – there was a dense indigenous population, living in sedentary communities and with a social organisation closely bound up with the communal use of land. In their attempt to preserve their identity, these *communities* clung to traditional forms of land use. During the colonial period the Spaniards, being limited in numbers, preferred to strengthen the communities in order to extract from them a surplus in the form of crops or labour. Spanish legislation and the action of the Religious Orders were directed to this end. In regions where there was a less dense population or where social structures were less bound up with the pattern of land utilisation, the communities tended to disappear and their surviving members were either absorbed by the *haciendas*, or began to live in isolation on the outskirts of the estates or of the administrative centres established by civil or religious metropolitan authorities.

In regions where agriculture was geared to the export market from the very beginning, the *hacienda* took the form of a commercial enterprise, frequently employing slave labour imported from Africa, as in the

---

[1] The term *hacienda* (or *fazenda* in Brazil) was originally applied to properties devoted to stock farming. In Brazil, *fazenda* tended to become widely used in a more general sense. In the Spanish-speaking countries, several terms are used to designate the large estate. The term 'plantation', in the sense of a large agricultural estate, is not used in Latin America. The terms *hacienda*, *latifundio* or *large estate* will here be used to refer generally to any large agricultural property with the dual connotation of a production unit and a type of social organisation.

case of Brazil and most of the Caribbean region. Given its greater capital requirements and its dependence on unstable foreign markets, the agricultural enterprise underwent prolonged periods of crisis and in some cases disintegrated into a number of small productive units devoted primarily to subsistence activities. In any event, wherever agricultural enterprises or plantations were set up, isolated farmers or smallholders moved in, either because the highly specialised commercial enterprise created a local market for farm products or was not in a position to absorb the natural increase in the free labour force it employed, or because in times of financial difficulty it laid off some of the labour it had attracted. Thus the smallholder – the starting-point for the future mass of *minifundistas* – had two different origins in the region: on the one hand there was the element composed of former members of indigenous communities that had broken up, who began to cultivate tiny individual plots of land for their own subsistence needs while at the same time spending the better part of the day working on the large estate; on the other, there was the element indirectly created by large-scale commercial agriculture both in its phase of expansion and in the periods of disintegration. In regions where land was abundant, these small farmers often performed a pioneering role, clearing new lands for farming and introducing commercial crops. However, given their rudimentary farming techniques, where land was scarce or controlled by the large estates, the population increase forced them to subdivide the land, leading to the achievement of a Malthusian balance between population and soil resources.

In sum, it can be said that although the *hacienda* was the basic element of the region's agricultural organisation, it nowhere existed entirely on its own. Roughly speaking, the different areas of the region can be divided into three broad groups: areas in which the large estate existed side by side mainly with the Indian community, areas in which it co-existed mainly with the small production unit, and areas in which it had virtually disappeared. The latter case is exceptional and occurred only in Haiti where the struggle for political independence took the form of a revolt against slavery. Here the abolition of slavery put an end to the system of agricultural organisation based on the large plantation, and the smallholding became practically the only form of organising production. The areas where the dominant pattern became *hacienda*–community were those in which there had been a relatively dense indigenous population and the Spaniards and *assimilados* had remained a small minority. Lastly, the large estate–small production unit pattern generally prevailed in areas where land was relatively abundant and where agriculture had been largely commercial in nature from the very beginning.

It was in the regions where the *hacienda*–community pattern prevailed that mounting agrarian unrest gave rise to the land reform movements that became a major landmark in Latin America's social evolution in the present century. The coexistence of *hacienda* and community took a number of forms. At one extreme we find the isolated estate, providing employment opportunities for some of the community's members but interfering hardly at all with community organisation. At the other extreme we find estates that *occupy* several communities and come to exercise strict control over all their activities. It is in the evolution of these relationships between estate and community that we can trace the roots of the major social tensions that were to trigger off the agrarian reforms of Mexico and Bolivia.

Agrarian reform in Mexico

In Mexico, relations between estate and community were influenced by the Reform movement of the mid-nineteenth century and by the intensification of economic development in the last quarter of that century. With the spread of the *hacienda* system in the country's central region, community lands had been appropriated and the communities confined to the poorer-quality lands. Dispossession and confinement drove many communities to close ranks and sharpened their hostility to the constituted power exercised through the *hacienda*. Convinced that progress presupposed the full enforcement of a private-property system and that the Mexican Indian would only be *free* when the archaic institutions that kept him in a fossilised state had been destroyed, as we have seen in chapter 7, Mexican Liberals encouraged the transfer to private hands of public lands used by the communities, and the transfer to private use, by members of the communities, of lands held communally. Many of the land concessions granted at the time were taken up by foreigners, who frequently started irrigation projects and introduced new farming techniques, heightening the contrast between their prosperity and the extreme poverty of the communities confined to the poorest lands. This situation sparked off a number of uprisings which led many landowners, backed by the central power to establish brutal systems of oppression.

Two underlying factors set the stage for the Mexican agrarian revolution: the existence of the community, with its bonds of solidarity strengthened by the circumstances outlined above, and the vigorous expansion of commercial agriculture, which had led to the expulsion of communities from most of the better lands available.[2] If community bonds had not existed, part of the displaced population would probably have emigrated to other regions, particularly to the south where new lands were still being brought under cultivation by means of rudimentary techniques.[3]

The Mexican Revolution, which started in 1910, paved the way for the communities to recover the lands that had been taken from them. Thus the initial uprising developed into a spontaneous and irreversible social movement, that radically altered the course of a political movement whose urban leaders seemed to want no more than the establishment of a democracy inspired by liberal ideas. The 1917 Constitution, by incorporating the principles that had fired the agrarian leaders, provided the basis for a process of social change that was to leave its mark on the Mexico of today. When the revolutionary process started there were some eight or nine thousand large estates in Mexico, controlling virtually all the good land in the country. Alongside these estates, four or five thousand Indian communities were eking out a living on poor quality lands, frequently on tiny plots. The *hacienda* system was spreading both in the southern part of the country and in the north, while in the central region it had already taken over all the best land.[4]

The three decades preceding the Revolution were a period of expansion for the *hacienda* which seemed to be an institution capable of bringing new areas under cultivation, of introducing new crops, making progress in the technical field, and of investing in capital improvements. However, it was not in a position to provide enough employment for the rural masses and it monopolised the best lands. Thus the root of the problem was of a social nature. The Mexican land reform was essentially designed to solve this social problem, an aim which accounts for the introduction of the *ejido* system.

Awareness that the indigenous communities had been robbed of their

---

[2] Between 1877 and 1907, Mexico's agricultural export production grew at the average annual rate of 6.4 per cent, increasing its share of the total from 4 to 20 per cent. This expansion was achieved, in part, at the expense of production for local consumption. Production of maize, the country's staple food, fell from 52 per cent to 33 per cent of the total. In per capita terms, the decline in maize production was 49 per cent. Thus, the agricultural surplus was increased at the cost of effectively sacrificing the rural population. For data see Leopoldo Solís M., 'Hacia un Análisis General a Largo Plazo del Desarrollo Económico de México' in *Demografía y Economía*, (Colégio de Mexico), vol. I, no. 1, 1967.

[3] On this point see Henri Enjalbert, 'Réforme Agraire et Production Agricole au Mexique (1910–1965)' in *Les Problèmes Agraires des Amériques Latines*.

[4] Cf. Rodolfo Stavenhagen, 'Aspectos Sociales de la Estrutura Agrária en México' in *Les Problèmes Agraires des Amériques Latines*.

best lands contributed to the popularity of agrarianist ideas in enlightened urban circles. In the south, where the plunder of communal lands had been widespread, the first plan for land reform, sponsored by Emiliano Zapata, had been proposed as early as 1911. A decree issued by Carranza in 1915 provided for restitution of the land wrested from the indigenous communities, and in 1917 the principle of agrarian reform was incorporated in Article 27 of the new constitution.

In practice, however, the problem was not simply the 'restitution of lands, woodlands, and waters' to communities able to prove that they had been dispossessed of these resources. From the moment the land question was raised (after 1912, armed groups of peasants, under the leadership of Zapata, began to invade and occupy land) the redistribution movement became widespread. *Peones* living on the *haciendas* and landless peasants, who depended, in one way or another, on the large estates but were not attached to indigenous communities, joined the agitation for agrarian reform.

The *ejido*[5] system was created to solve the problems of peasants who were unable to prove that they had 'owned' land and had been dispossessed. Nonetheless, the law established that any peasant claiming the right to land must be attached to a 'nucleus of population', even if he had joined it only six months before making his claim. Specifically, it was the 'population nucleus', recognised as such by the State, that was entitled to the grant of land as property. Moreover, the land was granted to the community as an inalienable right: under the provisions of the law, community property could 'in no case, and in no form, be alienated, ceded, transferred, rented, mortgaged, or encumbered, in whole or in part'. Ejidal property is thus a peculiar form of realty, subject to special statute. The 'population nucleus' comprising the ejidal community remains under the direct control of the State. The law provides that *ejidos* can be worked individually (each *ejidatario* being assigned an individual parcel of land) or collectively; however, this decision is the prerogative of the State: 'collective exploitation of the *ejido* can be

---

[5] The word *ejido* refers both to a community which has been granted land in accordance with the procedures set up by law under the constitution and to the communal land itself. According to Preston E. James, the word originated from the traditional organisation of the Spanish agricultural village, which held title in common to three kinds of land excluded from private ownership: areas devoted to the support of village government; common pastures and woodlands; and an open tract located just outside the village gate, used in common for a variety of activities but not for raising crops or grazing animals. This tract was known as the 'ejido', literally 'the way out', because of its location on the way out of the village. See Preston E. James, *Latin America*, rev. ed., New York, 1950, p. 549 (Translator).

sanctioned or revoked only by the President of the Republic' (Article 130 of the Federal Agrarian Reform Law).

The individual *ejidal plot* tended to become the effective unit of exploitation. Although it cannot be alienated or encumbered, it can be willed to the *ejidatario's* widow, children or dependents. An *ejidataria* (a woman who has been alloted a parcel of ejidal land) does not lose the right to cultivate her allotment if she married an *ejidatario*. In this way, the land is tied to the community, which frequently has access to other resources (pastures, woodlands, etc.) for use in common. Social life thus tends to be organised around common interests, in contrast with the former system of authoritarian control exercised by the large landowner over all activities on his estate.

The *ejido* came to constitute a political cell in the system of social organisation, and, after the creation of the National Peasant Confederation (CNC) under the Cárdenas government, it allied itself with the central authority to become one of the mainstays of the political party that controls the State. This does not mean that the peasantry became an active agent of the power system. The vacuum left by the displaced landowners was filled by urban groups who find a base of support in the *ejidatario* masses.

Mexican agrarian reform was a complex social process whose uneven development was to continue to the present day.[6] The distribution of land to the peasant masses entailed in the central area in particular, the break-up of the large estates. These were in most cases integrated units whose resources of soil, pastures, woodland and water were complementary, enabling them to attain a certain level of productivity and profitability. The break-up of these properties and their redistribution in small plots, where land use was dependent on rudimentary techniques, inevitably entailed a drop in productivity and reduction in the surpluses formerly available to the urban populations. It was natural therefore, that this should provoke several kinds of reaction. Consequently, in the period extending from 1920 to 1935, distribution of lands made slow progress and in large areas the agrarian reform programme made virtually no impression. On the other hand, it was soon realised that the agrarian reform would only achieve its objectives if it succeeded, at the same time, in bringing new land under the plough and increasing the irrigated areas. In 1926 a government commission – which later became a ministry – was appointed to study and carry out major

---

[6] An overall survey of the Mexican agrarian reform process and a description of its institutions is found in Moises T. de la Pena, *Mito y Realidad de la Reforma Agrária en México*, Mexico, 1964.

irrigation projects. At the same time an attempt was made to siphon off some of the pressure exerted by land-hungry peasants, by promoting the settlement of certain regions in the north which, although semi-arid, could support non-irrigated crops. The large cattle estates could cede some of their land without affecting their profitability; furthermore, the new agrarian legislation allowed *hacendados* to keep the nucleus of their estates with some 200 to 300 hectares of land, or 100 hectares in the case of irrigated farmland. This small private property, or so-called 'small estate', with access to abundant credit facilities rapidly became the cornerstone of the country's agriculture.

The Lázaro Cárdenas government initiated a new and decisive stage in the agrarian reform process. Between 1935 and 1940, 17.6 million hectares of land were transformed into *ejidos* encompassing 808,271 beneficiaries, whereas between 1916 and 1934 only 7.7 million hectares had been redistributed. The intensification of the process revealed a number of weak points in the new agricultural system that had been created in the country. The ejidos were generally too small, which meant that *ejidatarios* soon became *microfundists*. Since land reform was carried out in response to the demands of populations living within a 7-kilometre radius of the estate that was to be expropriated, claimants were frequently far too numerous to be accommodated on the available land. The situation was aggravated by the repatriation of large numbers of *braceros* (seasonal migrant workers), who had been forced to return to Mexico by the economic crisis in the United States. Under the three governments following the Cárdenas administration, i.e. up to 1958, there was a change of direction in agrarian policy: distribution of lands was reduced considerably and the permitted size of small private properties or 'small estates' was increased.[7] During this period, substantial investments were made to extend the crop lands in the large irrigated areas of the north. Half the new land brought under cultivation was distributed in the form of *ejidos*, and the other half was sold as private property in parcels averaging 30–60 hectares and in some cases as much as 100 hectares. The *ejidatarios* received plots averaging 4–6 hectares. These arrangements were severely criticised by the advocates

---

[7] The Agrarian Law provides 'exemption from expropriation for the purposes of assignment to new owners, enlargement of too small holdings, or creation of new population centres' for 'small properties in productive use' in respect of the following areas: 100 hectares of irrigated land; 200 hectares of unirrigated land; 150 hectares of irrigated land under cotton; 300 hectares of unirrigated land under specified cash crops, including sugar and coffee; and the number of hectares required to support up to 500 head of cattle (Article 249).

of land reform and there was a new change of direction under the presidency of López Mateos (1958–64) with a policy aiming to reserve all land brought under irrigation for crop farming, through the investment of public funds, for the creation of new *ejidos*.

An overall assessment of the Mexican agrarian reform is not an easy task. Its objective, which was to do away with the autocratic control exercised over the peasant population by the large estates and to give access to the land to the greatest possible number of people, has been partly achieved. The *ejido* system has proved an effective means of employing, and hence keeping on the land, a structural population surplus that would otherwise have failed to find jobs either in agriculture or in the urban areas. The fact that this population surplus remained on the land brought about a decline in the productivity of labour in some areas, and in certain regions there was a decline not only in the productivity of labour but also in the productivity of natural resources, with a fall in overall output.[8] The estate had been a capitalisation mechanism and its disappearance could have entailed a reduction in the formation of capital in the agricultural sector. This was avoided because in most cases the *haciendas* were whittled down to medium sized private properties (up to 300 hectares) which benefited from substantial public and private credit. The conversion to medium estates permitted the emergence of a type of agricultural enterprise which was in a better position to make full use of its land and water resources than the traditional *hacienda*.

The *ejido* system has been the subject of much controversy, in part because of the ambiguity that has characterised the implementation of the Mexican agrarian reform programme. Official statements continue to emphasise social objectives, but since 1940, agricultural policy has systematically pursued the objective of increasing the agricultural surplus extracted for urban consumption or export. At the same time, the 'growth at any price' strategy has led to the gradual abandonment of considerations of a social nature.[9]

Criticism of the *ejido* system follows two lines of argument. The first emphasises certain distortions resulting largely from the way in which policy has been implemented: the small size of the plots, leading to the creation of *minifundismo*, disguised renting of plots, etc. The other

[8] On this point see the summing up in Ramón Fernandez y Fernandez, 'La Reforma Agrária Mexicana: una Gran Experiencia' in *Les Problèmes Agraires des Amériques Latines*.

[9] Cf. Jesus Puente Leyua, 'Recursos y Crescimiento del Sector Agropecuario en México, 1930–1967', *El Trimestre Económico*, no. 150, April–June 1971.

emphasises the non-viability of an institution which is neither a collective form of land exploitation nor a system of private property. In this view, an *ejidatario* is merely a *minifundista* who does not even own the plot he farms: he can neither add to it nor sell it and if conditions are bad he has no option but to seek a solution outside the law.

The experience of the collective *ejidos*, enthusiastically promoted during the Cárdenas period, is of limited significance because of their subsequent evolution, in a climate of discouragement and even hostility. Many of these *ejidos* – a few hundred were created altogether – were given good farmland, devoted to commercial crops, which enabled them to survive and even to produce relatively favourable results in economic terms.[10]

There seems to be little doubt that collective farming facilitates the absorption of the manpower surplus by combining agricultural production with complementary activities. The most successful collective *ejidos* were precisely those with good land which had been used for crops whose earning power permitted investment in capital improvements and the creation of new forms of employment. The greatest difficulties in organising collective production were encountered when land grants were inadequate in size or quality and subsistence farming was the only feasible activity. In these cases, capital investment was dependent on credit, that is, on resources which had to be found outside the *ejido*. The official policy adopted was to direct the flow of resources channelled through the credit agencies – resources which were in short supply – to private properties where the land–man relationship was more favourable. This made it possible to maximise an agricultural surplus to be made available to the urban populations or exported.

At first, the size of the individual plots allotted to the *ejidatarios* was limited to 4 hectares. Subsequently, legal provision was made to increase this limit to 20 hectares for non-irrigated land and 10 hectares in the case of irrigated land (Article 220 of the Agrarian Law). But this measure did not increase the amount of land available for redistribution: it merely increased the size of the waiting lists for land in existing ejidal communities. In some regions, ejidal plots are under 1 hectare and at present the average size of an individual *ejido* plot is only 6.5 hectares.[11]

---

[10] For an analysis of the various aspects of the problem, see S. Eckstein, *El Ejido Colectivo en México*, Mexico, 1966.

[11] For an assessment of the role of the *ejido* in the social evolution of Mexico since the Revolution see François Chevalier, 'The Ejido and Political Stability in Mexico' in Claudio Veliz (ed.), *The Politics of Conformity in Latin America*, London, 1967.

The controversy aroused by the implementation of the agrarian reform and the understandable fears, exaggerated and exploited by its critics, that the *ejido* system would paralyse capitalisation in the agricultural sector and make the country dependent on food imports – which in fact did happen during the 1930s – contributed greatly to the preoccupation with agricultural production problems. Irrigation and other agricultural infrastructural works began to absorb a large proportion of public funds. The area of government-irrigated land increased from 25,000 hectares in 1930 to 265,000 in 1949 and 2,221,000 in 1960. During the same period the area of privately-irrigated land was reduced by more than 300,000 hectares.[12] Additionally, a network of specialised government banks was created to meet the requirements of the agricultural sector.

It is also worth mentioning the effects of land reform on the functioning of the Mexican State. The traditional estate, as an instrument for controlling the rural population, was the cornerstone of the power system on which the State was based. The possibility of carrying out a far-reaching industrialisation policy was blocked for many years by rural interests, since the landowners feared a rise in the prices of manufactured imports. With the elimination of this pressure group, the Mexican State was free to pursue an industrialisation policy, which has now been carried out without hindrance since the 1920s. When Cárdenas reformed the party controlling the country's political life to create a solid peasant-based organisation, the rural sector became a factor for stabilising the political system, since it could be mobilised by the State political machine.

According to the figures given in the latest census, there were around 20,000 *ejidos* in Mexico in 1960 with approximately 1.5 million active associates, representing a quarter of the country's agricultural labour force. Slightly over one-fifth of this labour force (22 per cent) consisted of property owners of whom two-thirds were smallholders owning plots of up to 5 hectares. The remaining 33 per cent were landless agricultural labourers. Between 1950 and 1960, the relative proportion of both *ejidatarios* and smallholders declined while that of owners of medium-sized and large properties and of wage-earners in particular, increased, rising from 46 per cent to 53 per cent.

When we consider today's agrarian structure in Mexico, after more than half a century of land reform, the most surprising feature is the persistence of property concentration in the non-ejidal sector. The 1960 census figures show that in that year 47.5 per cent of the country's

[12] Cf. Jesus Puente Leyua, op. cit., Table III.

farms were in the private sector, which accounted for 57 per cent of the cropland, 69 per cent of the irrigated land and 69 per cent of the agricultural capital. Furthermore, this sector absorbed 91.4 per cent of the fertilisers used in the country and contributed 59 per cent of the agricultural output. The degree of land concentration in the private sector is considerable since 66.8 per cent of farms, all with up to 5 hectares of land apiece, accounted for only 1.1 per cent of the farm area, and 10.8 per cent of the area under crops. On the other hand, farms of over 200 hectares, representing only 3.8 per cent of the total number of farm units, held 86.8 per cent of the total farm area and 52 per cent of the area under crops.

If we divide Mexican farms into three groups – private smallholdings or *minifundios*, medium-sized and large private estates and *ejidos* – we find that the first two groups employ approximately the same proportion of the rural labour force (27 and 28 per cent respectively) although the first group accounts for only 5 per cent of the cropland and the second for 52 per cent. On the other hand, the *minifundistas* produced 5 per cent of the farm output and the other private producers 54 per cent. Thus while the value of production per hectare in the two sectors is not very different, the value of production per worker on the *minifundios* is only 8 per cent of that in the other sector.

If we include the *ejido* system in the survey of Mexico's agrarian structure, that is if each parcel of ejidal land is treated as an individual farm, we find that the differences between the three groups are not significant when compared with Latin American countries where traditional agrarian structures have been maintained. In fact, *minifundios*, whether privately-held smallholdings or *ejidos*, accounted for 84.2 per cent of the farm units in Mexico in 1960, a proportion similar to that found in Guatemala where, as we noted in chapter 7, *minifundios* accounted for 88.4 per cent of farms. Medium-sized and large farms accounted for 2.1 per cent of the farm units in Guatemala and for 3.2 per cent in Mexico; they occupied 72.3 per cent of the arable land in Guatemala and 42.8 per cent in Mexico and their shares of the value of agricultural production were 57 and 54.3 per cent respectively. The ratio of the value of production of large multi-family farms to that of *minifundios* was 260:1 in Mexico, which is lower than the ratio of 339:1 indicated for Guatemala in chapter 7, but higher than the corresponding ratios for the other countries referred to in that chapter.

Analysis of the above data shows that the striking disparities in labour productivity observed in Mexican agriculture are essentially a reflection of the amount of capital invested per person employed, as well as of differences in technical levels corresponding to the different levels of capital accumulation. Thus, differences in size and type of farm do not appear to be the basic cause of the disparities noted.[13] The average value of agricultural production per unit of cultivated land is very similar for the three types of farm referred to above: the private *minifundio* produces 11 per cent more than the national average, the *ejido* 5 per cent less and the medium-sized and large private estate 3 per cent more.

Taking the period 1930–60 as a whole, we find that the agricultural labour force increased from 3.6 to 6.3 million, the cultivated area per worker from 1.98 to 2.17 hectares and the irrigated area per worker from 0.467 to 0.554 hectares. The considerable increase in production during this period has been attributed equally to the expansion of the cultivated area and to the increase in yields per hectare. Thus, the decisive factor in the increase of output was the major capitalisation effort promoted largely by the State. There is ample evidence to suggest that the investments made were mostly for the benefit of the medium-sized and large private estates. Since production per hectare in this group is not greater than in the other two, it must be concluded that the main effect of the investment pattern was to increase the labour productivity differential in favour of that particular sector. In fact, in 1960, labour productivity on the medium-sized and large private estates was 7 times greater than in the *ejido* sector and 12.6 times greater than on the private *minifundios*.

We may speculate as to what the results would have been, in terms of production growth, had investment been orientated in a manner less unfavourable to the two smallholding sectors. There is no reason to suppose that it would have been negative, since, as we have seen, output per hectare is similar on the three types of holding. It is certainly likely, however, that with a different orientation of investment there would have been a far less concentrated distribution of income in the agricultural sector and, consequently, the agricultural surpluses extracted from the rural masses for the benefit of other social groups, would have been much smaller.

The Mexican land reform effectively removed the *latifundio* as the basic structure for organising the labour of the peasant masses. This function was taken over by the State, which, by expropriating land, creating *ejidos*, determining their organisational structure (deciding whether they were to be farmed collectively or divided up into family plots) and controlling their access to credit through the specialised government credit agency, as well as through its orientation of public

[13] Cf. Jesus Puente Leyua, op. cit., and also S. Eckstein, op. cit., pp. 113 et seq.

investment funds and technical assistance services, has ensured the expansion of agricultural production and the creation of a considerable surplus whose utilisation is outside the control of the peasant population. This objective could only have been achieved because the cost of agricultural labour was kept extremely low, which in turn is a reflection of the slow growth of labour productivity on the *minifundios*, whether private smallholdings or *ejidos*, where capitalisation is negligible, agricultural techniques rudimentary and manpower, even when intensively used, continues to be under-employed.

Agrarian reform in Bolivia

Bolivia made the second major attempt witnessed in Latin America in the present century to bring about a change in social structures. It differed from the Mexican attempt in several respects although the starting-point for both was the same: conflict between community and estate. However, in contrast to the situation that existed in the days of Porfirio Díaz in Mexico, agriculture in Bolivia was not expanding on the eve of the revolution that set the stage for agrarian reform in 1952. As we have seen, in pre-revolutionary Mexico the *hacienda* was on the increase and had proved an adequate instrument for promoting capital formation and extending the country's agricultural frontier. The situation in Bolivia was entirely different, reflecting the greater lack of development in the country's economy as a whole. The *indigenous community*, which had maintained its close attachment to the traditional *ayllu*, was in 1952, as indeed right up to the present day, still of considerable importance in the Bolivian social structure. According to the 1950 census figures there were around 3,779 indigenous communities in the country, with a total population of about one million. Even though these figures have been challenged,[14] there can be little doubt that this traditional form of social organisation was the predominant pattern in Bolivia before the agrarian reform. These communities have evolved, and individual cultivation of the land has largely replaced the once prevalent system of farming communal plots. The large estate had penetrated less than in other Latin American countries and had also acquired certain features that distinguished it from those characterising the Mexican situation on the eve of the revolution. It has been estimated that in 1950 there were around 8,000 *haciendas* in the country (of which 6,000 had more than 500 hectares of land), on which some 200,000 indigenous families

---

[14] Cf. Henri Gumbau, 'Les Changements de Structure à la Suite de la Réforme Bolivienne' in *Les Problèmes agraires des Amériques Latines*, cit.

lived and worked. In that same year, there were not more than 50,000 smallholders, which indicates the secondary role of this type of farm organisation in the Bolivian context.

Almost without exception, the Bolivian *hacienda* was less an enterprise seeking to take over community lands in order to establish a new system of production based on modern techniques and aiming to maximise production, than a semi-feudal organisation designed to appropriate part of the community's production directly. It existed parasitically on the work of one or several 'captive' Indian communities, which maintained their traditional social institutions. The community was thus preserved as a framework for social organisation with its own traditional authorities, but its relations with the land were altered. Part of the land was divided into plots and assigned to individual families, while the part that had been communally owned, or its equivalent, was worked directly for the *hacendado*. The worker divided his time between his own plot of land and the estate lands, the latter taking up between three and five days of work a week, as in the *corvee* system of medieval Europe. The indigenous community, strictly controlled by the large estate, was entirely cut off from the outside world; internal monetary flows were reduced to a minimum and artisan activities to meet community requirements were encouraged. All economic and political contacts with the outside world were made through the *hacienda*. However, the most significant feature was the change in the relationship with the land which as we have seen, was inseparable from the community form of organisation. Since *free communities* existed side by side with 'captive' communities, the situation of the latter was considered a form of social degradation regardless of the material living conditions prevailing in each. Open conflict between *hacienda* and community, which flared up when some of the community's members were expelled from their land by estate owners with 'progressive' inclinations, was the exception. But such cases came to be increasingly important in the agrarian reform process, since the expelled *comuneros* went to the cities, where their awakened political consciousness was sharpened by the knowledge of the exploitation and plunder suffered by the indigenous population. Thus it was not the exploited community, deprived of its best lands, that rose in revolt but individuals who had been drawn into urban life. When the time came for a redistribution of land, these former *comuneros* occasionally came into conflict with those who had remained on the *hacienda*.[15]

The aim of the Bolivian agrarian reform was to do away with the exploitation of the community by the *hacienda*. This was attempted by

[15] See the study by Arturo Urquidi Morales, 'Las Comunidades Indígenas y su Perspectiva Histórica', in *Les Problèmes agraires des Amériques Latines*, cit.

breaking up the *hacienda* in areas where it had essentially been an instrument for exploiting the indigenous population, in other words, where it could be classified as a *latifundio*. In areas where the *hacienda* was classified as a medium property or *agricultural enterprise*, expropriation was restricted to lands exceeding the limits established by the law. These limits were variable and were determined in accordance with the nature of the agricultural activity. The immediate result of reform was the creation of smallholdings, nearly always *minifundios*, from the plots of land on the *hacienda* which had been cultivated by individual indigenous families for their own subsistence needs. The lands formerly cultivated for the estate owners were retained as communal property. The aim was not only to *free* the community but to maintain it as a framework for social organisation. Its members became smallholders but were still bound together by the tie of communal ownership of part of the redistributed lands.[16]

Agrarian reform was carried out largely under the direction of rural *syndicates*, which had been organised, under urban political supervision, on the large estates. The MNR (Movimiento Nacionalista Revolucionário), which had promoted the 1952 revolution, was a strictly urban-based political movement with a strong following among the miners. However, by displacing the traditional power structure, it considerably weakened the system of social control constituted by the large estates. Moreover, by bringing the spontaneous freedom movement of the communities into the revolutionary process, the MNR gave a far greater depth to this process than it would otherwise have achieved in a country where 80 per cent of the population lived on the land. A decade after the agrarian reform started, the government had granted about 200,000 titles in the Altiplano region, which meant that nearly all the families living on the former estates had become independent farmers.

Just as in Mexico the idea of organising labour along collective lines on the *ejidos* was gradually allowed to drop, so in Bolivia the aim of retaining part of the estate lands for collective farming and communal usufruct has gradually been abandoned. In the first place, to prevent individual plots from being too small, the communal lands have in many cases been reduced to very little. It should not be forgotten that on the former *haciendas*, these lands did not always justify commercial organisation since the property system was more a mechanism for extracting a surplus from the indigenous community than a form of agricultural

[16] For an overall analysis of the Bolivian agrarian reform see Henri Gumbau, 'Les Changements de Structure à la Suite de la Réforme Bolivienne' in *Les Problèmes Agraires des Amériques Latines*.

organisation. Barring fairly substantial investment, the only way to improve the community's living conditions was to allow it to keep its produce. In Mexico, as we have seen, the break-up of the large estates often meant a less-efficient utilisation of natural resources. In Bolivia, where the communities were already living on the estates and continued to practise the same rudimentary farming techniques, this problem was not so serious. The drop in the agricultural surplus available for the urban populations was inevitable in view of the improved standards of consumption of the rural masses living on the estates. Agrarian reform thus had a dual consequence: it altered the income distribution pattern in favour of the rural masses and it enabled the communities, formerly 'imprisoned' by the large estates, to recover their independence. Through the peasant syndicates, these communities were drawn into the political life of the country. The increase in the number of rural schools (which had been prohibited on the large estates) built and run by the communities themselves are an indication that their contact with the outside world is beginning to bear fruit.

The elimination of the authoritarian control exercised over the communities by the *haciendas*, the new status of *comuneros* as smallholders and their contacts with the outside world, created conditions for the rural population of the Altiplano to begin to emerge from the cultural and geographical isolation in which it had lived for centuries. This was a decisive step for the creation of a genuine national civil society in Bolivia. The increased mobility of the population may have far-reaching economic consequences, since Bolivia has abundant land and an extremely scattered population pattern. Both the indigenous free community and the semi-feudal system established by the *haciendas* had helped to preserve the ancient pattern of settlement, concentrated in the Altiplano and the valleys. Agrarian reform, by highlighting the problem of agricultural shortages in the urban areas, created a growing awareness of the need to open up new lands, which presupposes a greater population mobility than had traditionally existed in the country. To encourage this mobility, substantial infrastructure investments were needed after the reform. A new road was built linking Cochabamba with Santa Cruz and several facilities have been provided to encourage the colonisation of virgin land. A new agrarian structure is emerging in the tropical *llanos* (grasslands) of the Yungas area. The new pattern is not yet clear but large consortia organised along co-operative lines and modern capitalist enterprises have been established in these areas and are promoting the development of cash crops such as sugar, coffee, cotton and rice.

The Bolivian agrarian reform was an attempt to break down tradi-

tional social structures and is certainly the most important step taken
since independence towards the formation of a genuinely national
Bolivian society. The old *hacienda* system was a means of organising a
large proportion of the peasant population in a production pattern
which required them to perform hard labour in hopelessly inadequate
conditions of nourishment. One inevitable effect of agrarian reform in
the early years was 'decompression', that is the relaxation of strict
working routines. As a result, though the nutrition standards of the
rural population probably improved, there was a drop in productivity
and an even greater reduction in the surplus extracted from agricultural production. Between 1952 and 1957, output fell by 13 per
cent; in the next five years, however, production began to recover and
ten years after the beginning of land reform it had regained its 1952
level. In the following decade (1962 to 1972) agricultural production
averaged a growth rate of 3.4 per cent a year, representing a per
capita rate of 1 per cent. However, the living conditions of the peasant
population probably improved far more than these figures imply.

The contribution of the agricultural sector to the gross domestic
product, calculated at constant prices, fell from 31 to 20 per cent between
1952 and 1972. On the other hand, in 1972 the value of production per
person actively employed in the agricultural sector was no more than
one-quarter of the average value for all productive sectors. It must be
inferred, therefore, that a large proportion of the peasantry continues
to be integrated in a subsistence economy and has benefited hardly at all
from the productivity increases in other activities.

The abolition of the large estate reduced the degree of exploitation of
the peasant masses and improved their working conditions but it also
reduced the degree of integration of the agricultural sector in commercial circuits and in the social division of labour. This accounts for the
widening productivity gap between this sector and the economy as a
whole. There can be no doubt that the rural communities, after centuries
of dependence and servitude, were not equipped to take advantage of the
opportunities provided by the change in the structures of domination.
But it is also true that the Bolivian State neglected to provide the financial
and technical resources needed to raise agricultural productivity. Nor
was it prepared to promote the successful establishment of a new kind of
agriculture, different from the traditional pattern and capable of producing the surpluses needed for urban expansion, along the lines of the
Mexican experience. In sum, twenty years after the implementation of
agrarian reform, the problem of organising the country's agriculture to
meet its basic development needs has not yet been solved.

Agrarian reform in Peru

Peru, like Bolivia, is a country where the bulk of the rural population is still attached, in varying degrees, to indigenous communities. To what extent these communities derive from the pre-colonial *ayllu* or are largely the creation of the Spanish system of domination, is a problem that need not concern us here.[17]

In the 1940 census 4,600 villages were classified as indigenous communities and in the mid-1960s it was estimated that two-thirds of the agricultural labour force was drawn from members of these communities.[18] Unlike Bolivia, however, Peru had witnessed notable changes in its agricultural production patterns during the latter half of the nineteenth century: with the intensive penetration of capitalist forms of production in certain areas, there had been a considerable rise in productivity and greater assimilation of modern techniques. A distinctive feature of this development, in comparison with similar developments in Mexico, was that the penetration of capitalism in Peru contributed far less to the creation or sharpening of conflict between *hacienda* and indigenous community, since it mainly took the form of creating a pattern of agricultural production parallel to that of traditional agriculture, in which *hacienda* and community are attached to each other in symbiotic relationship.

Peru is divided into three agricultural regions with distinct ecological, social and economic conditions. In the mid-1960s, the country's agricultural labour force numbered 1,719 thousand workers, 16 per cent living in the *Costa* (Coastal region), 71 per cent in the *Sierra* (highlands) and 13 per cent in the *Selva* (jungle, that is the forested parts of eastern Peru). Labour productivity in the *Costa* was more than four times as high as in the *Sierra* and almost three times as high as in the *Selva*.[19] In the *Sierra* the situation was not very different from that in Bolivia before agrarian reform: the rural population was divided into *comuneros* and *hacienda Indians*, both living at subsistence level on tiny plots of land. With the increase in population, many *comuneros* had emigrated to the coast and more recently to the *Selva*. The *hacienda Indians* paid rent for their individual parcels of land in the form of work without pay for a specified number of days per week, or services to the estate owner: road

[17] For a survey of the controversial views on this subject see Fernando Fuenzalida Vollmar, 'La Estructura de la Comunidad de Indigénas Tradicional' in *El Campesino en el Peru*, Lima, 1970.

[18] Cf. Fernando Fuenzalida Vollmar, op. cit.

[19] Cf. Estevan Strauss, *Reestructuración del Espacio Económico Latinoamericano*, mimeograph, ILPES, 1969.

building (*faena*), transportation of produce (*propio*) and domestic work (*pongo*).[20] Thus, the *Sierra hacienda* was essentially of the traditional type, extracting a surplus from tenant-labourers whose numbers increased as the better lands were occupied. Only exceptionally, and then only relatively recently, was the pattern broken, with the emergence in the *Sierra* of estate owners interested in 'modernising' the land, that is, in depriving workers of the land they had traditionally used for their subsistence needs. 'Modernising' estates, organised for commercial farming, were established in the coastal region and the border valleys of the Amazon spur, areas with ecological conditions very different from those of the highlands, on land which had not attracted settlement by indigenous communities.

In sum, although the bulk of the rural population remained in the *Sierra*, a region of meagre soils, which was under increasing population pressure, the country's agricultural development was concentrated in the two border regions. The distinctive features of Peru's rural development have their roots in the particular relations that were formed between the area of traditional agriculture, which provided a reserve of manpower, and the border valleys.

The instability of the coastal sugar economy geared to the international markets, led to intense concentration of land ownership in the coastal valleys, and to increasing control over agro-industrial activities by foreign interests.[21] Labour relations took a strictly capitalist form and there emerged among the wage-earning masses a vigorous union movement without parallel in the Latin American rural world. In the valleys of the Amazon tributaries – a transition zone between the highlands and the Amazon region proper – agricultural development is more recent and has been based mainly on tree crops such as coffee, cocoa and fruit. The *Selva*, unlike the *Costa*, whose development took place at a time when there was far less pressure on *Sierra* land,[22] had a plentiful labour supply as well as abundant land, a combination which permitted the transplantation to the new areas of labour relations similar to those of traditional agriculture. Since ownership of land was controlled by a minority, the land itself could be used to pay for labour, following the patterns of the traditional share-labour arrangements of the *Sierra*. Nevertheless, the better quality and greater availability of land enabled

[20] Cf. Hugo Blanco, *Land or Death*, New York, 1972, p. 29.

[21] When the 1969 agrarian reform began, two-thirds of the capital invested in the agro-industrial complexes of the coastal region was foreign. See data, by enterprise, in Alfredo Barnechea, 'Pomalca: informe urgente', *Participación*, December 1973.

[22] The coastal region, in the early years of its agricultural development, had to resort to imported Asian labour, brought in under a system of semi-slavery.

the bulk of the *Selva* farm population to earn higher incomes and many workers were able to hire labour for their own parcels of land. On the other hand, given the nature of the crops, a large proportion of the labour force is not settled in the region, coming down from the *Sierra* only in the harvest season.

The precarious nature of labour relations, the strict control over access to land and the state of uncertainty and insecurity among populations in the process of losing their links with their traditional communities, created mounting social tensions, which culminated in open conflict, with occupations of land and outbursts of armed violence. It would be difficult to explain the direction taken by agrarian reform in Peru without taking into account the involvement of the armed forces in repressing these uprisings.

The Peruvian Agrarian Reform Law, promulgated on 24 June 1969 by the military government which had taken power in the previous year, was designed to be an instrument for the transformation of the country's economic, social and political structures. There can be no doubt that it represents a major step towards the integration of Peruvian civil society – until recently characterised by a stratification almost as sharply defined as the caste system – and towards changing the bases of the power system controlling the Peruvian State.

The most striking feature of the reform was the complete nationalisation of the agro-industrial complexes in the coastal region and their progressive transformation into co-operatives. Since wages in this sector were much higher (in some cases as much as five times higher) than peasant incomes in the *Sierra*, and since a large proportion of the investment is industrial, not agricultural, there would seem to be little doubt that the aim of expropriation was political rather than economic or social. In the *Sierra*, and in the border areas of the *Selva*, the main aims of the reform are to do away with forms of labour exploitation left over from colonial times; to put an end to the *minifundio*; and to introduce strong new forms of collective organisation for agricultural production, such as *peasant communities* and *sociedades de interés social* (societies of 'social interest', or associations serving the social interests of the community). Private property is maintained in cases where the land is farmed directly by the owner either individually or as the head of an enterprise, but maximum limits are laid down. In the *Costa*, the maximum permitted is 150 hectares of irrigated land and 300 hectares of unirrigated land; in other regions the maximum permitted areas are between 15–55 hectares of irrigated land and 30–110 hectares of unirrigated land. In all cases, these areas may be increased by one-third if wages are raised to at least 10 per cent above the legal minimum. Farms of less than 3 hectares and farms that cannot provide an income equivalent to a stipulated minimum for each region are to disappear.

The agrarian reform has been applied methodically, by regions, under the strict control of the authorities. Redistribution decisions or 'adjudications' have given preference to the peasants working on the land, but in the large majority of cases farms were reorganised as collective enterprises. Of the land expropriated up to 1973, some one and a half million hectares were distributed to agricultural *sociedades de interés social*, each receiving an average of more than 50 thousand hectares of land; a further one and a half million hectares were distributed to co-operatives, with allotments averaging 4,500 hectares; 365,000 hectares were given to 83 peasant communities and only 124,000 hectares to individuals, each peasant family receiving an average of 7 hectares of land.[23]

The Peruvian agrarian reform, unlike the other major land reforms carried out in Latin America, did not entail a drop in agricultural output. On the social plane, it undoubtedly had widespread repercussions, although the available information does not permit an accurate assessment of its impact. Nevertheless, the regions that benefited most were those where the living conditions of the population were relatively better than average. It is likely that the gap between the living standards of the coastal workers and the *Sierra* peasants has widened; while in the coastal region itself, disparities between members of co-operatives and other workers, and even between members of different co-operatives may have become more pronounced, because of disparities in land and water resources. The problem of improving the living conditions of the peasant masses concentrated in the *Sierra* has not yet been solved and awaits the creation of suitable conditions for the large-scale transfer of populations to the valleys of the Amazon tributaries.

The post-reform pattern of Peruvian agriculture is not yet clear. There seems little doubt that the emphasis is on the organisation of large agricultural units, outside the control of private capital. It must be conceded, therefore, that the Peruvian reform is not likely to follow the line that came to prevail in Mexico and Bolivia, where peasants freed from the *latifundio* became *minifundistas*, providing a manpower reserve for a private sector in which most investment was concentrated. But this different direction can be consolidated only if the co-operatives and *sociedades de interés social* succeed in the dual task of improving the living conditions of the rural masses and producing the agricultural surplus which the country needs for its development.

[23] Cf. ECLA, *Economic Survey of Latin America*, 1973, Table 160.

Agrarian reform in Chile

The Chilean case, better than any other, lends itself to the study of the nature and scope of Latin American land reforms, not only because the Chilean agrarian reform was carefully planned and methodically implemented but also because of the detailed information available on the country's agrarian structure before and after the reform effort.

In Chile, unlike the other cases studied, agriculture was not the country's main source of employment when land reform began: in 1970, only 22 per cent of the economically active population was employed in the agricultural sector, which contributed only 8 per cent to the formation of the gross domestic product. Furthermore, the State did not rely mainly on agriculture for the extraction of a surplus and nor did the country depend on this sector for the generation of its capacity to import. In these circumstances, there was some room for manoeuvre, making it possible to contemplate land reform without too many fears. This accounts for the consensus reached in the country on the question of agrarian reform and for its implementation on the basis of a law passed by a democratically elected government.

The first agrarian reform law, promulgated in 1962 by a conservative government, reflected the country's growing concern with the agricultural sector's failure to produce the surpluses required by urbanisation. In the two preceding decades agricultural output had not kept pace with the growth of the population, making it increasingly necessary for the country to import food: on the other hand, the standard of living of the peasant population was extremely low and was declining in relation to the national average. It was estimated that one-third of the agricultural population was unemployed despite the existence of idle land throughout the country, including under-utilised irrigated land. In sum, labour and land resources were used extremely wastefully, while the country became increasingly dependent on food imports, and living conditions in the rural areas deteriorated in relative terms. Evidence of these facts permitted the emergence of consensus on the need for structural reorganisation of the agrarian sector. Nevertheless, although agriculture contributed less than 10 per cent to the formation of the national product, the landowning class continued to wield considerable influence in the power system. In effect, the 1962 law was little more than a tactical diversion, a formal undertaking within the framework of the Alliance for Progress.

The proclaimed goals of the agrarian reform programme proposed by the Christian Democratic government in 1965 were far more ambitious: (*a*) to give land to thousands of peasant families; (*b*) to raise agricultural output; (*c*) to ensure active participation of the peasant masses in the social life of the nation.[24]

The Agrarian Reform Law finally approved in July 1967 authorised the expropriation of poorly exploited (abandoned or unused) properties, agricultural enterprises owned by joint-stock companies, and units larger than a specified basic maximum, which varied according to the quality of soil, but must always be the equivalent of 80 hectares of good irrigated land in the Greater Santiago area. Indemnification was provided for in the large majority of cases: 10 per cent of the compensation, assessed on the value of the land as declared by the owner for tax purposes, was payable in cash and the balance was to be paid in the form of government bonds, redeemable in 25 years and earning 6 per cent interest, with provision for adjustment in relation to the cost of living index for 75 per cent of the bond value. Expropriated land would be 'adjudicated' to those who worked it, but the law provided for a provisional system whereby an expropriated property could be managed jointly by the resident workers and the State for a transition period of 3 to 5 years. This provisional system, known as *asentamiento*, was the outcome of a compromise between those who wished to divide the land immediately with the workers, and those who, fearing that division would entail a drop in productivity, wished to establish some form of collective arrangement. At the end of the transition period, the peasants themselves were to decide on the form of production to be adopted on a permanent basis.

Between 1965 and 1970, the Christian Democratic government expropriated 1,408 properties, covering an area of 3,563, 554 hectares, including 290,000 hectares of irrigated land. Between January 1971 and June 1972, the Popular Unity coalition government expropriated 3,282 properties, with a total area of 5,296,765 hectares, including 371,000 hectares of irrigated land. From the data in Table 23.1 we can compare the country's post-reform agrarian structure with the situation that existed before reform.

Before the reform, the large estate sector – properties with over 80 basic irrigated hectares of land – comprised 4,876 units and accounted for more than 55 per cent of the agricultural land, measured in equivalent hectares. After the reform, there were less than 200 properties of this type, accounting for less than 3 per cent of the agricultural area. These figures clearly demonstrate that Chile's agrarian structure was *effectively transformed* within the limits provided for in the 1967 law.

[24] Solon Barraclough, 'Reforma Agraria: Historia y Perspectivas', *Cuadernos de la Realidad Nacional*, Santiago, March 1971.

TABLE 23.1 *Chile: Agrarian structure before and after land reform*

Tracts of land (in BIH[a])	Farm units (per cent)		Area (in BIH[a])	
	1965	1972	1965	1972
Less than 5	81.4	79.3	9.7	9.7
5–20	11.5	11.3	12.7	13.0
20–40	3.0	3.3	9.5	11.6
40–60	1.3	2.5	7.1	14.5
60–80	0.8	1.6	5.7	12.8
80 and over	2.0	0.1	55.3	2.9
Reformed sector	0.0	1.9	0.0	35.5

[a] Basic irrigated hectare: unit of measure equivalent to one hectare of irrigated land in the Greater Santiago area.
SOURCE: S. Barraclough and J. A. Fernández, *Diagnóstico de la Reforma Agraria Chilena*, Mexico, 1974, p. 38.

This change was brought about in part on the initiative of the land-owners themselves, who took advantage of the delayed passage of the law through Congress to subdivide their holdings. Indeed, the relative number of properties of between 60 and 80 basic irrigated hectares doubled and the area they occupied more than doubled; the same thing happened in the case of properties of between 40 and 60 basic irrigated hectares and, on a smaller scale, in the case of those with between 20 and 40 basic irrigated hectares of land. The *reformed sector*, created as a result of the application of the law, accounted for 35 per cent of the farm area. The relatively small number of units in this section (19 per cent of the total) is a consequence of the fact that the final form of organising production had not yet been decided. The number of workers effectively benefiting from the reform (those resident in the expropriated properties) was around 75 thousand in 1972, representing 11 per cent of the agricultural labour force.

From the properties expropriated under the Christian Democratic government, 628 *asentamientos* were formed. Since the workers on these settlements kept their individual parcels of land and received advances from the State which guaranteed them a minimum income regardless of their performance, they became the chief beneficiaries of the reform. Under the *Unidad Popular* government, the land reform agencies established 27 production centres (State farms), 150 agrarian reform centres (large, collectively-farmed units), 921 peasant committees (a variant of the *asentamiento*) and 318 *asentamientos*. Thus, the two governments, applying the same law, gave a very different direction to the agrarian reform. In the first case, the intention was to create a class of smallholders, farming economically viable units; in the second, the emphasis was on integrating the peasants into collectively-operated units.

The basic problem, however, was less the type of agricultural organisation to be adopted in the reformed sector than the number of persons who should benefit from the reform. In practice, the peasants consistently fought to keep the individual plots they had farmed under the old system of tenure, which reduced the amount of land available for collective farming. Since they also resisted attempts to incorporate casual workers in the reformed units, on any permanent basis, these temporary workers continued to be an exploited class. The *agrarian reform centres* were created in an effort to overcome these difficulties but, in practice, the form of holding that tended to prevail in the reformed sector concentrated the benefits of agrarian reform in the hands of the minority made up of the workers who had been living on the expropriated properties.

An overall assessment of the post-reform agrarian structure in Chile shows that three distinct sectors have emerged: the first, comprising the old *minifundios* and smallholdings, accounts for 22.7 per cent of the agricultural area (in basic irrigated hectares); the second, comprising the medium-sized private properties and the remaining large estates, accounts for 41.8 per cent of the agricultural land; and the third, comprising the reformed holdings, accounts for 33.5 per cent of the agricultural land. In 1972, the first sector produced 28 per cent of the farm output and employed 55 per cent of the agricultural labour force, the second produced 45 per cent of the output and employed 25 per cent of the labour force and the third produced 27 per cent of the output and employed 20 per cent of the labour force.[25] On the basis of these figures, and taking the first sector (I) as the base, we can establish the following indicators of agricultural performance in the three sectors:

	I	II	III
Value of production per BIH	100	68	62
Employment per BIH	100	24	23
Value of production per unit of employment	100	180	135

Comparison of the data for Sectors II and III shows that the agrarian

[25] Basic data from S. Barraclough and J. A. Fernández, op. cit.

reform apparently did not significantly reduce productivity per basic irrigated hectare but neither did it increase the capacity to absorb labour per unit of land. The difference in labour productivity is largely attributable to the fact that the private sector was able to keep its installations and remain flexible, showing a greater degree of capitalisation than in the reformed sector. Since the cost of labour employed in Sector II will continue to be influenced by the living conditions of the bulk of the population remaining on the *minifundios* of Sector I, whose income is of necessity much smaller than that of the peasants in the reformed sector, it is likely that there will continue to be a substantial surplus per worker in Sector II. As in the case of Mexico, this sector will tend to attract credit and other facilities, since the creation of the surpluses required by the urban population will be dependent on its dynamic growth.

The Chilean agrarian reform has practically done away with *latifundismo* and has provided the country with a broad sector of medium-sized farms. This will certainly have a positive effect on the use of land and water resources. On the other hand, it has benefited only a fraction (between 10 and 12 per cent) of the peasant masses. It is likely that these beneficiaries will join the new *rural middle class*, the creation of which seems to have been one of the principal objectives of the Christian Democrats who passed the 1967 law. But the problem of *minifundismo* and rural underemployment remains unsolved.

Unlike Peru and Bolivia, where there are still tracts of virgin land on the eastern slopes of the Andes which could be made available for settlement, in Chile, the enlargement of farmland is dependent on costly investments in irrigation works and soil improvement. Thus, while agrarian reform was a necessary condition for increasing rural employment and raising living standards among the peasant masses, it was not enough on its own. Since agricultural investment in Chile is not simply a problem of utilising an underemployed labour force, as in the case of new land settlements in countries with an expanding agricultural frontier, investment decisions must take into account the creation of alternative forms of employment, or the generation of the country's capacity to import, or both. Moreover, the social aims of the agrarian reform could not be achieved without a major restructing of the Chilean economy and Chilean society. The *Unidad Popular* government seemed to have understood the problem but consensus on the action to be taken was far from having been formed in Chile.

24 Economic aspects of the Cuban revolution

Singularity of the traditional Cuban economy

Cuba displays a number of peculiarities worth analysing separately in an overall study of the Latin American framework. Along with Puerto Rico, the island remained under Spanish rule until the beginning of this century, the colonial period having lasted almost a century longer in this area than in the rest of Latin America. When the Cuban people's struggle to win their independence created impediments to US trade, the United States government used the conflict as a pretext for taking over the remnants of Spain's former Empire in the Americas and Asia. Consequently, the Cuban National State started its independent life under the occupation of United States forces. This occupation has not yet entirely come to an end – the United States government still has a base on Cuban territory – and up to 1934 it could have been extended to the whole island at any time, 'in the interests of the Cuban people' as adjudged by the President of the United States, in accordance with the provisions of the famous 'Platt Amendment'. The delay of almost a century in starting the process of building a nation-state, and the particular circumstances attending its emergence under the tutelage of a powerful neighbour, make the Cuban process unique in the Latin American context. However, Cuba's singularity lies even deeper and its roots are to be found in the economic evolution of the island within the framework of the Antillean region.

The Spaniards first used the Caribbean islands as defence bases for their lines of communication with the mainland colonies. The indigenous populations, living at a rudimentary cultural level, were practically wiped out and extensive stock farming was established on the larger islands to supply the metropolitan fleets. From the seventeenth century, the smaller islands were occupied by the French and the English, who wanted to secure a foothold for an assault on the mainland. With a view to eventual penetration of the Spanish Empire, they encouraged white colonisation of the islands they had occupied, founding settlements of small planters who combined the growing of subsistence crops with the production of tobacco and indigo for the European market. These settlements, which had been of political value to the metropolitan countries because they could provide colonial militias[1] to be mobilised against the rich Spanish Empire, underwent profound changes during the latter part of the seventeenth century when the cultivation of sugar-cane was introduced into the islands by the Dutch settlers who had been driven out of the Brazilian Northeast. In fact, Dutch interests were responsible for developing sugar production in the Antilles. They financed sugar mills and the importation of slaves, provided technical assistance and guaranteed markets. Sugar ushered in a period of great prosperity for the island settlements, which had formerly lived in conditions of extreme poverty. But prosperity had its price: the social pattern of the islands was profoundly changed. White settlers emigrated, or became small planters marginalised on the poorest lands, while large sugar plantations were established, worked by Negro slaves imported from Africa and owned by a small number of wealthy proprietors or corporations of shareholders who lived in the metropolis. The island of Barbados offers a striking example of this process: between 1643 and 1667 the number of landowners in the island fell from 11,200 to 745 and the slave population increased from 5,680 to 82,023.[2]

While the French and English West Indies were becoming vast sugar plantations with a dense population of African origin, Cuba remained a scantily occupied territory of large cattle estates and small tobacco plantations. This situation is explained by the fact that Spain was herself a sugar producer and that the international sugar trade was almost entirely controlled by the Dutch. Consequently, although sugar was the most important commodity in international trade for more than two centuries, in the Spanish colonies it was produced for local consumption only. In the first half of the nineteenth century important changes occurred in the Antillean economy. The Haitian War of Liberation (1791–1804) brought about the collapse of the export economy of a colony that was at that time the world's leading coffee producer and one of the world's major sugar producers. The abolition of slavery in the

[1] Léon Vignols, 'Les Antilles Françaises sous l'Ancien Régime', *Revue d'Histoire Economique et Sociale*, 1928.
[2] V. T. Harlow, *A History of Barbados*, Oxford, 1926, p. 310.

English colonies in 1832, and in the French possessions in 1848, did not radically alter the living conditions of the Negro population but it did produce changes in the agrarian structure. Wherever land was available, even if of poor quality, former slaves tried to establish themselves as small independent producers, becoming subsistence farmers on *minifundios* in much the same way as in Haiti. However, since land was generally in short supply or held by the big plantation owners, the pattern that tended to prevail was a system whereby former slaves were obliged to combine subsistence farming on their own undersized plots of land with some form of wage labour on the plantation whenever this happened to suit the owners. It should be added that with the rise of beet sugar production, which had started during the Napoleonic Wars, the Antillean product began to lose its leading position on the world sugar market, largely as the result of the protection enjoyed by beet sugar on the European markets. To these factors for change in the pattern of the Antillean economy must be added the remarkable expansion of the United States market, whose geographical proximity made it the principal outlet for the region's exportable surpluses.

The expansion of Cuban sugar production in the nineteenth century took place with an eye to the US market, which was not bound by commercial treaty to other parts of the West Indies.[3] In this way, close commercial and financial bonds were established between the United States and Cuba during the colonial period.[4] The fight against Spanish rule, intensified after 1868, created a climate of insecurity for the big plantation owners with metropolitan connexions and facilitated the penetration of US interests. After 1901, with the elimination of Spanish power, and the American military occupation which lasted, with a number of interruptions, up to 1908, penetration of US business groups was consolidated and extended and, at the same time, the island's economy was completely transformed. Thus, in the short space of two decades – between 1901 and 1920 – the output of sugar rose from 1.5 million to 5 million tons, while radical changes were introduced into Cuban economic structures. Cane plantations spread rapidly and the amount of land controlled by the sugar corporations, largely foreign-owned, increased even more dramatically. Small planters were relegated to the tobacco-growing areas or to poorer lands on the lower slopes of mountains. The bulk of the rural population became agricultural labourers on the plantations, while the shortage of labour in the harvest season gave rise

[3] For data on Cuban sugar exports during the nineteenth century see Ramiro Guerra y Sánchez, *Azúcar y Población en las Antillas*, Havana, 1944.
[4] Cf. Julio Le Reverend, *Historia Economica de Cuba*, Barcelona 1972, pp. 205–6.

to a current of immigration mostly from the neighbouring islands.[5]

A comparison of the different forms of sugar economy in the Antilles will help us to identify certain distinctive features of the pre-revolutionary Cuban economy. To simplify, it can be said that three types of sugar economy existed in the region. In the first, which lingered on in Cuba until the end of the nineteenth century, we find slave labour, in the second a combination of rural wage earners and subsistence *minifundio* farmers, and in the third the prevalence of wage workers. The slave system, characterised by a marked rigidity in production costs – all costs were fixed since there was no difference between investments in equipment and in the labour force – was part of an economy completely geared to foreign trade. The system introduced into the English and French Antilles after the abolition of slavery brought an important element of flexibility, since the labour force could pay for itself, in part by growing subsistence crops. This greater flexibility of costs enabled sugar-cane growing to survive on several islands despite the impoverishment of soils and the difficulties created by the advent of beet sugar and the consequent increase in price instability.

The third type of sugar economy established itself in Cuba in the last century, spreading throughout the island once the last vestiges of slavery had disappeared.[6] Given the abundance of land suitable for semi-extensive use, it was possible to pay wages that were sufficiently high to offset the disadvantages of seasonal employment for the large majority of the labour force. This situation reflected the high rate of profits in the industry on the one hand and the relatively low cost of labour on the other, made possible by historical circumstances and by the inflow of immigrants from colonial and semi-colonial areas. It was likewise the result of the very special position of the industry since the high profitability of the sugar corporations was also based on a particular type of integration with the US economy whose negative aspects were to become evident only at a later stage, when the sugar economy was no longer in a position to absorb the increase in the labour force. It then became obvious that the Cuban sugar industry had to rely for its competitive edge on the availability of cheap labour, in other words on the almost complete lack of alternative sources of employment. The development of the sugar industry in Puerto Rico, where integration with the US economy took a different form, underlines the importance of this

---

[5] Cf. Ramiro Guerra y Sanchez, op. cit.

[6] Temporary bond labour was introduced in Cuba at the end of the nineteenth century, when Asian workers were brought in; it was of little significance, however, either in terms of labour relations, or as a source of manpower.

point. Since workers had the possibility of emigrating to the United States and since industrialisation created new employment opportunities in the island itself, there were serious obstacles to the development of the Puerto Rican sugar industry, whose output fell short of the basic quota it had been allocated by the US government. Consequently, despite a substantial rise in the productivity of labour – the number of workers on the cane plantations fell from 124,000 to 49,000 between 1934 and 1959 – Puerto Rican sugar production has declined since the Second World War.[7]

In the case of the Cuban economy, the cycle of expansion based on the export of sugar came to an end in the first half of the 1920s. This expansion was accompanied by a rise in the export coefficient and growing integration with the United States economy. At one point the sugar industry contributed as much as 30 per cent to the domestic product and accounted for 80 per cent of the export total. The situation of the Cuban economy during this period was in some respects similar to that of the Venezuelan economy in the 1950s, with the difference that, whereas prices on the international oil market were remarkably stable, sugar prices were – and indeed still are – extremely unstable. In the period immediately following the First World War, the price of sugar rose steeply, reaching a record level of 22 cents a pound, only to fall in the early 1920s to 4 cents a pound. The ensuing crisis revealed the vulnerability of the economic system that had been created in the country. Economic activity became increasingly dependent on US financial groups. The country's banking network was taken over largely by foreign banks and the very existence of an independent monetary system was seriously challenged. Cuba sheltered behind a preferential tariff system, exporting her sugar to the United States under conditions similar to those obtaining in the Lesser Antilles, whose exports were given preferential treatment by the respective metropolitan countries. The Reciprocal Trade Agreement of 1903, which had reduced US tariffs on Cuban sugar imports, also gave products from the United States preferential entry into the Cuban market. The system worked along the lines of a free trade area, enabling each country to specialise in those products it was best able to supply. In practice, however, Cuba was able to supply one product only, while the United States could produce a range of hundreds, if not thousands, of products. Moreover, the prices of such products were set in the US market, which meant that on average they would not fluctutate too far above or below the level of wholesale prices in the country, whereas sugar

[7] Rafael Picó, *Puerto Rico: Planificación y Acción*, San Juan de Puerto Rico, 1962.

prices were determined in the international market (the situation obtaining before the quota was fixed) in terms of the available surpluses in a large number of countries producing mainly for their own home markets. To accommodate fluctuations in external demand, sugar producers kept large tracts of land in reserve, which meant that land tended to be permanently under-utilised and its yield neglected.

The problems created by tariff disarmament vis-à-vis the United States could have been less serious had Cuba possessed an independent monetary system, a basic condition for the implementation of a policy designed to defend the domestic level of income. Cuban banks, predominantly foreign-owned, operated with a high liquidity ratio and held a large part of their assets in foreign currency. Consequently, a fall in the value of exports could create unemployment without causing serious balance of payments problems. This situation contrasted sharply with that in other countries of the region where a contraction in the value of exports had drastic effects on the balance of payments, forcing devaluation of the exchange rate and indirectly creating a protection mechanism akin to a rise in tariffs. The Cuban economy operated as if its circulating medium consisted entirely of foreign exchange, while the banking system enjoyed a liquidity ratio of 50 per cent. In sum, the country lacked the minimum decision-making autonomy necessary to initiate the processes that form a national economic system.

Reaction against the situation outlined above came in the latter half of the 1920s, leading in 1927 to a change in tariff legislation that became the starting-point for the first attempt to diversify the Cuban economy. The period saw the beginning of an industrialisation process resembling the process started in other Latin American countries in the late nineteenth century under the impulse of expanding exports. In Cuba, however, the process had barely begun before the 1929 crisis, which assumed catastrophic proportions for that country because of the complete lack of defence mechanisms. Following the announcement of protectionist measures by the US, the bottom fell out of the sugar market. With prices plummeting to incredible levels – the lowest level for 1932 corresponded to 2.5 per cent of the highest level reached in the preceding decade – the country's economic life was almost paralysed and the resultant unemployment rate can seldom have been paralleled in any other country.

Industrialisation being virtually non-existent, Cuba was in no position to handle this crisis like the other countries in the region with similar levels of per capita income and domestic markets of comparable size. In other words, the minimum conditions for starting an import-substitution process had not been created. It cannot be asserted categorically that if Cuban industrialisation had begun a decade earlier the country's evolution in the depression period would have proceeded along the same lines as that of the region's more developed countries. None of these countries was so closely bound to a dominant economy as to lack an autonomous monetary system, which was the case in Cuba. Import-substituting industrialisation in this period was promoted through inflation and exchange controls, a situation hard to envisage in the case of a country whose banking system was controlled from abroad. None the less, the crisis proved to be an acid test and the considerable influence exercised by foreign interests in the country is evident in the fact that a way out was sought in the direction of closer integration with the US economy.

In 1934 the US government abrogated the Platt Amendment as part of President Franklin D. Roosevelt's Good Neighbour Policy. The United States kept the Guantánamo military base but there was no longer any legal justification for the US government to exercise the right to intervene that it had claimed since the defeat of Spanish power. In that same year, the first steps were taken to link the Cuban economy more intimately to that of the United States, on a basis which experience had already shown to be non-viable. To counter the wave of protectionism that had swept the United States during the crisis, leading to a reduction of imports of Cuban sugar in favour of domestic production, including that of Puerto Rico and Hawaii, Cuban interests demanded a *quota* on the US market. As a result of this pressure, Cuba was assigned a basic quota of 28 per cent of the US market under the Costingan–Jones Law of 1932. The quota signified a guaranteed market share but this was substantially smaller than the proportion accounted for by Cuban sugar in the past. On the other hand, it created a new form of dependence: quota exports of Cuban sugar were sold at American market prices, which were well above prices obtaining in the world market and also more stable. In other words, Cuba was protected by a US government policy that had been designed to organise the domestic commodity market and to defend the real income levels of the country's farmers. In the same year that American legislation extended to Cuba some of the benefits arising from the New Deal Policy, the Cuban government signed a complementary trade agreement with the United States in which tariff disarmament was taken a stage further: the margin of preference in favour of US exporters was increased and new items were added to the list of products to be given preferential treatment.

Thus, just when the Cuban State was taking a decisive step towards consolidating its position following the repeal of the Platt Amendment, the Cuban economy became more dependent and less viable. Industrialisation was sacrificed – in this period several recently built factories were demolished and the equipment was sold to other countries in the region that were fostering the development of local industry – in favour of strengthening the sugar economy within a framework that implied its stagnation. The only rational basis for the guidelines implicit in this economic policy would have been a growing integration with the United States along the lines of the pattern that was to prevail in Puerto Rico after the 1940s. As it was, the stagnation of the sugar sector meant that land, labour and capital resources were considerably under-utilised. Since no Cuban product could hope to compete with US imports, these resources could not be utilised. The Puerto Rican solution was to subsidise investment in the island with funds provided by the US government, while at the same time encouraging the absorption of surplus manpower by the United States. In fact, within the space of a quarter of a century, the Puerto Rican population living in the metropolis equalled that remaining on the island.

In Cuba, where political developments had been moving towards the consolidation of a sovereign nation-state, the guidelines adopted in the early 1930s led to an inevitable impasse in the economic sphere. The export sector, on which all other economic activities were dependent, made no progress between the 1920s and the 1950s, while the country's population doubled. The economy tended to adapt itself to conditions of permanent underemployment of the country's labour force, a situation which led to the reinforcement of trade unions committed to defending stability in employment. Capital resources formed in the country tended to find their way abroad and the economy's investment rate was extremely low. Part of the resources available were invested in land, which was used to establish extremely unproductive cattle *latifundia*. Thus, the Cuban economy in this period was characterised by the persistence of a high unemployment coefficient, the export of capital, and the underutilisation of agricultural lands.

In the years following the Second World War, systematic studies of the Cuban economy undertaken by the country's economists and by international agencies drew attention to its intrinsic irrationality. As a result of these studies an attempt was made to provide the Cuban State with wider means of action, particularly at the monetary level. The Cuban National Bank was founded in this period and a number of other institutions were established with a view to promoting the country's development. After 1952 the government began to intervene directly in the marketing of sugar, through the National Bank. Unsold stocks were withdrawn from the market along the lines of the coffee policy adopted in Brazil at the beginning of the present century. The aim of this policy was to prevent crop fluctuations attributable to climatic factors from having an adverse effect on world market prices, while at the same time cushioning the impact of income fluctuations in the export sector on the economy as a whole. In addition to the attempts made to regulate the export sector, the Cuban government sponsored investment in the agricultural, livestock and manufacturing sectors with a view to promoting import substitution. It has been estimated that between 1954 and 1958 fixed capital investment in the manufacturing industry, financed largely by the State, amounted to 250 million dollars. Of this total, 68 million dollars were invested in oil refineries and 17 million dollars in the chemical industry. The pulp and paper industry, using cane bagasse as its raw material, began to develop in this period.[8] However, despite the new bearings in government policy, the annual growth rate of gross domestic product per capita between 1948 and 1958 was only 1 per cent, as compared with a rate of nearly 2 per cent for the region as a whole. It should be added that the counterpart to the State's efforts to finance the private sector's investments in the 1950s was a marked increase in the external debt and a no less considerable decline in the country's gold and foreign exchange reserves. Cuba was on the verge of a crisis which would have forced the government either to back down on its investment programme in order to build up its reserves of foreign exchange – at the cost of aggravating unemployment – or to take a decisive step forward in the direction of doing away with the preferential system and the reciprocity agreements that were subjecting the Cuban economy to semi-integration with the economy of the United States, in conditions tending to widen the gap between the living standards of the Cuban and American people.

Redistributive stage of the revolution

The 1959 revolution precipitated the course of events and impelled the country towards the second alternative at a spectacular pace. The reaction of the United States and the subsequent economic blockade of the island imposed by the Washington government, together with the sup-

---

[8] For a retrospective analysis of Cuba's industrial development see 'El Desarrollo Industrial de Cuba', a document presented by the Cuban government to the *Latin American Symposium on Industrialization* organised by ECLA in March 1966, and included in the ECLA publication of that name.

port given to the new Cuban government by the Soviet Union and other socialist countries, caused events to move with incredible speed, changing the very essence of the range of options arising out of the country's previous evolution. The revolution must be regarded as part of the formative process of the Cuban nation-state, a process that had begun with the country's struggle for liberation from Spanish power. But the later course of the revolution cannot fully be understood without taking into account the fact that the last act of this liberation process was played out against the United States at the critical time when the balance of nuclear power called for a strict demarcation of the spheres of influence of the two super-powers. Thus, the international circumstances surrounding the Cuban Revolution came to play a decisive role in the course it was to follow.

From an economic point of view, the evolution of post-revolutionary Cuba can be divided into two periods. The first is marked by a policy designed to change the power structure and the distribution of income; the second by a concerted effort to bring about the country's economic reconstruction.

The revolution's first major act in the economic sphere was the promulgation of an Agrarian Reform Law which differed from other Latin American land reform legislation in that it did not aim to divide up the land. The maximum landholding permitted was 30 *caballerias*[9] (402.6 hectares) and any land in excess of this area was expropriated. Where the land was already divided and had formerly been worked by tenant farmers or sharecroppers, it was distributed to them in parcels of 5 *caballerias*, i.e. 67 hectares, each. Where estates had been organised as a farming unit, the unit was preserved and co-operatives or State farms (*granjas*) were set up. Medium-sized properties of between 5 and 30 *caballerias*, permitted under this first reform, were done away with by the Second Agrarian Reform Law promulgated in October 1963. Essentially, the reform involved the abolition of rural rents formerly paid by some 100,000 small farmers, and the introduction of State control over all medium and large estates, formerly run as agricultural enterprises. The State was represented by a powerful institution created specifically for the purpose: the National Land Reform Institute (Instituto Nacional de la Reforma Agrária – INRA). Independent smallholders, both old and new, owning around 7.2 million hectares of land, were organised in a National Association of Small Farmers (Asociación Nacional de Agricultores Pequeños – ANAP). Medium and large farms, controlled by the

---

[9] One *caballeria* is equal to 33.16 acres.

State through INRA, account for around 11.4 million hectares divided into some 1,500 agricultural units.[10]

In addition to the agrarian reform, several other measures helped to change the pattern of income distribution.[11] In March 1959, urban rents were lowered by between 30 and 50 per cent and at the same time higher wages were paid to urban and rural workers. Government expenditure on social services (health, education and housing in particular) was raised from $390 million to $1,321 million. Conservative estimates have allowed that the sum effect of the various measures adopted between 1959 and 1961 was to transfer at least 15 per cent of the Cuban national income from property-owning groups to the working masses. The Cuban Revolution was thus, in its initial stage, closer to the distributive spirit of classic socialist ideology than to the developmental socialism that had prevailed in the Eastern European countries. In the latter case, income was transferred to the State with a view to raising the rate of capital formation.

The initial orientation of the Cuban Revolution may be accounted for by the fact that its leaders had been influenced by studies of the country's economy before the revolution, which invariably emphasised the existence of considerable unused productive capacity attributable to the lack of effective demand and the extremely inequitable distribution of income. It was felt that a policy directed towards remedying this situation would bring about a rapid growth of the product, although it would at the same time create balance of payments problems over the medium term. To forestall these problems the external sector of the economy would be brought under effective control. This policy was to lead the Cuban State to place the country's economic relations with the United States on a completely new footing. In fact, the margin of idle capacity in the industrial sector was substantial: ECLA has estimated that in the major branches of industry, including textiles, this margin was as high as 60 per cent in 1959. This explains why the domestic product was able to grow sufficiently in the first two years of the revolution to absorb a large part of the expansion of monetary demand brought about by the rise in wages.[12] The short-term elasticity of supply was not, however, confined

[10] For a complete survey of the Cuban land reform see Michel Gutelman, *L'Agriculture Socialisée à Cuba*, Paris, 1967, René Dumont, *Cuba, Socialisme et Développement*, Paris, 1964, and Julio le Riverend, 'Conclusiones sobre la Reforma Agrária en Cuba' in *Les Problèmes Agraires des Amériques Latines*.

[11] ECLA, *Economic Survey of Latin America, 1963*.

[12] For an introduction to this first stage of the revolution, from the economic point of view, see Dudley Seers (and others), *Cuba: The Economic and Social Revolution*, London, 1964.

to the manufacturing sector. The sugar harvest in 1961 was the second largest in Cuban history and between 1958 and 1962 rice production rose from 163,000 tons to 300,000 tons, maize production from 134,000 tons to 257,000 tons and production of beans from 33,000 tons to 78,000 tons.[13]

The lack of structural diversification in the Cuban economy meant that any attempt to speed up the rate of growth would bring immediate pressure on the balance of payments. It was thus only to be expected that the external sector would rapidly develop a severe foreign exchange bottleneck that was to determine the future course of the Cuban Revolution. Exchange control, the rationing of scarce foreign exchange, the need to find new markets for the country's sugar surpluses and new credit lines to finance imports of equipment, whose overall volume had to be rapidly increased, became pressing problems. This came at a time when the expropriation of land, largely owned by North American citizens, had led to the formation of a powerful pressure group in the United States violently opposed to any form of public or private co-operation between the United States and the revolutionary government in Cuba. The Cuban government began to diversify its sources of supply and it was the purchase of crude oil from the Soviet Union, to be refined at the island's US-owned refineries, that provoked the incident that was to snowball into the nationalisation of all property owned by North American citizens in the island whose assets were worth over 1,000 million dollars.

Whatever may have been the original intention of Cuba's leaders, there can be no doubt that after the severing of economic relations with the United States they were left with very little room to manoeuvre. With US supplies close at hand, the Cuban economy had traditionally operated with limited stocks, a far from negligible advantage. Once these stocks had been used up, the shortage of spare parts became a serious problem. Integration with the centrally planned economies called for a number of adjustments on the part of these and for radical changes in Cuban economic structures. Such changes could not be made overnight, and domestic supply problems of no mean order were to arise during the transition period. The gravity of these problems was apparently not grasped at first and it was thought that a concerted effort to promote import substitution both in the agricultural and in the industrial sectors would ease the pressure on the balance of payments within a reasonably short space of time. As a result of this policy, a large number of new projects were launched in the agricultural sector – the country had been largely dependent on imports of food in the pre-

---

[13] Michel Gutelman, *L'Agriculture Socialisée à Cuba.*

revolutionary era – and imports of industrial equipment were considerably stepped up. The consequences were extremely unfortunate: there was a drop in the productivity of the agricultural sector and the shift of factors away from sugar production began to affect the country's only means of earning enough foreign exchange to boost the dwindling capacity to import. As for the industrial sector, it soon became apparent that industry would continue to be heavily dependent on imported intermediate products for some time to come.

Besides the above-mentioned problems, we must bear in mind the speed with which the country's entire economic structure was changed. A vicious circle was created in which the government tended to bring all economic decisions under strict central control without having the technical and administrative resources needed for their implementation to be effective. Medium and large agricultural enterprises were taken over by the State at a time when large numbers of qualified technicians formerly employed in the agricultural sector were leaving the country. Similarly, the entire industrial sector was brought under direct State control when the majority of experienced managers and industrial engineers were emigrating.

The structural organisation of the industrial sector is based on several ministries – the Ministry of Industry, the Ministries of the Food, Sugar and Building Industries – and central government agencies such as the National Fisheries Commission and the Cuban Tobacco Institute. These various ministries and autonomous agencies control consolidated *enterprises* which in their turn are responsible for the direction of *establishments* or production units. By and large, the enterprises administer between 10 and 25 factories each. In 1964, 172 factories accounted for 70 per cent of the value of production and for 49 per cent of the labour force employed in the manufacturing sector.[14]

Given the lack of diversification of the industrial sector – the structure of the Cuban industrial system in 1964 resembled that of the Central American countries – and the poor development of local resources of raw materials, both agricultural and mineral, the import content of the industrial product is very high. As a consequence, to achieve a rise of one dollar in the output of the food industry, excluding sugar, 30 cents had to be spent on direct and indirect imported inputs. In the textile industry the amount required was 22 cents, in the chemical industry 34 cents, in the metal-using and engineering industries 43 cents, etc.[15]

[14] Government of Cuba, 'El Desarrollo Industrial de Cuba'.
[15] *Ibid.*

Reconstruction phase in the external sector

The new line of post-revolutionary economic policy began to take shape after 1963–4. In 1963 the balance of payments deficit amounted to 323 million dollars, corresponding to 37 per cent of the total value of imports and approximately 10 per cent of the domestic product. Sugar production, which had risen to 6,767,000 tons in 1961, i.e. 1 million tons above the average for the preceding decade, fell to 4,815,000 tons in 1962 and to 3,821,000 tons in 1963. The decline was in part attributable to extremely adverse weather conditions but there can be no doubt that the main reason was the reduction in the area planted to sugar cane – in some cases involving the ploughing up of highly productive cane lands – and the acute shortage of labour at the peak of the sugar harvest. The Cuban experience of this period made it very clear that to transform the economic structure of an underdeveloped country it is not enough to have a power structure with the ability to increase the capitalisation effort. It is equally necessary to have a certain margin of capacity to import, in the absence of which the assimilation of technological progress will be insufficient. Even if Cuba had shifted privately owned productive resources confiscated in the early stages of the Revolution towards capital formation – in the same way that the Eastern European countries channelled to this end resources taken from the agricultural sector – the possibility of transforming the economic structure would still have been dependent on the capacity to import, simply because the capacity to *transform* resources in an underdeveloped and under-industrialised economy is extremely limited. The Cuban Revolution had begun by redistributing income with a view to raising the consumption level of the masses, which meant not only that the rate of investment would fail to rise but that the capacity to import released by the reduction in consumption of the wealthy classes would be absorbed by the increase in imports of non-durable consumer goods or intermediate products and raw materials needed to produce such goods locally. In fact, the value of imports rose from 638 million dollars in 1960 to 867 million dollars in 1963 and 1,015 million dollars in 1964, the increment being financed entirely by external aid, almost exclusively provided by the Soviet Union. In 1964 the import coefficient was over 30 per cent, a level which, since 1930, had been matched in the region only by Venezuela.

The new policy directives formulated after 1963/4 were essentially aimed at the recovery of the capacity to import through the more systematic exploitation of the country's comparative advantages in sugar production and other agricultural and livestock products. Thus, Cuba returned to the basic pattern of her economic evolution but in a new context. The Soviet Union undertook to increase its imports of Cuban sugar from 2.1 million tons in 1964 to 5 million tons by 1970. Sugar prices seemed unlikely to create serious difficulties since, even if the Soviet Union paid prices well above those prevailing in the world market at that time, it would still be saving a considerable amount of money in view of the much higher costs of locally produced sugar.[16] In other words, the price paid could be twice the world market price and still represent only a third of local production costs. This example emphasises the considerable advantages to be gained from the organisation of international markets. By using Cuban imports to meet the rise in domestic sugar consumption, the Soviet Union was in a position to reduce the domestic prices of sugar while at the same time providing Cuba with a stable market for its exports over the medium term. During the 1960s, the Cuban government set a target of 10 million tons of sugar by 1970, which meant raising output by 50 per cent in terms of the level attained in 1961. In order to achieve this production target, the area under cultivation was substantially extended, but results were well below expectations because of the significant fall both in the yield per hectare and in the raw-sugar yield of the cane.

Since Cuba faces a shortage of water which must be shared with other crops, the possibility of expanding sugar production is limited by the availability of water and the relative cost of fertilisers. It is true that these constraints may be countered by improvements in the overall level of the country's agricultural techniques. Nevertheless, it must be borne in mind that the relative advantages of cane production largely reflect the low level of capital formation in the economy as a whole and the relatively abundant supply of comparatively cheap labour. Any change in these basic conditions will obviously affect the present comparative advantage of sugar.

In recent years the Cuban government has been assessing possibilities for developing new export lines. Stock farming is in a strong position in this respect and it is hoped to raise productivity substantially within the next few years. Cattle herds increased from 6.2 million head in 1963 to 7.1 million in 1970. Nickel has become an export item of increasing importance. Although its exploitation involves special technical problems, Cuba has exceptionally rich deposits. Coffee and citrus fruits are being planted or replanted with an eye to export possibilities, but the results have varied considerably.

[16] Cf. René Dumont, *Cuba, Socialisme et Développement.*

As a consequence of the new directives adopted, the area dedicated to a number of crops – maize, cotton, oilseeds and rice – has been reduced. Production of rice, which competes with sugar cane for irrigation water, fell from 237,000 tons in 1963/4 to 97,000 tons in 1967/8. As it was impossible to continue increasing imports, general rationing had to be introduced. On the other hand, to provide the investments required by the plan to expand the capacity to import, the industrial programme devised in the first stage of the evolution, with a view to promoting import-substitution, had to be altered, which implied scrapping a large number of projects for which equipment had already been imported. The industrialisation effort was slowed down and reorientated towards reinforcing the agricultural economy and taking advantage of the external economies it created. Top priority was given to industrial sectors related to agriculture such as chemical fertilisers – nitrogens and phosphates – and agricultural machinery. Food-processing industries, particularly dairy products and citrus juice industries, both partly geared towards the export market, have also been fostered, as has the fishing industry, whose output was raised from 35,600 tons in 1963 to 80,000 tons in 1969. Another development priority is the building materials industry. As a result of investment in the cement industry, its production capacity was increased from 800,000 tons to 2.2 million tons in the course of the 1960s.

The essential aim of Cuba's new economic policy was thus the recovery and expansion of sugar production with a view to providing the country with a basic capacity to import which will leave room to manoeuvre changing economic structures. We have already indicated that the results were disappointing. The 1970 harvest was 8,533,000 tons[17], only 26 per cent higher than in 1961. Moreover, average costs of production had increased considerably, making it imperative to change the emphasis of economic policy. Between 1971 and 1974, sugar production tended to stabilise at around 5.5 million tons, while at the same time greater efforts were made to expand the production of crops destined for the home market. As a result, rice production was raised to 326,000 tons in 1971, 38 per cent higher than the previous record in 1964. On the whole, food production, including animal protein products, increased significantly in the early 1970s, after having remained at a standstill in the preceding five-year period.

Throughout the latter half of the 1960s, the Cuban economy had been performing with a serious imbalance in the external sector. In 1968–9

[17] ECLA, *Economic Survey of Latin America*, Part I, Table 21.

the average value of exports was 658 million dollars, as against 1,128 million for imports. This meant that 48 per cent of the country's imports had to be financed from external credit, provided almost entirely by the Soviet Union. In 1970, however, the inflow of external funds was reduced to one-half the level of the previous year and in the first half of the 1970s, the situation improved considerably, as a result of the higher sugar prices on the free market. Sugar exports to the Soviet Union, which had accounted for 45 per cent of the total in 1970, fell to 31 per cent and 26 per cent in the next two years. This enabled Cuba to take advantage of the sharp rise in free-market prices, which had more than trebled during that period. Despite the continued rise in free-market prices in 1973–4, there is no guarantee that the relative prices of sugar will remain high in the future. The difficulties encountered during the renegotiation of the International Sugar Agreement in 1973 provide an unmistakable warning in this respect. The fact that the Cuban economy continues to rely mainly on sugar for the generation of its capacity to import, is a clear indication that its degree of external vulnerability remains high.

Up to the end of the 1960s the Cuban economy seemed to be groping towards an individual path of development.[18] The socialist ideals of its leaders, whose egalitarian aims have been given tangible expression in the concerted effort to bring about rapid improvements in the living conditions of the masses, affect the entire economic process. The remarkable victories scored in raising the educational levels of the masses and improving their health conditions, together with the mobilisation of the people and their integration into the political process, are ample proof of the outstanding ability of the revolutionary leaders. Nonetheless, the basic economic problem continued to stand: when would the country be able to count on a productive system capable of providing an increasing flow of goods and services that would allow the Cuban population to have access to the benefits of the technological revolution taking place on a world-wide scale? The plans implemented in the latter half of the 1960s represented an intermediate stage: they aimed to recover the capacity to import, thus reducing dependence on foreign aid, which for some time was a necessary condition for survival. A new stage began in the 1970s, with emphasis on raising labour productivity in all activities related to internal supply. The rapid increase in production during the period under review confirmed that a substantial proportion of the investments made in the 1960s, both in agriculture and in industry,

---

[18] A summary of the recent evolution of the Cuban economy (up to the beginning of 1967) is found in Robin Blackburn's article, 'The Economics of the Cuban Revolution', in Claudio Veliz (ed.), *Latin America and the Caribbean: A Handbook*.

had been under-utilised. With the adoption of a more realistic incentive policy, there was a notable rise in labour productivity as a result of the elimination of this margin of under-utilised capacity. On the other hand, the increased supply of goods permitted the absorption of part of the excess liquidity available in the consumer sector since the early days of the revolution, which in turn increased the labour supply. Thus, growth of the product was accompanied by a reduction in its social cost.

It should be borne in mind that the agricultural sector includes some 150,000 small farmers largely responsible for supplying the domestic market. In 1965 the private sector supplied 69 per cent of the vegetables, 68 per cent of the fruit, 58 per cent of the yams and tubers, 40 per cent of the milk and 32 per cent of the rice available for domestic consumption. Despite the fact that 43 per cent of the agricultural land is in the hands of the private sector, this sector had not been involved in agricultural planning, which tended to be over-rigid and could not be adapted to production units responsive solely to economic incentives. The decision announced in January 1968, to do away with the system whereby small private farmers were under contract to the State and had to hand over their surplus produce to public pooling and purchasing centres, regardless of fixed prices[19] and in exchange for standard inputs, seemed to indicate that Cuba was moving towards complete collectivisation of the agricultural sector. The experience of other socialist countries had shown that this would prove by no means an easy task. This tentative phase was prolonged by the fact that in Cuba the philosophical conflict underlying all socialist revolutions was particularly vital: a conflict between those who believe that the liberation of mankind (the destruction of the social and psychological structures that inhibit or deform human creativity) should precede the search for economic effectiveness and those who contend that no victory in the human sphere can be lasting if the material basis of society is not substantially broadened from the outset. The latter approach came to prevail at the beginning of the 1970s.

[19] Cf. Henri Denis, 'Le Socialisme Cubàin à la Recherche d'un Modèle Economique', *Le Monde*, 10 January 1968.

25 Present problems and prospects

After a century and a half of separation from their former European metropolises, the Latin American countries still present, jointly or severally, a profile not yet fully delineated. Each sub-region is at a different stage of a process of cultural homogenisation, of social and political modernisation and of an economic process that is in many respects *sui generis*. The institutions that formed the substratum of colonial society – the *hacienda*, the dependent indigenous community and the agricultural enterprise producing for export – remained virtually intact in the period that followed and provided the foundation for the formation of the nation-states. Economic development, insignificant in the three preceding centuries, gained momentum in the mid-nineteenth century, with the entry of the region into the system of international division of labour that emerged from the Industrial Revolution. Up to the beginning of the present century this development consisted in making extensive use of available land and labour resources for the purpose of specialising in the export of primary products. In many cases this required substantial infrastructural investment, generally financed abroad. Thus, the penetration of modern technology favoured the infrastructure rather than the directly productive activities.

Modernisation of infrastructures provided agglomeration economies favouring the urban populations, which began to increase in the last quarter of the nineteenth century as a reflexion of the expanding external sector and the final consolidation of the nation-states. With urbanisation, the transplanting of private and public consumption standards from countries with an industrial-based civilisation was intensified. Hence, modernisation was accomplished through the adoption of finished products and the transplantation of behaviour patterns related to the *use* of the product rather than through the assimilation of modern technology related to productive forms and processes. Adoption of higher standards of consumption, particularly in the public health sector, had a marked impact on the demographic situation. Death rates declined steadily, falling to levels similar to those obtaining in countries with far higher standards of living. On the other hand, birth rates remained very high since, in many essential respects, the living conditions of the broad mass of the population were unaffected by development. The growth of large urban nuclei, bringing changes in the process of capital formation – particularly with regard to building techniques – and the rising levels of living of part of the population, set in train an industrialisation process that was to open out in a number of directions and gain in depth as a result of the structural tensions created by the crisis in the export sector.

Given that the assimilation of technological progress at the level of the productive processes is the basis of economic development, the Latin American process should be approached from this particular angle. I have pointed out that in the phase of expanding primary exports the penetration of modern technology was virtually confined to the infra-structure sector. In the mineral-exporting economies, the enclave nature of the export sector prevented technical progress in this sector from having any significant effect on the economy as a whole. In the case of the farming and cattle-raising economies producing for export, whether because their comparative advantages were based on extensive use of resources or because their agrarian organisation did not favour capital-isation, experience showed that the assimilation of technical innovations would be slow or non-existent. The role of opening the door to the as-similation of modern technology on a wide front fell to the industrial-isation process. Simplifying, it can be said that assimilation of technical progress in Latin America took place initially at the level of consumption and that, strictly speaking, it was only after industrialisation that there was assimilation of technical progress at the level of the forms of produc-tion. This disparity was bound to create a number of problems and it was precisely in this area that economic development assumed the peculiar-ities characteristic of the region. Transplantation of a highly complex technology gave rise to a new type of dualism between highly capitalised productive units employing modern technical processes and productive sectors employing traditional techniques and having a low level of capital investment, a dualism superimposed on the former polarisation between market-economy sector and subsistence-economy sector.

Latin American industrialisation was just beginning when the inter-national economy entered a phase of important changes. The traditional system of international division of labour, based on the exchange of raw materials for manufactures, began to break down, giving way to decen-tralisation of industrial activity on a world-wide scale following the lead of large enterprises creating or controlling technical progress in the form of new products and new productive processes. In Latin America this process largely took the form of a progressive control of local manu-facturing activities, in sectors in which technological progress was most rapid, by large enterprises for the most part with head offices in the United States. The process of transmitting progress in technology, formerly implicit in the exportation of equipment and machinery traded for raw materials, now tended to take the form of international decentral-isation by the big industrial groups. This new form of technological deployment aggravated certain distortions that had emerged in the preceding period. Since technical progress implies a rise in the capital outlay per person employed – reflecting the particular conditions of the countries in the vanguard of the accumulation process, responsible for creating new techniques – assimilation of this process tends to provoke serious structural distortions, particularly if it is not accompanied by a significant increase in the overall product or if it means that a growing share of income accrues to foreign-owned factors and generates a flow of payments to be made abroad. In countries with a structural manpower surplus, where wage rates reflect the living conditions of the bulk of the population and not the degree to which technological progress has been assimilated, the benefits of increased productivity will tend to be con-centrated in the hands of owners and entrepreneurs. Hence the character-istic discontinuities in the demand schedule, comprising the demand of two distinct groups: a large group whose consumption remains undiver-sified and grows by the addition of new individuals only, and a minority whose demand is highly dynamic both qualitatively and quantitatively.

Thus, we find a pattern in which the spread of technical progress is decidedly slow and access to the benefits of increased productivity is restricted. The result is that large groups of the population constitute marginalised masses, virtually unaffected by progress. Even in countries where development has been steadier and more intensive, as in the case of Mexico, a large part of the population has failed to gain access to the benefits accruing from such development and the gap between this group and the medium- and high-income groups is constantly widening. The marginalised rural population, composed of minifundists and seasonal farm labourers, is extremely undernourished and has a life expectancy far below the national mean. In the urban areas, the phenomenon of marginalisation is more visible because of the precarious housing con-ditions.

A survey of the performance of the Latin American economy in the post-war period shows three easily identifiable periods: the first, which lasted until the end of the 1950s, is characterised by rapid growth; the second, which lasted into the late 1960s, evidenced a marked slackening in growth rates; and the third, which began around 1968, is distinguished by a renewed acceleration of the growth process. There can be little doubt that the major factors determining these trends were of external origin. In the first two periods, the decisive factor was the behaviour of the terms of trade, which improved substantially in the first half of the 1950s, only to deteriorate sharply in the first five years of the 1960s. In the third period, the behaviour of the terms of trade continued to play a key role but another major contributing factor was the high level of foreign capital inflows. This level, which had remained stationary at 1.5 billion dollars between 1961 and 1967, rose to 3.6 billion in 1971 and 5 billion in 1972 and 1973, a figure representing more than one-fifth of the value of the region's imports of goods and services. Interacting with these external factors, the process of industrial change went ahead: in the first two periods through industrialisation in the form of import-substitution and in the third through consolidation of the substitution process and promotion of manufacturing for export. The industrialisation process was accompanied by growing control of foreign groups over productive activities related to domestic markets.

In the early years of the 1960s, under the impact of the Cuban Revolution and the slackening of growth in countries such as Chile, Argentina and Brazil, there was an intensification of the debate over the real significance of the region's economic development. Latin Americans had become increasingly conscious of the high social cost of this development, of the non-viability of wider distribution of its benefits among substantial sectors of the population, and of the region's growing external dependence in respect of the operation of the productive system and the orientation of development. As a result, the preoccupation with *economic programming techniques* gave way to a concern with *integrated economic and social development strategies*. More and more studies appeared, proposing various development *styles* and development *models*, some emphasising the maximisation of growth rates, some the strengthening of national control over productive systems and others the need to widen distribution of the benefits of development. Thus, in Brazil, the emphasis was on the achievement of high growth rates for the gross domestic product; in Peru on the reinforcement of national power, embodied in the State, in relation to foreign groups and the local oligarchy which had traditionally controlled the economic system; while in Chile, the Popular Unity Government sought to bring about democratisation of the nation's wealth.

The very success of the Brazilian experience, however, helped to lay bare the essence of the problem, by exposing the ambiguity of a development concept understood in terms of the reproduction of cultural patterns transplanted from wealthier societies. The concentration of income and the enormous waste of resources following in the wake of development *at any cost*, gave additional ammunition to those who argued that if under-development, in its most anti-social aspects, is to be effectively eliminated, development must be an integral part of a broader social project. On the other hand, the brutal curtailment of the Chilean experience once more called attention to the restricted field of action open to the region's social reformers, subject as they are to enormous internal and external pressures.

Economic analysis is merely a first approach to the study of complex historical processes currently under way in Latin America. We must not forget that what is happening in this region continues to reflect the action of exogenous variables, since Latin American countries are dependent on exports of raw materials and imported technology. Moreover, the most up-to-date industrial sectors are integrated in financially powerful multi-national groups, operating with equally powerful political backing. On the other hand, the disparities among countries at different stages of economic growth and cultural homogenisation considerably limit the scope of any attempt to forecast trends. There can be no doubt that development based on exports of raw materials and import-substituting industrialisation has reached the limits of its possibilities, at least in the case of the region's largest countries. Similarly, the institutional framework inherited from the colonial period or established shortly after separation from the mother countries seems to have exhausted its possibilities of adaptation to development needs. It is understandable, then, that problems relating to structural reform should have become the region's foremost concern. Discussion has focused increasingly on the means to be used for a structural reconstruction whose basic features are becoming more clearly defined. Among the most relevant points emerging from the list of topics being debated in the region the following are worth singling out:

1. Re-entry of the regional economies into the expanding lines of the international economy. The organisation of commodity markets so as to assure relative stability for commodity prices and the possibility of establishing medium-term forecasts of demand are of general concern. The effort to attain these objectives is helping to create a united front among the countries of the region and to promote a more broadly-based understanding with the other countries of the Third World. The adop-

tion by countries producing commodities and raw materials of a common trade policy towards the highly industrialised countries helped to strengthen the bonds between the region's countries and enhanced its bargaining position in negotiations with the United States, the European Common Market, the Soviet Union and Japan.

2. Reshaping of economic relations with the United States. The evolution of such relations indicates that the region is becoming a source of foreign exchange earnings which the United States uses to cover part of its balance-of-payments deficit with other regions of the world. Latin America's share of US imports has been declining persistently, falling from around one-third in the early 1950s to one-quarter of the total by the end of that decade and to 12 per cent in 1970. The deficit in the region's balance of trade was 1,399,000 dollars in 1970, compared with an average deficit of 831 million dollars annually in the period 1966–70 and 266 million in 1961–5. The magnitude of the imbalance becomes apparent if we bear in mind that in 1970, the servicing of private US capital cost the region 1,693 million dollars. The situation hastened to become even more serious subsequently, since US exports to the region increased from 5.7 to 15.1 billion dollars between 1970 and 1974.

3. Reshaping of relations with the big international consortia. We have already seen that the most dynamic sectors of the Latin American economy have been increasingly controlled by international consortia. Apart from problems relating to the general orientation of development, the choice of production techniques and the application of resources to research within the region, there is the problem of the appropriation by foreign groups of a considerable proportion of the benefits of increased productivity. Given the oligopolistic positions they occupy and the price-leadership policies they pursue, multi-national enterprises are in a position to plan their expansion on the basis of self-financing, complemented where necessary by recourse to local banking systems. In fact, in economies characterised by a sizeable structural manpower surplus, as is generally the case in the region, the enterprises that dominate the market are in a privileged position for retaining all the benefits of increased productivity, deriving from advances in technology and from the external economies which such enterprises are able to reap. Repercussions on the balance of payments are obvious, a situation which in itself could unleash forces that would act as a brake on development. An exceptionally complex problem is involved and it cannot be solved at the cost of obstructing the channels through which technological progress is transmitted. Although discussion of this problem is still at the preliminary stage, there is every indication that the solution must

be sought in the creation of new forms of enterprise, enabling foreign groups to co-operate with national organisations, acting in accordance with plans which make assimilation of new techniques subordinate to clearly-defined social objectives.

A move towards the solution of these and other problems related to external relations would be inconceivable without a parallel effort to bring about structural reforms and create new forms of co-operation in the region. Of the items included in this second part of the agenda, particular significance attaches to the following:

(a) *Reconstruction of economic structures with a view to intensifying the assimilation of modern technology in all productive sectors.* In most of the countries concerned, the intensification of technological progress in the agricultural sector is absolutely essential in order to combat soil erosion and stop the destruction of other non-renewable resources; to increase agricultural production, and to improve the distribution of national incomes. These social objectives can only be achieved within the framework of a social reconstruction effort wider in scope than the agrarian reforms carried out in the region.

(b) *Formulation of employment policies capable of putting an end to the present process of growing social marginalisation.* The penetration of modern technology in an underdeveloped economy, within the *laissez-faire* framework, creates or aggravates the type of dualism on the social plane which has been described as 'marginalisation'. The problem is all too familiar. It can only be solved by adopting a policy designed to prevent the market system from destroying forms of employment that cannot be replaced. Discussion of this problem is leading to a drastic reformulation of the idea of development which had come to prevail in the region.

(c) *Reorganisation of the public sector.* Since the State must assume growing responsibility for promoting development, it will have to undergo profound modifications. New forms of organisation that make it possible to reconcile adequate standards of efficiency with the coherence of purpose inherent in public action are already being developed in the region. The creation of new public enterprises, operating in strategic sectors for the promotion of development or the defence of collective interests, has proved increasingly successful. Progress has been slow, however, in the creation of new instruments of international action and control over foreign enterprises.

(d) *The achievement of a minimum of technological autonomy.* Given the peculiarities of the region's natural resources, particularly in the case of the tropical and subtropical areas, and in view of the *sui generis* aspects of its economy, Latin America's development calls for a concerted effort in promoting technological research and the background sciences required to consolidate and develop research findings. This effort will have to be carried out almost exclusively by the public sector or in State-financed university institutions, inasmuch as control of a large part of the private sector by foreign groups tends to make enterprises dependent on research centres located outside the region.

(e) *Co-operation at the regional level.* Most of the problems referred to can be adequately approached only within a framework of effective regional co-operation. On the other hand, co-operation presupposes the existence of viable national structures from the point of view of development. In other words: structural reconstruction, the organisation of the State so as to equip it to take command of national development processes, and the attainment of forms of closer co-operation at the regional level are interdependent problems, for which solutions can be arrived at only by approximations based on parallel efforts. In present conditions of inadequate structures and external dependence, *integration* would lead the region to a new impasse in underdevelopment. At the same time, existing national decision-centres would be even further deflated. In view of the marked disparities in present levels of development and of the magnitude of the internal structural reconstruction effort required, there is every likelihood that the integration process will continue to make slow progress and to suffer serious setbacks, as was the case in Central America in the late 1960s. Nevertheless, new forms of regional co-operation may be found, not only in the sphere of international action but also in relation to solving common problems and achieving closer financial co-operation. The policy of the Andean Group for the common treatment of foreign capital is a striking example of the new forms of co-operation which are beginning to emerge.

Possibly in no other region of the Third World has the debate on development engaged so many minds over the last twenty-five years. And in no other region has it been so difficult to justify the highly precarious living conditions of the great majority of the population, given the abundance of natural resources and the proclaimed successes of development policies. The experience of these twenty-five years has shown that behind the region's superficial similarities, there is a wide variety of historical conditions, which makes it likely that the struggle to overcome underdevelopment will continue to take many forms. The common denominator seems to be the realisation that the *laissez-faire* approach, in the context of dependency, inevitably leads to the exacerbation of social disparities, and that structural change requires a far greater political effort than had previously been envisaged. The easy optimism of the 1950s gave way to the apprehensions, impatience and frustrations of the 1960s. As we enter the last quarter of the twentieth century, the prospects for the future are still uncertain and many perplexities remain. But there can be no doubt that the authoritarian control of the old élites has finally been broken, and that the people of the region have begun to participate in the making of their own history.

Bibliography

I. UNITED NATIONS DOCUMENTS

UNITED NATIONS, ECONOMIC COMMISSION FOR LATIN AMERICA (ECLA).

América Latina y la Estrategia Internacional de Desarrollo, UN, 1973.

América Latina y los Problemas Actuales de la Energía, UN, 1974.

América Latina y la Política Comercial Internacional, UN (E/CN.12/773), 1967.

Analyses and Projections of Economic Development, UN (E/CN.12/363), 1955.

La CEPAL y el Análisis del Desarrollo Latino-americano, UN(E/CN.12/AC. 61/10), 1968.

Contribución a la Política de Integración Económica de América Latina, UN (E/CN.12/728), 1965; also included in ECLA, *Hacia la Integración Acelerada de América Latina*.

El Desarrollo Agrícola en América Latina, UN, 1969.

El Desequilibrio Externo en el Desarrollo Económico Latinoamericano: el Caso de México, UN (E/CN.12/428), 1957.

Las Economias de Escala en Plantas Siderurgicas, UN, 1967.

The Economic Development of Latin America in the Post-War Period, UN, 1964.

Economic Bulletin for Latin America, UN, monthly.

Economic Survey of Latin America, UN, annual. *1949, 1963, 1965, 1966, 1967, 1970, 1971, 1973*.

Elementos para Elaboración de una Política de Desarrollo con Integración para América Latina, UN, 1969.

Estudio sobre la Distribución del Ingreso en América Latina, UN, 1967.

Evolución de la Integración Económica en Centroamérica, UN, 1966.

Hacia la Integración Acelerada de América Latina, Mexico, 1967.

La Industria Petroquimica en América Latina, vol.1 of ECLA, *El Proceso de Industrialización en América Latina*.

La Industria Quimica Latinoamericana en 1962–64, UN (E/CN.12/756), 1966.

La Industria Textil en América Latina, XII: *Informe Regional*, UN, 1968.

Integración, Sector Externo y Desarrollo Económico de América Latina, 1966.

An Introduction to the Technique of Programming, UN, 1953; also abbreviated as vol. I of ECLA, *Analyses and Projections*.

Latin America and the Second Session of UNCTAD, UN (E/CN.12/803), 1968.
Latin America and the UN Conference on Trade and Development, UN (E/CN. 12/693), 1964.
Latin American Symposium on Industrialization, UN, March 1966.
Las Máquinas-herramientas en el Brasil, UN (E/CN.12/633), 1962.
Las Máquinas-herramientas en la Argentina, UN (ST.ECLA/Conf.23/L 18), 1966.
El Mercado Comun Centroamericano y sus Problemas Recientes, UN, 1971.
Notas sobre la Economía y el Desarrollo de América Latina, UN, 1973.
Los Nuevos Precios del Petroleo y la Industria Electrica en América Latina, UN, 1974.
El Proceso de Industrialización en América Latina, UN (E/CN.12/716 rev. 1), 1966.
El Proceso de Industrialización en América Latina en los Primeros Años del Segundo Decenio para el Desarrollo, UN, 1974.
El Segundo Decenio de las Naciones Unidas para el Desarrollo, UN, 1969.
Tendencias y Estructuras de la Economia Latinoamericana, UN, 1971.
Theoretical and Practical Problems of Economic Growth, UN (E/CN.12/221), 1951.
ECLA and BANCO NACIONAL DE DESENVOLVIMENTO ECONOMICO. *Analise e Projeções da Economia Brasileira*, issued as vol. II of ECLA, *Analyses and Projections*.
A Evolução Recènte da Economia Brasileira, Rio de Janeiro 1967.
ECLA, FAO and INTERAMERICAN DEVELOPMENT BANK. *El Uso de Fertilizantes en América Latina*, UN, 1966.
UNITED NATIONS, FOOD and AGRICULTURE ORGANIZATION (FAO). *Prospects for Agriculture*, UN, 1972.
UNITED NATIONS. *Monthly Bulletin of Statistics: December 1967*, New York, July 1968. *Yearbook of International Trade Statistics*, New York, 1964.

2. OTHER WORKS

ABREU, J. Capistrano de. *Capítulos de História Colonial*, 5th ed. Rio de Janeiro, 1934.
ARAGÃO, José Maria. 'La Teoría Económica y el Proceso de Integración de América Latina', in *Integración*, no. 2, Buenos Aires, 1968.
ARCILA FARIAS, Eduardo. *Reformas Económicas del Siglo XVIII en Nueva España*, Mexico, 1974.
BAER, Werner. 'The Inflation Controversy in Latin America: A Survey', *Latin American Research Review*, II, no. 2, 1967.
BAER, Werner and MANESCHI, Andrea. *Import-substitution, Stagnation and Structural Change: an Interpretation of the Brazilian Case* (mimeograph), 1968.
BARNECHEA, Alfredo. 'Pomalca: Informe Urgente', *Participación*, December 1973.

BARRACLOUGH, Solon L. 'Reforma Agrária: História y Perspectivas', *Cuadernos de la Realidad Nacional*, March 1971.

BARRACLOUGH, Solon L. and FERNANDEZ, S. A. *Diagnóstico de la Reforma Agrária Chilena*, Mexico, 1974.

BARRACLOUGH, Solon L. and DOMIKE, Arthur L. 'La Estructura Agrária en Siete Paises de América Latina', *El Trimestre Económico*, April–June 1966.

BLACKBURN, Robin. 'The Economics of the Cuban Revolution', in Claudio Veliz (ed.), *Latin America and the Caribbean: A Handbook*, London, 1968.

BLANCO, Hugo. *Land or Death*, New York, 1972.

BOXER, C. R. *The Golden Age of Brazil, 1665–1750: Growing Pains of a Colonial Society*, Berkeley, Univ of California Press, 1962.

BRADING, D. A. *Miners and Merchants in Bourbon Mexico, 1763–1810*, Cambridge, 1971.

BRADING, D. A. and CROSS, Harry E. 'Colonial Silver Mining: Mexico and Peru' *The Hispanic American Historical Review*, November 1972.

BUNJE, Alejandro. *Riqueza y Renta de la Argentina*, Buenos Aires, 1917.

CAMACHO, Hugo Dario Montiel. *La Explotación del petróleo en Venezuela y la capitalización Nacional*, Mexico, 1967.

CECEÑA, José Luis. *Los Monópolios en México*, Mexico, 1962.

Centre National de la Recherche Scientifique. *Colloques Internationaux: Paris 11–16 October, 1965: Les Problèmes Agraires des Amériques Latines*, Paris, 1967.

Centro Latinoamericano de Demografia. *Boletín Demográfico*, July 1972.

CHAUNU, Pierre. *L'Amerique et les Amériques*, Paris, 1964.

CHEVALIER, François. 'The *Ejido* and Political Stability in Mexico', in Claudio Veliz (ed.), *The Politics of Conformity in Latin America*, London, 1967.

CHEVALIER, François. 'La Expansión de la Gran Propriedad en el Alto Peru en el Siglo XX', *Comunidades*, Madrid, May–August 1968.

CHILE. Universidad de Chile. Oficina de Planificación. *Antecedentes y Informaciones*, August 1974.

Consejo Latinoamericano de Ciencias Sociales. *La História Económica en América Latina*, Mexico, 1972.

CHONCHOL, Jacques. 'Land Tenure and Development in Latin America', in Claudio Veliz (ed.), *Obstacles to Change in Latin America*, London, 1965.

CORTÉSCONDE, R. 'Problemas del Crecimiento Industrial, 1870–1914', S. Torcuato di Tella and others, *Argentina, Sociedad de Masas*, Eudeba, Buenos Aires, 1965.

CÓSIO VILLEGAS, Daniel. *História Moderna de México*, VII, *El Porfiriato: Vida Económica*, Mexico, 1965.

COSIO VILLEGAS, Daniel. *El Sistema Politico Mexicano*, Mexico, 1972.

CUMBERLAND, Charles C. 'The Díaz Régime as Background for the Revolution' in Lewis Hanke (ed.) *History of Latin American Civilization*, 2 vols. Boston, 1967.

CUNNINGHAM, W. *The Growth of Modern Industry and Commerce: Modern Times*, Part I, Cambridge Univ. Press, 1921.

DELAVAUD, Collin and others. *L'Amérique Latine: Approche Géographique Générale et Régionale*, Paris, 1973.

DENIS, Henri. 'Le Socialisme Cubain à la Recherche d'un Modèle Economique', *Le Monde*, 10 Jan. 1968.

DÍAZ-ALEJANDRO, Carlos F. 'El Grupo Andino en el Proceso de Integración Latinoamericano', in *Estudios Internacionales*, July–September 1960.

Essays on the Economic History of the Argentine Republic, Yale University Press, 1970.

'An Interpretation of Argentine Economic Growth since 1930', *Journal of Development Studies*, Oct. 1966 and Jan. 1967.

DONGHI, Tulio Halperin. *História Contemporanea de América Latina*, Madrid, 1969.

DUMONT, René. *Cuba, Socialisme et Développement*, Editions du Seuil, Paris, 1964.

ECKSTEIN, S. *El Ejido Colectivo en México*, Mexico, 1966.

ELLICOT, Gerald. 'The Fishing Industry of Peru', in Claudio Veliz (ed.), *Latin America and the Caribbean: A Handbook*, London, 1968.

ENJALBERT, Henri. 'Réforme Agraire et Production Agricole au Mexique (1910–1965)' in Centre National de la Recherche Scientifique, *Les Problèmes Agraires des Amériques Latines*.

FERNANDEZ Y FERNANDEZ, Ramón. 'La Reforma Agraria Mexicana: una Gran Experiencia', in Centre National de la Recherche Scientifique, *Les Problèmes Agraires des Amériques Latines*.

FERRER, Aldo. *La Economía Argentina*, Mexico, 1963. English edition: *The Argentine Economy:* translated by Marjorie M. Urquidi, Berkeley, Univ. of California Press, 1967.

FUENZALIDA VOLLMAR, Fernando. 'La Estructura de la Comunidad de Indigenas Tradicional', in *El Campesino en el Peru*, Lima, 1970.

FURTADO, Celso. *Análise do 'Modelo' Brasileiro*, Rio de Janeiro, 1972.

'The External Disequilibrium in the Underdeveloped Economies', *The Indian Journal of Economics*, April 1958.

Formação Económica do Brasil, Rio, 1959. English edition: *The Economic Growth of Brazil: a Survey from Colonial to Modern Times*, tr. by Richard W. de Aguiar and Eric Charles Drysdale, Berkeley, Univ. of California Press, 1963.

Subdesenvolvimento e Estagnação na América Latina, Rio de Janeiro, 1967.

Teoria e Politica do Desenvolvimento Econômico, Editora Nacional, São Paulo, 1967.

Um Projeto para o Brasil, Rio, 1968.

GERMANI, Gino. *Política y Sociedad en una Época de Transición*, ed. Paidos, Buenos Aires, 1962.

GONZALEZ CASANOVA, Pablo. *La Democracia en México*, Mexico, 1965.

Government of Cuba. 'El Desarollo Industrial de Cuba', in ECLA, *Latin American Symposium on Industrialization*.

GRUNWALD, Joseph. 'The Structuralist School on Price Stabilisation and

Economic Development: The Chilean Case', in A. Hirschman (ed.) *Latin American Issues*, New York, 1961.

GUERRA Y SANCHEZ, Ramiro. *Azúcar y Población en las Antillas*, Havana, 1944: translated as *Sugar and Society in the Caribbean: an Economic History of Cuban Agriculture*, New Haven, Yale University Press, 1964.

GUMBAU, Henri. 'Les Changements de Structure à la suite de la Reforme Bolivienne' in Centre National de la Recherche Scientifique, *Les Problèmes Agraires des Amériques Latines*, Paris, 1967.

GUTELMAN, Michel. *L'Agriculture Socialisée à Cuba*, Maspero, Paris, 1967.

HAMILTON, E. J. *American Treasure and the Price Revolution in Spain, 1501–1650*, New York, 1934.

HANKE, Lewis. 'The Imperial City of Potosî, Boom Town Supreme' in Lewis Hanke (ed.) *History of Latin American Civilization*, 2 vols. Boston, 1967.

HARLOW, V. T. *A History of Barbados*, Oxford, 1926.

HUMPHREYS, Robert A. *Latin American History: a Guide to the Literature in English*, Oxford, London, 1960.

Instituto Brasileiro de Geografia e Estatística. *Anuário Estatístico do Brasil, Quadros Retrospectivos, 1939–40*.

Instituto Interamericano de Estudios Juridícos Internacionales. *Instrumentos Relativos a la Integración Económica en América Latina*, Washington, 1964: translated as Inter-American Institute of International Legal Studies, *Instruments Relating to the Economic Integration of Latin America*, Oceana Publications, Dobbs Ferry, 1968.

Instituto Interamericano de Estadística, *América en Cifras*, 1965, 1972.

Instituto Latinoamericana de Planificación Económica y Social. *Discusiones sobre Planificación*, Mexico, 1966.

Instituto para la Integracion de America Latina. *El Proceso de Integración en América Latina: 1968–71*, Buenos Aires, 1972.

Interamerican Development Bank. Montague Yudelman (ed.), *Agricultural Development in Latin America: Current Status and Prospects*, 1966.

Interamerican Committee for Agricultural Development. *Tenencia de la Tierra y Desarrollo Socio-Economico del Sector Agricola*, Washington Pan American Union, 1965–1966.

JARA, Alvaro, *Problemas y Métodos de la História Económica Hispanoamericana*, 2nd ed., Universidad Central de Venezuela, Caracas, 1969.

Guerre et Societé au Chili, translated by Jacques Lafayette, Paris, 1961.

Tres Ensaios sobre Economía Minera Hispanoamericana, Santiago, 1966.

KEITH, Robert G. 'Origen del Sistema de Hacienda' in *La Hacienda, la Comunidad y el Campesino en el Peru* (Instituto de Estudios Peruanos. Colección Peru Problemas no. 3), Lima, 1970.

KINDLEBERGER, C. P. *Foreign Trade and the National Economy*, Yale University Press, 1962.

KLAREN, Peter. *La Formación de las Haciendas Azucereras y los Origenes del APRA*, Lima, 1970.

KUZNETS, Simon. *Modern Economic Growth*, Yale University Press, 1966.

LAMBERT, Jacques. *Amérique Latine: Structures Sociales et Institutions Politiques*, Paris, 1963, 2nd ed. 1968. English ed. *Latin America: Social Structure and Political Institutions*, translated by Helen Katel, Berkeley, Univ. of California Press, 1967.

LARRALDE, W. 'Primeiros Ensaios de Reforma Agraria em Venezuela' in Centre National de la Recherche Scientifique, *Les Problèmes Agraires des Amériques Latines*.

LE RIVEREND, Julio. 'Conclusiones sobre la Reforma Agrária en Cuba' in Centre National de la Recherche Scientifique, *Les Problèmes Agraires des Amériques Latines*.

História Económica de Cuba, Barcelona, 1972.

MANESCHI, Andrea. *Aspectos Quantitativos do Sétor Publico do Brasil de 1939 a 1970*, São Paulo, 1970.

MARTNER, Gonzalo. *Planificación y Presupuesto por programas*, Mexico, 1967.

MELLAFE, Rolando. 'Problemas Demográficos e História Colonial Hispanoamericana' in *Temas de História Económica Hispanoamericana*, Paris, 1965.

MILLER PAIVA, Ruy and others. *Brazil's Agricultural Sector: Economic Behaviour, Problems and Possibilities*, São Paulo, 1973.

MONBEIG, Pierre. *Pionniers et Planteurs de São Paulo*, Paris, 1952.

NAVARETTE, Ifigenia N. de. *La Distribución del Ingreso en el Desarrollo Económico de México*, Instituto de Investigaciones Económicas, Mexico, 1960.

NOVOA MONREAL, Eduardo. *La Batalla por el Cobre*, Santiago, 1972.

NOYOLA, Vazquez Juan. 'El Desarrollo Económico y la Inflación en México y Otros Paises Latinoamericanos', *Investigación Económica*, XVI, no. 4, Mexico, 1965.

NURKSE, Ragnar. 'Trade Theory and Development Policy', in H. Ellis (ed.), *Economic Development for Latin America*, International Economic Association Conference 1957, Macmillan, London, 1961.

OLIVEIRA, Julio. 'La Teoria no Monetaria de la Inflación, *El Trimestre Económico*, Jan.–Mar. 1960.

PAN AMERICAN HEALTH ORGANIZATION. *Proyecciones Cuadrienales*, Ministerios de Salud, 1972–1975.

Panorama Economico, Santiago, July 1969.

PENA, Moisés T. de la. *Mito y Realidad de la Reforma Agrária en México*, Mexico, 1964.

PEREIRA, José C. *Estrutura e Expansão de Industria em São Paulo*, São Paulo, 1967.

PICÓ, Rafael. *Puerto Rico: Planificación y Acción*, San Juan de Puerto Rico, 1962.

PINTO SANTA CRUZ, Aníbal. *Chile, un Caso de Desarrollo Frustrado*, ed. Universitaria, Santiago de Chile, 1962.

'Estabilidad y Desarrollo', *El Trimestre Económico*, Jan.–Mar. 1960.

PINTO SANTA CRUZ, Anibal and DI FILIPPO, Armando. 'Notas sobre la Estrategia de la Distribucción y la Redistribucción del Ingreso en América Latina', *El Trimestre Económico*, April–June 1974.

POBLETE TRONCOSO, Moisés. *La Reforma Agraria en América Latina*, Bello, Santiago de Chile, 1961.

PREBISCH, Raúl. 'El Falso Dilema entre Desarrollo Económico y Estabilidad Monetaria', *Boletín Económico de América Latina*, March 1961.

Nueva Política Comercial para el Desarrollo, Fondo de Cultura Económica, Mexico, 1964.

PUENTE LEYVA, Jesús. 'Recursos y crescimiento del Sector Agropecuario en Mexico, 1930–1967', *El Trimestre Económico*, April–June 1971.

PUIGGROS, Rodolfo. *História Económica del Río de la Plata*, 3rd ed. Buenos Aires, n.d.

REYNOLDS, Clark Winston. *Essays on the Chilean Economy*, 1965.

SEERS, Dudley. 'Inflación y Crecimiento: Resumen de la Experiencia Latino-americana' in *Boletín Económico de América Latina*, Feb. 1962.

SEERS, Dudley, and others. *Cuba: the Economic and Social Revolution*, London, 1964.

SÉRGIO, Antonio. *Breve Intepretação da Historia de Portugal*, Lisbon, 1972.

SILVA HERZOG, Jesús. *História de la Expropriación de las Empresas Petroleras*, Mexico, 1964.

SÓLIS, M. Leopoldo. 'Hacia un Análisis General a Largo Plazo del Desarrollo Económico de México' in Colégio de México, *Demografia y Economía*, I, no. 1, Mexico, 1967.

SOTELO, Ignacio. *Sociologia de América Latina*, Madrid, 1972.

SOZA VALDERRAMA, Hector. *Planificación del Desarrollo Industrial*, Mexico, 1966.

STAVENHAGEN, Rodolfo. 'Aspectos Sociales de la Estrutura Agrária en México' in Centre National de la Recherche Scientifique, *Les Problèmes Agraires des Amériques Latines*.

Sept Thèses Erronées sur l'Amerique Latine, Paris, 1973 (published in English as 'Seven Fallacies about Latin America' in Petras. J. and Zeitlin, M. (eds.) *Latin America: Reform or Revolution?*, Greenwich, 1968, 13–31.

STEIN, Stanley J. *The Brazilian Cotton Manufacture: Textile Enterprise in an Underdeveloped Area, 1850–1950*, Harvard University Press, 1957.

STRAUSS, Estevan. *Reestructuración del Espacio Económico Latinoamericano* (mimeograph), Instituto Latinoamericano de Planificación Económico y Social, 1969.

SUNKEL, Osvaldo. 'La Inflación Chilena: un Enfoque Heterodoxo', *El Trimestre Económico*, Oct.–Dec. 1958.

TAMAGNA, Frank. *Central Banking in Latin America*, Mexico, 1965.

TAPIÉ, Victor-L. *Histoire de l'Amérique Latine au XIXe Siècle*, Paris, 1945.

TAVARES, Maria de Conceição. *Da Substituiçao de Imporraçoẽs ao Capitalismo Financeiro*, Rio de Janeiro, 1972.

URQUIDI, Victor, L. *Teoría, Realidad y Posibilidad de la ALALC en la Integración Económica Latinoamericana*, Mexico, 1966.

Viabilidad Económica de América Latina, Mexico, 1962.

The Challenge of Development in Latin America, translated by Marjorie M. Urquidi, Pall Mall Press, London, 1964.

URQUIDI MORALES, A. 'Las Comunidades Indígenas y su Perspectiva Histórica' in Centre National de la Recherche Scientifique, *Les Problèmes Agraires des Amériques Latines*, Paris, 1967.

VÉLIZ, Claudio (ed.). *Latin America and the Caribbean: A Handbook*, London, 1968.

Obstacles to Change in Latin America, London, 1965.

The Politics of Conformity in Latin America, London, 1967.

VICENS VIVES, Jaime. *Bibliógrafia Histórica de Espana y Hispanoamérica*, Barcelona, 1953.

VIGNOLS, Léon. 'Les Antilles Françaises sous l'Ancien Régime', *Revue d'Histoire Economique et Sociale*, 1928.

VILLA MARTINEZ, Rosa Olivia. *Inflación y Desarrollo: el Enfoque Estructuralista* (Thesis), Universidad Nacional Autónoma de México, 1966.

VILLANUEVA, Javier. *The Inflationary Process in Argentina, 1943–1960* (mimeograph), Buenos Aires, 1964.

WALTERS, R. F. *Shifting Cultivation in Latin America*, UN FAO, 1971.

WHITAKER, Arthur P. 'The Failure of the Huancavelica Mercury Mine' in Lewis Hanke (ed.) *History of Latin American Cultivation*, 2 vols. Boston, 1967.

WIONCZEK, Miguel S. 'Central Banking', in C. Veliz (ed.), *Latin America and the Caribbean: A Handbook*, London, 1968.

WIONCZEK, M. S. and others. *Latin American Economic Integration*, Praeger, New York, 1966.

YATES, P. L. *Forty Years of Foreign Trade*, Allen and Unwin, London, 1959.

ZAVALA, Silvio. *Las Instituciones Jurídicas en la Conquista de América*, Madrid, 1935.

Index